On the Relation Between Science and Religion

George Combe

CAMBRIDGE UNIVERSITY PRESS

Cambridge New York Melbourne Madrid Cape Town Singapore São Paolo Delhi

Published in the United States of America by Cambridge University Press, New York

www.cambridge.org
Information on this title: www.cambridge.org/9781108004510

© in this compilation Cambridge University Press 2009

This edition first published 1857
This digitally printed version 2009

ISBN 978-1-108-00451-0

This book reproduces the text of the original edition. The content and language reflect the beliefs, practices and terminology of their time, and have not been updated.

CAMBRIDGE LIBRARY COLLECTION

Books of enduring scholarly value

Religion

For centuries, scripture and theology were the focus of prodigious amounts of scholarship and publishing, dominated in the English-speaking world by the work of Protestant Christians. Enlightenment philosophy and science, anthropology, ethnology and the colonial experience all brought new perspectives, lively debates and heated controversies to the study of religion and its role in the world, many of which continue to this day. This series explores the editing and interpretation of religious texts, the history of religious ideas and institutions, and not least the encounter between religion and science.

On the Relation Between Science and Religion

George Combe (1788-1858) rose from humble origins to tour widely in Europe and the United States lecturing on phrenology, the popular Victorian belief that character traits were determined by the configuration of the skull. His most famous book, The Constitution of Man, published in 1828, put forward a naturalist agenda and sold approximately 350,000 copies, distributed by over 100 publishers, by 1900. In 1857, Combe published On the Relation between Science and Religion. He describes his childhood bafflement as to how God governs the world, his delight on observing the laws of nature, and his disillusionment with human social organisation. He denounces dogmatism and sectarianism, and argues insistently that religious leaders should encourage the study of science as revealing God's governance, rather than discourage it. He proposes that phrenology sheds light on the divine purpose and moral laws through an improved understanding of the workings of the human mind (identifying 'affective' and 'intellectual' areas of the brain responsible for traits such as 'benevolence', 'wonder', and 'hope'), and criticises both scientists and religious leaders who maintain that higher thought and moral behaviour has nothing to do with the brain. His book ranges widely across the concerns of Victorian educated classes, referring to books (including Paley's Natural Theology as well as the phrenology works of Gall and Spurzheim), statistics on church attendance, popular views on Eastern religions, spiritualism, and Roman Catholicism, and current affairs. It is a fascinating document of its time, and addresses questions many of which still resonate today.

Cambridge University Press has long been a pioneer in the reissuing of out-of-print titles from its own backlist, producing digital reprints of books that are still sought after by scholars and students but could not be reprinted economically using traditional technology. The Cambridge Library Collection extends this activity to a wider range of books which are still of importance to researchers and professionals, either for the source material they contain, or as landmarks in the history of their academic discipline.

Drawing from the world-renowned collections in the Cambridge University Library, and guided by the advice of experts in each subject area, Cambridge University Press is using state-of-the-art scanning machines in its own Printing House to capture the content of each book selected for inclusion. The files are processed to give a consistently clear, crisp image, and the books finished to the high quality standard for which the Press is recognised around the world. The latest print-on-demand technology ensures that the books will remain available indefinitely, and that orders for single or multiple copies can quickly be supplied.

The Cambridge Library Collection will bring back to life books of enduring scholarly value across a wide range of disciplines in the humanities and social sciences and in science and technology.

ON

THE RELATION

BETWEEN

SCIENCE AND RELIGION.

BY

GEORGE COMBE.

Ταράσσει τοὺς ἀνθρώπους οὐ τὰ πράγματα, ἀλλὰ τὰ περὶ τῶν πραγμάτων δόγματα· οἷον θάνατος οὐδὲν δεινόν, ἐπεὶ καὶ Σωκράτει ἂν ἐφαίνετο· ἀλλὰ τὸ δόγμα τὸ περὶ θανάτου, ἐκεῖνο τὸ δεινόν ἐστιν.—EPICTETUS, *Enchir.* 10.

TRANSLATION.

"Men are harassed not by things but by the notions they form of things; death, for example, is nothing terrible, for if it were, it would have appeared so to Socrates; but the notion that death is something terrible, is the really terrible thing."

"Impiety clears the soul of its consecrated errors, but it does not fill the heart of man. Impiety alone will never ruin a human worship. A faith destroyed must be replaced by a faith. It is not given to irreligion to destroy a religion on earth. It is but a religion more enlightened which can really triumph over a religion fallen into contempt, by replacing it. The earth cannot remain without an altar, and God only is strong enough against God!"—LAMARTINE'S *History of the Girondists* (vol. i. p. 156; Bohn, 1848).

FOURTH—AND PEOPLE'S EDITION,
Price Two Shillings.

EDINBURGH:
MACLACHLAN AND STEWART.
LONDON: SIMPKIN, MARSHALL, AND CO.
1857.

The Right of Translation is Reserved by the Author.

To CHARLES MACKAY, Esq., LL.D.

My Dear Sir,

A friendship of long duration, admiration of your genius, and cordial sympathy with the purposes to which you have devoted it, induce me to dedicate this volume to you as a mark of affection and esteem.

I am,

My Dear Sir,

Yours very sincerely,

GEO. COMBE.

Edinburgh, 31st March 1857.

TABLE OF CONTENTS.

	Page
INTRODUCTION.	
CHAP. I. On the present state of the relation between Science and Religion,	1
II. Definition of the words Science and Religion, and Elucidation of the complex character of Religion,	15
III. Sect. I. Of the Physical Elements of Man,	23
II. Of the Mental Organs and Faculties of Man,	29
III. Of the Particular Faculties of the Mind, their cerebral organs, modes of activity, and uses and abuses,	33
IV. Is Man naturally a Religious Being?	34
V. Is Man naturally a Moral Being?	45
VI. Is there any Natural Standard of Moral and Religious Truth?	47
IV. Of the extent to which Man is able to discover the Ultimate Elements or Essence of the External World,	51
V. Of God,	66
VI. Can we trace Divine Government in the Phenomena of the Physical and Moral Worlds? And if so, by what means is it maintained and rendered efficient?	82
Sect. I. Of the Government of the Physical World,	82
II. Can we discover the Means by which the Moral World is Governed?	84
III. Of Life—Health—Disease—and Death,	89
IV. Of the Divine Government of Human Actions,	109
V. Means by which the Individual Human Faculties, as Moral Forces, are regulated in their Action,	118
VI. Effects of the Predominance of particular Groups of Organs in Individuals in determining their qualities as Moral Agents,	130
The effects of Predominance of Size in the Animal Region of the Brain,	132
Effects when both the Animal and Intellectual Organs are large, and the Moral Organs are small,	136
Effects when the Animal, Moral, and Intellectual Regions of the Brain, are all large and nearly equally balanced,	139

CONTENTS.

	Page
CHAP. VI. Sect. VI. Effects when the Moral and Intellectual Organs are large in proportion to those of the Propensities,	144
Rammohun Roy,	145
Effects of Special Combinations of the Mental Forces as they occur in Individuals,	150
Robert Burns,	154
Note on Mr Hugh Miller,	157
VII. Of Nations considered as Moral Forces,	160
VII. Historical Evidence that the Divine Government of Nations is Moral,	171
VIII. Is this World, such as it now exists, an Institution?—Or is it the Wreck of a better System?	179
Sect. I. Is this World an Institution?	ib.
II. Is this World the Wreck of a better System?	185
IX. Practical Considerations,	191
Sect. I. How should we act, if the World is an Institution?	ib.
II. The consequences which have followed from the prevailing religious Dogmas,	218
X. Conclusion,	253

APPENDIX.

No. I. Names of the Phrenological Organs and their situations in the head, referred to in page 33,	261
II. Evidence of the Influence of the Brain on Feeling and Thought, referred to on page 28,	262
III. Descriptions of Heaven and Hell, &c., from Catechism by Joseph Hay, A.M., Minister, Arbroath, referred to on page 233,	264
IV. On Man-Concocted Articles of Faith, referred to on page 233,	266
V. Definition of the "Personality" of the Deity,	268
VI. On the Worship of the Shakers, referred to on pages 204 and 213,	269
VII. Letters from the late Dr Samuel Brown to George Combe, on the Natural Evidence for the Existence and Attributes of God, and other topics,	270
VIII. Note on Dr M'Cosh's "Method of the Divine Government,"	276
IX. Note on "Faith in God and Modern Atheism compared," by James Buchanan, D.D., referred to in the Introduction, page xxx.,	277
X. Speech of Lord John Russell on Teaching Natural Theology in Common Schools,	277
XI. Recommendations to teach Physiology in Common Schools, referred to on page 257,	278

ADVERTISEMENT.

The substance of this work appeared first in the Phrenological Journal, vol. xx., published in 1847.

The present, or *fourth* edition, which is greatly enlarged, consists of—

Copies at 5s. each,	500	
People's edition, copies at 2s. each,	1500	
Total,	——	2000 copies.

The working classes are indebted to the generosity of R. F. Breed, Esq., Ballaughton House, Douglas, Isle of Man, for the People's Edition, he having desired its publication, and provided funds to cover the extra expense attending it.

Edinburgh, 31st March 1857.

INTRODUCTION.

The present work first appeared in 1847 as a pamphlet, and attracted considerable attention. It has for some time been out of print, and as it continues in demand, I have been led by circumstances to enlarge it in the present edition. As the investigation contained in it is of great extent, and embraces a consideration of the present religious creeds of Europe, I shall introduce it by a brief notice of the incidents which led me to take an interest in the subject. By pursuing this course, I shall be under the necessity of introducing a portion of my personal history—which may expose me to the charge of vanity and egotism; but on the other hand, the narrative will shew that the questions here discussed have long formed topics of earnest and serious consideration in my mind, and that the views now advanced are brought forward in no light spirit, but are founded on deep and solemn convictions.

An event so common and trivial as almost to appear ludicrous when introduced into a grave discourse, but which is *real*, gave rise to the train of thought which is developed in this work. When a child of six or seven years of age, some benevolent friend bestowed on me a lump of sugar-candy. The nursery-maid desired me to give a share of it to my younger brothers and sisters, and I presented it to her to be disposed of as she recommended. She gave each of them a portion, and when she returned the remainder to me, she said, "That's a good boy—God will reward you for this." These words were uttered by her as a mere form of pious speech, proper to be addressed to a child; but they conveyed to my mind an idea;—they suggested intelligibly and practically, for the first time, the conception of a Divine reward for a kind action; and I instantly put the question to her, "*How* will God reward me?" "He will send you everything that is good." "What do you mean by 'good'—Will he send me more sugar-candy?" "Yes—certainly he will, if you are a good boy." "Will he make this piece of sugar-candy grow bigger?" "Yes—God always rewards those who are kind-hearted."

I could not rest contented with words, but at once proceeded to the verification of the assurance by experiment and observation. I forthwith examined minutely all the edges of the remaining portion of sugar-candy, took an account of its dimensions, and then, wrapping it carefully in paper, put it into a drawer, and waited with anxiety for its increase. I left it in the drawer all night, and next morning examined it with eager curiosity. I could discover no trace of alteration in its size, either of increase or decrease. I was greatly disappointed; my faith in the reward of virtue by the Ruler of the world received its first shock, and I feared that God did *not* govern the world in the manner which the nursery-maid had represented.

Several years afterwards, I read in the Grammatical Exercises, an early class-book then used in the High School of Edinburgh, these words: "*Deus gubernat mundum,*" "God governs the world." "*Mundus gubernatur a Deo,*" "The world is governed by God." These sentences were introduced into the book as exercises in Latin grammar; and our teacher, the late Mr Luke Fraser, dealt with them merely as such, without entering into any consideration of the ideas embodied in them.

This must have occurred about the year 1798, when I was ten years of age; and the words "*Deus gubernat mundum—Mundus gubernatur a Deo,*" made an indelible impression, and continued for years and years to haunt my imagination. As a child, I assumed the fact itself to be an indubitable truth, but felt a restless curiosity to discover *how* God exercises his jurisdiction.

Some time afterwards, I read in the Edinburgh Advertiser, that Napoleon Buonaparte (instigated and assisted, as I used to hear, by the devil) governed France, and governed it very wickedly; and that King George III., Mr Pitt, and Lord Melville, governed Great Britain and Ireland—not very successfully either, for I read of rebellion, and murders, and burnings, and executions in Ireland; while in Scotland my father complained of enormous Excise duties which threatened to involve him in ruin. I saw that my father ruled in his trade, and my mother in her household affairs, both pretty well on the whole; but with such evident marks of imperfection, that it was impossible to trace God's superintendence or direction in their administration.

In the class in the High School of which I was a member, Mr Luke Fraser seemed to me to reign supreme; and as I felt his government to be harsh, and often unjust, I could not recognise God in it either. Under his tuition, and that of Dr Adam, the Rector of the High School, and of Dr John Hill, the Professor of Latin in the University of Edinburgh, I became acquainted with the literature, the mythology, and the history of Greece and Rome; but in these no traces of the Divine government of the world were discernible.

These were the only governments of which I then had experience, or about which I could obtain any information; and in none of them could I discover satisfactory evidence of God's interference in the affairs of men. On the contrary, it appeared to me, that one and all of the historical personages before named did just what they pleased, and that God took no account of their actions in this world, however He might deal with them in the next. They all seemed to acknowledge *in words* that God governs the world; but, nevertheless, they appeared to me to *act* as if they were themselves independent and irresponsible governors, consulting only their own notions of what was right or wrong, and often pursuing what they considered to be their own interests, irrespective of God's asserted supremacy in human affairs. Most of them professed to believe in their accountability in the next world; but this belief seemed to me like a rope of sand in binding their consciences. They rarely hesitated to encounter all the dangers of that judgment when their worldly interests or passions strongly solicited them to a course of action condemned by their professed creeds.

From infancy I attended regularly an evangelical church, was early instructed in the Bible, and in the Shorter and Larger Catechisms, and the Confession of Faith of the Assembly of Divines at Westminster; and read orthodox sermons and treatises by various distinguished authors. In the Old Testament there were narratives of God's government of the Jewish nation, by the exercise of special acts of supernatural power, and I understood this as a clear and satisfactory exposition of Divine government. In the New Testament, also, certain special acts of Divine interference with the affairs of men were recorded, which likewise gave me great satisfaction, as evidences that God governs the world; but I never could apply these examples to practical purposes.

I learned, in some way which I do not now recollect, that during many ages after the close of the Scripture records, the Roman Catholic priesthood had asserted that such acts of special supernatural administration continued, and that they themselves were the appointed instruments through whose medium it pleased God thus to manifest his power. But I never *saw* instances of this kind of government in my own sphere of life.

In the course of time I read arguments and criticisms which carried with them an irresistible conviction, that these pretensions of the Roman Catholic priesthood had been pious frauds practised on an ignorant and superstitious people. Here, then, was another shock to my belief that God governs the world; and the difficulty was increased by an obscure impression, that notwithstanding this denial by the Protestant divines, of the continuance of a special supernatural Providence acting through the Roman Catholic priesthood, they and their followers seemed to admit something very similar in their own favour.* As however, I could not discover, by observation, satisfactory evidence of special acts of Divine interference in human affairs, taking place in consequence of *their* solicitations, any more than in consequence of those of the Roman Catholic priesthood, I arrived at the conclusion that all special acts of Divine administration had ceased with the Scripture times; and thus I was again sent adrift into the great ocean of doubt, and no longer saw traces of the *manner* in which God governs the world in our day, whatever He might have done in the days of the Jewish nation.

As I advanced in understanding, my theological studies

---

* See examples in point in Chapter I.

rather increased than diminished these perplexities. I read that "not a sparrow falls to the ground without our heavenly Father," and that "the very hairs of our heads are numbered;" which seemed to indicate a very intimate and minute government of the world. But, simultaneously with this information, I was taught that God forgives those who offend against his laws, if they have faith in Jesus Christ and repent; and that He often leaves the wicked to run the course of their sins in this world without punishing them, reserving his retribution for the day of judgment. This seemed to me to imply that God really does not govern the world in any intelligible or practical sense, but merely takes note of men's actions, and commences his actual and efficient government only after the resurrection from the dead.

During the time these speculations engaged my attention, my mind opened to the import of the Calvinistic theology which had formed the staple of my religious instruction. I was taught to repeat the Catechism from which an extract is given on page 186, and I attended regularly a church in which Calvinism was preached by one of the ministers, in a form which, to me, was very terrible. Conscious of being no better than my fellow-creatures, I could discover no reason why, if any were to be passed over to the left hand at the day of judgment, I should not be one of the number. The narrative of the sufferings and death of Jesus Christ, excited in me only strong feelings of compassion for Him, and of indignation against his persecutors. I was overwhelmed by the terrors of a future judgment, and wished myself an inferior animal without a soul. So deep and habitual was the gloomy impression, that summer was rendered appalling by the prospect of thunder storms, in one of which I might be struck instantaneously dead and precipitated in a moment into everlasting misery. In the autumn evenings, I used to climb high up on the rocks of Edinburgh Castle, which overhung my father's house, and gaze with intense interest on "The Evening Star," or planet, that shone with resplendent brilliancy in the wake of the departed sun; I longed to see into its internal economy, and thought: "Oh! could I but discover that summer and winter, heat and cold, life and death, prevail in you as they do here, how happy should I be! I should then believe that this world is not cursed, but that you, the planet,—and we, the earth,—are both such as God intended us to be!"

The distress occasioned by these impressions was aggravated by finding such doubts and difficulties described in the Catechism "as punishments of sin," and ascribed to "blindness of mind, a reprobate sense, and strong delusions." I believed this to be the fact, because at that time I had not heard or read a word calling in question the absolute truth of the doctrines of the Catechism. The only information I then possessed about "unbelief" and "unbelievers" was derived from sermons preached against them; and it was not till a much later period that I became convinced that the feelings now mentioned arose from the intuitive revulsion of the moral, religious, and intellectual faculties with which I had been endowed, against the dogmas of Calvin.

The only relief from these depressing views of man's qualities and condition was afforded by the perusal of "Ray on the Wisdom of God in Creation," and subsequently "Paley's Natural Theology." At first, I feared that their views also were "strong delusions," but as my understanding gained strength, these works confirmed my faith that God does govern the world; although, owing to their containing no clear exposition of the *manner* in which He does so, they conveyed rather an impression than a conviction of the fact. Moreover, as I never saw any person *acting* on that faith, it maintained itself in my mind chiefly as an impression; and it thus remained for many years, not only without proof, but often against apparent evidence to the contrary. My course of inquiry, therefore, was still onward; and with a view to obtaining a solution of the problem, I studied a variety of works on moral and metaphysical subjects; but from none of them did I receive any satisfaction.

In point of fact, I reached to man's estate with a firm faith that God governs the world, but utterly baffled in all my attempts to discover *how* this government is effected. Intercourse with society revealed to me that my earnest and literal application of the Calvinistic doctrines was idiosyncratic, and that ordinary believers were in the habit of modifying the sense in which they accepted them, pretty much to suit their own tastes. When I suggested that this was practising conventional hypocrisy, I was told that no other course was left open to a young man who depended on public opinion for success in his profession; for were he to disclose his dissent from the religious standards of the country, he would be branded with the stamp of infidelity, suspected of immorality, and obstructed in every step of his career. Besides, it was hinted that Scripture itself recognises the admissibility in such cases of compliance with the established forms of worship, even when these are idolatrous. See 2 Kings, chap. v., verses 17, 18, and 19.*

The feeling of disappointment became more intense in proportion as a succession of studies presented to my mind clear and thoroughly convincing evidence, that in certain departments of nature God does unquestionably govern the world. When, for example, I comprehended the laws of the solar system, as elucidated by Copernicus, Galileo, Newton, and Laplace, and perceived the most perfect adaptation, harmony, and regularity, pervading the revolutions of the planets and their satellites, the conviction that God governs in that system was at once irresistible, complete, and delightful. The planets, however, were far away, and I longed to discover the same order and harmony on earth; but in vain.

My next studies were Anatomy and Physiology. From these sources new light broke in upon my mind. Clear, however, as the examples of Divine government afforded by these sciences appeared to be, I found no application made of them beyond the domains of surgery. No practical inference was deduced from them to regulate human conduct in the ordinary circumstances of life. When I left the medical school, all traces of the government of God in the world were lost, and my feeling of disappointment returned.

Chemistry was the next science which engaged my attention, and in the qualities and relations of matter, it presented

* " Naaman" (the leper, captain of the host of the King of Syria) " said" (to Elisha who had cured him by bidding him wash in Jordan), " Shall there not then, I pray thee, be given to thy servant two mules' burden of earth ? for thy servant will henceforth offer neither burnt-offering nor sacrifice unto other gods, but unto the Lord. In this thing the Lord pardon thy servant, that when my master goeth into the House of Rimmon to worship there, and he leaneth on my hand, and I bow myself in the house of Rimmon : when I bow myself in the House of Rimmon, the Lord pardon thy servant in this thing. And he said unto him, *Go in peace.* So he departed from him a little way."

extraordinary illustrations of Divine government. In the revelations made by this science, I discovered powers conferred on matter, capable of producing the most stupendous results, yet all regulated in their action with a degree of precision that admitted of even mathematical and arithmetical computation, and appeared irresistibly to proclaim the all-pervading God. Yet when I left the chemical laboratory and returned into the world of business, these delicious visions fled, and I could no longer trace the Divine government in the affairs of men.

In this condition of mind I continued for several years, and recollect meeting with only two works which approached to the solution of any portion of the enigma which puzzled my understanding. These were "Smith's Wealth of Nations," and "Malthus on Population." The first appeared to me to demonstrate that God actually governs in the relations of commerce; that He has established certain natural laws which regulate the interests of men in the exchange of commodities and labour; and that those laws are in harmony with the dictates of our moral and intellectual faculties, and wisely related to the natural productions of the different soils and climates of the earth.

I first read the work of Mr Malthus in 1805, and he appeared to me to prove that God reigns, through the medium of fixed natural laws, in another department of human affairs —namely, in that of population. The facts adduced by him shewed that the Creator has bestowed on mankind a power of increasing their numbers much beyond the ratio of the diminution that, in favourable circumstances, will be caused by death; and, consequently, that they must limit their increase by moral restraint; or augment, by ever-extending cultivation of the soil, their means of subsistence in proportion to their numbers, or expose themselves to the evil of being reduced by disease and famine to the number which the actual production of food will maintain. These propositions, like the doctrines of Adam Smith, met with general rejection; and their author, far from being honoured as a successful expounder of a portion of God's method of governing the world, was assailed with unmitigated abuse, and his views were strenuously resisted in practice.

Bishop Butler also threw a flash of light across the dark

horizon; but it was only a flash. He announced clearly the great principle of a moral government of the world by natural laws; but he did little to elucidate the *means* by which it is accomplished. In consequence of his not understanding the means, his views in regard to the Divine government of the world, although in the main sound, are not practical. He was compelled to resort to the world to come, in order to find compensation for what appeared to him to be imperfections in the moral government of this world, in some instances in which a more minute knowledge of the mode of God's present administration would have convinced him that the apparent imperfection is removable on earth.

During the continuance of these perplexities, this consideration presented itself to my mind,—that in every department of nature, the evidences of Divine government, of the mode in which it is administered, and of the laws by which it is maintained, become more and more clear and comprehensible, in proportion to the exactness of our knowledge of the objects through the instrumentality of which it is accomplished.

Although, in this manner, partial light appeared to dawn on the government of physical nature, the administration of the moral world remained a complete enigma, and it was not until a comparatively recent period that glimpses of order began to appear in it also. It was Dr Gall's discovery of the functions of the brain that led me by imperceptible steps to the views on this subject which are presented in the present volume; and they rest on it alone. I mention this fact, because I am well aware that this discovery continues to be ignored or rejected by almost all men of science, and by the people in general of Europe. Nevertheless, I have a complete conviction, founded on observation and experience extended over forty years, that, although far from perfection, it is essentially founded in truth, that its doctrines require only to be tried by the standard of nature to be accepted by men of ordinary honesty and intelligence, and that enough is ascertained to warrant the inferences here deduced.

It becomes important, therefore, in support of the basis on which the most important conclusions of this work are founded, to endeavour to throw light on the causes of the long rejection of Phrenology.

In 1812 I attended a course of Lectures on Anatomy and Physiology delivered by Dr John Barclay, then the most esteemed teacher of these sciences in Edinburgh; and after a display of the mechanical structure of the brain, by slicing it across from side to side, commencing at the top, which occupied four hours, I heard him declare that the functions of its different parts were unknown. I had previously studied mental philosophy in the standard works on the subject, and knew that in them no exposition was given of organs by which the different faculties act, or are influenced. When, therefore, Gall's doctrine that particular mental powers are connected with different portions of the brain was announced in England by Dr Spurzheim, I was convinced that neither anatomists, physiologists, nor mental philosophers, were in possession of any knowledge whatever on the subject; nevertheless, they rejected it with contumely and disdain. At first I was led away by the boldness and confidence of their condemnation; but after attending a course of lectures by Dr Spurzheim, and seeing the evidence he presented in proof of the discovery, I was puzzled to account for the unmeasured abuse that was heaped on it by men of almost all conditions and attainments, in absolute ignorance of its merits.

In the course of reflection, it appeared to me that this state of public opinion arose from inattention to two facts which were indisputable, and which were decisive as to the competency of the objectors, in the actual state of their knowledge, to pronounce any rational judgment on the subject: these were—First: That structure does not reveal the vital functions of organs; and, Second: That we have no consciousness, of the functions of the different parts of the brain. Now, the acutest intellect having no knowledge of the functions of the brain except that derived from structure and consciousness, was absolutely incapable of telling whether Gall's views were true or false. Nevertheless, this was the actual condition of mind of the opponents, and it continues to be the state of most of those who reject Phrenology in the present day.

On the 5th May 1819 I communicated these propositions to Dr P. M. Roget, who had then published in the Supplement to the Encyclopædia Britannica a pretended refutation of Gall's "Cranioscopy," &c., and challenged him to confess or deny their truth and relevancy in relation to the question in hand.* But he answered that the essential point at issue is: "Whether there really exists such a uniform correspondence between certain forms of the head, skull, or brain, and certain characters of mind, as can be distinctly recognised by observation;" and that, in his opinion, the evidence derived from the observations of Drs Gall and Spurzheim "is quite inconclusive." In reply, I wrote that if the object be important, and if there be *no method* of attaining it, except that followed by Gall and Spurzheim, why, if their evidence was insufficient, did he not proceed to observe nature and seek for evidence of his own? He rejoined: "My comments of course applied solely to the evidence brought forward by its founders, Drs Gall and Spurzheim; I accordingly thought it right to omit all reference to my personal experience on the matter, more especially as I was not exactly writing in my own name; and I felt it nowise incumbent on me to lay the foundations of any similar system myself, or presume to direct others in the pursuit, by laying down a plan of operations to be followed for that purpose."

I have referred to this correspondence because it represents the condition of mind of the men who rejected Dr Gall's discovery forty years ago, and whose writings and authority formed the public opinion on it at that time. I can safely affirm that, after the most careful study of the objections, the conviction was irresistibly forced on me that their authors *had not made themselves acquainted* with the evidence adduced by Drs Gall and Spurzheim, and had never seriously considered the propositions that *Gall's method is the only one by which the object can be reached*, and that every person who has not resorted to the practice of it, is absolutely and necessarily ignorant whether his discoveries are true or false.

The only exception to this style of condemnation known to me was presented by Mr John Abernethy, who said: "I see no mode by which we can with propriety admit or reject the assertions of Drs Gall and Spurzheim, *except by pursuing the same course of investigations which they themselves have followed;* a task of great labour and difficulty, and one which, for various reasons, I should feel great repugnance to undertake."†

* See the correspondence in my translation of Gall on the Cerebellum, p. 217.
† Memoir of John Abernethy, by George Macilwain.

These observations are worthy of the honest and powerful mind that uttered them. The study *is* difficult, perhaps the most difficult of all subjects of scientific inquiry. The difficulties arise from the following circumstances. Phrenology is the Physiology of the Brain; and is not, and cannot become, an *exact*, but must ever remain an *estimative* science. In no department of Physiology can mathematical measurements be applied to determine the *size* of organs, on which, *cæteris paribus*, the amount of their vital power depends. We must *estimate* their size by tact, improved by experience. Again, the force of a vital function cannot be mathematically measured, but must be *estimated*. In Phrenology, therefore, we have to learn —1st, To know the exact situation of each organ; 2dly, To estimate its absolute size, and its size in relation to the other organs; 3dly, To discover the primitive faculty on which each particular mental manifestation depends; to *estimate* the strength of that faculty; and then to compare its strength with the size of its organs; 4thly, To discover by observation and experience what changes in the *direction* of the faculties are occasioned by the combinations of their organs in different degrees of relative size; 5thly, To estimate the effects of temperament and training on the *strength* and *activity* of the faculties; 6thly, To pursue these inquiries in a wide field of active life, and to devote time, observation, and intelligence to the study, with a sincere desire to arrive at truth. All this *is possible—has been done*—and may be accomplished by an inquirer of adequate ability who will qualify himself for conducting it by obtaining knowledge of the method and principles through which success can be attained. But it is no undue pretension to affirm that not one of the persons who so authoritatively pronounced Phrenology to be false, *had* qualified himself, in this manner, to form a judgment on the subject. In point of fact, as already observed, they were wholly unaware of their own incompetence, for the reasons before assigned, to form any rational opinion on its merits.

Yet the generation of Lecturers and Professors,* Preachers,

---

* The University of Edinburgh possesses two Professors who form exceptions to the observations in the text. Professor Gregory has long been a strenuous advocate of Phrenology; and Dr Laycock, Professor of the Practice of Medicine, without enrolling himself as a Phrenologist, recognises the soundness of its general principles, and applies them to cerebral pathology.

INTRODUCTION.   xvii

Reviewers, mental philosophers, and the reading public, who continue to reject Phrenology, have almost universally derived their opinions of it from the representations given by those guides whom they implicitly followed in their youth. Lord Jeffrey denied that the mind in its higher functions uses organs at all; and Dr William Stenhouse Kirkes, in his Handbook of Physiology recently published, informs us that " the reason, or spirit of man, which has knowledge of Divine truths, and the conscience, with its natural discernment of right and wrong, *cannot be proved to have any connection with the brain.*"* The reader will judge of the soundness of this statement by comparing it with the observations made on pages 27 to 32, and 42 to 44, of this volume, and also the facts adduced in the Appendix, No. II.

The young men of the present generation continue to imbibe the prejudices of their teachers without examination, and to retail them. Two examples have recently appeared in Edinburgh. Mr Edward Haughton, M.R.C.S.E., has published " The Criticism of an Essay" (by Mr Herring) " on Phrenology, read at the Hunterian Medical Society;" which criticism is remarkable only for puerility of thinking, and ignorance of the writings of the controversialists who have preceded him; and obviously owes its origin to a desire to gratify " Dr J. Hughes Bennett, Professor of the Institutes of Medicine in the University of Edinburgh, &c., &c.," to whom it is dedicated. The views of Phrenology communicated by this gentleman to his students may be inferred from the " Criticism."

The second example is afforded by Mr Thomas Spencer Baynes, LL.B., in a eulogy by him on Sir William Hamilton, published in the " Edinburgh Essays." He informs us that Sir William " proceeded to test the worth of Phrenology by an examination" of the facts on which it " professed to be wholly founded." " He selected several of the leading points laid down as the physiological basis of the system, such as the relative size and function of the cerebellum, the age at which the brain is fully developed, the presence and value of the frontal sinus—and found, after a series of experiments, that the dictum of the phrenologist on each point was not only

* 3d Edition, p. 453.

erroneous, but absolutely false." This is strong language; and Mr Baynes, after what I am about to mention, will perceive that he has exposed himself to the application of it to himself.

First—Sir William Hamilton, in contradiction to the Phrenologists, asserted that "the cerebella of the two sexes absolutely are nearly equal,—the preponderance rather in favour of the women." But Dr John Reid, Chandos Professor of Anatomy and Medicine in the University of St Andrews, afterwards published* the average result arrived at by him, after weighing 53 male brains and 34 female brains, as follows:—

Male.   Female.

Cerebellum, 5 oz. 4 dr.—4 oz. 12¼ dr.; difference in favour of the male, 7¾ dr.

Dr Reid's investigations were continued by Dr T. B. Peacock. He informs us that his tables† include the weights obtained by both Dr Reid and himself, and "are based on 356 weights of the encephalon." He states the average weight of the cerebellum in 57 males between 25 and 55 years of age, at 5 oz. 2·6 dr.—and in 34 females between the same ages, at 4 oz. 12·4 dr; making a difference in favour of the male of 6·2 dr., in direct contradiction to Sir William Hamilton's assertion.

Secondly—As to the Frontal Sinus. By an arrangement between Sir William Hamilton and me, Professors Christison and Syme, and the late Dr John Scott, were chosen as a court of inquiry to test the validity of Sir William Hamilton's objections against Phrenology, and they began with the frontal sinus. After hearing Sir William Hamilton at great length on the subject, the umpires unanimously set aside all the skulls produced by him, as insufficient to support his propositions; and the proceedings under the reference never went farther. Their verdict is printed verbatim in the Phrenological Journal, vol. v., p. 34.

Thirdly—Mr Baynes alludes to a correspondence between Sir William Hamilton and Dr Spurzheim, and says: "But the points at issue were never brought to a decision, as Dr Spurzheim refused to submit them to any adequate and impartial judges, demanding instead that they should be discussed before a popular assembly, and decided by the voice of a public

---

* London and Edinburgh Monthly Journal of Medical Science for April 1843.

† Published in the same Journal for August and September 1846.

meeting. *Of course Sir William Hamilton had too much respect for himself and the scientific questions at stake, to bring them before such an utterly incompetent tribunal."* Now, this statement betrays culpable ignorance of the facts, or a reckless disregard of truth; for Sir William Hamilton addressed his first attack on Phrenology and Phrenologists to a popular audience of ladies and gentlemen assembled by advertisements, and he renewed his assaults before the Royal Society of Edinburgh, also a public body. (See Phrenological Journal, vol. iv., p. 378.) In a letter dated 18th February 1828, " Dr Spurzheim returns compliments to Sir William Hamilton," and says, " Sir William Hamilton *publicly* attacked Phrenology before Dr Spurzheim visited Edinburgh; it is now Sir William Hamilton's duty to prove *publicly* his assertions. Dr Spurzheim, therefore, repeats for the fourth and last time that he is willing to meet Sir William Hamilton before the public." Again, on 29th February 1828, Dr Spurzheim writes that he "would have thankfully availed himself of a private meeting with Sir William Hamilton, and received from him private instruction in Anatomy and Physiology; but since Sir William *publicly* attacked Phrenology and its believers, Dr Spurzheim can meet him only before the public." (Phrenological Journal, vol. v., pp. 39-42.) In the words in italics, Mr Baynes has, through sheer ignorance, I presume, of the facts about which he was writing, pronounced a severe censure on the object of his eulogy. Neither party, probably, desired to constitute the public a "tribunal" to "decide" the questions at issue; but as Sir William Hamilton, by addressing a popular audience, had obviously intended to influence public opinion *against* Phrenology, Dr Spurzheim was certainly entitled to insist on having a public opportunity to refute his objections.

So little consideration have physiologists bestowed on the question of the best *method* of discovering the functions of the brain, that Dr Carpenter, no mean authority, says* that "All our positive knowledge of the functions of the nervous system in general, save that which results from our own consciousness of what passes within ourselves, and that which we obtain from watching the manifestations of disease in man, is derived from observations of the phenomena exhibited by ani-

* Principles of Human Physiology, p. 681. *Fourth Edition.*

mals, made the subjects of experiments; and in the interpretations of these, great caution must be exercised." Here, then, Dr Gall's method of comparing the strength of particular mental manifestations, such as Benevolence, Self-esteem, Love of Children, and so forth, in healthy human beings, with the size of particular parts of their brains, as a means of discovering the healthy functions, is absolutely ignored; while we are referred to consciousness as one source of knowledge of these functions, in utter disregard of the fact that consciousness does not reveal to us even the existence of the brain, much less its functions. If it did, how could men like Jeffrey and Dr Kirkes deny the necessity of organs of any kind in performing the higher operations of the mind? He refers to morbid manifestations of mind, or Mental Pathology, as the second source of knowledge; but in regard to all other vital organs, it is held that Pathology is rendered much more instructive when preceded by a sound physiology; in other words, it is advantageous to know the function of an organ in its healthy state, in order to arrive at a sound judgment concerning the effects of disease in altering that function.

Dr Draper, an eminent American physiologist, entertains views widely different from those of Dr Kirkes. He says: "Nearly all philosophers who have cultivated, in recent times, that branch of knowledge (Metaphysics), have viewed with apprehension the rapid advances of Physiology, foreseeing that it would attempt the final solution of problems which have exercised the ingenuity of the last twenty centuries. In this they are not mistaken. Certainly it is desirable that some new method should be introduced, which may give point and precision to whatever metaphysical truths exist, and enable us to distinguish, separate, and dismiss what are only vain and empty speculations."*

Religious prejudice has constituted another obstacle to the progress of Phrenology. The functions of the brain being unknown, and the whole phenomena of consciousness having been habitually ascribed to an immaterial mind acting independently of organs, there was a shock to religious feeling

---

* Human Physiology, &c., by John W. Draper, M.D., *New York*, 1856, p. 259.

against Dr Gall's discovery, which expressed itself in a variety of ways. No rational person is ever heard casting ridicule and reproach against the structure and functions of the lungs, the heart, the stomach, or any other organ, the structure and uses of which are known; because these are acknowledged to bear conspicuous indications of Divine Wisdom and Goodness. But, apparently owing to the structure and functions of the brain being unknown, they met with very different treatment. Gall's description of its uses was made the subject of every vulgar jest that petulant ignorance could invent; the cry of materialism was raised against it; and it has been charged with degrading man to the level of the brutes. These objections appear to me to be the consequences of sheer ignorance. I have accompanied religious and intelligent persons to the Phrenological Museum, and shown to them the small brain that is invariably accompanied by idiotcy; casts of the heads of executed criminals, exhibiting a large development of the base, and a deficient development of the upper or moral and religious portions of the head, and often a deficient development of the anterior lobe, devoted to intellect. In contrast to these, I have drawn their attention to casts of the heads and brains of men of high moral, religious, and intellectual endowments, and pointed out the differences in the proportions of these regions, between their heads and those of the criminally disposed. And I have placed before their eyes a large collection of the skulls of men and women of different nations, and pointed out the predominant development of the moral and intellectual regions in the most highly civilized; and the defective development of these in the savage and barbarous races; and I have said to these visitors: "These forms and proportions are natural: they proceed from God's laws governing our organism: Gall did not make them; he only called attention to their significance." But even such an appeal was ineffectual to rouse their serious attention. Their minds were so completely preoccupied by spiritual notions, that the ideas of the brain being an Institution of God, and of its different forms and proportions having any significance worthy of their attention, did not penetrate their intellects. They continued to laugh and joke, and object, and ridicule the whole subject, as if the brain were mere waste matter placed within the skull to give it weight, and keep it steady on the shoulders. I recollect, in particular, addressing in this manner one very intelligent religious person, of some scientific and literary attainments. He afterwards wrote an article in the North British Review, in which he spoke sneeringly of Dr Gall as "the man of bumps;" apparently without considering that God made the brain, and that as the brain gives form to the skull, it follows that if Gall be "the man of bumps," *a fortiori* is the Deity "the God of bumps!" The writings of religious men against the Physiology of the Brain are full of similar stolid manifestations of impiety.

How differently Mr Abernethy looked on the human structure is beautifully expressed in the following extract from his Memoirs before cited. He mentions that Galen said: "In explaining these things" (the structure and functions of living organisms and the laws by which these are regulated), "I esteem myself as composing a solemn hymn to the great Architect of our bodily frame, in which I think there is more true piety than in sacrificing whole hecatombs of oxen, or in burning the most costly perfumes; for, first, I endeavour from His works to know Him myself, and afterwards, by the same means, to shew Him to others, to inform them how great is His Wisdom, Goodness, and Power."

It is only the circumstance of little having been known of the structure* and functions of the brain before Dr Gall discovered them, that, in my opinion, can account for such irrational treatment as Phrenology has received from the religious world. But in this respect, it has only shared the fate of all other important discoveries that have gone greatly beyond the limits of contemporary knowledge. The earth continued to whirl men round on its surface every twenty-four hours, while they were stoutly denying that it did so; and they in vain appealed to the evidence of their senses to prove that it stood still. The solution of the question lay beyond the sphere of their senses. In like manner, our contemporaries are actually manifesting their different emotional and intellectual faculties with a degree of energy, corresponding, *cœteris paribus*, to the size of their brains, even when they

---

* See evidence as to the discovery of the structure of the brain, in the Appendix, No. III., to my work, "Phrenology applied to Painting and Sculpture."

are using those very organs in denying the fact. They in vain appeal to the testimony of their own consciousness for evidence to support their denial; for, as the proof of the rotation of the globe lay beyond the domain of the senses unaided by science, so, as already observed, the evidence of the functions of the brain lies out of the region of consciousness. So thoroughly, however, was the conviction that the earth stands still, ingrained in men's minds by the appearances of the heavens and the earth; so strongly was it supported by tradition as ancient as the human race, by books of the highest scientific authority, and by religion; that even after demonstrative evidence was produced of the fact of its motion, men could not imagine or believe it, but retained the established convictions and transmitted them to their children. In 1671, thirty years after the death of Galileo, and two years after Newton had commenced lecturing in Cambridge, Dr John Owen, the most eminent divine among the Independents, describes the Copernican System as " the late hypothesis fixing the sun in the centre of the world—built on fallible phenomena and advanced by many arbitrary presumptions against evident testimonies of Scripture, and reasons as probable as any which are produced in its confirmation." (*Prelim. Exerc.* xxxvi. to Hebrews, § 16, p. 636; *Edit.* 1840.)

A parallel example of the extreme difficulty which even superior men experience in embracing new ideas is presented by the cases of Dr Thomas Brown and Dr John Abercrombie. Both of these persons were practising physicians in Edinburgh, and both of them published works on mental philosophy. As physicians, both of them treated mental maladies as diseases of the brain; but, as metaphysicians, both discussed mental phenomena as if the mind were wholly independent of organs! A general reference to the brain as the organ of the mind may be found in their works, but they ignored the dependence of particular mental powers on particular portions of the brain, and were blind to all the consequences that flow from this fact. In like manner, so deeply and extensively is the conviction entertained that the feeling and thinking entity of man is something which acts independently of matter, and so strongly does this notion appear to be supported by consciousness; by nearly the universal acknowledgment of mankind, past and present; by the authority of the profoundest investigators of mental science; and by nearly all the religious teachers of all countries,—that no amount of evidence of the influence of the brain on the mental manifestations has been able to shake the belief of the great majority of the people of this age on the subject. It was only after successive generations, denying the earth's rotation, had been buried, and after the lapse of ages, that prejudice so far gave way that the demonstration of its motion was allowed to reach the minds of the young in their education. After this was achieved, the new doctrine was regarded by all instructed persons as a fact which had always been true, and with which every other well-ascertained phenomenon in nature was, and always had been, in accordance. It is probable, therefore, that it will be only after several more generations, practically denying the functions of the brain, have passed away, that serious attention will be generally bestowed on the evidence of its being the organ of the mental functions, and the chief instrument by means of which the government of the moral world is conducted; and only after the lapse of a long series of years will a just appreciation of the importance of Gall's discovery have so far triumphed over an ignorant prejudice against it, that it will be generally taught to the young as science. When this shall have been accomplished, educated men will allow that it has always been a fact, and they will proceed to bring their other ideas of nature into harmony with it, and to act upon them. The confusion which has so long appeared to reign in the moral world will then probably begin to disappear, and man will find himself master of his own destinies, to an extent of which at present no adequate conception can be formed.

But the grand religious objection to Phrenology has been, that it leads to materialism. It appears to me that man possesses no faculties which enable him to discover the essence of things, and that, therefore, he is incapable of arriving at any certain conclusion concerning the nature of the thinking entity in man and animals. But even assuming that it is the living brain which thinks and feels, those who urge this as an objection, appear never to have considered that if *God* has seen proper to employ the ten inorganic substances named on page 23 (to which Dr George Wilson has added

Fluorine), as materials with which to constitute the body and brain, and to endow them, while so employed, with all the vital and mental functions they possess, cerebral matter cannot be to *man* a fit object of aversion, contempt, and ridicule. I beg religious readers to look on this figure

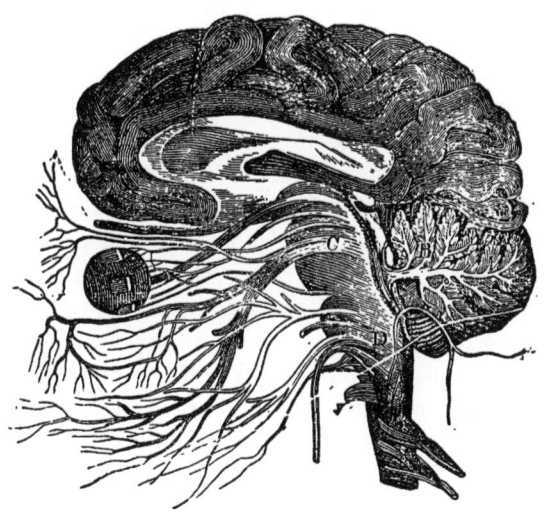

Here we perceive the nerves of all the senses entering into the brain, and the spinal cord proceeding from it; and we know that the cord sends forth nerves, one set of which conveys the mandates of the will down to, and the other conveys sensation up to it from, all parts of the body. I appeal to every reflecting person who believes in God, whether this complicated structure, with these connections, should continue to be treated only with contumely and aversion, as has been the practice in times past, or whether we should not approach the investigation of it with that seriousness of feeling which we exhibit in studying the other portions of the human structure which we believe to be of Divine origin. This appeal is specially necessary, because it is chiefly through the influence of religious persons that, even in the few schools into which Physiology has been introduced as a branch of instruction, the functions of the different parts of the brain, as organs of particular mental faculties, continue to be deliberately excluded.

This religious opposition to Phrenology appears more strikingly impolitic and absurd when we consider the present state of the dogmatic faith of the British Empire. The failure of the means of religious·instruction hitherto employed has forced itself upon the attention even of religious men. The Rev. R. C. Savage, A.M., Vicar of Nuneaton, &c., in a Letter to the Earl of Denbigh, says :* "We find this melancholy fact recorded against us, that on the census Sunday in March 1851, out of our population of 475,013, only 75,706 attended any place of worship connected with the Church of England ; and that the whole amount of persons (including the Sunday Schools) attending *any* place of worship in Warwickshire on that day was only 142,227, leaving 332,786 in this county who were absent from the worship of Almighty God on that day." In Birmingham and Coventry, the proportions of persons absent from public worship on that day to those present were similar to the foregoing; and the Reverend Vicar observes, that "it cannot be said the churches were deserted and the chapels filled ; your Lordship will observe there were more vacant sittings in the places of dissenting worship than in the churches" (P. 6). "But here is the fearful fact, that out of a population (in Birmingham) of 232,841, only 45,544 attended any place of worship in the morning ; only 6877 in the afternoon ; and only 33,564 in the evening. And the numbers in the morning and afternoon would include many of the Sunday School children, of whom there are 21,406 !" (P. 7.)

Mr Savage adds : "Surely, My Lord, this is a startling fact, which, while it arouses our fears and calls forth our sorrow, should awaken also our deepest sympathy in searching out the cause of this disregard for, and neglect of, the ordinances of religion and the services of the Church." (P. 6.)

"And this leads to our *Second point*, a consideration of the Remedy most suitable to meet this alarming, but true, representation of our present social condition. The great question doubtless is, how shall this threatening evil be met and be dissipated ? how shall the masses of the population be delivered from the spiritual and moral pestilence which is already so fearful, and which by every day's delay grows into more overwhelming certainty of desolation and ruin to all that we hold

---

* London : Seeley, Jackson, and Halliday. 1856.

dear and sacred? An increase of Churches—an increase of the Pastorate—an increase of the means of Education and of children brought under the influence of our Schools, both day and Sunday—the erection of Reformatories for juvenile offenders—the establishment of ragged schools—these no doubt are all needed, and are all valuable and indispensable helps to the Church in the great work which is now before her—*but these do not accomplish it.* These do not reach the evil in all its varied ramifications; some touch it at one point and some at another; but still the evil exists and is daily increasing.—*We want an agency which will reach where these do not reach, and which will aid and strengthen them where they do.*" (P. 16.)

The agency which he recommends is "the employment of pious, sober-minded, and judicious *Laymen*, properly qualified to work under the Clergyman, in reading the Scriptures and visiting from house to house, and thus to invade and penetrate the dark dense mass of ignorance, prejudice, and irreligion, which exists to the expression of the Church's sympathy and of her care for immortal souls." It is implied that only the old formulas are to be used, and the old doctrines inculcated by these laymen, in the face of all the experience here recorded of the want of power in these to interest and attract the people! As the foregoing representation applies more or less to every part of Great Britain and Ireland, I have taken the liberty, in the following work, to suggest something additional to the means recommended by Mr Savage; and, however erroneous my views may appear, it is clear that *something* besides the system that has failed is needed, to carry forward the civilization of the country; and, perhaps, in a multitude of counsellors, wisdom may be found.

A grand obstacle to the discovery of remedies for these evils has been raised by the practice of many religious persons of denouncing as infidels and "bad men" all who dissent from the accredited standards of faith and suggest improvements on them. This conduct has at length led to a reaction, which is constantly gaining strength. Within the last twenty years not only various doctrines, but, in some instances, the whole fabric of Christianity itself, have been subjected to numerous searching, logical, and temperate assaults. In support of this remark, it is necessary only to refer to the following among many similar works which have appeared within that time: Froude's Nemesis of Faith:—T. Parker's Discourse of Matters pertaining to Religion:—Religious Thoughts of a Believer in Nature:—Greg's Creed of Christendom:—Mackay's Progress of the Intellect:—De Wette's Introduction to the Old Testament, translated by T. Parker:—Eichhorn's Introduction to the same:—Chevalier Bunsen's " Gott in der Geschichte:"—Macnaught on Inspiration:—Donaldson's "Christian Orthodoxy," and "Jasher:"—" Hebrew Records," by Dr Giles:—Dr Davidson's vol. in new edition of Horne's Introduction:—Coleridge's Confessions of an Inquiring Spirit:—Jowett's Commentary on Paul's Epistles:—F. Newman's Phases of Faith, and other works:—The Westminster Review, passim:—National Review, January 1857; Article, "Spurgeon and his popularity."

I give this list to impress, if possible, religious persons with a perception of the position of Religion in the present day, in the hope of inducing them to listen with patience and candour to suggestions offered in the spirit, not of destruction* but of improvement. As it is chiefly through the periodical press that they seek to cast obloquy on reformers, I beg to call their attention to the passage quoted from Lamartine on the title page of this work, and recommend the following examples of liberality to their imitation.

In " Lowe's Edinburgh Magazine" for July 1848, said to have been an organ of the Free Church, the following observations occur:—" Now let speculative Philosophy take warning and encouragement from the progress of Geology, if it would assert its own honour, or offer a spontaneous testimony to the majesty of truth. And for ourselves, we hesitate not to aver, that the honest truth-seeking infidel, when handling the pure symbols of some favourite science, which he knows dispassionately

---

* In a work entitled "At Home and Abroad," containing selections from the correspondence of the late Countess D'Ossoli (Margaret Fuller), lately published in the U. S., we find the following account of Thomas Carlyle and his conversation: "He has touched the rocks, and they have given forth musical answer; little more was wanting to begin to construct the City. But that little was wanting, and the work of construction is left to those that come after him; nay all attempts of the kind, he is the readiest to deride, fearing new shams worse than the old, unable to trust the general action of a thought, and finding no heroic man, no natural king to represent it, and challenge his confidence." In Chap. I. I have freely availed myself of Mr Carlyle's powerful eloquence in exposing error. I should doubly rejoice should he now try to extinguish the foregoing reproach by making equally splendid efforts to build up a new fabric of truth.

and loves disinterestedly, will make a larger contribution towards the advancement of even religious truth, because undesignedly he explores and interprets the operation of harmonious law in the universe of God, than the rigorous and bristling divine, who, with iron tongue and leaden brains, would engulph both science and religion under the crushing terrors of one enormous anathema."

"An Atheist," says the "Nonconformist," a religious newspaper conducted with great liberality and ability, "is not to be tabooed. He is not to be thrust out of the pale of humanity. Our puritan forefathers would have branded and imprisoned him; we would reason and plead with him. To us he is, and to them he ought to have been, a man and a brother. If he really believes there is no God (*prove* it he cannot), the 'portentous heroism' of such a creed awakes within us thrilling emotions of wonder and surprise. And if with this no-belief he connects a life irreproachable and unselfish, if with this no-belief he associates high patriotic yearnings and generous political sentiments, and if with this no-belief never a word of scorn or cankering hate for those who are entrapped by 'superstition' escapes his lips, then we dare not despise, much less loathe, such a man: we can give him the right hand of true friendship, and not fearing that he will make us worse, we will try to make him better. By all means let the Atheist have free speech, let him address the public ear by the press and by the platform with most unchartered liberty; we would no more denounce him than we would attempt to silence him. He has as much right to speak *his* conviction as we ours. And not only so, it is his duty to do this. Suppression of thought leads to suppression of truth. Concealment of conviction becomes an extinguisher of truth." (*The Nonconformist*, Dec. 1852.)

Such sentiments as these do more to sustain Christianity than the most fiery denunciations against Atheists and Atheism. The former proceed from the moral emotions, and are addressed to the same emotions in other men; the latter flow from the animal propensities, which alone they evoke.

In the same commendable spirit writes Dr James Buchanan, Divinity Professor in the Free Church College at Edinburgh, in his late work, entitled "Faith in God and Modern Atheism compared, in their Essential Nature, Theoretic Grounds, and Practical Influence;" Edinburgh, 1855. He argues with the Atheists as if they were thinking beings, possibly lovers of truth; and in contending with other classes of men to whose opinions he is more or less opposed, he writes with a like degree of candour and moderation. Though myself so unfortunate as to be one of the objects of his hostile criticism (see Appendix, No. IX.), I have read with pleasure several passages in which the study of the laws of nature is strongly recommended by him. "It is not true," says he, "that there is any real or necessary antagonism between the laws of nature and the prerogatives of God; on the contrary, let our knowledge advance, until *all* the phenomena both of the Material and Moral worlds shall be reduced under so many general laws, even then Superstition might disappear, but Theology would remain, and would only receive fresh accessions of evidence and strength, in proportion as the wise order of nature is more fully unfolded, and its most hidden mysteries disclosed." (Vol. I., p. 485.) Again: " On the ground of analogy, we think it highly probable that every department of nature *is* subject to regular and stable laws; and on the same ground we may anticipate that, in the progressive advance of human knowledge, many new fields will yet be conquered, and added to the domain of Science." (Vol. II., p. 194.) In regard to Phrenology, he admits that it no more leads to materialism than do similar facts which everybody recognises (vol. II., pp. 73, 90–93); and that "the mere proof of the soul's being an immaterial substance would not necessarily infer its being also immortal." (Vol. II., p. 121.)

To prevent misunderstanding, I beg here to explain the meaning which is attached in the following work to the expressions," Laws of Nature" and " Natural Laws." Every object and being in nature has received a definite constitution, and also powers of acting on other objects and beings. The action of the forces is so regular, that we describe them as operating under laws imposed on them by God; but these words indicate merely our perception of the regularity of the action. It is impossible for man to alter or break a natural law, when understood in this sense; for the action of the forces and the effects they produce are placed beyond his control. But the observation of the action of the forces leads man to draw rules from it for the regulation of his own conduct, and these rules are called natural laws, because Nature dictates or prescribes them as guides to conduct. If we fail to attend to the operations of the natural forces, we may unknowingly act in opposition to them; but as the action is inherent in the things, and does not vary with our state of knowledge, we must suffer from our ignorance and inattention. Or we may know the forces and the consequences which their action inevitably produces, but from ignorance that through them God is dictating to us rules of conduct; or from mistaken notions of duty, from passion, self-conceit, or other causes, we may disregard them, and act in opposition to them: but the consequences will not be altered to suit our ignorant errors or humours; we must obey or suffer. Further explanations on this subject are given on pages 97 and 208 of the present work.

It is proper also to mention that many passages and ideas that have already appeared in my other works are here reproduced, not as new truths, but as the foundations of a new application of them. Only two alternatives were presented to me; either to refer the reader to these passages scattered over several works (which would have broken all continuity of argument), or to reproduce them; and I have adopted the latter as the more convenient course for the reader.

Finally—The same propositions are frequently repeated in the different chapters of this work, and I wish to explain that this has been done intentionally; because my object has been, if possible, to break up some old religious associations, in order to facilitate the introduction of new ideas; and it appeared to me that a single cold announcement of the new suggestions, however clear and logical, would have little effect in accomplishing this end.

ON THE

RELATION BETWEEN SCIENCE AND RELIGION.

CHAPTER I.

ON THE PRESENT STATE OF THE RELATION BETWEEN SCIENCE AND RELIGION.

THE Reformation in the sixteenth century produced a powerful effect on the European mind. The miracles, precepts, and sublime devotional effusions of the Old and New Testaments, excited, with deep intensity, the religious sentiments of the people, and introduced ardent discussions on temporal and eternal interests, which, unfortunately, were followed by furious and desolating wars. Freedom on earth, and salvation in heaven or perdition in hell, were the mighty topics which then engaged public attention.

In the beginning of the seventeenth century, a generation born and educated under these exciting influences, appeared upon the stage. The Reformation was then consummated, but the duty remained of acting it out in deeds. The new generation had read in the Books of the Old Testament of a people whose king was God; whose national councils were guided by omniscience, and whose enterprises, whether in peace or war, were aided and accomplished by omnipotence employing means altogether apart from the ordinary course of nature. The New Testament presented records of a continued exercise of similar supernatural powers; and the great lesson taught in both seemed to that generation to be, that the power of God was exercised as a shield to protect, and an irresistible influence to lead to success and victory in secular affairs, *those who believed and worshipped aright*, who embraced cordially the doctrines revealed in the sacred volumes, who abjured all self-righteousness and self-reliance, and who threw themselves in perfect confidence and humility on Him as their King, protector, and avenger.

A

In the first half of the seventeenth century, the active members of society in England and Scotland embraced these views as principles not only of faith but of practice. With that profound earnestness of purpose which is inspired by sincere conviction of religious truth, they desired to realize in deeds what they professed as faith. As remarked by Thomas Carlyle, that generation "attempted to bring the Divine law of the Bible into actual practice in men's affairs on the earth." In the contests between Cromwell and the Covenanters, we observe both parties claiming to be "the people of God;" both asserting that they were directed by Divine influence, and supported by Divine power, even when in hostile collision with each other. It is necessary only to read attentively Cromwell's letters and speeches, and the contemporary narratives of the Covenanters, to be satisfied of this fact. Each party ascribed its successes to the Divine approval of its conduct and belief, and its calamities to displeasure with its unbelief or other sins. When Cromwell overthrew the Scotch, and "had the execution of them," in other words, the slaughter of them, for many miles in the pursuit, he called it "a sweet mercy," vouchsafed to him by God, to whom he devoutly ascribed the glory. After mentioning his victory at Dunbar, the trophies of which were about "three thousand Scotch slain," "near ten thousand prisoners," "the whole baggage and train taken," with "all their artillery, great and small," he adds, "It is easy to see the Lord hath done this. It would do you good to see and hear our poor foot to go up and down making their boast of God."*

The Covenanters held the same belief; but, somewhat inconsistently, while they confessed that their own religious unworthiness had brought upon them the Divine displeasure, they denied to Cromwell the right to interpret the victory as a manifestation of the Divine approval of *his* faith, principles, and practice:—They endeavoured to represent it as merely "an event;" for which Cromwell rebukes them in the following words:—"You (the men of the Covenant) say that you have not so learned Christ 'as to hang the equity of your cause upon events.' We (for our part) could wish that blindness had not been cast upon your eyes to all those marvellous dispensations which God hath lately wrought in England. But did you not solemnly appeal (to God) and pray? Did not we do so too? And ought not you and we to think, with fear and trembling, of the hand of the great God in this mighty and strange appearance of His, instead of slightly

* Letter XCII., Cromwell to Lenthal, dated "Dunbar, 4th September 1650." (Carlyle's Cromwell, vol. ii. p. 41.)

calling it an 'event?' Were not both your and our expectations renewed from time to time whilst we waited upon God, to see which way He would manifest himself upon our appeals? And shall we, after all these our prayers, fastings, tears, expectations, and solemn appeals, call these bare 'events?' The Lord pity you."*

While the people of that age entertained these views of the manner of God's administration of secular affairs, they were equally convinced of the supernatural agency of the devil, and with similar earnestness acted on this conviction. They ascribed their sins to Satanic influence on their minds, and attributed to the exercise of Satanic power many of the physical evils under which they suffered. They imagined that this power was exercised by the devil through the instrumentality of human beings, and burned thousands of these supposed agents of the fiend, under the name of witches. This belief lingered among the Scotch people a century later. In February 1743 the "Associate Presbytery" of the Secession Church passed an " Act for renewing the National Covenant ;" and among other national sins which they confessed and vowed to renounce is mentioned, " The Repeal of the Penal Statutes against Witchcraft, contrary to the express laws of God, and for which a holy God may be provoked, in a way of righteous judgment, to leave those who are already ensnared to be hardened more and more, and to permit Satan to tempt and seduce others to the same wicked and dangerous snare."

These were the views of God's providence entertained by the religious men of the seventeenth century. Those who were not penetrated by a deep sentiment of religion acted then, as the same class does now, on the views of the order of nature with which their own experience and observation, aided by those of others, had supplied them. They did not trouble themselves with much inquiry whether this order was systematic or incidental, moral, or irrespective of morality; but acted as their views of expediency dictated at the moment. It is with the opinions of the religious and earnest men of that century that we are now principally engaged.

In commenting on that period, Thomas Carlyle observes, in his own quaint style, that " the nobility and gentry of England were then a very strange body of men. The English squire of the seventeenth century clearly appears to have believed in God, not as a figure of speech, but as a very fact, very awful to the heart of the English squire." He adds,

* Letter XCVII., Cromwell to "The Governor of Edinburgh Castle," dated "Edinburgh, 12th September 1650." *Lib. cit.*, vol. ii. p. 65.

"We have wandered far away from the ideas which guided us in that century, and, indeed, which had guided us in all preceding centuries; but of which that century was the ultimate manifestation. We have wandered very far, and must endeavour to return and connect ourselves therewith again."*

I ask, How shall we return? This is a grave question, and the answer demands serious consideration.

The grand characteristic of the Jewish dispensation, on which chiefly these views of the Divine government of the world were founded, was, that it was special and supernatural. In the seventeenth century the people possessed very little correct scientific knowledge of the elements, agencies, and laws of inorganic and organic nature. The Scriptures constituted almost the sole storehouse of deep reflection and profound emotion for that age; and in the absence of scientific knowledge, they fell naturally into the belief that, as the Scriptures were given for guides to human conduct, the same scheme of Providence, physical and moral, which had prevailed in ancient times, must still continue in force. Their conviction on this point appears to have been profound and sincere, and they attempted to act it out in deeds.

But was there no error of apprehension here? Were they not mistaken in believing that the course of Providence was the same in their day as it is described to have been among the Jews in the times of the Scripture records? A brief consideration of their actions, and the results of them, will perhaps throw some light on this question.

They assumed that the supernatural agencies which Scripture told them had been manifested under the Jewish dispensation might still be evoked, and would, in some form or other, be exerted for their guidance and support, if they appealed to God, and called for them in a right spirit. Hence, instead of studying and conforming to the laws of nature, they resorted to fastings, humiliations, praise, and prayers, as practical means not only of gaining battles and establishing political power, but of obtaining Divine direction in all the serious affairs of life. Their *theology* and their science, so far as they had any science, were in harmony. They did not recognize an established and regular order of nature as the means through which God governs the world, and to which He requires man to conform his conduct; but regarded every element of physical nature, and every faculty of the human mind, as under the administration of a special and supernatural providence.

* *Lib. cit.*, vol. i. pp. 3 and 87.

They viewed God as wielding all these elements arbitrarily, according to His will; *and on that will they believed they could operate by religious faith and observances.* In principle, their view of the nature of the Divine administration of the world was similar to that entertained by the Greeks and Romans. Homer's priests and heroes offered supplications to the gods for direct interference in favour of their schemes, and their prayers are represented to have been occasionally successful in eliciting supernatural aid. Cromwell, and the men of his age, with more true and exalted conceptions of God, believed in His still administering the affairs of men, not by means of a regular order of causes and effects, but by direct exercises of special power.

I should say that in this condition of mind they were inspired by pure and exalted religious emotions, but misled by great errors in theology. It was under the influence of such views of the Divine administration, that the existing standards of the Church of England, and of the Presbyterian Church of Scotland, were framed; and hence perhaps arose the very meagre recognition of the order of God's providence in the course of nature, as *religious* truth, and as a system of practical instruction for the guidance of human conduct, which characterizes them.

After that age, however, the human understanding, by a profounder and more exact study of nature, obtained a different view of the course of Providence in the administration of temporal affairs. Science revealed a system in which every object, animate and inanimate, appears to be endowed with peculiar qualities and agencies, which it preserves and exerts with undeviating regularity, as long as its circumstances continue unchanged; and in which each object is adapted, with wisdom and benevolence, to the others, and all to man. In the words of the Rev. Mr Sedgwick, science unfolded a fixed order of creation, so clear and intelligible that "we are justified in saying that, in the moral as in the physical world, God seems to govern by general laws."—" I am not now," says he, " contending for the doctrine of moral necessity; but I do affirm, that the moral government of God is by general laws, and *that it is our bounden duty to study those laws, and, as far as we can, to turn them to account."*

Here, then, an important revolution has been effected in the views of profound thinkers, in regard to the mode in which Providence administers this world. Science has banished from their minds belief in the exercise, by the Deity, in our

---

* A Discourse on the Studies of the University (of Cambridge). By Adam Sedgwick, M.A., &c., 3d edition.

day, of special acts of supernatural power, as a means of influencing human affairs, and it has presented a systematic order of nature, which man may study, comprehend, and follow, as a guide to his practical conduct. In point of fact, the new faith has already partially taken the place of the old. In everything physical, men now act more on the belief that this world's administration is conducted on the principle of an established order of nature, in which objects and agencies are presented to man for his study,—are to some extent placed under his control,—and are wisely calculated to promote his instruction and enjoyment. Some individuals adopt the same view in regard even to moral affairs. The creed of the modern man of science is well expressed by Mr Sedgwick in the following words:—" If there be a superintending Providence, and if His will be manifested by general laws, operating both on the physical and moral world, *then must a violation of these laws be a violation of His will, and be pregnant with inevitable misery.* Nothing can, in the end, be expedient for man, *except it be subordinate to those laws the Author of Nature has thought fit to impress on his moral and physical creation.*" Other clergymen also embrace the same view. The Rev. Dr Thomas Guthrie, in his pamphlet, " A Plea for Ragged Schools," observes, that " They commit a grave mistake, who forget that injury as inevitably results from flying in the face of a moral or mental, as of a physical law."

This revolution in practical belief, however, is only partial; and the great characteristic of the religious mind at the present day is its aversion to the doctrine of an intelligible, moral, and practical system of government revealed by God to man in the order of nature for the guidance of his conduct, and that correct expositions of this system possess the character of *religious truths.* This unbelief in an intelligible and practically useful Divine government in nature affects our religion, our literature, and our conduct. I put the following questions in all earnestness:—Are the fertility of the soil, the health of the body, the prosperity of individuals and of nations—in short, the great secular interests of mankind—now governed by special acts of supernatural power? Science answers that they are not. Are they, then, governed by any regular and comprehensible natural laws? If they are not, then is this world a theatre of anarchy, and consequently of atheism; it is a world without the practical manifestation of a God. If, on the other hand, such laws exist as science proclaims, they must be of Divine institution, and worthy of all reverence; and I ask, In the standards of what church, from the pulpits of what sect, and in the schools of what denomination of Christians, are these laws taught to either the young or old as religious truths of Divine authority, and as practical guides for conduct in this world's affairs? If we do not now live under a special supernatural government of the world, but under a government by natural laws, and if these laws are not studied, honoured, and obeyed as God's laws, are we not actually a nation without a religion in harmony with the true order of Providence, and therefore without a religion adapted to practical purposes?

The answer will probably be that this argument is infidelity; but, with all deference, I reply that the denial of a regular, intelligible, wisely adapted, and divinely appointed order of nature, as a guide to human conduct in this world, is practical atheism; while the acknowledgment of the existence of such an order, accompanied by the nearly universal neglect of teaching and obeying its requirements, is real infidelity, disrespectful to God, and injurious to the best interests of man. We cannot consistently believe that God answers the *prayers* of the Mahommedans, Hindoos, Persians, and Chinese, for we deny the soundness of their faith; nor that, as in the case of the ancient Jews, He exercises a special providence for their guidance to temporal prosperity, and for their consolation in affliction and in the hour of death: and yet, if God really governs the world, his laws must apply to these nations as well as to ourselves.

The churches which have at all recognised the order of nature, have attached to it a lower character than truly belongs to it. They do not recognise it as religious, *i.e.*, as an administration of Divine origin, deserving of reverential obedience. They have treated science and secular knowledge chiefly as objects of curiosity and sources of gain, and have given to actions intelligently founded on them the character of prudence. So humble has been their estimate of the importance of science, that they have not systematically called in the influence of the religious sentiments to hallow, elevate, and enforce the teachings of nature. In most of their schools the elucidation of the relations of science to human conduct is omitted altogether, and catechisms of human invention usurp its place.

Society, meantime, including the Calvinistic world itself, proceeds in its secular enterprises on the basis of natural science, so far as it has been able to discover it. If practical men send a ship to sea, they endeavour to render it staunch and strong, and to place in it an expert crew and an able commander, as conditions of safety, dictated by their conviction of the order of nature in flood and storm. If they are sick, they resort to a physician to restore them to health, according to the ordinary laws of organization. If they suffer famine from wet seasons, they drain their lands; and so forth. All these practices and observances are taught and enforced by men of science and the secular press, as measures of practical prudence; but few churches recognise the order of nature on which they are founded, as an object of reverence, and a becoming subject of religious instruction.

On the contrary, from the days of Galileo to the present time, religious professors have too often made war on science, on scientific teachers, and on the order of nature, and many of them still adhere, as far as the reason and light of the public mind will permit them, to their old doctrine of an inherent disorder reigning in the natural world. That disorder prevails is undeniable; but science proclaims that it is to a great extent owing to man's ignorance of his own nature, and that of the external world, and to his neglect of their relations. Many theologians do not recognise such views, but proceed as if human affairs were, somehow or other, still, in our day, influenced by special manifestations of Divine power. Mr Plumptre is reported, in the *Times*, to have said, in his place in Parliament, while discussing the famine in Ireland in 1846–7, through the failure of the potato crop, that "He did not mean to enter at large into the question where the guilt which had drawn down upon them this tremendous dispensation lay, whether that guilt lay with the people or the rulers; but he could not help expressing what he considered to be a well-founded opinion, that the rulers of this country had deeply offended, by some acts which they had recently placed on the statute-book, and which, in his belief, were calculated to bring down the Divine displeasure on the land; but into this he would not enter."

It is conjectured that this Honourable Gentleman had in view the grant to the Roman Catholic College of Maynooth, or the repeal of the corn-laws, as the "act" which, in his opinion, was calculated to bring down the Divine displeasure on the land. Be the acts what they may, the speech implied that, in his opinion, sin in the people, or in their rulers, had led to a special deflection of physical nature from the ordinary course, in order to produce a famine, for the punishment, not of the special offenders, but of men, women, and children promiscuously, many of whom had no control over the transactions. These notions would be unworthy of notice, except that they are still embraced as religion by large numbers of our people. In the olden time, eclipses were viewed as portentous announcements of Heaven's wrath against the sins of men; but the discovery of unswerving physical laws, by which the motions of the heavenly bodies are regulated, and in virtue of which the certain occurrence of eclipses can be predicted, has expunged that superstition from the civilized mind. Nevertheless the same blind love of the wonderful and mysterious, which led our ancestors to quail before a natural and normal obscuration of the sun, leads the unenlightened mind in our day to see in sin the causes of such visitations as cholera and agricultural blights, instead of looking for them in physical conditions presented to our understandings as problems to be solved, and to be then turned to account in avoiding future evils. Examples are frequently occurring of this conflict between the views of men who acknowledge a practical natural Providence, and those who do not.

Archbishop Whately, in his "Address to the Clergy and other Members of the Established Church on the use and abuse of the present occasion" (the famine in Ireland in 1846–47), says—

"But advantage has been taken of the existing calamity to inculcate, with a view to the conversion of persons whom I believe to be in error, doctrines which I cannot but think utterly unsound, and of dangerous tendency, by arguments which will not stand the test of calm and rational examination. There are some who represent the present famine (as indeed they did the cholera some years back) as a Divine judgment sent for the punishment of what they designate as national sins, especially the degree of toleration and favour shewn to the members of the Church of Rome. Now this procedure, the attributing to such and such causes the supposed Divine wrath, is likely, when those of a different creed from our own are thus addressed, to be by some of them rejected as profane presumption, and by others *retorted*. When once men begin to take upon them the office of inspired prophets, and to pronounce boldly what are the counsels of the Most High, it is as easy to do this on the one side as on the other. Roman Catholics who are told that a pestilence or a famine are sent as judgments on the land for the toleration of Romanism, may contend that, on the contrary, it is the Protestantism that is the national sin. And without the evidence of a sensible miracle to appeal to, neither party can expect to convince the other.

"When Israel was afflicted with a famine, in the days of Elijah, on account of the idolatry of those of the people who had offended the Lord by worshipping Baal, the idolaters might have contended that the judgment was sent by Baal against the worshippers of Jehovah, *had not* the prophet expressly denounced that judgment *beforehand*, and foretold both the commencement, and afterwards the termination, of the drought, besides calling down the fire from heaven upon the altar. This it is that enables us to pronounce that that famine was a Divine judgment sent for the sin of Israel, and for *what* sin. And it is the same with the many similar cases that are recorded in Scripture. That Sodom and Gomorrah were destroyed on account of their abominable wickedness we *know*, *because Scripture* tells us so. And that Ananias and Sapphira were struck dead for tempting the Spirit of God we know, and all present knew, *because* the Apostle Peter announced beforehand their fate. and declared the crime which called it down. But for any uninspired man to take upon him to make similar declarations respecting any one of his neighbours who may die suddenly, or concerning any city that may be destroyed by a volcano or an earthquake, is as irrational and presumptuous as it is uncharitable and unchristian."

Another example is presented by a letter addressed by Lord Palmerston, as Home Secretary, to the Presbytery of Edinburgh, in answer to their inquiry whether he intended to advise the Queen to order a day of fasting, humiliation, and prayer, to be held in Scotland, in order to supplicate Divine Providence to stay the cholera which afflicted the people in 1854:—

" The Maker of the universe has established certain laws of nature for the planet in which we live, and the weal or woe of mankind depends upon the observance or the neglect of those laws. One of those laws connects health with the absence of those gaseous exhalations which proceed from over-crowded human beings, or from decomposing substances, whether animal or vegetable; and those same laws render sickness the almost inevitable consequence of exposure to those noxious influences. But it has at the same time pleased Providence to place it within the power of man to make such arrangements as will prevent or disperse such exhalations, so as to render them harmless; and it is the duty of man to attend to those laws of nature, and to exert the faculties which Providence has thus given to man for his own welfare.

" The recent visitation of cholera, which has for the moment been mercifully checked, is an awful warning given to the people of this realm, that they have too much neglected their duty in this respect, and that those persons with whom it rested to purify towns and cities, and to prevent or remove the causes of disease, have not been sufficiently active in regard to such matters. Lord Palmerston would, therefore, suggest that the best course which the people of this country can pursue to deserve that the further progress of the cholera should be stayed, will be to employ the interval that will elapse between the present time and the beginning of next spring in planning and executing measures by which those portions of their towns and cities which are inhabited by the poorest classes, and which, from the nature of things, must most need purification and improvement, may be freed from those causes and sources of contagion, which, if allowed to remain, will infallibly breed pestilence, and be fruitful in death, in spite of all the prayers and fastings of a united but inactive nation. When man has done his utmost for his own safety, then is the time to invoke the blessing of Heaven to give effect to his exertions."

The majority of the Presbytery expressed great dissatisfaction with this communication, and refused to acknowledge that cleansing the town would be a becoming substitute for a day of fasting, humiliation, and prayer, as a means of averting cholera. The civic rulers of Edinburgh, however, acted on it, and with very beneficial effects; for the disease fell far more lightly on the city on this occasion than at the previous visitation in 1831.

It is impossible that the public mind can advance in sound and self-consistent practical principles of action in this world's affairs, while conflicting views of science, religion, and the course of God's Providence, are poured forth from the pulpit and the press ; and it is equally impossible that the youthful mind can be trained to study, reverence, and conform to the course of God's Providence, while that Providence is treated with so little consideration by those who assume the character of accredited expositors of the Divine will.

The questions, then, Whether there be an intelligible course of nature revealed to the human understanding, whether it should be taught to the young, and whether the religious sentiments should be trained to venerate and conform to it as of Divine institution ? are not barren speculations respecting dogmas and doctrines. They touch a highly momentous practical principle. While an impassable gulph stands between the views of God's Providence on which society in its daily business acts, and the religious faith which it professes to hold, the influence of the latter on social conduct must necessarily be feeble and limited. It is a matter of great importance to have the principles of action and of belief brought into harmony. Nothing can retard the moral and intellectual advancement of the people more thoroughly than having a theology for churches and Sundays, and a widely different code of principles for everyday conduct; and yet this *is*, and *must continue to be*, the case with all the Christian nations, while they fail to recognise and to study the order of Providence in nature as a divinely appointed guide to human action.

A second Reformation in religion is imperatively called for, and is preparing. The devout teacher will recognise man and the natural world as constituted by Divine benevolence and wisdom, and adapted to each other for man's instruction and benefit. He will communicate to the young a knowledge of that constitution and its adaptations, as the basis of their religious faith and practice in reference to this world. Until this change shall have been accomplished, religion will never exert its due influence over human affairs.

Thomas Carlyle, in treating of the opinions of the seventeenth century, observes, that " the Christian doctrines which then dwelt alive in every heart, have now in a manner died out of all hearts,—very mournful to behold ; and *are not the guidance of this world any more.*" Dr Chalmers also says :—
" As things stand at present, our creeds and confessions have become effete, and the Bible a dead letter ; and that orthodoxy which was at one time the glory, by withering into the inert and lifeless, is now the shame and reproach of all our churches." Again : " There must be a most deplorable want amongst us of ' the light shining before men,' when in-

stead of glorifying our cause, they (men like **Thomas Carlyle**) can speak, and with a truth the most humiliating, of our inert and unproductive orthodoxy." Though in some respects erroneous, this representation is literally true in the sense in which I have explained the fact. It is chiefly in regard to the continuation of the special supernatural agency of God in this world, that the belief of the seventeenth century has practically gone out. It has not been abandoned in direct terms; on the contrary, it is retained in the standards and instructions of the churches, and is embraced, or attempted to be embraced, by many individuals: but, in point of fact, it is no longer felt to be a reality by modern enlightened Christians.

"Nay, worse still," continues Mr Carlyle, "*the cant of them does yet dwell alive with us;* little doubting that it is cant." With the *ignorant*, it is *not* cant, but a sincere, although a sadly confused belief. The strong-minded and well-informed men who have abandoned the ancient faith, are *wrong* in supposing that it is cant in their weaker brethren. They are themselves to blame for not honestly disabusing them, and informing them that the belief of the seventeenth century was, in this particular, a mistake, and that it no longer constitutes a practical rule of action. Mr Carlyle proceeds: "*In which fatal intermediate state, the eternal sacredness* of this universe itself, of this human life itself, *has fallen dark to the most of us.*" This is lamentably true. The religious sentiments are not permitted practically to recognise the mode of God's administration in the ordinary course of nature, as revealing his laws for the guidance of human conduct. We really *are* in the intermediate state here described. The old belief *has* partially died away; and our churches scowl upon the new belief, which perhaps may help to restore "the eternal sacredness of this universe itself, and of this human life itself."

In Germany, which led the way in the first Reformation, the same truth has forced itself on the attention of religious men. Dr Tholuck, professor of theology in the university of Halle, who is well known in this country as a distinguished evangelical Protestant divine, remarks:—

"We live in an age when mankind is particularly rich in means to render the elements and nature subservient to their will. We live in a time when the individual becomes every day more independent of restraining power; and if in the same measure in which this might, and dominion, and richness in means, increases, the fear of God, and the consciousness of dependence on him, decreases more and more; when all these gifts and all these means, instead of being used in the service of God, and of his kingdom, are used in the service of selfishness and our own enjoyment; when man;

through this dominion, becomes day after day more free from earthly restraints, but each day more and more a slave to his earthly passions ; when blinded man builds altars, and sings praises to his own skill and wit, instead of to his Heavenly Father, from whom cometh every good and perfect gift —oh ! have not even the ancients foretold, what must become of such a generation in that wonderful fable of the daring of Prometheus, who, with violent hands stole from heaven its vivifying fire ? What we here speak of is no anxious dream, no unreal imagination ; no ! *undeniable is the existing tendency in this generation, to consecrate the temple which our pious forefathers reared to their Father in heaven, to man, the fleeting son of an hour."*

Who is to blame for this forgetfulness of God by the cultivators of science, but the churches that have omitted to teach the sacred character of Nature, and to acknowledge her instruction as Divine ?

To those whose understandings have embraced the views which I am now advancing, and whose religious sentiments have been interwoven with them, " this eternal sacredness" stands forth in all the beauty, brightness, and intensity, which it ever possessed in the minds of the men of the seventeenth century. Mr Carlyle adds : " We think *that* too," (viz. the " sacredness of the universe,") " cant and a creed." Yes— men of science, whose religious sentiments have never been led to recognise the Divine adaptations in nature as proclamations of the Divine will and attributes, but who have pursued their investigations from intellectual or interested motives alone, *do* regard the views which I am now advocating as " cant and a creed." To such individuals I can only say that the religious sentiments exist in man ; that the experience of all ages shews that in youth they may be directed to almost any object, and will thereafter cling to it as sacred throughout life ; and the question is—Whether their legitimate direction is exclusively to dogmas and formulas of belief in reference mainly to another world, framed by fallible men in the dark ages as true interpretations of Scripture ; or also towards that revelation which is addressed by the great Ruler of the universe to man in nature, and adapted to promote his improvement and enjoyment ?

If we can persuade the people that the course of nature, which determines their condition at every moment of their lives, " is the design—law—command—instruction (any word will do), of an all-powerful though unseen Ruler, it will become a religion with them ; obedience will be felt as a wish and a duty, an interest and a necessity." The friend from whose letter I quote these words adds : " But *can* you per-

* A Selection from the University Sermons of Augustus Tholuck, D.D., &c., p. 181. London, Seeley, 1844.

suade mankind thus ? I mean, can you give them a *practical conviction ?*" I answer: In the present unsatisfactory condition of things, the experiment is at least worth the trying. Whatever objections may exist to this proposal, *something* is needed to reconcile religion and science; for, as Mr Carlyle remarks, " the old names suggest new things to us— not august and divine, but hypocritical, pitiable, and detestable. The old names and similitudes of belief still circulate from tongue to tongue, though now in such a ghastly condition: not as commandments of the living God, which we must do or perish eternally; alas, no, as something very different from that."

CHAPTER II.

DEFINITION OF THE WORDS SCIENCE AND RELIGION, AND ELUCIDATIONS OF THE COMPLEX CHARACTER OF RELIGION.

In an enquiry into the relation between science and religion, it is necessary to define what is meant by these terms. By science, then, I understand a systematic exposition of correctly observed facts concerning the constitution, qualities, modes of action, and relations of the objects of nature.

It is unnecessary to enlarge on the definition of science; but, as much obscurity exists with respect to the nature and objects of religion, it may be useful to enter more fully into an elucidation of this subject.

It is generally acknowledged that there is a distinction between the emotional and intellectual faculties of men, but the mind being considered by many persons as a single power, the distinction is, in their view, one of nomenclature merely. Phrenological observations lead to a different view.

There is in the brain an organ for each primitive emotion, and one for each primitive intellectual faculty. And not only are these organs distinct from each other in space, but the natural vigour of each emotion, and of each intellectual power, depends on the size and condition of its organ.

Religion is not a product of intellect alone. No kind, quantity, or quality, of intellectual conceptions, will generate religious emotions. On the other hand, the religious emotions which prompt us to reverence and adore, cannot reach definite objects without the aid of the intellectual powers. These objects, also, may be physical or mental. Entwine the reverential emotions from infancy with the statue of Jupiter, and it will become a religious object: connect them with dogmas and articles of faith, and these will be reverenced as religious truths.

The kind of intellectual conceptions with which the religious emotions may be associated, will depend upon the strength and cultivation of *both* of these orders of faculties. If the religious organs be naturally very large and much exercised, and those of the intellect feeble and undisciplined, the emotions may be trained to invest almost any objects with the attribute of holiness and to regard them with reverence. For example, in ancient Egypt, reptiles and birds were objects of religious veneration. In Hindostan, Juggernaut is worshipped; in Greece and Rome, Jupiter and Apollo, Juno, Venus, and Diana, and many other imaginary beings, were adored as deities. In these countries, the religious emotions were trained from infancy to reverence the statues of these imaginary personages as worthy of religious homage.

The intellectual faculties not only perceive the external objects represented as sacred, but receive the instruction concerning their qualities, which the religious teachers of the people choose to communicate; and the combination of the religious emotions with these ideas constitutes the religion of the various worshippers. When the silversmiths of Ephesus shouted, "Great is Diana of the Ephesians!" it is insinuated that they knew that she was only an idol, and affected reverence for her merely for the sake of gain, because they made shrines for her temple. If this surmise be correct, their intellects were so far enlightened that the association between *their* religious emotions and her statue and temple was dissolved; she was no longer an object of reverence to them; but at the same time they knew that this connection still subsisted in the minds of the people, and they relied on the strength and sincerity of the popular belief as the means of exciting opposition to the apostle.

When, on the other hand, the intellectual organs are powerful and well cultivated, and those of the religious emotions feeble and little exercised, the individual will, with great difficulty, attain a strong living religious character. He may try to believe dogmas, perform ceremonies, and conform to observances; but he will feel, and penetrating observers will discover, that the unction of piety is not a powerful element in his mental constitution.

Religion, in the common acceptation of the term, means a system of divine faith and worship, and thus used it expresses only external objects. In the present treatise, I consider it as a mental state, made up of certain emotions and intellectual conceptions. In this subjective sense, these two are necessary to constitute religion.

As this proposition is a fundamental one in the discussions on which we are about to enter, and as it will probably be new to some readers, a few illustrations of it may be useful. In the following instances objects possessing in themselves no sacred qualities, are invested with such a character by becoming associated with the religious emotions.

In England, for example, grave-yards and churches are consecrated, and in Scotland they are not. What constitutes consecration? A Bishop performs certain ceremonies, reads certain prayers, and declares the ground holy and set apart to receive the bodies of believers, there to rest till the resurrection. In like manner he declares the church to be sacred, and dedicates it to the worship of God. In England, the religious emotions are, from infancy, entwined with these ceremonies and objects; and in the mind of the thoroughbred-Church of England Christian, in whom the religious organs are large and active, these places actually become sacred. He shudders at the idea of being buried in unconsecrated ground, and is shocked at the proposal to transact secular business in a church. If there were a naturally sacred character in the burial-ground and church, consecration would be unnecessary; and as it is incredible that the ceremonies change their nature, the change can occur only in the minds of the people. How are these acts viewed by the staunch Scotch Presbyterian,—one trained from infancy to venerate Calvin and John Knox, the Shorter Catechism, the Westminster Confession of Faith, and his own church-ceremonies, and taught, moreover, that Episcopalians and Bishops persecuted his ancestors to death, and still profess a religion closely allied to that of the Church of Rome? To such a person, the ceremonies of consecration appear as unmeaning and unreal as the incantations of the witches in Macbeth; the grave-yard appears to him merely a piece of ground, and the church four walls and a roof; and he regards the sacred or holy character in which these appear to the Englishman as a superstitious fancy! And why does he do so? Because he views them through his intellect alone, which experiences no emotions; while, from infancy, feelings of hatred have been associated in his mind with the Episcopalian doctrines and ritual.

With the sound Scotch Presbyterian no edifice is sacred. In Edinburgh, a theatre was long used on week days for the drama, and on Sundays as a church. The English Churchman would have revolted at this practice. A congregation of the Free Church of Scotland worshipped in a music-hall; and in the new cemeteries, a portion of the ground is consecrated for the burial of Episcopalians, and the remainder is unconsecrated for Presbyterian use. A line on the ground-plan or a walk in the grave-yard distinguishes the parts, but no demarcation indicative of difference of character is discernible.

During the agitation for repeal of the corn law, a deputation of English Repealers visited Scotland. A meeting was advertised to be held in the county-hall in a provincial town but it was found too small, and the meeting adjourned to a large Dissenting chapel close at hand. One of the English leaders, in whom the organs of the religious emotions were large, and who had been trained to reverence churches and chapels as sacred edifices, was prepared to deliver a regular secular speech adapted to a popular audience in the county-hall; but he told me that the moment the adjournment to a chapel was announced, the intended tone of his speech appeared to him in utter discord with the sacredness of the place; and although he was informed that the chapel was not consecrated, that it was often used for public meetings, and was regarded merely as a secular edifice; and although his intellect recognised the truth of these assurances; his religious emotions could not be subdued, and his speech was grave and solemn, and very unlike that which he had intended to deliver.

I have occasionally heard irreverent remarks made by earnest uncompromising Presbyterians on the Episcopalian observances of Christmas Day and Good Friday; while some English visitors to Scotland have expressed their astonishment at the superstitious solemnity with which certain days, destitute of all scriptural sanctity,—namely, the Fast days preceding the administration of the sacrament,—are there observed as holy.

The name given to the intellectual ideas which enter into the composition of religion is THEOLOGY. It means the notions which we form concerning the Being to whom, or the objects to which, our reverential and devotional emotions should be directed.

> " Lo the poor Indian! whose untutored mind
> Sees God in clouds, or hears him in the wind."

This is the theology of the Indian. The Hindoos and Mahommedans have embodied their theology—in other words, their notions concerning the objects to be reverenced and worshipped—in books. The emotional faculties of the people being trained to reverence, as Divine revelations, the narratives and dogmas which these books contain, the compound becomes in their minds religion. Hence, an individual may be highly religious, and know nothing of theology beyond the narratives and dogmas which have been entwined with his religious emotions from his infancy; while another may be a profound theologian, acquainted with the original languages of Scripture, skilled in all the controversies which have taken place concerning the authors by whom its different parts were written, the time and order of their appearance, their title to the attribute of inspiration, and the true meaning of their texts, yet not be religious. In point of fact, experience shows that, in many instances, the more an individual knows of these subjects, the less religious, in the common acceptation of the word, he becomes—*i.e.*, his reverence for the special dogmas and observances, which in his youth he was trained to regard with religious awe, diminishes.

The difference between religion and theology, which I have here endeavoured to indicate, may be farther illustrated by comparing them to the warp and woof of a web. The weaver fixes in his loom, first, long threads stretching out directly from his own position, and these are called the warp. Then he puts thread upon a shuttle, which he ever and anon casts between the long threads, and these cross threads are called the woof. The web or cloth is composed of the two series of threads closely pressed together. Now, in our present problem, the native sentiment of reverence and devotion may be likened to the warp. It is the foundation or first element of the web. The theological ideas may be considered as the cross thread or woof. As the shuttle adds the woof to the warp to make the cloth, the intellect adds theology, or particular notions about God, to the emotion, and the two combined constitute what we commonly call religion. The Hindoo religion is the primitive pure emotion, with such intellectual ideas as the priests of the country have been able to weave into it. The Mahommedan and Christian religions may be described in similar terms; and thus it is that the composite web of reverential emotion and intellectual ideas which each nation has formed for itself, is called its religion. The compound nature of this web is not usually perceived by its votaries. The Hindoo regards his sacred web as altogether pure religion; and the Mahommedan, and the Christian, of whatever sect, do the same.

The primitive emotion, when energetic and excited, is so overpowering, that it carries the whole mind captive. When it acts blindly, it dethrones reason, stifles conscience, and enlists every passion to vindicate the honour and glory of the Being whom it has been trained to reverence. When the woof of error has been added in infancy, and the web of superstition formed, every thread—that is to say, every notion concerning God, and his priests, and man's duty to both—becomes sacred in the eyes of the devotee, and stirs the emotion into a glow of rapture if gratified, and of pain, accompanied by indignation and fury, if offended. In this state of mind, barbarous nations plunder and slay in honour and to the glory of their gods.

In Christian nations, analogous phenomena appear. We all profess to draw our religion from the Bible; but in Scotland, one woof is woven into the warp, in England another, in Ireland a third, in Germany a fourth, in Russia a fifth, and so on. In Scotland, my own country, the woof consists of certain views of God, of human nature, and of man's state, duties, and destiny, embodied in the Shorter Catechism and the Confession of Faith. In our infancy these are woven by our parents and clergy into the very core of our religious emotion, and the resulting texture is our religion. The union is so intimate, and the web so firmly knit together, that most of us have no conception of anything being religion except this our own compound web of devotion and intellectual doctrine. The doctrine is to us as sacred as the emotion, and he who controverts it is regarded as the enemy of our religion. In barbarous ages, Christian men, acting under this impression, burned individuals who controverted their interpretations of Scripture; and in our own day, they calumniate them as Infidels, and obstruct their social advancement. Nevertheless, the doctrine which they thus regard as unquestionably Divine is a mere human woof composed of inferences drawn from particular texts of Scripture, by mortal men assembled at Westminster in the 17th century; men fallible like ourselves, and many of them more ignorant; though its intimate union with our devotional emotion is apt to incapacitate our mind from so regarding it.

We obtain direct and irresistible proof that such is the fact, by merely crossing the Border, or St George's Channel. In England, the woof is composed of the Liturgy and the Episcopalian Catechism. The Englishman, into whose devotional emotion the doctrines of these books have been woven from infancy, cannot conceive of anything but his own web of opinion being the true religion. If ignorant and prejudiced, he regards the Scottish Theology with indifference, aversion, or contempt; and in a similar state of mind, the Scotsman repays his contumely by treating English Theology in a corresponding spirit. When enlightened, although they differ in opinion, they regard each other with respect. Cross the Channel, again, to Catholic Ireland, and there you find that the Pope and Councils have fashioned other standards of faith, and that the priests have woven them into the warp of the Irish mind, and this web constitutes its religion.

Nay, the clergy of different sects have woven notions about church government and ceremonies into the warp, and made these also appear portions of religion; and men fight for and defend them with as much zeal as if they were attributes of God.

We can now understand why it is that we are afflicted with such deadly strifes and hatred in the name of religion. "The clouds that intercept the heavens from us, come not from the heavens, but from the earth." The thing we call religion is a compound web; and when our neighbour shows us his threads of religious opinion, and calls them Divine, we, into whose minds they have not been woven, survey his fabric with the eye of reason, and pronounce it to be partly pure and partly spurious. Our neighbour's devotional feeling receives a rude shock; he becomes angry, and attacks our web of religion in his turn, and treats it in a similar way. Neither of us, in general, is capable of examining closely and calmly the threads that constitute the woof of his own web, and hence discord between religious parties is interminable.

In the prevalent creeds, nature is not recognised as sacred; no dogmas are founded on scientific truth and systematically combined with the religious emotions, so as to invest them with a religious character. This appears to be the true cause why no practical natural religion exists, and why none can be formed until we venture on a new religious Reformation. It explains also why "the eternal sacredness of this universe itself, of this human life itself, has fallen dark to the most of us." Meanwhile, the union between the religious emotions and the prevalent dogmas, being cemented by no natural bond, is in constant danger of dislocation, either by forcible and confident appeals made by other pretending authorities to the religious emotions themselves, as in the case of Mormonism, or by the teachings of science rendering it impossible for the intellect to recognise the truth of the established doctrines. The absence of a rational foundation for their faith was recently shown by the prevalence, even among the educated classes, of belief in spirit-rapping and table-turning. Professing to believe in the sublime doctrines of heaven and hell, and some of them in that of purgatory, they actually embraced the notion, and earnestly acted on it, that the spirits of the dead could be evoked from those awful abodes, and induced to answer the most trumpery questions by the invocation of practitioners who made gain of the popular credulity. The same class of persons possessed so little knowledge of the laws of physical nature, and so little reverence for the power and wisdom of Him who established them, that they indulged in the wildest dreams of tables being moved and made to perform wonderful evolutions by mysterious influences, in contradiction to the order of nature revealed by previous knowledge and experience.

Is the human mind to continue for ever having its religion stamped upon it, like a pattern on potters' clay, and to retain and act upon it through life, irrespective altogether of a foundation in nature? And can religions that repudiate, or at least neglect nature, and rest chiefly on human interpretations, formed in dark and unscientific ages, of sacred books, be calculated to promote the civilization of man amidst the blaze of light and reason which are every hour revealing the imperfections of the popular notions, and their conflict with the works and will of the Almighty? Let us not shrink from answering these questions, but boldly, yet humbly, inquire into the resources afforded by the present state of knowledge for improving our religious systems.

To attain this object, it appears necessary to inquire whether science affords a foundation for a natural theology and a natural religion? To answer this question, we must consider, 1*st*, The natural evidence for the existence of a Supreme Being; 2*dly*, Whether we can trace Divine government in the phenomena of the physical and moral departments of the world? 3*dly*, If such government be discernible, by what means it is maintained and rendered efficient? 4*thly*, Whether specific duties are revealed and prescribed to man by this government, and what these are?—The answers to these questions will constitute our natural theology;—and, *lastly*, Whether by entwining with the religious emotions the views of God, of His government, and of the duties which He prescribes, we shall be able to confer a religious character on these truths, and thus constitute a natural religion? If we succeed in those objects, we shall render science sacred, invest the practical duties of life with a religious character, and produce a faith calculated to expand and purify itself by every advance in the discovery of truth, and to reinforce, by all the power and fervour of our highest emotions, the progress of mankind towards the utmost degree of improvement and happiness which their nature is fitted to attain.

Before, however, entering on the consideration of these subjects, it may be useful to enquire into the extent of our knowledge of man himself, and of his capacities for discovering and comprehending scientific answers to these questions. This, therefore, shall be our next object.

CHAPTER III.

OF MAN.

SECTION I.—OF THE PHYSICAL ELEMENTS OF MAN.

THE human body is an organised compound substance, but its known elements belong to the inorganic kingdom. All its parts are formed from the blood, and the blood consists of two ingredients—fibrine and serum. Fibrine is identical in its composition with muscular fibre, and serum with white of egg. These two substances contain ten chemical elements: namely, oxygen, hydrogen, nitrogen, carbon, phosphorous, sulphur, chlorine, potash, soda, and lime. Iron and certain fatty substances also are found in the blood.

At present, the primitive organic form is considered to be a cell. The tissues which enter into the structure of complex organs are regarded only as the means for supplying the conditions requisite for the vital operations of the cells. Different cells have different properties; one set of cells, for example, separates certain elements from the blood and forms bones, another set forms nerves. The cause of the formation of the cell, and of different cells possessing different properties, is unknown. Many physiologists name it the vital force, and regard it as the source of growth and reproduction. Several of the conditions under which cells develope themselves into complex organs are known; but it is unascertained whether their evolutions are the result merely of properties possessed by matter in its inorganic form, or of matter and some new force added to it. It has not been proved that inorganic matter can become organised simply by the powers known to be inherent in itself. Organic substances and beings exist, and possess the power of absorbing and converting inorganic matter into organic; but science has not revealed how the first of them became organic, and whence they derived this power of assimilation. Suffice it, therefore, here to observe, that out of inorganic elements, cells and various tissues are formed. These, in the progress of growth, are developed into specific organs, such as the bones, muscles, nerves, lungs, and so forth, each having a peculiar function. The action of the elements out of which these cells, tissues, and organs are formed is precise and uniform; and the compound organism, called the human body, appears as evidently to be a result of design as a clock, a steam-engine, or any other mechanical production of human skill, only immeasurably transcending, in the offices which it performs, and in the admirable contrivances by which these are accomplished, every combination by mortal skill. The following arguments in favour of a vital principle have frequently been used.

It is said, for example, that, strictly speaking, the elements before named are only the chemical residuum after the vital power has ceased to act; but it does not necessarily follow that these, in the same forms and proportions in which they are found after death, constitute all that enters into the composition of the body while alive. · The vital force may be some element still unknown, which combines with them and forms a new compound, but which escaping at death leaves these elements as a mere residuum. Water, the steam of water with its prodigiously expansive power, and ice, are all composed of oxygen and hydrogen; but their characteristics are widely different, according to the amount of heat which they contain; and *heat* is still an unknown force or action, for it is not now regarded as a substance. In like manner, be the vital principle what it may, we must constantly bear in mind that a living man may consist of substances different from every thing we know chemically, and different from the elements present in his body in a state of death: in the actual condition of science, the difficulty of ascertaining what he really is, seems insuperable; for we cannot discover it from consciousness, and chemical analysis of the body is impossible without killing it. Blood, when drawn from the body, dies, and so do all other parts when separated from the living organism.

Another theory of life dispenses altogether with a vital principle as a force distinct from matter. According to it, there is no evidence to prove the existence of any particular vital principle, but life may be referred to a more complicated action of the common properties of matter than we see in inorganic substances. When carbon and oxygen, for instance, are brought together under certain circumstances, carbonic acid is formed. Why this happens, we cannot tell; and we content ourselves with saying, that the union takes place according to chemical laws—in other words, that, in the same circumstances, these substances constantly and unvaryingly combine in the same manner. Certain properties have been bestowed upon carbon and oxygen by the Author of Nature, and these never alter. We can scarcely form a notion of what they are in themselves. On this point our present chemical knowledge is meagre in the extreme. As already observed, when carbon and oxygen meet under certain circumstances they form carbonic acid, but we understand nothing of various important modifications which ensue by the addition of nitrogen and hydrogen. A grain of wheat is composed of oxygen, hydrogen, nitrogen, carbon, and some alkaline and earthy salts. The different atoms are so constituted, that, in certain circumstances, a disturbance of them takes place—motion ensues, and different additional changes of matter follow, all according to the fixed properties of the different atoms. So long as the grain of wheat remains unaltered, so long as its atoms retain their original position and their original powers of action upon each other, it retains the capability of being called into life; that is, of passing through a series of changes totally independent of any volition on its part, but which ensue according to laws analogous to those which guide the motions of a watch, only much more complicated in their nature. The great problem would be to arrange the atoms of matter in such a way, that, in certain circumstances, wheat, or oats, or barley, should be the produce of the atomic changes in the elements which are common to all of these substances. This seems to have been done by the great Intelligent Cause at the commencement of nature; and laws of reproduction being established, the organised kingdom seems to proceed without any more direct supervision than is bestowed upon the inorganic world. Indeed, many authorities now maintain that both are subject to similar laws. This is a startling view when we compare man with a stone; but it is less so when we pass from a stone to a shell, from a shell to a piece of wood, from that to a sponge, from a sponge to blubber, and so on up to man. The extinction of life seems to be nothing more or less than a disturbance of the movement of the atoms, similar to that which occurs when we blow out a candle. The properties of the atoms of the candle remain the same, but the circumstances in which they are placed are different, and the phenomena which accompany their future motions, if heat be not reapplied so as to produce ignition, are also different. I need not go farther into the matter. These observations will give the reader a view of the nascent ideas on the subject now entertained in Germany, and I give them only historically as such.

The advocates of this theory ask the question:—If life be due to a vital principle, what becomes of it in frozen fishes, and dried animalculæ, some of which may be retained in a desiccated condition for years? According to the new theory, the conditions of change were simply removed; restore them, and *life*, that is, motion of their particles, returns. When a man faints and falls into the water, he is much more likely to be restored to animation, even after a considerable period of immersion, than if he had fallen in while the vital changes were in full activity: The vital functions go on more slowly in a fainting man, than in one in full health and activity; and less oxygen being needed, want of respiration is not so soon fatal. His condition is analogous to that which occurs in hybernating animals, and in men who in India are temporarily buried, and revive.

I have observed that those in whom the organs of Wonder, Imitation, and Ideality, are large, are predisposed to regard life as a distinct force superadded to matter; while those in whom these organs are moderately developed, and in whom Causality and Comparison are large, are inclined to prefer the latter theory, or some one analogous to it. They ascribe to matter, when placed in certain circumstances, the power of assuming organic forms and maintaining organic action, as one of its own attributes.* By such of them as are Theists, however, this power is regarded as derived from the Deity. As before remarked, there is no satisfactory evidence to show that inorganic matter can organise itself.

Many divines, as well as philosophers, have held the opinion that man has no spiritual substance or soul distinct from the body, but becomes extinct at death, and so continues till the resurrection. Among these are Milton,† Locke,‡ Bishops Sherlock§ and Law,|| Dr John Taylor,¶ Dr Priestley,** Robert Hall,†† and Archdeacon Blackburne;‡‡ to whom may be added Bishop Watson, although, being naturally averse to dogmatism on subjects so abstruse, he went no farther than to say that he thought the point doubtful—declaring that he was "not disturbed at his inability clearly to convince himself that the soul is or is not a substance distinct from the body;"§§ that

---

* See an Inquiry into the Opinions, Ancient and Modern, concerning Life and Organization. By John Barclay, M.D. Edinburgh, Bell and Bradfute, 1822.
† Treatise on Christian Doctrine, vol. i., p. 250.
‡ The Reasonableness of Christianity as delivered in the Scriptures; at the beginning.
§ Discourses vi. and xlix.; Sherlock's Works, ed. 1830, vol. i., p. 124, and vol. ii., p. 431.
|| Considerations on the Theory of Religion, 5th ed., pp. 49, 186; and more particularly, Discourse appended to it (pp. 343–429) on the Nature and End of Death under the Christian Covenant.
¶ Letter to Bishop Law, quoted by the latter, p. 422.
** Disquisitions relating to Matter and Spirit. Lond. 1777.
†† Letter to his Congregation at Bristol in 1790, quoted in the Encyc. Brit., 7th ed., vol. xi., p. 115.
‡‡ Blackburne's Works, vols. ii. and iii.
§§ Anecdotes of his own Life, 2d ed., vol. i., p. 24.

" he despaired of ever seeing the question clearly decided, whether the brain is the efficient or the instrumental cause of sensation ;"* and that " if the Gospel is not true, he could have no expectation of a future state."†

The discovery of the cause of life or the nature of the vital principle may be *practically* important; because if man could find it out and ascertain the conditions under which it acts, he might acquire the power of influencing the formation of organisms at their source, and hence might modify the whole series of their actions. Theologically considered, however, this discovery appears to be unimportant; because if we admit the existence of God, and believe that in calling man into existence He had a purpose, we cannot conceive that He should have chosen a wrong substance out of which to fashion him. We may rest assured that the object of man's existence, be it what it may, will be accomplished, of whatever essence his organism consists.

I may add, that the opinion is now very general among thinking men, that the question of immortality has no dependence on that of the immateriality of the soul and possibility of its separate existence, but that, whatever the nature of the soul is, it can be immortal or mortal only by the will of God.‡

Some of the advocates of a superadded vital principle entertain the notion that it is spiritual or immaterial, and that it acts even in the present life independently of matter. This, however, appears to me to be an error. Even assuming the existence of a separate and superadded vital principle, it does not follow that the body, compounded of it and matter, possesses the attributes generally ascribed to an immaterial being or soul; or that the vital principle, while forming a part of the living organism, is emancipated from the laws and control of matter. A more reasonable proposition would be, that the unknown principle, when combined with diversities of organic structure, would produce diversities of living powers. Combined with the organism of vision, for example, we may suppose that it would produce vision: but vision is not emancipated by it from the influence of matter; on the contrary, this sense is affected by every cause that changes the condition of the structure, and is exercised according to fixed laws, which are embodied in the science of optics. The same remarks apply to the organs of hearing, touch, taste, and smell. And not only so, but the vital principle, combined with one portion of

---

* Anecdotes of his own life, 2d ed., vol. ii., p. 400.   † Ib., vol. i., p. 395.
‡ This opinion is expressed by Dr John Taylor in a passage quoted by Bishop Law, p. 423; by Dugald Stewart, Prelim. Disert. to Encyc. Brit., p. 58; and by sundry other writers mentioned in the Phren. Jour. xv. 348. See Locke's opinion on the subject in detail, Phren. Jour. xvi. 60; and Baron Smith's, xvi. 287.

the brain, may be supposed to produce the emotion of Veneration; with another portion the sentiment of justice; with another the power of perceiving melody; with another the power of conceiving efficiency; and every one of these emotions and powers will be liable to be improved, deranged, or destroyed, by chemical and mechanical causes which affect the structure. A few drops of prussic acid will extinguish their action; a certain dose of chloroform, morphia, or alcohol, will excite, a larger dose will suspend, and a still larger dose will destroy them. Be the compound of the vital principle with the chemical elements, therefore, what it may, it is able, up only to a certain point, and under regulated conditions, to resist the usual agency of chemical forces, and at all times its condition is liable to be changed by them as well as by functional action. There is thus no warrant for assuming that the phenomena of life, including volition, emotion, and intelligent judgment, are in this world performed by a being unconnected with, and independent of matter. Some evidence on this subject is given in the appendix, No. II.

The human body appears to be a mechanism constructed to grow for a certain number of years, to remain nearly stationary for a certain time, then to commence a process of decay, and finally to suffer dissolution, all its parts reverting to the inorganic state.

Each tissue preserves its state of health, unless forced into morbid action by influences foreign to itself; and when it is disordered, a series of changes commences in it, the tendency of which is to restore it to the healthy condition. The great organs of the body, composed of these tissues, retain in their compound state the same property of self-preservation. As long as the conditions under which they were brought to maturity remain unchanged, they continue sound, and their action is normal. When disordered, they also commence a series of actions to regain the state of health;—if unsuccessful, the changes end in death.

Each is endowed with a specific function, such as digestion, respiration, or secretion; and health and life depend on the combined, harmonious, and normal action of the whole. "The action of every tissue thus contributes, by virtue of its natural constitution, both to its own preservation, and to the function of the compound organ into the formation of which it enters. By the same law the action of every compound organ contributes in like manner both to self-preservation and to the more general welfare of the body. Every one of these actions is regulated by fixed laws."*

* Dr Combe's Physiology of Digestion, Preface.

SECTION II.—OF THE MENTAL ORGANS AND FACULTIES OF MAN.

We become acquainted with mental states, and also with the external world, its relations, and its causes, by means of our mental faculties. Let us, therefore, next inquire into these.

Although all our knowledge of mental phenomena is derived from consciousness, consciousness, as a direct source of information, gives no intimation whatever of the *causes* of our sensations, feelings, perceptions, and judgments. We are conscious only of these mental states and acts themselves. We may discover by observation and reflection the objects which excite them, and the circumstances in which they arise; but after we have ascertained these, we are not advanced one step in our discovery of the *cause* of the powers themselves.

Moreover, we have no *consciousness* of the *substance* of which the thinking part of us is composed. This is another important proposition which it is necessary to keep in view in our subsequent investigations. The name "Mind," has been given to the collective powers of sensation, feeling, perception, and judgment, of which we are conscious; and as the phenomena which they produce are unlike any acts or states which are observed in inanimate matter, mind has been assumed to be something altogether different from matter, and its substance or essence has, in contradistinction to that of matter, been called spirit.

But, apparently, mind, as something distinct from matter, as a spirit, or an immaterial essence, is absolutely unknown to us, and the popular opinion to the contrary seems to owe its origin to our being unconscious while in health of the influence of the brain in acts of feeling and thinking. The logical conclusion to be drawn from the facts known to us is, that mind is an aggregate of individual powers of sensation, emotion, perception, and judgment, each of which depends for its action in this world on the size and condition of a particular part of the brain; that each stands in definite relations to the others, and to a certain class of external objects; and that each may exist, strong or weak, in a state of health or disease, cultivated or uncultivated, in the same individual. A man, for example, may have powerful vision, and dull hearing; or he may be blind, but not deaf; or he may have had his eye-sight greatly improved by exercise, or impaired by intense study. Another man may possess a powerful sentiment of Benevolence, and a weak sentiment of Veneration; his faculty of

Veneration may have become diseased, while his sentiment of Benevolence has remained sound; Veneration may have been cultivated while Benevolence has been left dormant, or *vice versa*. Nay more, each of the cerebral organs, be its ultimate elements what they may, acts as a mental force, and produces distinct moral or intellectual results, analogous to the effects produced by the different qualities of matter.

If we could enter fully into the consciousness of individuals, we should discover that in each the mind was as distinctly and powerfully affected by these differences in the condition of the various organs and faculties, as the body is by differences in the condition of its separate organs; and that instead of a distinct mind or spiritual being existing in each of us, the exact counterpart of the mind of all other individuals, and uninfluenced by the organism, each of us is a compound of many mental attributes, which differ individually in intensity in different persons, and render the consciousness or mind of each of us only a modified type of that of our fellow men. The man whose brain is small, and whose lungs and abdomen are large, would err grievously if he supposed that all other men in their bodily constitutions were exact types of himself, felt as he felt, and could act only as he could act; were he to write books or legislate on such an assumption, he would only propound or enact error. Just so an individual deficient in Benevolence or Veneration, who should assume mankind in general to feel in those departments of emotion exactly like himself, would be grievously mistaken; and were he to institute a series of practical arrangements, or to found a school of philosophy or a sect in religion, on such a basis, he would carry with him only those whose minds were constituted like his own.

Since consciousness, then, makes us acquainted only with our own mental states, and affords no information concerning the causes of them, our next inquiry is, Whether *observation* leads to any more extended knowledge? It unfolds to us certain causes which affect our mental condition, of which causes consciousness gives us no intimation. To borrow an illustration from the body: consciousness gives us no intimation of the existence of the spinal cord, or of the nerves of sensation and motion proceeding from it, which are ramified on the muscles and skin. We are conscious of volition to move the limbs, and of the cold and heat which ice and fire occasion; but in a state of health we have no consciousness whatever of the existence of the organs by means of which these actions and sensations are produced. By observation, however, of the structure of the parts, and of the effects of injuries of them, we have discovered that for the powers of voluntary motion and sensation in the limbs, we are absolutely dependent on the nerves and spinal marrow. In like manner, although, in a state of health, we are unconscious of the existence of the brain, and of its influence on our mental states,* yet observation throws an important light on this subject. It makes us acquainted with a pulpy substance, composed partly of white and partly of grey matter, consisting of many distinguishable parts. Into it all the nerves of the external senses enter, and with it the nerves of all the other parts of the body are in connection. Observation, in short, enables us to discover that this part is the organ of the mind, and that by its structure, size, age, and health, all mental states, in this world, are affected or modified. Without it there is no consciousness: when it is impaired, our mental faculties suffer a corresponding enfeeblement, and when it is excited, they glow with a corresponding fervour.

As these facts appear to me to be of *fundamental importance* in forming sound conclusions regarding the means or instruments through which the moral government of the world is conducted, I beg to refer the reader to the evidence of them contained in the Phrenological works named below.†

Consciousness localises the mental acts in the head, and gives us a full conviction that they are performed there, although it does not reveal what substance occupies the interior of the skull, or the influence of that substance on our powers of thinking and feeling. It is worthy of observation also, that the po-

---

* Some individuals have stated that in health they are conscious of the existence of the brain and of its functions; but it is clear from the general ridicule with which Dr Gall's announcement of its functions was received, that these must be exceptional cases.

† Sur les Fonctions du Cerveau, et sur celles de chacune de ses Parties. Par F. J. Gall, M.D. Paris, 1825. 6 vols. 8vo.

Phrenology, or the Doctrine of the Mind, and of the Relations between its Manifestations and the Body. By J. G. Spurzheim, M.D. London, 1825.

A View of the Philosophical Principles of Phrenology. By J. G. Spurzheim, M.D. London, 1825.

Phrenology in connexion with the Study of Physiognomy. By J. G. Spurzheim, M.D. London, 1826.

A System of Phrenology. By George Combe. 5th ed. Edinburgh, 1843. 2 vols. 8vo.

The Phrenological Journal, 1824–1847. 20 vols. 8vo.

The effects of morbid states of the brain on the mental powers is illustrated also in the following works. If the public were familiarly acquainted with the facts recorded in these, and other authorities, they could not continue to view any psychological system which omits the consideration of the brain as of practical value:—

Annals of Phrenology, No. 1., Boston, U. S., Oct. 1833, p. 37.

Medico-Chirurgical Review, No. 46, p. 366, Oct. 1835.

Nouveaux Elémens de Physiologie, 7th edit., ii. 195-6.

Hennen's Principles of Military Surgery.

Principles of Medicine. By Samuel Jackson, M.D.

Elliotson's Blumenbach, 4th edit., p. 283.

Remarks on the Influence of Mental Cultivation, &c., upon Health. By Amariah Brigham, M.D. 2d edit., p. 23. Boston, U. S. 1833.

pular notions of the independence of the mind on the body are modern, and the offspring of philosophical theories that have sprung up chiefly since the days of Locke. In Shakspeare and the older writers, the word "brains" is frequently used as implying the mental functions.

The cases which are supposed to contradict these assertions are easily explained. It is often said of persons dying at an advanced age that their mental faculties remained entire to the last. The real meaning of this phrase is, that the patients were not deranged; that is to say, that, in so far as they were capable of manifesting the mind, their faculties acted normally: but it is a complete mistake to suppose that their minds were then as capable of profound investigation, of vivid emotion, and of energetic action, as in the maturity of life. Sometimes cerebral excitement from *disease* renders the mind particularly brilliant, however weak the body at large may be. The fact of the mental powers being the last to fade, is explained by the circumstance, that the brain and nervous system suffer the least diminution of size in the general decay of the corporeal frame.*

The bearing of these facts on the moral government of the world will be subsequently explained. Meantime, I may remark, that all reasoning on the mind, its phenomena and laws, which overlooks the influence of the brain,—and all reasonings on mind in general, and on the individual faculties of man in particular,—which omit consideration of the effects of the size and condition of the special organs on the manifestations of these faculties, are in a scientific, as well as a practical point of view, defective in a fundamental element of truth. In considering a compound result, our judgments become sound only in proportion to our recognition of *all the causes* which contribute towards its production. We may reason on gravitation as an abstract force, irrespective of the material substances which gravitate; but until we ascertain the qualities of physical objects which affect their gravitating power, we shall never attain to either a scientific or a practical comprehension of it. A feather and a piece of lead, of the same size, both gravitate, but with very different degrees of energy. A theory of gravitation ignoring the influence of density, would be somewhat analogous to a system of mental philosophy, omitting the influence of its brain and of the individual parts on the mental manifestations.

* The brain and spinal cord lose only 0·019 of their original substance in a warm-blooded animal starved to death. Of the fat, 0·933 parts are lost; of the blood, 0·750; of the muscles, 0·423; of the organs of respiration, 0·222; and of the bones, 0·167. Chossat, Recherches Experimentales sur l'Inanition, p. 92. Paris, 1843. See also The Physiology of Digestion, by Andrew Combe, M.D., p. 86. Edit. 1849.

SECTION III.—OF THE PARTICULAR FACULTIES OF THE MIND, THEIR CEREBRAL ORGANS, MODES OF ACTIVITY, AND USES AND ABUSES.

These subjects are treated of in detail in the phrenological and other works before named (page 31); to which I beg leave to refer. In the Appendix No. I. a list of the organs, and an outline of their positions in the brain, are given, to assist such readers as may not have access to these works; but as they embrace only names and divisions of space, they are not meant as substitutes for the treatises. It is necessary here only to recapitulate the following general conclusions, which are considered as ascertained :—

1*st*, That men in general, in the state of health, have no consciousness of the existence or uses of the brain.

2*dly*, That in consequence of this want of consciousness, men, in general, in all ages, have ascribed the phenomena of sensation, emotion, and thought, exclusively to a spiritual entity which they have named the Mind.

3*dly*, That certain facts discoverable by observation, demonstrate that the brain is the organ of the mental functions, and that no consciousness, and no mental manifestations, take place, in our present state, without its agency.

4*thly*, That the *condition* of the brain affects both the *power* and the *quality* of the mental manifestations.

It is of much importance in this inquiry to bear in mind that the size and condition of particular parts of the brain determine the degree of energy and activity of particular faculties of the mind. For example; if the part of the brain which serves to manifest the emotion of Veneration be very deficient, that emotion will be very imperfectly known through the consciousness of the individual; and no external influences hitherto discovered, falling within the sphere of natural action, will enable him to experience it in a normal degree. If that part be very large, and his temperament be active, he will be conscious of strong emotions of that description, and will feel great pleasure in religious exercises. And if that part become diseased, the effect may be prostration or extinction of the emotion, if the disease destroy the organ; or a morbid exaltation of it, if the malady excite the cerebral convolutions into abnormal vivácity, without impairing their structure. And so of all the other mental faculties and their organs.

Each mental faculty is a distinct power, the strength of which depends, as I have said, on the size and condition of its organ; and each has a prescribed sphere of action which is regulated by fixed laws. For example, Acquisitiveness is the desire for property. Its power and activity depend on the size and condition of its organ. Property can be called into existence only by complying with certain conditions woven into the order of nature, and not dependent on the will of man; and it can be distributed so as to produce general well-being, only according to certain rules, also fixed by the nature of things and beings, and not alterable by man. If, in any individual, the desire be too feeble, or too strong, or be unguided by knowledge, and if, in consequence, it acts in contravention of those rules, disappointment and suffering will ensue ; and the same propositions may be stated in regard to all the other faculties.

The key to the moral government of the world, therefore, is to be found in a knowledge of these mental forces and of the laws to which they are subjected.

The evidence on which certain mental organs are considered to be ascertained, and the existence and functions of others rendered probable, is stated in the works on Phrenology before mentioned. It is not considered necessary to enter into a detailed statement of that evidence here ; because this may be seen in the works alluded to, and because I here assume that the present treatise will have no practical influence, until, by the advance of the public mind, that evidence and its consequences shall have been studied with the attention and earnestness which so important a subject demands.

SECTION IV.—IS MAN NATURALLY A RELIGIOUS BEING?

As our ideas of physical things are formed through the medium of faculties which are common to all the race, it would be possible to arrive at unanimity of opinion concerning them, provided every individual possessed the faculties in an equal degree of perfection, and had applied them in the same direction, and with equal assiduity. But as the organs of the external senses and of the intellectual faculties differ widely in size, quality, and cultivation, in different persons, this unanimity is unattainable. The same remark applies to the religious and all the other emotions. If religious emotions exist, and if their organs were equally large and active, equally cultivated, and directed to the same objects, in all men, all would be equally religious ; but as these organs differ in size, activity, and cultivation, in different persons, some are ardently religious, while others deny the existence of religious emotions altogether. The emotions, moreover, are differently directed in different individuals ; and hence, unanimity in regard to the objects to which they should be addressed, is not to be expected.

These facts do not lead logically to universal scepticism; because they do not deny the existence of religious emotions and their organs. On the contrary, by establishing the existence of organs for the religious emotions, while we show how widely their size, cultivation, and direction, differ in different persons, we remove the objections to the existence of religion which these differences naturally suggest. In proportion as men reach the highest points of cerebral development, temperament, and cultivation, the nearer will they approach to unanimity in regard to moral and religious truths. The same form and size of brain and cultivation may be found in a sincere Roman Catholic and a sincere Protestant; but their faculties having been directed to different objects in their youth, each has failed to give the same consideration to the objects venerated by his neighbour which he has given to his own.

Organs for the following emotions have been discovered and proved to exist in man: viz., WONDER, IDEALITY, VENERATION, HOPE, CONSCIENTIOUSNESS, and BENEVOLENCE. In the works of Drs Gall and Spurzheim, and other writers on Phrenology, and in the Phrenological Journal, the history of the discovery, and a mass of evidence in support of the organs are given. Those readers who desire seriously to investigate the basis on which this treatise rests, will naturally examine these works, and appeal to nature; and it is therefore unnecessary for their satisfaction to detail the evidence here. Individuals, again, who regard this work as a collection of mere speculative opinions, like the philosophies of ethical writers who were unacquainted with Phrenology, or of those who choose to ignore it, would treat any amount of narrated evidence only as words; and it is, therefore, unnecessary to state it for *their* edification.

OF THE ORGAN OF WONDER.

The primitive function of this faculty appears to me to be to produce the love of the new. Its gratification is accompanied by an emotion which we name surprise; and as this feeling is highly pleasurable, it prompts us to pursue the new, and leads to inventions in art, and discoveries in science. The faculty is adapted to the constitution of the external world; for the whole of nature, animate and inanimate, is in a continual state of decay and renovation. Carlyle has well remarked, that the whole of this world is habitually in a state of revolution. Nothing stands still. This faculty renders the new agreeable to us, while Destructiveness places us in harmony with the dissolution of the old.

Ideality produces the peculiar emotion which is experienced when we behold beautiful objects; and it gives a desire to improve everything, and to advance constantly towards perfection. When it acts in combination chiefly with our emotional and observing faculties, it may stimulate the intellect to imagine poetical scenes which cannot stand the test of scientific analysis; and it frequently is thus employed. In like manner, a high degree of development or morbid excitement of the organ of Wonder, by giving an intense desire for the new and strange, may prompt the intellect, when uninstructed in science, to imagine a supernatural world, which reason cannot penetrate or recognise. Fairy-land, and the witch scene in Macbeth, may be cited as examples.

This organ, when very large and active, or when morbidly excited, leads to a belief in ghosts, spirits, and a spiritual world, in which the human mind is supposed to act independently of matter. These notions bear the same relation to it that the imagery of poetry bears to Ideality. They gratify the emotion, although rigid science ignores them. A full account of the discovery and effects of the organ of Wonder is given in Gall's work, Sur les Fonctions du Cerveau, tome v., p. 341; in Dr Spurzheim's "Phrenology," p. 206; and in my System of Phrenology, vol. i., p. 449, 5th edition.

In the Phrenological Journal, vol. i., pp. 541 and 553, the subject of spectral illusions, or apparitions, is largely discussed, and evidence adduced that they result from morbid action of the organs of the observing faculties. The organ of Wonder, when very highly developed, and also when diseased, stimulates these organs into a state of abnormal action, and causes them to generate apparitions or spectral illusions. There is evidence that the organ of Wonder is not sufficient by itself to give form and colour to spectral illusions, but that these originate in the abnormal activity of the perceptive organs. In the same work, vol. v., p. 594, a case is recorded in which diseased structure was found under the portion of the cranium lying above the organ of Wonder; and the patient, an educated man of 41 years of age, had long complained of being tormented by invisible beings, whose agency and influence he felt, but whom he never could see. In him the observing organs were not affected.

As a contrast to this instance, the case of an old gentleman of 94 years of age is described in the same journal, vol. x., p. 352, in whom disease, indicating chronic inflammation, was found in the falx and in the dura mater, covering Firmness,

Benevolence, Veneration, Imitation, and Wonder, on both sides, and in the portion of the skull covering the organ of Wonder, on the left side, which was thickened by descent of the inner table; and there were indications also of chronic inflammatory action and other disease in the anterior lobe. He never was insane, but he saw visions, coloured, and of various forms, which he knew to be spectral illusions; and he lost the knowledge of the meaning of words, while he knew objects and judged of them soundly. Additional cases of spectral illusions are recorded in vol. v., pp. 210, 319, 430; —and at p. 504 of the same volume the subject of witchcraft is discussed in connection with this and other organs.

A gentleman in whom the organ of Wonder is large, and the reflecting organs are fully, although not largely developed, told me that when a marvellous incident or miraculous narrative is presented to him, his instinctive tendency is to believe it. In its mere marvellousness, it possesses to him so great an interest that he is disposed at once, and with pleasure, to embrace it as true. An effort of his intellect is required to arrest his tendency to believe, and to enable him to subject the narrative to a philosophical investigation.

Here, then, we discover an organ which, in a state of high development and activity, and also in one of disease, gives a love of the supernatural; and which, when acting with the perceptive organs in a morbid condition, produces spectral illusions, which the ignorant mistake for supernatural appearances.

I have observed, that when this organ and that of Veneration are large, and there is a nervous or sanguine temperament, and even when the intellectual organs are well developed, a strong predisposition exists to believe in spiritual beings and agencies. It is this combination which, when unguided by science, produces belief in spirit-rapping, table-turning, and other supernatural phenomena, about which so much has recently been published. Persons thus constituted recoil from such investigations as that in which we are now engaged, as repugnant to their feelings. There is in nature no evidence accessible to man of the existence in this world of creatures unconnected with matter; but we appear to be capable of recognising the existence of intelligence, design, power, and other mental qualities behind the screen of matter, although our own faculties are not adequate to the discovery or comprehension of the nature of the Being who manifests them. Wonder appears to stand related to this supernatural power in a way somewhat analogous to that in which Benevolence stands related to pleasure and pain in sentient beings. Pain, which Benevolence desires to remove, and pleasure, which it loves to augment, are not material objects, but emotions produced by nervous matter existing in certain conditions and under certain relations to external objects. It is through the organ of Benevolence that emotions of joy or pity arise in us when we contemplate certain states of pleasure or of pain in other sentient beings; and this occurs although we do not yet know the molecular condition of the organism which causes any of these feelings to arise. In like manner, Wonder starts into action when the intellect contemplates the agencies and relations of things, and seems to generate a belief in the existence of a supernatural power, although the intellect cannot penetrate into the mystery of what the nature of this power is.

When the organs of Wonder and Veneration are very deficient in an individual, and his intellectual organs are powerful and trained in science, he regards the wonderful and supernatural with dislike. All discourses about the undemonstrable appear to him to be dreams, and he is apt to despise the intellects of men who seriously believe in a supernatural power and intelligence which has given properties to matter, and placed its action under laws, and which makes its existence felt by man, although he is incapable of thoroughly comprehending and defining it. In this respect the disputant resembles the man who, being extremely deficient in the organs of Time and Tune, pronounces music to be merely a confused noise.

VENERATION, HOPE, AND IDEALITY.

Dr Gall discovered this organ by observing the heads of persons particularly prone to devotional exercises, one of whom was his own brother. He studied the heads of many devotees praying before the altars in the Roman Catholic churches of Germany, and arrived at conviction of the situation and functions of this organ. It is regarded by phrenologists as fully supported by irrefragable evidence.

The function of the faculty is to produce the emotion or sentiment of reverence or veneration in general, on perceiving an object at once great and good. It and the organ of Wonder form the emotional fountains whence natural religion springs, and the combined action of the two produces adoration. They are aided by Ideality and Hope.

The organ of Ideality gives rise to the love of the perfect, and when acting with Veneration, leads to the desire of perfection in holiness. The organ of Hope produces the expectation that we shall realise what we desire, and, when added to this combination, produces faith and confidence, that somehow or other, somewhere or other, and at some time or other, this condition of perfect holiness will be attained.

These emotions are particularly grand, pleasing, soothing, or exciting, according to the degree in which their organs are possessed, and the manner in which they are addressed by external influences. They exercise a powerful influence on all the other faculties, and, when vividly active, frequently overpower reason. To those in whom they are large and active, religious exercises afford the greatest pleasure, and are invested with deep solemnity and interest. When the organ of Veneration alone is large, and it has been directed chiefly to persons of high rank, it is often found venerating them and their station, and producing little regard for religion; but the emotion is still one of reverence, the object only being changed.

When this organ is very small, the emotion of reverence is scarcely experienced. Fear of future punishment and hope of future reward, love of approbation, the expectation of worldly advancement, and other motives, may lead persons thus organized to profess an interest in religion, and to show great zeal for articles of faith, the church, and other objects and observances connected with public worship; but they, nevertheless, are feebly moved by genuine sentiments of devotion. I have observed that individuals who have large organs of Wonder and Veneration, and who, by training, have been deeply imbued with certain theological opinions, will, nevertheless, if their organs of Benevolence, Conscientiousness, and intellect be large and well cultivated, not hesitate to modify their articles of faith according to their own convictions of truth; while, on the other hand, those persons in whom the last named organs are deficient, and who, nevertheless, profess a profound reverence for religion, are the grand sticklers for creeds, articles of faith, and the forms and ceremonies of public worship. The *moral sentiments* not being powerful in their minds, they lean on religious dogmas for guidance and support, and conclude that these are equally needed by all other persons: hence they attach an undue importance to them, and insist on every believer embracing the identical opinions which they entertain. The more strongly both the moral and religious emotions exist in any individual, along with vigorous and enlightened intellect, the more firmly does he rely on their native power and efficacy for good; the less he cares for formulas; the more large-minded and tolerant he becomes in his estimates of the faith of other men who differ from him, and the more progressive is he in his own opinions.

The religious emotions are liable to be invaded by disease. Dr A. Combe thus describes religious insanity :—

"Religious fanaticism, or excessive and ill-directed activity of Veneration and some other sentiments, has long been regarded as a most fruitful source of insanity, and is a pure specimen of a functional cause. It was so frequent at a former time in France, that out of many cases in regard to the causes of which Pinel could procure information, nearly one-fourth arose from religious enthusiasm carried to excess. But, in these instances, it almost invariably happened that some one or more of the lower propensities had been in a state of active alliance with misdirected devotion, and brought about a conflict in the mind, which the organism could not withstand.

"It is quite certain, for instance, that every new sect that appears inflicts mental derangement upon numbers of its votaries; and the more violent, startling, and extraordinary the doctrines enforced, and the wider the difference between them and those previously entertained, the more extensively will nervous disease and insanity follow; for in the same proportion will their extravagancies be calculated to interest the greater number of powerful faculties, exalt the healthy action of the brain, and excite to disease. And, accordingly, in speaking of the form of mental derangement generally arising from this cause, under the name of *devout melancholy,* 'there are,' says an author whose writings are remarkable for sagacity and accuracy of observation, 'few practitioners who have not had opportunities of seeing some shocking instances of this disease. The greatness and excellence of the object, and the satisfaction the soul experiences in giving itself up to the contemplation of the Almighty, excite too lively a sensation, and *produce in the brain a tension too violent and too continual to be supported* for a long time without injury; it soon throws the mind into fanatical madness, and exhausts the body. I have seen the most amiable young persons, led away by an erroneous system, fade and fall away into decay, neglecting the duties of their calling, in order to give up their thoughts wholly to the Supreme Author of their being, who could not have been more properly glorified than by a strict attention to those duties.'*

"The preceding is a sketch evidently drawn from nature, but an example or two will make its accuracy more striking, and its utility more evident to the unprofessional reader:—A lady of middle age who had always been cheerful and regular in her devotions, went, during the winter, on a visit to a family—

---

* Tissot on the Diseases of Literary and Sedentary Persons, p. 68.

followers of Swedenborg. Being pressed, she went and heard their doctrines propounded, and, for the first time, began to doubt the truth of her own views. She returned to London in great disquietude of mind, and in this state accompanied her mother to church on Easter Sunday, and remained to receive the sacrament. But when the cup was presented to her, she was greatly disconcerted and confused to perceive that not a single drop of wine remained for her. She hurried home in dismay, declared she was lost and rejected of God : and furious mania soon came on, of which she was afterwards cured.* In this patient, functional excitement of the organs of the religious sentiments was obviously the cause of the disease that overset reason. But a still more striking instance of over-excitement of Veneration and the other religious feelings, leading to cerebral disease and insanity, is the case of a young gentleman, educated, by his father's particular desire, in the strictest principles of religion, under the care of several divines in succession, each of whom ' was enjoined to be very attentive to his religious instruction. Many of the most abstruse doctrines of theology were pressed upon him. His mind, consequently, became partially bewildered and enfeebled, and impressed with the most visionary images. At length, he conceived that his sole duty was to pray for the remission of his manifold sins, and to study the Bible and particular homilies. Accordingly, if he walked out when the devotional fit came upon him, he cared not in what puddle he knelt; or if at his meals, his food was quitted for prayer. Soon his spiritual extravagances were so many, and, if interrupted, his violence so great, that he was pronounced insane,'† and removed to Dr Burrows' establishment, where he recovered, but afterwards relapsed, and died maniacal. Numerous other examples might be quoted, but it is altogether unnecessary, as, unhappily, they are so common that almost every one must have met with them even in private life. In a few cases, I have known pain in the region of the head, corresponding to the organ of Veneration, much complained of.

" Besides this more simple kind of morbid excitement of Veneration, there are several varieties in which the organs of Wonder, Hope, Conscientiousness, and Ideality, seem to be also implicated. Where Wonder is joined to Veneration, the attention of the patient is generally first strongly attracted by the more mysterious parts of our religious faith, and the whole powers of the mind are devoted to their contemplation or solution, till involuntary excitement be produced, which ends in the subversion of health and reason, and leaves the mind a prey to visions,

* Burrows' Commentaries, p. 40. † Ibid., p. 43.

and to the permanent belief and fear of every species of supernatural agency.

"When Hope and Veneration are the faculties to which the functional excitement extends, brilliant anticipations and confident expectations of a happy futurity mark the character. Under such a form of disease, a lady, mentioned by Pinel, evidently laboured, who became insane in consequence of her husband's misfortunes, and who found delightful consolation, first, in long meditations and fervent prayer, and, subsequently, in ecstatic fits, during which she believed herself raised to the bosom of Divinity, and which, from excessive cerebral activity, soon terminated in unequivocal insanity.

"Conscientiousness and Veneration, similarly affected, and joined to Cautiousness, give rise to that deplorable form of melancholy in which the patient is so overwhelmed by the sense of his guilt in the sight of God, that he cannot for a moment turn his mind to the hopes held out in the gospel to the repentant sinner; but passes his days and weeks in the deepest remorse, insensible to every other impression. Dr Perfect gives an instructive example of this kind in a man, naturally of a cheerful disposition and lively imagination, and moderate in his enjoyments. Some conversations which he had with a sombre and melancholy Methodist, made an entire change in his views. He renounced all, even the most innocent indulgences, gave himself up to solitude, and from that time regarded an eternity of suffering as his inevitable destiny. The Supreme Being was represented to him by his friend as cruel, revengeful, and delighting in the torment of his creatures. These notions led to sleeplessness, constant moaning, black despair, and a tendency to suicide. But in the course of some time, Dr Perfect, assisted by a clergyman of true piety and an enlightened mind, and by a proper moral and physical regimen, succeeded in restoring him to health and happiness.

"Much alarm has unnecessarily been expressed by seriously disposed persons at the assertion that madness can ever be caused by indulgence of devotional or religious feelings, to whatever excess these may be carried; and no little obloquy has been thrown upon those observers whose experience has compelled them to state the fact. Even in France, where religion is certainly not cultivated with extreme ardour, public opinion on this subject was so strong some years ago, that Pinel, then the head physician of the largest asylum in Europe, and the best acquainted with the facts and history of insanity, was so much afraid to brave its censures, that while, on the one hand, he expressed his conviction that ' nothing is more common in hospitals than cases of alienation produced by too exalted devotion, by scruples carried to a destructive excess, or by religious terrors;' he yet felt constrained, by public opinion, to 'suppress his daily notes, containing a mass of details of this kind' which had come under his observation, and to take his examples 'elsewhere than in his own country,' or, in other words, from the works of English authors! Surely religion rests on too firm a foundation to require such a sacrifice of truth and candour to supposed expediency and bigotry. And if, in any circumstances, the exercise of our devotional feelings even *seems* to bring on the loss of reason, it is surely not only allowable, but a *positive duty*, for the professional writer under whose cognisance these things occur, to investigate accurately, and state fearlessly, the conditions under which he has seen them happen, that others may be preserved in time from a similar affliction."*

In contradiction to these views, and as illustrative of opinions still very prevalent even among intelligent men, I may quote the following observations on insanity made by Dr Heinroth, in a work published by him at Leipsic in 1837:—

"Insanity," says he, "is the loss of moral liberty; it never depends on a physical cause; it is not a disease of the body, but a disease of the mind—a sin. It is not, and it cannot be, hereditary; because the thinking I, the soul, is not hereditary. Only the constitution and temperament are transmissible by generation, against the influence of which every individual whose parents have been insane, should oppose a strenuous resistance, in order that he may not become alienated. The man who, during his whole life, has before his eyes and in his heart the image of God, has no occasion to fear that he shall ever suffer the loss of reason. It is clear as the light of day, that the torments of the unhappy persons known as bewitched and possessed, are the consequences of exaltation of their remorse of conscience. Man has received not reason alone as his inheritance; he has besides a certain moral power which cannot be conquered by any physical power, and which never gives way except under the weight of his own faults."

This passage is quoted and answered by M. Leuret, physician to the hospital of Bicêtre in Paris, as follows:—

"It contains as many errors as phrases. To say that a man will never become deranged, if, during his whole life, he has had in his heart the image of God, is to misunderstand the innumerable cases of insanity produced by an ascetic life and superstition; to impute the sufferings of those who believe themselves bewitched and possessed by devils, to the remorse

* Observations on Mental Derangement. By Andrew Combe, M.D., pp. 184-189.

of their consciences, is to calumniate a class of unfortunate individuals who often have committed no other wrongs than the one of exaggerating their own faults, or even ascribing to themselves some which they have never committed; to maintain that man possesses a moral power which cannot be overcome by any physical power, is to ignore the effects of injuries of the head, of swallowing certain poisonous substances, of inflammation of the membranes of the brain, and other causes, in producing mental derangement; to refuse to acknowledge that insanity is transmissible by generation, is to reject the evidence of experience, and to deny facts which every day presents to observation. Dr Heinroth admits that the temperament and constitution are transmissible. Be it so; but all the temperaments and every constitution are seen in a lunatic asylum. Insanity is not hereditary because the soul is not hereditary! A splendid reason! What do you know about the soul, and what need have you to introduce here points of religious belief? Observe nature, meditate on the facts which she presents to you, and you will reject these doctrines, in place of supporting them by arguments, the falsity of which is apparent to every understanding."*

We are now prepared to answer the question, "Is man naturally a religious being?" If organs of Wonder, Veneration, Ideality, and Hope, exist, and are endowed with the functions here ascribed to them, it is certain that religious emotions and desires are natural to man. The public mind will, in its own season, investigate the evidence of the existence and functions of these organs; and when it does so, doubt on the subject will vanish. The different degrees of development of them in different persons, also, will explain the circumstance of some individuals being deeply interested in, and others being indifferent about religion; and put an end to the fears which many persons in whom the organs are moderately developed, entertain about religion being constantly in danger from speculations regarded as subversive of devotion. It will then be understood that it will be as impossible to destroy religion, as to obliterate parental affection, the love of property, or any other natural desire which is based on a cerebral organ. It will then also be seen that superstition is the aberration of those faculties acting in ignorance of the natural sciences; and that, especially, our unconsciousness of the functions of the brain and of its action, has led to many errors in religious belief. Desires, for example, generated by the spontaneous action of the organs of the animal propensities,

* Du Traitment Moral de la Folie, p. 146.

have been mistaken for suggestions of the devil ; while the joy and fervour arising from a similar action of the religious organs have been mistaken for direct influences from Heaven.

The history of man, in almost every age and country, affords evidence of the innateness of the religious sentiment in his mind, though its intensity, like that of all other emotions, is different in different individuals and nations. If the existence of musicians, musical instruments, orchestras, music halls, and crowds of listeners, indicates that a love of melody and harmony is natural to the highest portion of our race, so must the existence of priests, temples, churches, and vast assemblages of worshippers in the same countries, be accepted as proof that religious emotions also are part of the natural constitution of the same minds.

SECTION V.—IS MAN NATURALLY A MORAL BEING?

The organs of BENEVOLENCE and CONSCIENTIOUSNESS are distinct from, and independent of, those of Wonder and Veneration, and they constitute the chief fountains of moral emotion. Veneration also may be said to belong to the moral faculties, but the emotion which it produces is more peculiarly religious.

The organ of Benevolence was discovered by Dr Gall, and he remarks that he collected so great a number of facts in regard to it, " that there is no fundamental quality or faculty whose existence and organ are better established than those of Benevolence." This conclusion appears to me to be supported by innumerable facts. The organ gives the desire of the happiness of others, and produces delight in the diffusion of enjoyment. It disposes to active goodness, and, in cases of distress, to compassion. It corresponds to the sentiment of " Charity" described by St Paul, to that of " Goodness of Nature," by Lord Bacon, and to the quality of " *Philanthropia*" of the Greeks.

When the organ is large, there is a strong natural inclination to kindness, and great pleasure is felt in promoting the welfare and enjoyment of all sentient beings. When the organ is small, there is indifference to the welfare of others ; and if the organs of the propensities, with Self-Esteem, be large, and Conscientiousness deficient, intense selfishness will be the result.

The organ of Conscientiousness gives the love of the true in contradistinction to the false,—of the real in contradistinction to the pretended, and of the genuine in contradistinction to the factitious. It produces also the feeling of duty, obligation, or incumbency. When the organ is large and active, it is attended with a sense of its own paramount authority over every other faculty, and it gives its impulses with a tone which appears like the voice of Heaven ; but it requires the aid of the other emotional faculties and intellect to guide it to justice.

The intellectual faculties investigate the qualities and relations not only of external objects, but of the desires and emotions which arise in the mind itself. They, however, do not *produce* these desires and emotions; and, consequently, unless the special organ on which each of these depends is active, the intellect cannot become acquainted with it.

For example, as Causality and Comparison cannot attain to a knowledge of melody without the aid of the organ of Tune, neither can they reach a knowledge of the emotion of kindness and compassion, or the disinterested love of the happiness of others, without the assistance of the organ of Benevolence; nor, according to my view, can they attain to a knowledge of the desire to act justly, to fulfil duty, and to discharge faithfully obligations undertaken, unless aided by the organ of Conscientiousness. The intellect alone may judge of *legal* obligation ; because it is sufficient of itself to discriminate whether " it is so nominated in the bond ;" but without the aid of the organ of Conscientiousness, it cannot arrive at a sound conclusion whether the thing " nominated in the bond" is *naturally* and intrinsically, irrespective of the bond, incumbent or not incumbent on him whose signature it bears.

It is the faculty of Conscientiousness, then, which produces the feeling of natural right on the part of one person to demand, and of natural obligation on another to perform, for which we have no single definite expression in the English language. What is commonly called justice, is the result of this sentiment acting in combination with the intellectual powers, the latter investigating the motives and consequences of the actions, on the justice or injustice of which Conscientiousness is to decide; but they do not feel the peculiar emotion which I have attempted to describe. Persons in whom the organ of Conscientiousness is very deficient, give the name of justice to the dictates of Benevolence or Veneration, or to the enactments of the law; but when the organ is large, the individual not only does not limit his sentiments of obligation by the requirements of the statute-book, but in some instances he will acknowledge that he has no *natural* title to what the civil law places at his disposal, and in other cases that he lies under a *natural* obligation to perform what the law does not enforce. In short, he feels within himself an inward law of duty, independently of the dictates of Benevolence and Veneration, and of the terms of statutory enactment. In the words of St Paul, he is a law unto himself. When the organ is very deficient this desire of acting justly is not experienced, and the individual generally takes the laws of his country, the precepts of his religion, or the opinions of his own social circle, as his standards of justice, duty, and obligation.

Mr John Stuart Mill, in the sixth book of his Logic, appears to recognise the fact that our desires of improvement proceed from the propensities and sentiments, but that these give mere desires, and cannot direct us *how* to satisfy themselves. Knowledge of the means of doing so must, he says, be acquired by the intellect. This rule applies to all our faculties of desire and emotion; and much confusion of opinion would be avoided if it were generally known that adequately developed organs of *both* sets of faculties, emotional and intellectual, together with a sufficient knowledge of nature, are necessary to sound judgment regarding what is beneficial, what is just, what is true, what is holy, and what is beautiful.

There is thus a foundation in nature for morality, distinguishable from that for religion. This being the case, it follows that one individual may be naturally moral who is not naturally religious, and another may be naturally religious who is not naturally moral, according as the one group of organs is large and the other small in his brain. Many persons hold religion to be the sole foundation of morality, and believe that religion rests on revelation alone. They also hold, that religion necessarily embraces morality. But these are assumptions at variance with the facts of cerebral physiology, and also with the experience of human actions.

SECTION VI.—IS THERE ANY NATURAL STANDARD OF MORAL AND RELIGIOUS TRUTH?

Much has been written about the existence of a natural standard of moral and religious truth. If by this phrase we mean a test which may be applied to all moral and religious emotions, sentiments, and opinions, and conformity to which will induce *all* men to admit them to be sound and true, then no such standard exists. A particular emotion, or opinion, which is recognised to be natural, just, and true, by a man in whom Veneration and Conscientiousness are large, may be regarded as a factitious intellectual error by another in whom these organs are very deficient. The same proposition may be repeated in reference to the other moral and religious faculties. Again, two individuals, whose moral and religious organs are equally well developed, may view the same religious doctrines quite differently, as truth or error, according as their faculties have been trained to reverence or condemn them. Moreover, great differences in religious feeling and perception are produced by the temperament and state of health of the individual. The whole organism must be in a state of complete health to enable us to reach the soundest views of religious truth. If the nervous system be in a morbid condition, depressing impressions will be received equally from the Bible and from nature. A patient, for example, labouring under *delirium tremens* may perceive the devil rushing out of the wall of his room ready to seize him; or one whose digestive organs are greatly disordered, may see all the external world enveloped in gloom and misery. In civilized life, in consequence of our habits not being yet founded on physiological knowledge, few persons enjoy complete health; and from this cause, many of us live habitually under erroneous impressions of the true nature of man, and its capacities for improvement in knowledge and enjoyment. Thus no series of moral and religious propositions can be announced, which all men, whatever be their original mental constitution, whatever their cultivation and training, and whatever their state of health, will acknowledge to be sound and true.

Notwithstanding all those obstacles, however, *degrees of probability* of moral and religious truth may be estimated. The more favourable the original cerebral constitution of an individual, the higher the cultivation bestowed on his mental faculties, and the wider his sphere of information and experience, the higher authority he becomes in questions of moral and religious truth; and men in general will recognise his views to be true in proportion to the degree in which, in the constitution of their own brains, in the cultivation of their own faculties, and in the scope of their own observations, they approximate to his standard. By improving, therefore, the sources from which moral and religious truth are derived, namely, development of brain, and cultivation, higher degrees of such truths will constantly be attained; and there will be a corresponding approach among mankind to unanimity. If design, order, and regularity exist in the constitution of this world, it is presumable that the soundest and most comprehensive views of these will be reached by the best constituted and best instructed minds. Moreover, if man is a progressive being, it is to be expected that the order of nature will be found to be constituted in harmony with his highest state of development and instruction, and that a great part of the disorder which he now sees and laments will be seen to arise from his own ignorance of himself, of external nature, and of their true relations to each other. I have elsewhere remarked, that the exquisite fineness of the notes which Paganini elicited from the violin (in quality they seemed more pure, rich, and ethereal than any sounds that matter could be supposed capable of emitting), was the result of his extraordinary development of the organs of Tune and Time, combined with an extremely sensitive nervous and bilious temperament. Until an individual thus endowed, and thoroughly trained to the practice of the art of music, appeared, the high capabilities of wood and catgut to yield notes of such exquisite melody were unknown; and a similar reflection may be applicable to the entire system of nature. The physical and moral world may be full of divine qualities and delicious harmonies, if we only had superior minds endowed with sufficient knowledge to evoke them.

In the existing state of philosophy, the reasonings and practical suggestions even of the highest and best instructed minds constitute very imperfect guides to moral and religious truth: because the individuals are still very imperfectly acquainted with the grand elements out of which these truths must be educed, namely, their own nature, and that of the external world; and not only so, but, from ignorance of the same kind, those persons to whom such views as these are addressed, try them by the standard of their own feelings, observations, and reflections, however imperfect and limited these may be, and condemn or approve, simply according to the impressions made on their minds in this condition. Moreover, if there be, as I contend, a systematic arrangement in the physical and moral worlds, there will be an external standard by which to try the opinions of men; namely, *the results which they produce when reduced to practice.* If nature be arranged in relation to the highest condition of the human faculties, then those individuals whose cerebral organs are most favourably developed, and whose faculties are best trained and most highly instructed, will possess a corresponding superiority over less gifted persons, in discovering, appreciating, unfolding, and practically following forth the course of nature. Such minds saw the accordance of the principles of free trade with the order of nature, and were able to expound *à priori* their certain beneficial consequences when practically adopted; while men in whom the organs of the moral sentiments and Causality were less developed, or less cultivated and instructed, saw only ruin to public interests in the adoption of the scheme. The practical results of any code of morality, or religious faith, will, after a sufficient trial, always reveal whether it be in accordance with the order of nature or not; for

D

well-being is the certain result of our opinions and conduct when in harmony, and suffering and discontent the inevitable consequence of them when at variance, with the real constitution of the physical and moral worlds.

It may be supposed, that, by means of this external standard, ethical and religious truth may be demonstrated to the conviction of all men; and this appears to be believed by some advocates of utility as the test of duty. But without an adequate development of brain, and high training and instruction of the moral and intellectual faculties, people experience great difficulty in perceiving and appreciating what constitutes even the elements of their own happiness, and a still greater difficulty in discovering the means of realising it. The low-brained, ill-fed, ignorant Celt clings to his filthy cabin and idle life, and turns a deaf ear to our exposition of the happiness which he would experience from habits more in accordance with his physical and mental constitutions. If, therefore, the views which I am now endeavouring to explain should ever become the basis of general opinion and action, we may expect that an individual who perceives in himself deficiencies of brain, or information, or both, which prevent his reaching the elevated emotions and profound views of his better constituted and instructed brethren, will be more disposed than he is at present, when he believes himself to be a normal specimen of human nature, to allow himself to be guided by superior minds. On the other hand, he who possesses higher cerebral power and more extensive information than the person who assumes the office of directing his judgment and controlling his conduct, will appeal to the higher standard of his own perceptions and the consequences of his opinions, and in everything relating to his own welfare and that of his dependants, he will act according to his own convictions. Such a man will be disposed to obey the laws and observe the customs of the country in which he lives, in so far as this is necessary to the peace of society, even although he should perceive them to fall far short of his own standards of truth, justice, and utility; but he will only the more earnestly strive to induce his compatriots to amend their principles and practice.

In order to judge soundly of the relation between Science and Religion, it is necessary that we should understand how far our faculties are capable of penetrating into the constitution and qualities of Nature. This, accordingly, shall form the next subject of inquiry.

CHAPTER IV.

OF THE EXTENT TO WHICH MAN IS ABLE TO DISCOVER THE ULTIMATE ELEMENTS OR ESSENCE OF THE EXTERNAL WORLD.

I HAVE already referred to phrenological works for a list of the faculties of the human mind, so far as they have been proved to be elementary by observation of the brain. The enumeration is not complete, nor are the functions of all of them delineated with scientific precision. Improvement is expected in both particulars; but the essential character and sphere of activity of each appear to me to be so far ascertained, that we may draw inferences from them, which, although liable to be modified in consequence of subsequent observation and analysis, will probably not be altered in their essential aspects. I now proceed to inquire into the extent to which these faculties enable us to discover the ultimate elements of our own nature and that of the external world.

In treating of our own nature, let us begin by considering the mind.

1st, I repeat the observation, for it is practically too little attended to, that Mind in the sense of spirit, or of an entity existing and acting in this world independently of matter, is absolutely unknown to us. We are conscious only of mental states and acts, and these have been ascertained always to depend in this life on corresponding conditions and actions of the brain. Whether, therefore, we contemplate the beauties of external nature, listen to the roar of the cataract, or raise our minds to God in the loftiest aspirations of religious adoration, a certain cerebral condition is indispensable in this world to the experience of the perceptions and emotions. Every philosophy, and every religion, which ignores this fundamental fact of our being, and its consequences (which shall be subsequently explained), is imperfect; and when it contradicts them it is false and injurious. It is in vain to exclaim that this fact leads to materialism, and is therefore dangerous. If it lead logically to materialism, then materialism must be true; it must be an institution of God, and must have been devised by His wisdom, and established by His goodness; and there would, therefore, be not only folly, but impiety, in rebelling against it. If, on the other hand, it does not lead logically to materialism, then the exclamation is groundless, and it is our duty to consider to what other logical conclusions it leads; and this shall be done in a subsequent chapter.

2*dly*, Our subjective knowledge, or knowledge of ourselves derived from consciousness, cannot in this life go beyond the limits of the functions of the cerebral organs. A dog cannot by any possible course of instruction or communication be made to comprehend a question in algebra, the revolution of the globe, the beauties of Shakspeare, or the sublime devotional feelings inspired by the oratorio of "The Creation." Its mental organs are not fitted to reach these conceptions and emotions. In like manner, all ideas and emotions which transcend the sphere of action of the mental organs of any particular human being are inappreciable and inconceivable by him. If the organ of Tune be very deficient, he cannot perceive or imagine melody; if Veneration be very deficient, he cannot comprehend the nature of the devotional emotion; and if Conscientiousness be very deficient, the feeling of justice is equally an inscrutable enigma to his mind, although he may possess other organs in a high degree.

3*dly*, The external world and the constitution of our cerebral organs are adapted to each other. Man appears to be a part of a great system, and he, as the rational observer, interpreter, and to some extent the deputed administrator of a portion of it, cannot correctly appreciate his own position, privileges, powers, and duties, until he has become acquainted with the external world, with himself, and with the reciprocal relations between them. One grand element in this knowledge, and that which is necessary to render all the others productive of happiness, is an intimate and correct knowledge of his own constitution, physical and mental; which, until the functions of the brain and the nervous system were discovered, it was impossible for him to attain.

We have already seen that we have no consciousness whatever of the substance or essence of the thinking principle; let us now inquire into the extent to which man can discover the nature or essence of the external world.

The means by which we gain knowledge of the external world are the external organs of our Senses, and cerebral organs.

The external senses generally recognised are those of FEELING, TASTE, SMELL, HEARING, and SIGHT. Each of these senses depends for its power of action on a specific organism, which stands in communication, through specific nerves, with a particular portion of the brain. All of these parts must be in a state of normal development, health, and efficiency, as indispensable conditions of our receiving, through them, correct intimations of the external world, and, in some respects, of the state of our own internal being. When the conditions do not exist, the corresponding perceptions fail to arise; and when they are deranged, the perceptions are impaired, disordered, or perverted, according to the extent of the aberration of the organs from their normal state.

The function of the senses is to bring us into communication with the external world. We have no consciousness of the existence of the organs of sense, or what functions are performed by them. We are conscious of hearing, seeing, smelling, tasting, and touching; but in performing these acts in a state of health, we neither feel nor perceive the part which the organic apparatus plays in executing them. When the organs are obstructed, diseased, or impaired, we become aware of their influence; but this is accomplished by acts of observation and reflection, and not by our normal intuitive consciousness. One great advantage of this constitution is that our attention is directed at once to the objects to be perceived, which are of the chief interest to us; the organic apparatus meanwhile performing its functions unobtrusively but efficiently, under its Author's care.

When an external object makes an impression on an organ of sense, the organ transmits it to the brain, and by means of internal cerebral organs, we *perceive the object*. Previously to every perception, there must be an impression on the organs of sense; and the function of these organs appears to consist in receiving and transmitting this impression to the organs of the internal faculties. Except when excited by an external cause, the organs of sense, in a state of health, do not transmit any stimulus to the brain; in other words, they do not possess the attribute of *spontaneous* activity.

The functions of every sense depend on its peculiar organism: and no preceding exercise or habit is necessary in order to acquire the special power of any sense. The organism of each sense performs its functions in consequence of its own innate constitution and the relations which it bears to external objects. If it be perfect, the functions are perfect also; and if it be diseased, the functions are deranged, notwithstanding all previous experience. The relations of each sense are determinate, and the impressions received are subject to positive laws.

The faculties which take cognizance of the external world, and also to some extent of our internal condition, receive the impressions made on the senses; and we proceed to inquire into the kind and extent of the knowledge which they enable us to acquire. Each mental power depends on a specific portion of the brain. When it is wanting, a certain range of knowledge is excluded. If the ears and the portion of the brain in direct connection with the auditory nerves be perfect, we may hear sounds; but if the organs of Tune be extremely deficient, we shall be unable to distinguish those qualities and relations of sound which constitute melody. If the eye, the optic nerves, and the parts of the brain in which the latter terminate, be perfect, we may see the form of objects; but if the organ of Colouring be very deficient, we shall be incapable of distinguishing their colours. If the organs of the perceptive faculties be very large and active, their range of perception is enlarged and increased in intensity; but their perceptions cannot pass beyond the limits assigned by their natural constitution and established relations. Disease in the organs impairs or deranges their functions.

Sir William Hamilton gives the following account of our knowledge of matter. "The necessary constituents," says he, "of our notion of matter, the primary qualities of bodies, are thus all evolved from the two catholic conditions of matter— (1), the occupying space; and (2), the being contained in space. Of these, the former affords (A) trinal extension, explicated again into (1), divisibility; (2), size, containing under it density or rarity; (3), figure; and (B) ultimate incompressibility; while the latter gives (A) mobility, and (B) situation." "The primary qualities of matter thus develop themselves out of the original datum of substance occupying space."—(Dissertations, Note D, § 2, in Hamilton's edition of Reid's Collected Writings.) Observations on the functions of the brain lead us to a different view. Our belief in the *existence* of *substance*, seems to me to result from the activity of Individuality excited by an external corporeal object; our perception of the form, size, colour, density, resistance, position in space, divisibility, and mobility of a corporeal object, are the direct results of the activity of the organs of Form, Size, Colour, Weight, Locality, Eventuality, and Comparison, excited by certain qualities possessed by matter. A few elucidations may be necessary to explain this doctrine.

The faculty of INDIVIDUALITY, gives us the belief of the *existence* of the external world and of ourselves. It forms the class of ideas represented by substantive nouns, when used without an adjective, as *rock, man, horse*. When, by means of the organs of sense, and the internal perceptive organs, we receive impressions of form, colour, size, &c., Individuality produces in us the conviction that the objects making these impressions exist; but here its powers terminate.

The physical qualities of substances are discovered by means of the organs of FORM, SIZE, WEIGHT, COLOURING, and TUNE. Each of these has received a specific constitution, and our power of acquiring the perceptions of the qualities to which it is related, depends on the degree of perfection of the organ. When large, we have strong and clear, when small, faint and imperfect, and when diseased, deranged perceptions.

These organs cannot discover the essence of the externa objects which produce the perceptions of their qualities. They give rise merely to the perceptions, and there their functions end. The organ of Colouring, for instance, receives from the eyes impressions which produce in it perceptions of colour; but it cannot discover what the efficient cause is, why grass appears green, gold yellow, and silver white. And so with the other organs for the perception of the qualities of external bodies.

These organs are constituted with so specific a relation to the qualities and modes of action of physical nature as it now exists (in what from its adaptation to these organs, I may be allowed to call its normal state), that they would be unfitted to a different constitution of physical objects, and would become useless were even the normal condition of actual nature much altered. The weight of the body, and the strength of the muscles, are so exactly adapted to the actual force of gravitation in our globe, that were this force greatly increased, our present constitution continuing unchanged, we should stick immoveably to the ground; while, if it were much diminished, we should, by our present muscular efforts in walking, bound into the air at every step. The faculty of Weight and Momentum is the mental power by means of which we estimate, intuitively, the force of gravitation, and adapt our muscular efforts to its influence. In a world in which there was no gravitation (such as a disembodied spirit may be supposed to inhabit), this power would be useless.

In like manner, the organ of Colouring is adapted to a scene of existence in which there is light, and to those degrees of temperature which exist in this world. Were there no light, vision would cease, and colour disappear; or were the temperature of external objects only moderately raised above its present standard, most of the beautiful variegated tints of nature would vanish.

The organ of Tune affords, if possible, a still more striking example. External objects are endowed with certain powers of vibration. These obey fixed laws, many of which have been observed and ascertained. The air has been rendered capable of transmitting these vibrations to the ear, and the ear to the brain; and from *its* excitement, the organ of Tune produces those intensely pleasurable perceptions to which we give the name of melody. The qualities of the vibrations are adapted to our emotional, as well as to our intellectual faculties; and the most rapturous devotion, affection, terror, hope, or pity, may be called into existence by strains addressed to the faculties on which these feelings depend. But again I remark, that all this exquisite pleasure is the result of the constitution and adaptation of the qualities of things to each other. Change the condition of the sonorous body, of the air, of the ear, or of the organ of Tune, and all the effects are changed. How an immaterial being could perceive or produce melody is to us utterly inconceivable.

Similar observations may be made in regard to all the faculties which take cognizance of the qualities of external objects. Their organs and external nature are so exactly adapted to each other, that a great change in the condition of either, would derange or extinguish our existing perceptions. The yellow aspect of nature in jaundice is a familiar example; the incapacity of a man whose brain is disordered by alcohol to adapt himself to the law of gravitation is another; to which many more might be added. One practical inference which may be drawn from these facts is, that the more highly the brain is developed, it becomes a more powerful instrument for penetrating into the constitution of nature.

Having considered the existence of physical objects and their qualities, we may survey the phenomena which they exhibit, or their modes of action. The faculty of Eventuality observes these, and also the phenomena of our internal being. A horse at rest is an object related to Individuality; a horse in motion, to it, and also to Eventuality. This is the faculty which comprehends the ideas signified by active and passive verbs. Its function is limited to observing phenomena, and it takes no cognizance of their causes or consequences, beyond observing each consequence as a new phenomenon following after the one that preceded it. Eventuality may be used in this manner to observe consequences. The lower animals possess it; a dog, for example, that has been accustomed to see game killed by means of a gun, will shrink and shew signs of fear when the gun is pointed at itself. In this instance, it appears to connect the consequence, physical injury, with the explosion of the gun, as a mere event; for we have no reason to believe that it comprehends fully the process of causation through which the effect is produced.* In the house of a friend whom I used to visit in the country, there was a tame monkey. His sons knocked down apples for it from a tree with a bow and arrows; and the monkey had so far observed the connection between the use of them and the fall of the apples, that when it saw the bow and arrows in the hands of the boys, it used to run to the tree and wait in expectation of its repast. By my suggestion, on a particular day, they did not use them, but laid them down beside the monkey and retired. It continued to sit and look at them and at the tree, but although its hands and arms were adapted to the use of them, it never attempted to apply them. An internal faculty, the one which supplies the notion of causation, was wanting. The organ of CAUSALITY, therefore, is necessary to communicate the *idea of causation*; and there are men in whom it is so deficient, that they regard the external world almost exclusively as a collection of objects and qualities, exhibiting multifarious phenomena. They have no vivid impression of efficiency in the antecedent to produce the sequent, and, in consequence, have no comprehension of nature as a scheme or system of reciprocally-adapted qualities and modes of action in the objects and beings which compose it. This topic will be resumed in treating of the faculty of Causality.

Individuals in whom the organ of Eventuality is deficient, are unobservant of phenomena and events.

As a source of information, Eventuality does not go beyond simple observation of action.

There are faculties which take cognizance of the abstract relations of things: These are LOCALITY, ORDER, NUMBER, and TIME. LOCALITY is the power by which we take cognizance of relative position; ORDER, of the physical arrangement of objects; NUMBER, of their numbers; and TIME, of duration. None of these relate to the qualities of physical objects; but both ORDER and NUMBER presuppose the existence of such objects, to be arranged in space and enumerated. Our conceptions of space, number, and time, have no limits. The faculties which form these ideas lose themselves in the infinite. In exercising them we are capable of rising above this earth and its qualities; but when we do venture on such excursions, our faculties return freighted with knowledge of only one truth—that nature, in its full extent, is unfathomable by our feeble powers.

* The question whether certain species of the higher mammalia do not possess in some degree perception of the relation of cause and effect, is attended with difficulty, for the elephant, horse, and dog modify their conduct to a certain extent according to circumstances; but none of them applies causes to reach distant results, as man does.

The practical point to be kept in view in regard to the faculties mentioned in the preceding paragraph is, that they convey to us no knowledge of any object, being, mode of being, or event; but are confined to the formation of abstract ideas of space, number, and duration.

The faculty of LANGUAGE enables us to invent arbitrary signs and sounds, which we associate with external objects, and also with internal sensations, perceptions, thoughts, desires, and emotions, so as to render them expressive of these to other individuals who have been taught to form corresponding associations. This faculty has no knowledge of the objects themselves which it names. Its functions begin and end in giving us the power of inventing, learning, and using words, as arbitrary signs of our knowledge and mental states. It is, therefore, the source of no new ideas concerning the external world, ourselves, or of the relations between us and them.

It is of importance in relation to the purpose of the present treatise to mention, that the *signification* of words is learned through the medium of the faculties which take cognizance of the things indicated by them. Thus, if a rose be shewn to a child or a native of a foreign country, and the tint be submitted to their observation, and the word " red" be uttered as expressive of it, they may appreciate its meaning, and afterwards use it as a general term indicating that colour. But if an individual have been born blind, no definitions, explanations, or illustrations, will suffice to convey to his mind a conception of the colour of a rose. He may learn that a rose has a quality which persons with perfect senses perceive, but which he cannot comprehend, and which they name a red colour; and he may learn to use this term as they use it: but still it will remain meaningless to him, except as an intimation of his own deficiency in an interesting field of perception. Similar observations apply in the case of all the faculties. When the organ of Tune is very deficient, the individual cannot comprehend the mental state indicated by the word "melody;" when he is very deficient in Causality, the impression of the link of connection between an event and its antecedent, expressed by the word " cause," does not reach him, let us define it to him ever so clearly; and if Veneration be very deficient, neither the emotion produced by that faculty, and named reverence or devotion, nor the mental state indicated by these words, can be appreciated by him, and no explanations will suffice to convey the meaning of them to his mind.

When this fact in our constitution becomes familiarly known, and when Phrenology has been taught as a department of Natural Science, many practical errors in human conduct will cease. In education, language will no longer be held to imply knowledge of things, and be taught as a substitute for it. And persons very deficient in particular emotional and intellectual organs will learn to appreciate their own mental condition in these particular departments; they will recognise that, in regard to them, they resemble the man born blind in relation to the colour of the rose. If the defect be in Veneration, for example, they will cease to deny the existence of a natural sentiment of devotion; if it be in Causality, they will not regard themselves as authorities in denying causation. Or if they do, an instructed society, perceiving the deficiencies in their organisms, will judge for themselves to what extent it is right to ascribe importance to opinions, doctrines, or practical projects, proceeding from such defective brains. Moreover, the converse rule also holds good, viz., The larger an organ is, the more favourable the development of the other organs with which it is combined, and the higher the temperament and the mental cultivation of an individual are, the greater will be his power of comprehending and expounding the true nature of things; and therefore the fuller and more correct will be the meaning which he will attach to words, and the higher authority will he be in indicating their meaning to others.

It follows from these premises, that no spoken or written communication can extend our previous knowledge of things, qualities, and mental states, unless we understand the meaning of the words in which it is expressed. We all feel this when visiting a country, with the language of which we are not acquainted. It is exemplified also in addressing, in their own languages, illiterate savages on subjects of high moral and intellectual importance. The emotions and conceptions which constitute the subjects of such discourses are unknown to them, partly through great deficiencies in the development of their brains, and partly through imperfect civilization. Their languages contain no terms expressive of them, and hence the speaker cannot convey to them his conceptions and emotions, when they transcend the powers of their own languages. Moreover, by means of words no communication which transcends the sphere of the human faculties can be rendered comprehensible to any body.

The last class of faculties by means of which we gain knowledge of the external world and of ourselves, are the REFLECTIVE POWERS. These are COMPARISON and CAUSALITY. They produce certain abstract ideas, and minister to the gratification of all the other faculties.

COMPARISON enables us to compare objects, and also feelings

and thoughts, and to discover their resemblances, differences, and analogies. The faculty of Tune may compare different notes, but it takes no account of colours, and cannot, therefore, compare a tone and a tint. COMPARISON appears to do so, and to discriminate their analogies and to decide on their harmonies or discords. When the organ is large and active, it gives high powers of discrimination in these relations; when small, there is a corresponding deficiency in this talent.

This faculty does not introduce us to any new qualities of objects or things. It enables us to discern their relations, and, aided by Causality, to observe their adaptations. For example, when by means of the faculties before named we have discovered the existence and qualities of the eyes and of the sun, this faculty and Causality discern certain relations between them, and give rise to the perception of the adaptation of the one to the other. Although the relations which Comparison and Causality perceive are not things, and the faculties may therefore be said to form only abstract ideas, yet the relations and adaptations themselves are real, and the knowledge of them is indispensable to human well-being. Without this knowledge man would be a creature of a lower grade.*

THE FACULTY OF CAUSALITY.

Dr Thomas Brown, in defining a cause, says: " A cause, in the fullest definition which it philosophically admits, may be said to be *that which immediately precedes any change, and which, existing at any time in similar circumstances, has been always, and will be always, immediately followed by a similar change.* Priority in the sequence observed, and invariableness of antecedence in the past and future sequences supposed, are the elements, and the only elements, combined in the notion of a cause." This appears to me to be a definition by means of Individuality and Eventuality, of the function of Causality, and to be incomplete. When we treat of a primitive power of the mind, all that we can do is to describe it, to state the objects to which it is related, and to give it a name. We cannot, by means of a definition, enable a person who never experienced its activity, to understand what it is. The definition of Dr Brown describes, with sufficient accuracy, the

---

* Mr H. C. Watson, in an able essay published in the Phrenological Journal, vol. vi. p. 389, suggests, that the simple function of Comparison is probably "a perception of conditions;" and in this view Dr Vimont coincides. Dr Spurzheim dissented, and maintained the views given in the text. A brief outline of the facts and arguments by which their respective views are supported is given in the System of Phrenology, vol. ii. p. 156.

circumstances in which the notion of causation is excited; but it does not indicate what seems to me to be the chief idea of a cause, and which is derived from another primitive mental faculty. In addition to the invariable sequence which Eventuality perceives, a notion of power or efficiency in the antecedent to produce the consequent, appears to me to arise in the mind, when contemplating instances of causation; and this notion is formed by means of the organ of Causality.

We have no knowledge of substance, except as it is unfolded to us in its qualities; yet we have a firm conviction that substance exists. We see only sequence in causation; yet we have an irresistible conviction that something exists in the antecedent having power to produce the consequent. Individuality gives the first, and Causality the second conviction, and both give belief in the *existence* of something, the essential nature of which is *unknown*.

It is said, that it is only by experience, or by observing the invariableness of the sequence, that we discover the connection of cause and effect; and this is true: but in this respect Causality does not differ from the other faculties. Caloric, as existing in nature, is one thing, and the sensation of heat produced by it in the human body is another. Before we can experience the sensation, heat must be applied to the nerves; but even after the sensation has been felt, we know nothing about what caloric is in itself, or *how* it comes to have the quality of causing the sensation. All that we discover is, that caloric, be it what it may, exists; and that it is capable of producing certain effects on matter, and of exciting in the living body that peculiar feeling which we name heat or warmth. The same holds in regard to Causality. Before we can know the existence of a cause, it must manifest itself by producing an effect. The application of caloric to the nerves produces the feeling of heat; and the presentment of an instance of causation excites in Causality the notion that a cause exists. A great deficiency of this organ renders the intellect nearly blind to causation, and unfits it for forming comprehensive and consecutive views of the causes of events. A person in whom the organ of Tune is very deficient, cannot perceive melody at all; one in whom it is better developed, but still small, perceives melody while a musical instrument is sounding, and he may enjoy it and judge of its qualities from the impression it makes; but he will be unable to recal a note when the instrument has ceased to act, which a person with a high development of the organ can do. In like manner, an individual in whom Causality is very deficient, sees two events occur that are actually related to each other as cause and effect, and yet he forms no notion of this connection; they appear to him simply as two events, one succeeding the other. If the organ be a little larger, but still small, he may have the notion of causation while he sees the phenomena, but he will be unable to recal the idea when they have ceased to appear, and he will experience no desire to investigate the relation between them, as one of causation. When we state a logical argument to men thus constituted, they perceive the steps of it as we proceed, and if it be sound they will acquiesce in our conclusions, and they may remember these as matters of fact; but they will be as incapable of recalling and restating the different links of the chain of reasoning as the person deficient in Tune is of reproducing the notes which he has heard. At the bar, such persons are incapable of making a reply, because their brains cannot retain and reproduce, with a view to refuting, the arguments of their opponent. In science, they extol the all-importance of facts, and depreciate hypothesis and theory; while in morals and religion they imperfectly, and with difficulty, penetrate to motives and causes of action. Another effect of great deficiency in the organ is an incapacity in the individual to bring the future results of existing causes home to his present consciousness. In consequence of this incapacity he lives in the present. Being incapable of tracing the connection of causes with effects, he does not appreciate those which are calculated to produce distant good; the good itself, therefore, is regarded by him as speculative or visionary; it does not interest him, and he confines his efforts to the attainment by direct means of immediate objects. He calls himself a practical man, and, being unaware of his own mental deficiency, is prone to underrate the judgment of those who are able to see farther than himself. When, on the contrary, the organ of Causality is large, active, and well-cultivated, causation is perceived to pervade the system of nature so far as it is known by man.

We are now prepared to consider some points which have occasioned great and animated discussions among the metaphysical writers of the old schools. It has been stated, that Individuality takes cognizance of objects that exist. A tree, a ship, a mountain, are presented to our view, and ideas or perceptions of them are formed; and the perception is followed by an intuitive belief in their existence. Bishop Berkeley objects to the belief in their existence as unphilosophical; because, says he, the perception or idea is a mere mental affection, and no reason can be assigned, why an external object must be believed to exist, merely because we experience a mental affection. A smell, for example, is nothing more than a certain impression on the mind, communicated through the olfactory nerves. But no necessary connection can be perceived between this affection, and belief in the existence of a rose: the mind may undergo the affection called a smell, just as it experiences the emotion called joy, and a material object may have as little to do in causing the one as the other. Hence Dr Berkeley concluded, that we have philosophical evidence for the existence only of mind and mental affections, and none for the existence of the material world. Hume carried this argument farther, and maintained, that as we are conscious only of ideas, and as the existence of ideas does not necessarily imply the existence of mind, we have philosophical evidence for the existence of ideas only, and none for that of either matter or mind. Dr Reid answered Berkeley's objection by maintaining, that the belief in external objects, consequent on perceiving them, is intuitive, and hence requires no reason for its support.

Phrenology enables us to refer these different speculations to their sources in the different faculties. Individuality (aided by the other perceptive faculties), in virtue of its constitution, perceives external objects, and its action is accompanied by intuitive belief in their existence. But Berkeley employed the faculty of Causality to discover *why* it is that this perception is followed by belief; and because Causality could give no account of the matter, and could see no necessary connection between the mental affection called perception, and the existence of external nature, he denied that that nature exists. Dr Reid's answer, translated into phrenological language, was simply this:—The cognizance of the existence of the outward world belongs to Individuality: Individuality has received its own constitution and its own functions, and cannot legitimately be called on to explain or account for these to Causality. In virtue of its constitution, it perceives the existence of external objects, and belief in that existence follows; and if Causality cannot see *how* this happens, it is a proof that Causality's powers are limited, but not that Individuality is deceitful in its indications.

Another class of philosophers, by an error springing from an analogous source, have denied causation. When Eventuality contemplates circumstances connected by the relation of cause and effect, it perceives only one event following another in immediate and invariable sequence. For example, if a cannon be fired, and the shot knock down a wall, Individuality and some other perceptive faculties observe only the existence and appearance of the powder. Eventuality perceives the fire applied to it, the explosion, and the fall of the building, as events following in succession; but it forms no idea of power in the gunpowder, when ignited, to produce the effect. When Causality, on the other hand, is joined with Eventuality in contemplating these phenomena, the impression of *power* or *efficiency* in the exploding gunpowder to produce the effect, arises spontaneously in the mind, and Causality produces an intuitive belief in the existence of this efficiency, just because it is its constitution to do so; and it is as absurd for Eventuality to deny the existence of some quality in the powder which gives rise to this feeling, because only Causality perceives it, as for Causality to deny the existence of the external world, because only Individuality perceives it.

There is no reason to believe that the qualities and relations of external nature, made known to man through these faculties, embrace all that it possesses. Indeed, the reverse is obviously the fact. INDIVIDUALITY reveals to us only the *existence* of substance, and we possess no faculty for discovering its essence or ultimate nature. The researches of chemists lead us to believe in the existence of atoms obeying certain laws of attraction and repulsion, as the ultimate form in which matter exists; but this is mere matter of inference. No one has yet seen or felt these atoms in their individual state; and even although this point were reached, the problems of their essence,—of the causes which have produced them and endowed them with their properties of attraction and repulsion,— and the nature of these powers of attraction and repulsion, would still remain to be solved. The faculty of Causality, as we have seen, affords no aid in penetrating into these mysteries. It appreciates only the existence of the powers which the supposed atoms manifest, and, from these manifestations, connects them in its own conceptions with their effects. But it is quite conceivable that a being endowed with additional and higher faculties than man possesses, might be capable of penetrating more deeply into the arcana of nature than we. The monkey, from wanting organs of Causality, cannot comprehend the causation embodied in external nature, and cannot profit by applying it to his own advantage as man does. A being endowed with faculties which should enable him to perceive intuitively the nature and relations of physical objects and beings, might not only perceive every thing at a glance which man can learn only by multiplied observations and experience, but he might thereby acquire a power of combining and applying the forces of nature far transcending that assigned to the human race. Man, apparently, is only entering on his career in this world as a moral and intellectual being, and commencing his studies of Nature, and the application of her powers. Future investigations may add incalculably to his knowledge and power; but we may safely predict that no part of that knowledge will differ in kind from what we now possess, or go beyond the limits of the faculties which have been bestowed on him. New organs in the brain may be discovered for mental powers of which we are conscious, such as the perception of heat and cold, roughness and smoothness, and others; but no new mental powers themselves could be added to our present endowment without changing our nature. Add Causality equal to man's to the dog, and it would on longer be a dog. Give us faculties capable of discovering the ultimate nature and relations of things, and we should cease to be human beings.

If the foregoing considerations be well founded, they appear to shew that man is constituted with a special reference to the existing state of the physical world, and that *it* is framed with a corresponding relation to his endowments; whence the inference seems to follow that practically, the sphere of his duties, and the fountains of his sufferings and enjoyments, will, to a great extent, be found by studying, comprehending, and acting in conformity with these arrangements. Moreover, as these are divine institutions, they, and the consequences that flow from them, may be regarded as forming a sacred woof which may, with great advantage, be woven into the warp of our religious emotions, and thus be made to constitute the texture of a natural religion. Do they not also set boundaries to our powers of receiving the revelation of supernatural truths, and go deep into the question as to the capacity of our nature, as it is now constituted, for existing in a state of being different from that which prevails in this world? The late Dr Chalmers appears to have had some glimpses of this inference, for I heard him preach an eloquent discourse, subsequently published, the object of which was to shew that there must be a new *earth*, as well as new heavens, for the future abode of man, to afford scope for the exercise and enjoyment of his natural faculties; in other words, that his existence in a sphere in which there is no matter, would imply a radical change of his whole nature—not simply his reproduction as man, with his capacities purified and enlarged, but amounting to the substitution of a new and different being in his place.

CHAPTER V.

OF GOD.

THE highest object to which the religious emotions of any people are directed, constitutes their God. When their notions concerning that object are combined with the religious emotions, the object becomes sacred, is hallowed and adored; and these opinions become the grand foundation of the rest of their faith. The natural mental process by which ideas of God have been formed appears to be the following. The faculties of Wonder and Veneration give us a tendency intuitively to believe in a supernatural cause of the remarkable phenomena of nature which we see and feel, but cannot comprehend. The faculties of Individuality and Imitation prompt us intuitively to personify abstract ideas and active powers. The Greeks and Romans, unable to account scientifically for the cause of the winds, ascribed it to a supernatural power, personified it, and called it Æolus, or the God of the Winds. Roused to admiration by the teeming fertility of the soil, and unable to comprehend its cause, they attributed it also to a supernatural power, and personified it; and as, in the animal economy, the producer is feminine, they were led by analogy to invest it with this sex; hence arose the Goddess Ceres. These nations multiplied deities to represent the causes of all the interesting and impressive phenomena of nature of which they could give no other account, including human passions, emotions, and intellectual powers. Mars was the God of War, the personification of Combativeness and Destructiveness; Minerva the Goddess of Wisdom, the personification of the moral sentiments and intellect; and so forth.

These notions being entwined in youth with the religious emotions of the people, became religious truths, and led to important results. First—They diverted the national mind from inquiring into the natural causes of the phenomena, which they accounted for by ascribing them to the agency of these supernatural powers; and hence, when evil overtook them, such as famine, or shipwreck, or pestilence, they ascribed it to the displeasure of Ceres, or of Æolus, or of Jupiter. Instead of endeavouring to remove its natural causes, or to use measures to protect themselves, as far as possible, against their influence, they sought to discover why the supernatural Power was offended, and how it might be appeased, and its favour secured; and ascribing to it their own passions and emotions, they sacrificed animals and occasionally men to assuage its anger, and offered incense, sang praises, and presented gifts, to gratify its senses and its Love of Approbation.

Secondly—These errors having become sacred, prompted the people to regard every one who desired to deliver them from their superstitions as a blasphemer and contemner of the Gods, and to slay him.

The Jews were taught higher conceptions of the great supernatural Power named God. Their Scriptures represent Him as existing in the form of a Man; for we are told that God made man after his own image, which implies that God had a form like the human; and it is narrated that, on one occasion, Moses saw a portion of God's person like the hinder parts of a man. Moreover, the Jewish Scriptures ascribe to God human passions: He is angry, jealous, revengeful, capable of being moved from his object by entreaty, and pleased with praise, sacrifices, and incense. Along with these qualities they ascribe to Him the sublimest attributes which the human faculties can conceive: Unity, eternal existence, ubiquity, omniscience, omnipotence, and all the human virtues.

These ideas of God were woven into the religious emotions of the Jewish people, and became the foundation of their religion. They were greatly superior to those of the Greeks and Romans, and of other contemporaneous nations; and this superiority has been one natural cause why the Jews have maintained themselves as a distinct people after their expulsion from Judea, when living in society with the professors of all the other creeds of the world.

Mahometan writers recognise, to some extent, the distinction between theology and religion, and name the first *Imân*, and the second *Din*. Mahomet was the founder of this faith, and he appears to have borrowed his ideas of God from the Jews. He " emphatically proclaims that there is but one God, the Creator and Governor of the universe—omnipresent, eternal, omniscient, omnipotent—most holy, wise, good, and merciful." In the Koran, we find these words:—" God! there is no God but he, the living, the self-subsisting; . . . he knoweth that which is past, and that which is to come; . . . his throne is extended over heaven and earth, and the preservation of both is no burden to him. He is the high and mighty." (*Koran* ch. vi.) And again: " He hath spread the earth as a bed for you, and the heaven as a covering; and hath caused water to descend from heaven, and thereby produced fruits for your sustenance. . . . He directeth whom he pleaseth into the right way. God knoweth that which ye do; . . . and whether ye manifest that which is in your minds, or conceal it, God will call you to account for it, and will forgive whom he pleaseth, and will punish whom he pleaseth; for God is almighty. Your God is one God; there is no God but he—the most merciful." (*Koran*, ch. ii.)

" In the creed of Islam, the Christian doctrine of the Trinity is distinctly repudiated. In the Mahometan Confession of Faith, it is declared, ' As he never begot any person whatsoever, so he himself was begotten by none: as he never was a son, so he never hath been a father.'

" In their search after the true ideal of the Divine nature, the faithful are directed to the works of creation and the benign agencies of providence—to the sun and stars, to the clouds, to the rain and winds, and their vivifying influences on the animal and vegetable world—as ' *signs* to people of understanding.' (*Koran*, ch. ii.) But, looking to the mutability and the limited existence and duration of all mere earthly and sensible objects, idolatry and creature-worship are denounced, as suggesting low and unworthy ideas of the Divine nature and character. ' Whatever rises,' says the Koran, ' must set; whatever is born, must die; and whatever is corruptible, must decay and perish.' (Ch. vi.) On such grounds, the worship of saints and images, and the use of pictorial or other representations of living things, was strictly forbidden.

" The belief in *angels*, which from time immemorial had been universal throughout the East, was adopted into the creed of Islam.

" As to the Koran, Mahometans were required to believe that it was not the work of the Prophet himself, but that it was an emanation from ' the very essence of God;' that it was preserved from all eternity, near the throne of God, on a vast table, called ' The preserved Table,' on which were also inscribed the Divine decrees, relating to all events, both past and future; and that the angel Gabriel was sent down with a transcript from it to the lowest heaven, from whence he revealed it to Mahomet, from time to time, in successive portions, as circumstances required. A view, however, of the entire volume of Scripture, bound in silk, and adorned with precious stones, was vouchsafed to the Prophet once a-year; and during the last year of his life he was twice indulged with that privilege."*

The notions of God, before quoted, form the great foundation

---
* Cyclopædia of Religious Denominations.

of the Mahometan religion. The doctrines and practices of the Koran derive their sanctity from being believed to be revelations of His will. Some of these doctrines harmonize with the order of God's natural providence, but many of them are at variance with it; and the whole being entwined with the religious emotions in the minds of the people, the two form together their religion.

Observations similar to those already made in regard to the religions of Greece and Rome apply to this faith. It averts the Mahometan mind from inquiring into the course of God's natural providence, paralyzes the intellect by limiting the scope of its pursuits, diverts the moral and religious emotions from their highest objects, and renders sacred every error which the Koran contains. It thus constitutes a huge barrier to progressive civilization.

Mahometans propagate their religion by the sword, and succeed. They force the parents in the conquered nations to allow their children to be taught religion by the Mahometan priests. These find little difficulty in entwining the Koran with the religious emotions of the young, and in one generation produce many sincere believers in the imposed faith. These are constantly augmenting, until the whole people become Mahometans.

The Christian religion overthrew the religion of Greece and Rome, and took its place. In the age when this happened, little natural science existed; printing had not been invented, books were scarce and dear, and the mass of the people could neither read nor write. In Italy, the clergy introduced into the Christian worship the use of pictures, in which were represented God the Father, under the form of an old man; Jesus Christ the Son, as a young man; and the Holy Spirit as a dove; and they trained the people to regard these three as one, the only true God. They ascribed attributes and offices to each of these persons, founded on interpretations of Scripture; and these notions constitute the general Christian opinion of God. They entwined them with the religious emotions, and thus formed them into important elements of the Christian faith.

They also led the emotions to reverence the Scriptures as the only revelation of the Divine will; but they did not trust the people with the sacred books themselves. They formed dogmas out of them, and trained the people to reverence these as an epitome, and as correct interpretations, of the sacred volume. Moreover, the Roman Catholic clergy assured the people that the true meaning of Scripture was, in some instances, obscure; that, in their state of unavoidable ignorance, they might err in their interpretations of it and peril their souls; that the Pope and assembled clergy were far better judges of its import; and thus they persuaded the laity to dispense with the exercise of their own judgment, and to accept, reverence, and believe whatever the clergy represented to them to be Divine truth.

Great knowledge of human nature was displayed in this proceeding. In a barbarous age, the emotions were necessarily much more powerful than the intellect, and by authoritatively presenting to them images and dogmas, and rendering these sacred by entwining them with the emotions, the clergy constituted this compound, religion. By excluding the privilege of private judgment, they aimed at securing perfect unity of faith and doctrine in the church, and conferring repose of mind on the individual believer.

Had it been possible to maintain the intellect of the laity permanently in the condition in which it was when this system of religion was founded, and had the clergy abstained from violating their own precepts in their practical conduct, the Roman Catholic faith might have had an indefinite existence over Europe. But the invention of printing conferred on the people the power of reading, and this roused their intellectual faculties, and prompted them to inquire into the accordance of their religion with Scripture; while the dissolute character of the clergy at the same time, shocked their moral faculties, and a reformation of religious doctrine and observances ensued.

The Reformers continued to preserve the association between the Scriptures and the religious emotions of the people unbroken, and recognised these writings as Divine revelation; but they asserted the right of the laity to read and interpret the Bible for themselves. They abolished the use of images and pictures, and dissolved the connection between these and the religious emotions. The only intellectual object which the leaders of the Reformation at first presented to the laity, as a substratum for their religious emotions, was the Scriptures. If the right of private judgment had been intended to be a reality, they should have left every Christian to extract the true meaning of the sacred volume for himself, and to combine it with his own religious emotions, and thus to constitute an individual religion. This would have been the infallible result of consistent action on their own principles; because, as no two individuals possess the intellectual and emotional organs developed in precisely the same degree of absolute and relative size, men's natural powers of interpreting Scripture differ, while differences in cultivation and literary and historical acquirements also lead to variety of interpretations.

The importance of this remark will be more readily appreciated when we consider that the Bible contains no system of theology, but is composed chiefly of narratives, descriptions, sublime effusions of devotional emotion, and much sound morality, bound together by no striking logical connection.

The leaders of the Reformation were not slow to perceive the consequences of this state of things. To found a sect, a series of dogmas must be extracted from the Bible, and the religious emotions must be trained to accept and reverence them as religious truths. The Reformers carried this principle into practice, framed epitomes of Scriptural doctrine, and taught the laity to believe in them as sound manuals of Divine revelation.

The present religions of Europe consist of dogmas compiled, or deduced in distant ages, from the Bible, by men ignoran- of natural science and of the real order of the Divine governt ment on earth. These have been intertwined, from generation to generation, with the religious emotions, and are all sacred in the eyes of believers. So completely is this the case, that when a clergyman is accused of preaching heresy, he is not allowed to appeal to the Scriptures to prove the soundness of his views; but his doctrine is tried by the standards of his church, and he is condemned if he has deviated from their text, whatever the Scriptures may prove to the contrary.

We read the Koran with our intellect alone; and in consequence of our religious emotions never having been intertwined with its text, it bears no aspect of sacredness to us. On the other hand, we find great difficulty in reading the Bible, and our religious formulas, with our intellect alone; because our religious emotions have been trained from our infancy to venerate the former as Divine revelation, and the latter as true interpretations of it. When the Mahometan reads the Bible, he judges of it by his intellect, or tries it by the Koran; and finding in it some parts like his own sacred standard, he approves of these, but finding other portions in discord with it, these he condemns. The Mahometan will never judge soundly of the Koran until he becomes capable of trying it by his intellect alone, and comparing it with the laws of God inscribed in the Book of Nature. When he shall become capable of this comparison, he will accept as Divine only such of its doctrines as harmonize with natural truth.

In a future chapter I shall inquire to what extent our Christian formulas are aiding or impeding our civilization; meantime I cast no imputation on the compilers of these formulas. They are not chargeable with disrespect to God in omitting to direct the religious emotions to His works and agency in nature; because at the time when they wrote, there were few expositions of these deserving the name of science, or worthy of being combined with the religious emotions and rendered sacred. And even now I have no charge to prefer against the clergy who still fail to teach the sacred character of nature, and who conscientiously substitute these dogmas in its place, although in many respects at variance with what appears to me to be the order of God's moral government of the world; because, until the functions of the brain, and the dependence of moral phenomena on these, were known, they had no adequate natural standard by which to try the truth and utility of their dogmas. No charity, however, can absolve them from the duty of inquiring into the facts now presented to their consideration, and giving effect to their legitimate consequences.

We have hitherto considered the Greek and Roman notions of God derived from the simple suggestions of the human faculties acting in the absence of scientific knowledge of nature; and also those derived by other nations from books believed by them to be Divine. We may now briefly inquire into the opinions concerning God which may be legitimately drawn from nature in the present state of our knowledge.

The first difficulty that meets us in this inquiry arises from the depth to which, during our whole lives, our religious emotions have been imbued with dogmatic ideas on the subject. Notions concerning the existence and attributes of God were impressed upon us by our mothers and nurses at the first dawn of our intelligence; were multiplied and ingrained in us in our youth by perusal of the Scriptures, and instruction in catechisms and articles of faith; and enforced in adult life by the pulpit, the press, and the general voice of society. To unravel the threads of this religious web, and to discover how many of them we owe to God's revelations of Himself in His works, and how many to human instruction; and moreover to discriminate the real title of the threads of human construction to form parts of the web of belief at all, may baffle the acutest understanding. Nevertheless, if we direct our attention to the Hindoo, Mahometan, or any other false religion, we shall have little difficulty in perceiving how important it would be to succeed in such an analysis of their notions of God, with a view to redeeming them from the practical consequences of their erroneous opinions concerning His nature and His will. The errors in doctrine of the Koran, when evolved into practice as the will and command of God, are sources of innumerable temporal evils in Mahometan society, with which reason and experience endeavour in vain to cope. Could we shed into the Mahometan's mind a clear perception of those among his opinions which harmonize with views of God and of His mode of governing the world, correctly drawn from the study of His works, and enable it to distinguish these from the other portions which rest on the authority of Mahomet, we should make some progress towards his release from the superstitions that are degrading his faculties and impeding his civilization.

There is reason to believe that a similar process of analysis of the threads of their faith might benefit the European nations also; because nothing is more certain than that although all profess to derive their views of God and of His will from Scripture, not only do nations and sects, but individuals also of the same sect, differ widely from each other in their opinions regarding these momentous subjects. Every one, therefore, cannot be holding the truth; and error developed into practice must lead to disaster in Europe, as certainly as in Turkey or Hindostan. Let us, therefore, at least attempt to discover what lessons unaided nature teaches us in regard to this question.

There are two opinions regarding the natural sources of our belief in the existence of God—one, that it is intuitive; and he other, that it is a deduction of reason. In Chapter IV., p. 54, I have endeavoured to shew that the organs of our senses, and those of our mental faculties, are adapted, by their inherent constitution, to external nature, and that it is in virtue of the powers bestowed on them, and of this adaptation, that we arrive at intuitive belief in the existence and qualities of external objects. Reason may assist us in examining and analysing the circumstances in which these intuitive convictions arise, but it cannot account for them. In the science of Optics, for example, we find expositions of the compound nature of light, and of the kinds of surfaces which reflect the green rays, and cause these objects to appear to us green; of others that reflect the red rays, and are seen by us as red, and so forth; but we see no necessary connection between the appearances of these surfaces and their power to reflect different rays, or between these rays and our own mental perceptions of colour. Our perceptions, and the convictions which attend them, are pure intuitions, and are the results simply of the constitution of our faculties and their adaptations to external nature.

Now, it appears to me that by the constitution of the mental faculties, particularly those of Wonder, Veneration, and Ideality, and their relations to external objects, belief in a supernatural Power arises intuitively in the mind of an individual possessing a well-constituted brain, from the perception and comprehension of the qualities, phenomena, and relations of the outward world. Reason may investigate the circumstances under which this intuitive belief arises, and extend and deepen it; but it is not its source. This view is fortified by the fact that we find the existence of a supernatural power recognised by all the races of men whose brains are even moderately developed in the organs before named, however ignorant of science they may be.

The qualities or attributes of this Power are deductions of reason, and nations and individuals view these differently, according to the differences that exist in the development of their brains, or in their intellectual cultivation. Revelation forms no exception to this rule. The nature of God (Unity or Trinity), and His attributes, are apprehended differently by different minds, all drawing their conclusions from Scripture. Some believe that the First Person of the Trinity possesses qualities that rendered it indispensable for Him to demand the sacrifice of the Second Person as the sole condition on which He could forgive the sins of mankind; while others consider this to be an erroneous interpretation of Scripture concerning the character of God. Many other discordant views of the Divine nature and attributes are known to prevail even among the sincerest Christians; and these shew that the Bible does not protect us from forming different opinions of its import when differences exist in the development of our brains and in our intellectual cultivation.

The manner in which reason may throw light on the circumstances in which our intuitive belief in God arises may now be considered.

If the definition of a cause given by Dr Thomas Brown, namely, that "priority in the sequence observed, and invariableness of antecedence in the past and future sequences supposed, are the elements, and the *only* elements, combined in the notion of a cause," be correct, it appears to me to be impossible to elucidate or strengthen by reason our intuitive belief in the existence of a God. On that supposition, the whole external world will exhibit only a succession of phenomena. However regular the sequences may be, and for however long a period they may have been observed, nothing seems to be implied in mere sequence that indicates anything beyond the phenomena themselves, and the circumstances in which they occur.

When, however, as formerly remarked, the organ of Causality is largely developed in an individual, the perception of antecedence and sequence in phenomena is accompanied by a mental state additional to that described by Dr Brown; viz., a belief, intuitive and irresistible, that, in the antecedent, there exists a quality of *power* or *efficiency* to produce the sequent. The proper function of Causality is to produce this belief, and it is only when the antecedent is thus viewed that it can properly be called a cause. There may be complex antecedents to one effect, but on analysing them, we recognise those only as causes in which we discern active power. Everything else belongs to the category of circumstances.

Let any one, for example, observe the appearances of the clouds as they float along a summer sky, borne onward by a gentle breeze, and let him note their forms, colours, magnitude, and density, and try to draw conclusions regarding the succession of forms or other attributes, which will characterize the clouds floating on a similar breeze to-morrow. Here, there are antecedents and subsequents in abundance; but we soon discover that the clouds exhibiting these phenomena do not enable us to draw conclusions in regard to the succession of future clouds. The reason of our hesitation is, that we have no *belief* of the antecedent cloud being the *cause* of the characteristics of the one that succeeds it. There is the absence of that regularity in the sequence which indicates the relation of cause and effect; but it is not the mere absence of this order which we recognise,—its absence suggests the thought that the antecedent cloud is not the cause of the appearances of the subsequent one, and we are prompted to search deeper, in order to discover what the cause is. We may discover substances, agents, or forces, such as are treated of in the science of Meteorology, more adequate to produce the effects. As formerly observed, however, Causality appears to produce only a belief in efficiency, without giving us a notion of the *nature* of the efficient cause; just as Individuality and the other observing faculties seem to produce in us a belief that matter exists, without revealing to us its essence or origin.

The mental process by which conviction of intelligence in a cause is attained may be illustrated by referring again, even at the expense of repetition, to the sun and the eye as an example. These objects exist, and the one is obviously adapted to the other; the sun to give light, and the eye to receive it, modify it, and thus enable us to see. The eye and sun did not arrange this relationship themselves. If these are contemplated, no necessary connection can be perceived between the two. There is nothing in the sun that necessarily implies the existence of eyes; and nothing in the eye that necessarily implies the existence of the sun. Nevertheless, the relationship of adaptation exists between them. Comparison and Causality, if adequately developed, cannot ascribe *adaptation* to either of the two structures, because both are required to render it possible. The adaptation, therefore, not being an attribute of either, and yet the perception of it being called forth in the mind by the contemplation of the objects, the hypothesis of the existence of an intelligence external to both the eye and the sun, which instituted it, seems alone capable of accounting for it. All nature is full of adaptations. The structure of the lungs is adapted to the air, and that of the muscles to the force of gravitation; the structure of plants is adapted at once to the sun, the air, and the soil; and so forth. Causality and Comparison, therefore, are furnished with such innumerable examples of what appear to them to be designed adaptations, that they cannot rest in the assumption that these are merely accidental or inherent qualities of matter. It has been said, that as science advances, the Deity recedes: If by this is meant that his irregular action is more and more excluded as a hypothesis or belief, the statement is correct; but in the sense that the evidence of his existence, power, and wisdom, becomes feebler, it is a mistake. The most stupendous idea of the universe that has yet been formed is that which supposes every fixed star to be a sun like our own, with planets circling round it, and the whole to be revolving round a more gigantic and hitherto undiscovered central orb. But this hypothesis assumes that the stars move round the central sun in virtue of forces of the same nature and obeying the same laws as those which prevail in the Earth; so that, even according to this view, the Deity is as directly influencing our planet as the heavenly host. The faculties of Causality and Comparison, judging from these data, support our intuitive belief that an extramundane Power and Intelligence exists, and that it instituted those *adaptations.**

It is objected that reason does not warrant our belief in the *self-existence* of God; and some affirm, that, for any thing we know to the contrary, the Ruler of the world may himself own a superior, and have been created. Their argument is stated in this form: " You who believe in God from intuition, must submit your belief to the scrutiny of reason. If you admit that every being must have a cause, then this Being himself

---

* In the System of Phrenology, I remarked that in individuals who are unable to see evidence in nature of the existence of a Supreme Intelligence, the organ of Causality is small. This was a premature conclusion; for I have since known men in whom the reasoning organs were amply developed and well cultivated, who assured me that they could not reach the conviction of the being of a God. I have known some such men equal, in point of integrity and practical benevolence, to the most orthodox believers. I am unable to predicate on what peculiarity of cerebral structure and condition in their case, this want of theological belief depends; but unless mankind, in all ages, have mistaken a mere phantom of imagination for a conviction of the understanding, or an intuitive truth, some peculiarity in the cerebral constitution of such persons will doubtless be found.

is an effect. You have no warrant in your intuitions, and there is no evidence from reason of his *self-existence* or *self-creation;* and, as he does exist, you must assign *a cause of him,* on the same principle that you regard him as the cause of the material creation." The atheists carry this argument the length of an absolute denial of God, in respect that it is only the *first cause* that, according to them, can legitimately be regarded as Deity; and the first cause, say they, is to us unknown.

The following answer to this objection may be considered. The knowing faculties *perceive objects directly*, and Causality *infers* qualities from manifestations. To be able to judge thoroughly of any object, the *whole* of these faculties must be employed on it. When a watch, for example, is presented to us, the knowing faculties perceive its spring, lever, and wheels, and Causality discerns the object or design. If the question is put, Whence did the watch proceed?—from the nature of its materials as perceived by the knowing faculties, Causality infers that it could not make itself; and from discovering intelligence and design in the adaptation of its parts, this faculty concludes, that its cause must have possessed these qualities, and therefore assigns its production to an intelligent artificer. Suppose the statement to be next made—" This artificer himself is an existence, and every existence must have a cause; who, then, made the watchmaker?" In this case, if no farther information were presented to Causality than what it could obtain by contemplating the structure of the watch, the answer would necessarily be, that it could not tell. But let the artificer, or man, be submitted to the joint observation of the knowing faculties and Causality, and let the question be put, Who made him?—the knowing powers, by examining the structure of his body, would present Causality with data from which it could unerringly infer, that although it perceived in him intelligence and power sufficient to make the watch, yet, from the nature of his constitution, he could not possibly have made himself. Proceeding in the investigation, Causality, still aided by the knowing faculties, would perceive the most striking indications of power, benevolence, and design in the human frame; and from contemplating these, it would arrive at a conviction, that the watchmaker is the work of a great, powerful, and intelligent Being. If, however, the question were repeated, " Whence did this Being proceed?" Causality could not answer, any more than it could tell, from seeing the watch alone, who made the watchmaker. The perceptive faculties cannot observe the substance of the Maker of the human body; His existence is suggested by Comparison and Causality; and all that they can accomplish is to infer his existence, and his qualities or attributes, from perceiving their manifestation. They have no data for inferring that He had an antecedent.

The argument now stated is objected to in a letter written to me by a deceased friend of great talents and attainments, on the following grounds:—"The argument of Design," it is said, " is *à posteriori*. It is an argument of analogy. It ascends from the known to the unknown. The subjects of the analogy are the works of man, a watch, a code of laws, or any other human contrivance, on one hand: and the phenomena of Nature on the other. The former, the watch, &c. are known to have been designed by the human Designer, Man; the latter, the phenomena of Nature, are inferred analogically to have been designed by the Unknown, but sought, Designer, God. Well, it appears to me that an analogy to be good for demonstration, must be extensible, at least in its essence, equally to both of the terms of the analogy. Now, man, the known Designer, invents or designs by discovering laws external to and independent of himself, and then applying these laws to the sure production of effects which he desiderates. (Black discovers latent heat, Watt applies that discovery in a desiderated direction, and the steam-engine is brought to perfection.) Therefore, the Unknown Designer, who is inferred by this analogy, does, for all the analogy makes good, simply discover truth external to, and independent of Himself, and then applies that truth to the production of effects (the phenomena of Nature), which he desiderates. This is not God, the eternal, almighty, and every way infinite One, whose existence the argument professes to demonstrate."

The argument from reason maintained in the preceding pages, may no doubt fall short of this demonstration; but it appears to me that the Supernatural Designer does much more than, like man, invent or design by discovering laws external to, and independent of Himself. The bodies of the mammalia are composed of the chemical elements named on page 23; and out of these, the Unknown Designer has formed different organisms which manifest very different qualities. The tiger and the lamb, the horse and the owl, man and the ape, are all composed, so far as we have yet discovered, of these ten elements. We have found out many of the laws which the elements obey in entering into combinations, and are able to produce from them many admirable new results: but we have never been able to convert them, by any skill of our own, into organized beings; much less to make those specific combinations of them which constitute different organisms, capable of manifesting different qualities. Even supposing Mr Cross to have produced by electricity the lowest species of organized being out of inorganic matter, still he could not give form and properties to that being at his will. It was at best a reproduction of a known organism. But the Unknown Designer appears to encounter no such difficulties. The ten elements, when wielded by Him, take every variety of Form, and manifest the most diverse qualities. Nay, He endows the structures with powers to be exerted contingently—powers which are ready to act when circumstances require their action, or to remain latent for ever. The blood of animals, for example, is possessed of the quality of repairing losses and injuries which may be sustained by their organisms, so that if a muscle is injured, it shall deposit muscular fibre, and if a bone is broken, it shall deposit osseous matter, in the places and quantities necessary to restore the parts to health and efficiency. But life may be passed without these parts sustaining any injury; and in this case the powers are never evoked into action. These phenomena indicate to Comparison and Causality that the Unknown Contriver possessed over the ten elements a command indescribably superior to that which we can wield.

Again, Man has in vain attempted to produce a perpetual motion; but the Supernatural Power appears to have found no difficulty in doing so. The revolution of the planets round the sun, and of the satellites round their principal planets, are examples in point. We comprehend the laws which govern these evolutions, and see uniformity and design manifested in them, but we cannot even conjecture how the planets were formed, and how their powers of motion were communicated to them. The only inference we can legitimately draw appears to me to be that intelligence and power produced these stupendous phenomena, and that the author of them is not a mere analogue of human power and intelligence, but that He deals with matter as its master. When we see things done with matter which man in vain attempts to accomplish, it seems a logical inference that the Unknown author of the things is not, like man, a mere worker on materials possessing properties which he cannot change, but one who, in a far higher degree, and to an extent unknown to us, commands their very essence, and applies them according to his will. We cannot discover limits to this power in the Unknown Designer, and hence we call him God.

This argument does not profess to demonstrate *all* the attributes of God; but only His existence, and such of His attributes as our limited faculties are capable of comprehending.

Our notions of the latter will be constantly augmented in number, and rise in sublimity in proportion to our advance in correct knowledge of their manifestations in nature. At present, we have scarcely started in our career of discovery of these, because, hitherto we have wanted the grand element necessary to comprehend God's mode of governing the most important departments of this world, viz.—knowledge of the means by which moral phenomena are produced and regulated.

Dr Vimont remarks, that we cannot fully comprehend God without being his equal; just as a dog cannot comprehend the human mind, in consequence of its utter want of several of the human faculties.

Hobbes, in his Treatise on Human Nature, has stated a somewhat similar view. "Forasmuch," says he, "as God Almighty is incomprehensible, it followeth that we can have no conception or image of the Deity; and, consequently, all his attributes signify our inability and defect of power to conceive anything concerning His nature, and not any conception of the same, except only this, That there is a God. Thus all that will consider may know that God *is*, though not *what* he is."

It has been objected, that although our intuitive perceptions, and also inferences drawn by Causality and Comparison may lead us to believe that God *has* existed, we see no evidence that he *now* exists. I reply that the manifestations of his agency, power, wisdom, and goodness, *continue* to be presented to us every moment, and that we have no data for concluding that the *cause* has ceased, while the effects continue.

The impossibility of the human faculties fully comprehending God has forced itself on some of the great minds who attempted to describe the Deity in Scripture. The definition of Him, as "I am," assumes that all is implied in the simple fact of his existence; and the question, "Canst thou by searching find out God? canst thou find out the Almighty unto perfection?" coincides with the views now suggested.

If these opinions of the limitation of human capacity in attempting to comprehend God be well founded, all discussions about the manner in which He exists must be futile, and to my mind they are highly irreverent. Locke defines a "person" to be "a thinking, intelligent being, that has reason and reflection, and considers itself as itself, the same thinking thing in different times and places." In this sense of the word our intellectual faculties lead us to assign a personal character to the Deity, although we can form no well-grounded notions concerning his form, his substance, his size, or his mode of living.

An article in the *Edinburgh Review*, generally ascribed to the Rev. Mr Sedgwick, expresses a similar view:—

"What know we," says he, "of the God of nature (we speak only of natural means), except through the faculties He has given us, rightly employed on the materials around us? In this we rise to a conception of material inorganic laws, in beautiful harmony and adjustment; and they suggest to us the conception of infinite power and wisdom. In like manner we rise to a conception of organic laws—of means (often almost purely mechanical, as they seem to us, and their organic functions well comprehended) adapted to an end—and that end the well-being of a creature endowed with sensation and volition. Thus we rise to a conception both of Divine Power and Divine Goodness; and we are constrained to believe, not merely that all material law is subordinate to His will, but that He has also (in the way He allows us to see His works) so exhibited the attributes of His will, as to shew himself to the mind of man as a personal and superintending God, concentrating His will on every atom of the universe."

Many persons believe that we owe our knowledge of the existence of God to the Bible; but this is a mistake, for it commences with expressions which obviously assume His existence as a fact.

Instead of vainly attempting to define so sacred an object as God, and one so far transcending our power of comprehension, let us inquire into the manifestations of His Will presented to us in Nature; and first as to the means by which He appears to govern the world.

CHAPTER VI.

CAN WE TRACE DIVINE GOVERNMENT IN THE PHENOMENA OF THE PHYSICAL AND MORAL WORLDS? AND IF SO, BY WHAT MEANS IS IT MAINTAINED AND RENDERED EFFICIENT?

SECTION I.—OF THE GOVERNMENT OF THE PHYSICAL WORLD.

ALL matter appears to exert force. The particles of the diamond cohere with so intense an energy, that it requires great mechanical power to separate them. The mountains seem inert, but they are constantly pressing downwards towards the centre of the earth. Water slumbering peacefully in the bosom of a lake, is exerting a pressure on the bottom and sides, and is in fact operating with a force similar to that which it manifests in rushing over the precipice. In the latter case, we perceive the force only because there is no counterbalancing resistance to arrest its action.

Farther, the forces of different substances act on each other, and produce important results. Oxygen acting on sulphur, in certain circumstances, combines with it and produces sulphuric acid, a highly corrosive liquid. Under the influence of heat, the same gas combines with carbon, and produces a gas destructive of animal life. If this reciprocal action of corporeal substances were indefinite and unlimited, the physical world, apparently, might lapse into confusion, chaos might come again, and the earth could afford no abiding place for animated beings. How is this result obviated? And by what means are order in the arrangements and regularity in the evolutions of matter preserved?

Each elementary substance manifests the tendency to undergo changes, and to act on other substances, only in certain ways and under certain conditions. The formation of crystals, and the cohesion of the particles of a liquid metal on cooling, are examples of the tendency of elements of the same kind to combine with each other in a specific manner; while the combination of different chemical elements, always in certain definite proportions, in constituting a new compound, is an example of the regulation of the powers of distinct substances in acting on each other. By investing the elements of matter with definite tendencies, and subjecting them to definite restraints, God appears to have made a provision for the maintenance of order and regularity in physical nature, which commends itself to the human intellect as simple and efficacious, and to our sentiments as admirable and exquisitely beautiful. After perceiving it we are able to contemplate the ceaseless changes proceeding in the material world, without apprehensions of confusion. The rocks are riven by the lightning, worn by the flood, or disintegrated by the frost, and their particles are swept into the sea; but other regulated forces are there forming new combinations of them, and new rocks, possessing the same characteristics as the old, will in future time emerge from the deep.

The Divine government of the physical world thus becomes manifest to us through the perception of order and regularity in the action of matter; and the means by which it is accomplished appear to be the endowing of these with definite forces, and enabling them to act on each other only in definite modes. As our faculties cannot penetrate behind the screen of matter, we can study the method of the Divine government *only in the means by which it is conducted;* and under this view science is an exposition of the order of Providence in governing the world. Every action of matter is a manifestation of Divine power, and when it is so regarded, is calculated to challenge the highest reverence of our emotional faculties. Astronomy, Chemistry, and the other physical sciences, unfold to us the forces and arrangements through which the changes of the seasons, the fertility of the soil, and the food of man and animals are produced. Famine and overflowing abundance, with all their physiological and moral consequences, are the results of the action of these forces; and we must extend our knowledge of them, and adapt our conduct to their operation, if we desire to understand and to conform to the Divine government. Natural philosophy consists of a description of the manner, so far as man has discovered it, in which the stupendous universe of suns and worlds, stretching beyond the scope even of our imaginations, are bound together and regulated; and mechanical science is an exposition of the conditions under which God has enabled us to control and apply a variety of the powers of nature. The forces of matter in the same circumstances, act with so much regularity and precision, that we are able to employ even mathematical proportions as means of measuring and calculating their effects.

In investigating physical forces and their relations and consequences, we may employ the intellectual faculties exclusively; and, in this case, our observations and conclusions are scientific in their character. The moral and religious emotions not being engaged in the investigation, there is nothing directly *moral* or *religious* in the knowledge which constitutes pure physical science. It is advantageous that science should be thus cultivated for its own advancement, because excited emotions disturb and often mislead the intellect. But, from the teacher's desk, from the moral and religious chairs of our universities, and from our pulpits, the intellect and the moral and religious sentiments should act together in communicating the truths of science as expositions of the means by which God governs the world. These sentiments would give to the intellectual instruction that exciting and hallowing influence which is indispensable to evolve reverence at once for the Ruler of the world, and for the means by which His government is conducted. It is difficult to perceive how otherwise the aid of the religious emotions can be obtained towards leading men seriously to regulate their conduct in conformity to the order of nature. Religion and science have never been thus systematically combined in the general instruction of the people; and hence the barrenness of science in moral and religious fruits, and of religion in the practical advancement of secular well-being.

If the views now advanced are sound, it appears to follow that Divine government is conspicuous in every well-understood department of physical nature, that it is accomplished by endowing physical substances with definite properties, and that *the evidences of this government, of the mode in which it is administered, and of the laws by which it is maintained, will become more and more clear and comprehensible, in proportion to the exactness of our knowledge of the objects through the instrumentality of which it is accomplished.* It is only where we are altogether ignorant of the causes of phenomena, or where our knowledge of them is vague and general, that confusion appears to reign; while intimate knowledge constantly reveals order and harmony.

SECTION II.—CAN WE DISCOVER THE MEANS BY WHICH THE MORAL WORLD IS GOVERNED?

By the government of the moral world, I mean the regulation of the phenomena exhibited by conscious and intelligent beings. We may first consider the case of the lower animals. Order and law appear to govern in the highest degree their production and action. They are all composed of the ten chemical elements before named, but the most rigid restrictions have been placed on the manner and conditions under which these shall combine in forming each species of animal. Man has not succeeded in imitating these combinations, and has not been able to manufacture a living organism. How are the characteristics of each species of animated beings instituted and preserved, so as to render each permanent, without any one of them changing its nature, and without the possibility of their generally amalgamating, and thus producing monstrosities, ending in ultimate and universal confusion? Apparently, by imposing impassable restraints on the action of the atoms of matter, when combining to form their organisms. The sheep and wolf cannot combine their blood and qualities by propagation; and although the horse and ass produce the mule, which appears an exception, it cannot continue its own race. Here, then, law and order are conspicuous.

When the animal is produced, its unconscious and conscious actions are equally regulated. Each species finds itself in circumstances in which external things are adapted to its organism—the water to the fish, the land to the quadruped, and the air to the bird. Each species possesses an apparatus for breathing, and the air is found to be adapted to all; each has digestive organs, and peculiar food related to these organs is provided for each variety,—grass for the ox and sheep, and flesh for the tiger and lion.

Ascending to their conscious actions, we find the swallow inspired with the inclination and capacity to build its nest; the beaver its hut; the bee its cells; with unerring precision: while the fox practises cunning, and the cock manifests courage, without experience or being taught.

Directing our attention still upwards, we find the very existence of the different species of the lower animals placed under regulations. At a meeting of the British Association (in 1856), Sir William Jardine read a communication on the progress of the artificial propagation of salmon in the Tay, a subject on which he was specially authorised to report by the Association. In the course of his remarks, Sir William is reported to have stated, " that it has been found that one of the worst enemies of the salmon ova in the breeding beds is the larvæ of the May-fly, a creature which in its turn was preyed upon by the common river trout. Now, the practice had prevailed in rivers preserved for salmon-fishing of destroying trout, though this fact shewed that the numbers of trouts ought not to be unduly diminished, as by keeping down the May-fly they aided in propagating salmon. As an illustration of this law of nature, he pointed out, that in parts of the country in which hawks had been ruthlessly extirpated, with the object of encouraging the breed of game, wood-pigeons had increased to such an extent as to have become a positive nuisance, and most injurious to the farmer; and *he shewed the danger incurred by unduly interfering with the balance established by nature among wild animals."*

How, then, are these specific qualities and powers of action, these adaptations, restrictions, and reciprocal checks, through which universal order is instituted and preserved among beings destitute of reason, and unconscious of the place and duties allotted to them in the world—produced? It appears to me that this is accomplished by the endowment of the material elements of which they are composed, with specific powers of action, and placing every one of these under restraints which it cannot surmount. It is in the organisms of the animals that we find the instruments of the Divine government of their actions revealed, and it is through the study of the qualities of these instruments that we discover the laws of this government.

Stupendous and admirable as these examples of Divine government are, our dogmatic religion not only ignores them, but excludes their being converted into religious truths by association with our religious emotions. Although the natural history of animals is taught meagerly in a few schools, and more largely in our universities, it is the physical appearance and habits of the different species that form the grand elements of this instruction: the view now given of these as examples of the Divine government on earth, is omitted, and by many persons it is objected to as disguised infidelity, or as a new religion. If the young were taught to perceive and comprehend the prevalence of law and order in the government of the inferior races, and to view this as a manifestation of the power and wisdom of God, it would greatly augment the interest with which they would study the physical and organic qualities and actions of the creatures; and it would also prepare their minds for the all-important truth, that man is placed under a similar regime himself. The evidence of this fact shall form the next subject of our consideration.

By the moral government of the world in relation to man, is meant the control and direction maintained by the Divine Ruler over human actions, by means of which He leads individuals and the race to fulfil the objects for which he instituted them. The problem is to discover the reality of this government; and this may perhaps be best accomplished by considering the *manner* in which it is accomplished. As previously observed, our ancestors in the seventeenth century believed this government to be conducted by special acts of supernatural interference on the part of God with human affairs. Science has banished this idea, and has substituted in its place the notion that the moral world also is governed by natural laws; but it has made small progress in unfolding what these laws are, and how they operate. The consequence is, that, at this moment, the great body of the people entertain no serious or practical conviction that such a government exists; and that even enlightened men have no systematic or self-consistent notions concerning the *mode* in which it is conducted. They acknowledge in words that there *is* a Divine government in the moral as well as in the physical world, and that it is by natural laws; but here they have stopped, and most of them are silent concerning the *mode* of that government. In consequence of the exclusion, effected by science, of the notion that special acts of Divine interference now take place in human affairs, the religious teaching founded on that principle has become effete. It has not been formally given up, but it is no longer of practical efficacy. Hence we are at this moment really a people without any acknowledged, self-consistent, satisfactory, or practical notions concerning the moral government of the world; in other words, concerning the order of God's providence in governing the condition and actions of men, and educing from them the results which He designed.

How is this deficiency to be supplied? Apparently in the same manner in which we have supplied other defects of our knowledge of the order of God's providence in the physical and organic kingdoms. Do we know intimately the machinery by means of which the government of the moral world is maintained and conducted? The answer must be in the negative. Have we applied such science of the body as we possess to guide us in discovering the principles on which health, disease, and death are dispensed to man? Have we any science of mind resembling in precision, minuteness, and certainty, the sciences of astronomy and chemistry? Monsieur De Bonald, in words quoted by Mr Dugald Stewart, answers the question. "The diversity of doctrines," says he, "has increased from age to age with the number of masters, and with the progress of knowledge; and Europe, which at present possesses libraries filled with philosophical works, and which reckons up almost as many philosophers as writers; poor in the midst of so much wealth, and uncertain, with the aid of all its guides, which road it should follow;—Europe, the centre and focus of all the lights of the world, has yet its *philosophy* only in expectation."*

---

* Stewart's Preliminary Dissertation to the Encyclopædia Britannica, vol. i. p. 230.

If the science of mind be as indispensable to our understanding the *manner* in which the Divine government of human actions is conducted, as is the science of matter to our comprehending the order of that government in the physical world, and if Monsieur De Bonald's description of the condition of mental science be correct, there is no cause for surprise at the darkness which envelopes us in regard to the government of the moral world.

It is too certain that Monsieur De Bonald is in the right; for although man has received a material body, has been placed in a material world, been subjected during his whole life to material influences, and can act on the external world only through the instrumentality of material organs, nevertheless, in the most esteemed treatises on the philosophy of mind, moral and intellectual faculties are described without mention of special organs, or of the influence of these in modifying the manifestations of the faculties; and without taking much notice of the relation of each faculty and organ to the other faculties and organs, or to external objects. In many standard works on Christian theology also, not only is all this knowledge omitted, but it is often denounced as degrading materialism and dangerous infidelity. Here, then, a dark abyss of ignorance, apparently impassable, breaks off all practical knowledge of the organic conditions under which mind is manifested, and also is acted upon by external moral and physical objects. And if our knowledge of the order of God's providence can increase only with our knowledge of the *means or instruments* through which He administers it, are we to sit quietly down, and allow this state of ignorance to continue for ever?

The reason why it has continued in the department of mind so long has already been mentioned. In a state of health, most men have no consciousness of the existence and interposition of material organs in thinking. They are conscious of thoughts and feelings, but not of organs; and people have been taught to ascribe all the phenomena of consciousness to *mind alone.* Consequently, they are offended with those who refer such phenomena in any degree to the influence of organs. Nevertheless, facts which are revealed by the most ordinary *observation,* shew, that mental organs exist, and have been endowed with specific powers, and been placed in specific relations to each other and to external objects, and that they manifest and determine the nature and modes of action of the forces which produce the phenomena of the moral world. May not the key to a knowledge of the manner in which God governs the world of mind, then, be found in the study of these organs, and their laws and relations? One point seems to be clear enough; namely, that if God *has* instituted mental organs, and ordained their functions, their constitution and laws must be adapted to the constitution and laws of all the other departments in creation; and that, therefore, a correct knowledge of the relations of the world of mind to the world of matter, must be unattainable, while we remain in ignorance of the mental organs.

A knowledge of these organs, therefore, and their relations and laws, appears calculated to form a bridge across the abyss of ignorance, which has hitherto concealed from our view the manner in which the Divine government of the moral world in the department of mind is conducted.

Let me ask, why should we be so deeply in the dark concerning the laws according to which life, health, talents, dispositions, and individual and social happiness, are dispensed to man? This question may, perhaps, be answered by asking others. Do we know intimately the *causes* which produce health and disease? The laws of action of these may regulate the endurance of life. Do we know the causes which give rise to the different dispositions and capacities of men? The degrees in which these causes are combined may be eminently influential in determining individual endowments. Do we know the precise social effects which these dispositions and capacities are fitted, in the case of each person, to produce, when permitted to act blindly, to act under false or imperfect information, or to act under a clear and correct knowledge of the real nature and relations of things? On the extent of this knowledge may depend our capacity to discern the causes of social happiness or misery, and to augment or diminish our own share of them. Do we know whether these causes and effects, whatever they may be, are to any extent subject to human control? and if so, *how* we may control them? If they are not subject to man's jurisdiction, do we know whether he has it in his power to modify, in any degree, his own conduct, in relation to their agency, so as to diminish the evil or increase the good which they are calculated to produce?

To nearly all of these questions only a negative answer can be given; and I suspect that in this ignorance lies the grand obstacle to the discovery of the mode in which God governs the moral world.

SECTION III.—OF LIFE—HEALTH—DISEASE—AND DEATH.

Life and health are the foundations of human well-being on earth; and in Chap. III. a brief exposition has been given of the elements of the human body, and the results of their combination into a living organism.

DEATH is perhaps the most solemn and momentous subject which can engage the consideration of Man. According to the dogmas of most of the religious sects of Christendom, it is a penalty inflicted by God on all mankind for Adam's first transgression; and it is also the awful portal through which each individual is ushered into everlasting happiness or misery. According to this view it is a dire calamity, which we must submit to with all the patience and resignation we can command, hoping for heaven as a solace under its pressure and a refuge from its terrors. According to the prevalent dogmas, however, these consolations are reserved only for the true believers of each sect; the adherents of the other sects—those which believe in "soul-destroying errors,"—and also all mankind who have not known Christianity, or who have not believed that interpretation of it which each sect holds to lead to salvation,—being doomed inexorably to death on earth and to never-ceasing misery hereafter.

At the time when these views were framed into dogmas, and woven into the core of the religious emotions of Europe as Divine truths, there was no science of geology revealing the condition of the earth and its inhabitants during millions of years before man appeared; no science of chemistry unfolding the elements of which man is composed and their relations to the things of this life; no science of physiology indicating the structure, functions, and relations of the different parts of the organism of man, and shewing their peculiar adaptation to this world. When we contemplate the facts brought to light in these sciences, we discover that death was an institution of nature, reigning among the inhabitants of the earth, through countless ages before a trace of man has been discovered; that there is a general resemblance between his structure and theirs; that his organism is constituted to receive its origin from previously existing organisms, to increase by assimilating the chemical elements of organized bodies with its own tissues, to reach maturity, then to decay, and finally to die; death being the resolution of its parts into their original elements.

According to the lights of science, therefore, death is an institution of nature; this conclusion becomes more certain in proportion to our advance in knowledge of our own constitution, of that of external objects, and of the relations established between them.

Here, then, is a conflict between the prevailing dogmas of Christendom, and science. Death viewed as a penalty is an incubus, a terror, and an affliction, calculated to darken the whole of life; and to those whose self-appreciation is governed by conscientiousness, who can discover no reasons why *they* should have been elected from all eternity to enter in at the strait gate, while countless millions of their fellow-creatures, equal, and some of them superior to themselves in every estimable quality, should have been consigned to never-ending suffering—to such minds the dogmatic sequel to death unspeakably augments its terrors. The grand remedy presented by each sect for this overwhelming evil, which it has conjured into existence, is belief in its own dogmas; and, according to them, no ray of consolation can be derived from any other source.

Viewed as a natural institution, death wears a different aspect. When we investigate the organism of man, we find it constituted in harmony with death. Organs of Destructiveness enable us, when in full health and actively employed, to live amidst the daily extinction of animal and human life, without finding it appalling and overwhelming. We enjoy repasts composed of the flesh of dead animals, and are gay and joyous over them. By the appointment of nature, they nourish and replenish us with vigour to discharge our moral and intellectual duties. In a state of health we pass the funerals of human beings in the streets, and look at the array, rarely stopping in our career of business or pleasure to moralize on the uncertainty of life. The dogmas represent this indifference as sin; science regards it as the result of the adaptation of our mental faculties to the circumstances in which they are destined to act. Nature prevails, and man in health and activity rarely thinks of death with fear. The pulpit often recalls it to our recollection; but, guided by dogmas which contradict nature, it only invests it with unauthorized terrors, and, by misdirecting our understandings, allows it to afflict us with evils, which, under a system of sounder instruction, might be avoided. It discourses largely of death as the prelude to a day of terrible retribution: but it is silent as to the causes of its premature occurrence, which, by separating husband and wife in the prime of life and in the full tide of domestic felicity, inflicts the deepest anguish on human affection; or, by removing children in the dawn of their existence, spreads desolation in the parental bosom; or, by cutting short the career of genius, or of manly vigour in its zenith, deprives society of all that the possessors of these gifts might have contributed to its welfare. These constitute the grand evils of death, and they are to a great extent avoidable: yet the pulpit chants dirges over their occurrence, points to them as the punishments of sin, refuses to recognize them as the temporal consequences of the infraction of the laws of health, which, being of Divine origin, it is its bounden duty to teach and enforce; while it calumniates as infidels all who attempt to shed light on this anomalous state of things. To this line of conduct, however, there are admirable exceptions, worthy of all reverence and sympathy; but I speak of the general style of preaching the dogmas of Christendom from the pulpit. One legitimate office of the pulpit, in relation to this subject, appears to me to be to warn us of our liability, by neglect and infringement of the laws of health, to bring upon ourselves the terrible sufferings that naturally accompany disease and premature death, and to teach us that it is a religious duty to study these laws and to obey them.

As we proceed in our scientific investigations, we discover that the human organism, when soundly constituted at birth and placed in normal circumstances during life, is framed to act without pain or suffering for seventy years at least; that after fifty, a process of insensible decay commences, accompanied by changes in our feelings and desires preparing us for death, and that when the extreme of life is reached, the harmony between our desires and death is complete. We do not then find death to be either a penalty or a calamity.

Viewed as an institution, it is obviously the means through which, in a world of limited space, the exquisite enjoyments of love between the sexes, and parental affection, are provided for; and it is through death that the errors, prejudices, and obstructions which impede the civilization and enjoyment of the race, are removed, by introducing the young, ingenuous, and enterprising, to mount higher and higher in the path of improvement. Viewed in this light, and deprived of its penal and portentous character, death is bereft of its most formidable features. We of this generation, into whose minds its terrible aspects have been deeply engraven by our spiritual instructors, can scarcely form a correct idea of the light in which it will appear to those who shall have been taught from infancy to regard it as an institution of God, intended not for our affliction, but as a necessary element in His plan of government, accompanied by innumerable advantages to ourselves, and, at the natural close of life, deprived of its terrors, by the accommodation of our feelings to its approach.

The dogmas derive their chief support from the facts that death is intuitively dreaded by most people, and that it is occasionally the cause of the deepest afflictions that darken the lot of man. How then shall we reconcile these facts with the notion of death being a beneficent institution? The explanation appears to me to be this—It is death in youth and middle age that wears these aspects, and is attended with these sufferings; but such deaths are not natural institutions, but accidents arising from human ignorance, and regardlessness of God's laws. We have been endowed with intelligence to discover our position on earth, and the duties it requires of us; and in proportion as we shall adequately comprehend the one and fulfil the other, we shall find premature death, and its general precursor, disease and pain, gradually diminishing. So far, however, as can at present be discerned, we cannot foretell the ultimate cessation of evil on earth; the power in our organism to repair casual injuries, and our faculties of Combativeness, Destructiveness, Cautiousness, and Secretiveness, appear to be constituted in direct relation to a world in which there shall always be a *liability* to evil; but, on the other hand, our moral and intellectual endowments, by giving the desire and capacity for progressive improvement, seem to indicate that advance in happiness is possible, and part of the plan of our being. Let us then investigate the causes of disease and premature death, and try to discover in what circumstances they occur, and what character they bear in the moral government of the world.

From an attentive study of our constitution, it appears that the Divine Ruler has conferred on man a system of organs of respiration, a heart and bloodvessels, a stomach and other organs of nutrition, and so forth; that to each of these He has given a definite constitution; and that He has appointed definite relations between each of them and all the others, and between each of them and the objects of external nature: and I now add that experience teaches us that *life and health accompany the normal and harmonious action of the whole; and that disease, pain, and premature death, are the consequences of their disproportionate and abnormal action.*
The study of the structure, functions, relations, and laws of these vital parts, then, appears to me to be *the true mode of investigating the principles according to which God dispenses life, health, disease, and death in this world;* in other words, *the mode in which He governs in this department of creation.** This view becomes more reasonable when we consider that hitherto no institution has been discovered in nature the direct object of which is to produce evil; that all known Natural Institutions appear to be calculated to produce a preponderance of good;

---

* In prosecuting this idea, my late brother, Dr A. Combe, was my constant coadjutor and guide.

and that God has given us faculties which enable us, within certain limits, to observe, understand, and act, according to the laws which regulate the forces that most directly affect our well-being.

Let us endeavour, then, to bring this idea to the test of observation and reason. With this view we may select the endurance of life as the first subject of our consideration.

It is beyond the compass of our faculties to discover why the world was constituted such as it is; but we must take the facts of nature as they exist; and I conclude that death in old age cannot be prevented by human intelligence and power. That the endurance of life, however, within prescribed limits, is subject to human influence, appears undeniable. That it depends on regularly operating causes, is rendered obvious by the records of mortality. The registers of burials kept in the different countries of Europe present striking examples of uniformity in the number of deaths that occur at the same ages in different years. So constant are these results, while the circumstances of any country continue the same, that it is possible to predict, with nearly perfect certainty, that in England and Wales, of 1000 persons between the ages of 20 and 30, living on the first day of January in any one year, ten will die before the first day of January in the next year.*

Uniformity in the numbers of events bespeaks uniformity in the causes which produce them; and uniformity in causes and effects constitutes the fundamental idea of government. If, then, these deaths do not occur arbitrarily or fortuitously, but result from regularly operating causes, the following questions present themselves for solution:—Are these causes discoverable by human intelligence? If they are so, can that intelligence modify them? If not, can an individual adapt his own conduct to their operation so as to influence their effects? These questions are important, equally in a religious and a practical point of view. If the causes are constant and inscrutable, and their action irresistible, it follows that, in regard to death, we are subject to a sublime and mysterious fatalism; in short, that the Mahometan doctrine on this subject is true. If, on the 1st day of January in any one year, 1000 youths, in the vigorous period of life, know, with nearly positive cer-

* I have selected the example of deaths from ages between 20 and 30, because, as will afterwards be shewn, during this interval the conditions of life seem to be to a great extent under human control. In later periods, from 70 to 80, or 80 to 90, they are not so. The human frame then obeys the law of its constitution—it decays and dies; but it does so under no inscrutable law. The causes of its decay are palpable, and the effects are obviously designed. The individual who suffers has then no duty but submission to the will of the Being who conferred life on him at first as a gratuitous boon, and who is entitled to withdraw it when the objects for which it was given have been accomplished.

tainty, that ere the clock strikes twelve on the night of the 31st of December, ten of their number will be lifeless corpses; and if, nevertheless, not one of them be able to discover who are to be the victims, or to employ any precautions to avert the blow from himself,—what is this but being subject to a real fatalism?

If, on the other hand, the causes *are* discoverable, and if the individuals subject to their influence possess also the power of modifying them, or of accommodating their own conduct to their action, and of thereby changing their influence on their own condition for good or evil, Divine government will not only be discerned in the event, but that government will present a widely different aspect. Instead of a course of mysterious fatalism, it will be a system of causation, regular in its action, scrutable in its principles, designedly adapted to the physical, moral, and intellectual nature of man, and as such presented to him for the cognisance of his intelligence, the respect of his moral feelings, and the practical guidance of his conduct. In discovering the causes of the ten deaths, and their modes of operation, we shall acquire a knowledge of the principles on which God administers life and death to men at the age between 20 and 30. We shall obtain a glimpse of the order of God's secular providence in this department of his kingdom. If this view be erroneous, there appears to be no alternative to the conclusion that, in regard to life and death, we are the subjects of a despotic fatalism. Let us inquire, then, whether the causes are scrutable, and whether human power is capable of modifying their influence.

If we desire to know by what laws God governs the sense of hearing—that is to say, under what conditions he bestows this boon upon us, and continues it with us—we shall best succeed by studying the structure and modes of action of the ear, and examining its relations to the air, to the constitution of sonorous bodies, to the brain, and also to the digestive, respiratory, and circulating systems of the body, on the action of which the sense of hearing indirectly depends. It is no abuse of language to say, that, in studying those details, we should be studying the conditions under which, within certain limits, we may retain, forfeit, improve, or impair the sense of hearing, pretty much at our discretion. In the structure, the functions, and the relations of the ear, we should discern the manifestations of God's power and goodness, and a clear exposition of the principles on which He administers this sense. In the means by which we are permitted, within certain limits, to destroy or to preserve, to impair or to invigorate our hearing, we should discover the evidence of His government not being a despotism or a fatalism, but a system of regular causation adapted to our constitution and condition, and presented to us for the investigation of our intelligence, and the guidance of our conduct. In the constitution of the sense and the appointment of its relations, which man cannot alter, God's sovereignty is made apparent. By connecting certain beneficial consequences with the actions done in accordance with that constitution and those relations, and certain painful consequences with actions done in discordance with them, which consequences also man cannot alter, the Divine Ruler preserves His own sway over the sense, and over all who possess it; while, by endowing man with intellect capable of discovering that constitution and its relations, with religious emotions enabling him to respect it, and with power, within certain limits, to act in accordance or discordance with it, and thereby to command the favourable or the adverse results at his own pleasure, human freedom is established and guaranteed; and man appears as a moral, religious, and intelligent being, studying the will of his Creator in His works, worshipping Him by conforming to His laws, and reaping the rich rewards of enjoyment destined to him as the consequences of his fulfilling the objects of his being. By those means the Divine government is maintained simultaneously with man's freedom.

The same propositions may be stated in regard to all the other parts of the human organism; and hence it seems to follow, that God has revealed to man the laws according to which He dispenses life and health, and actually invited him to take a moral and intelligent part in acting out the scheme of His providence for his own advantage.

The practical conclusion which I draw from these considerations is, that an intelligent individual who should know the structure, and functions, and laws of health, of the vital organs of the human body—the quality (*i.e.*, whether strong or weak, sound or diseased) of the constitution which each of the thousand persons had inherited from his progenitors,—and the moral and physical influences to which each should be subjected, could predict, with a great approximation to accuracy, *which* of the thousand would die within the year. If this view be correct, the ten deaths in the thousand, which, in the present circumstances of social life, appear like the result of a fatal fiat, would become merely the exponent of the number of individuals in whose persons the conditions of health and life had *de facto* been so far infringed as to produce the result under consideration; without necessarily implying, either that these conditions are in themselves inscrutable, or that the course of action which violates them is unavoidable. The sway of fatalism would disappear, and in its place a government calculated to serve as a guide to the conduct of moral and intelligent beings would be revealed;—a government, of which causation, regular in its action, certain in its effects, and scrutable in its forms, would constitute the foundation.

Moreover, it would follow from this view, that in the administration of God's secular providence in consigning ten individuals out of a thousand to the grave, and leaving nine hundred and ninety alive, as little of favouritism as of fatalism is to be discovered. The only sentence which each individual would find recorded regarding himself would be, that he must either fulfil the conditions of health, or suffer the consequences of infringing them.

It may be objected that it is impossible for any one individual to acquire all the requisite information; but this objection is foreign to the question. The real point at issue is, whether this knowledge exists and is necessary to our wellbeing during life. If it is so, we must teach it in schools and from the pulpit as Divine truth, and we must train the young and counsel the adult to act on it in their habitual conduct.

The greatest obstacle to this consummation is found in the difficulty of persuading the public mind that this knowledge *is* Divine truth, and that the practice of it is a religious duty. One cause of this difficulty appears to consist in certain erroneous notions which are entertained concerning the nature and object of the sufferings which attend infractions of the laws of nature. The inflictions under *human laws* have no natural, and therefore no necessary, relation to the offence they punish. There is no natural relation, for example, between stealing and mounting the steps of a tread-mill. When, therefore, it is asserted that under the Divine government an individual, by infringing the laws of health, may incur disease and pain, and bring himself to a premature grave, many readers regard this as teaching that the result is a *punishment*, in the dictionary sense of the word—namely, an "infliction imposed in vengeance of a crime;" and when they think of their own deficient instruction, and of the difficulties in learning and obeying the laws of health, they are shocked by the idea of their being *punished* for this ignorance. But the difficulty disappears when the word is differently defined. By punishment, I mean the natural evil which follows the breach of each physical, organic, and moral law. I regard the natural consequence of the infraction, not only as inevitable, *but as pre-ordained by the Divine Mind*, for a purpose. That purpose appears to me to be to deter intelligent beings from infringing the laws instituted by God for their welfare, and to preserve order in the world. When people, in general, think of physical laws, they perceive the consequences which these produce to be natural and inevitable; but they do not sufficiently reflect upon *the intentional pre-ordainment* of these consequences, as a warning or instruction to intelligent beings for the regulation of their conduct. It is the omission of this element that renders the knowledge which is actually possessed of the natural laws, of so little use. The popular interpretations of Christianity have thrown the public mind so widely out of the track of God's natural providence, that *His object or purpose* in this pre-ordainment is rarely thought of; and the most flagrant, and even deliberate infractions of the natural laws, are spoken of as mere acts of imprudence, without the least notion that the infringer is contemning a rule deliberately framed for his guidance by Divine wisdom, and enforced by Divine power.

In considering *moral* actions also, the public mind leaves out of view *the natural and inevitable*. Being accustomed to regard human punishment as arbitrary, and capable of abeyance or alteration, it views in the same light the inflictions asserted to take place under the natural moral law, and does not perceive *divine pre-ordainment and purpose* in the natural consequences of all moral actions. The great object which I have had in view in "The Constitution of Man," is to shew that this notion is erroneous; and that there is a natural pre-ordained consequence, which man can neither alter nor evade, attached to the infringement of *every* natural law.

To express this idea correctly a term is required, something between simple "consequence" and "punishment." The former fails to convey my idea in its totality, and the latter adds something to distort it. I find it difficult to discover an appropriate word; but hope that this explanation will render the idea itself comprehensible.

If, then, we could convey to the public mind a just appreciation of these principles, would it, or would it not, be possible for an intelligent person to acquire from his parents, his teachers, the pulpit, his medical advisers, books, and his own observation and experience, a knowledge of the conditions of life and health *in relation to himself*, sufficient for his guidance in the ordinary circumstances of life? And I ask whether, if thus instructed in these rules, trained from his infancy to venerate and observe them as Divine institutions, and also supported in doing so by social manners and public opinion, he could then, in an adequate degree, comply with the conditions of health, and escape from the supposed fatal list? I can perceive no reason for answering in the negative. If, in the first hundred years after the members of any community began to act on those principles, one individual in the thousand could escape from the list, and reduce the mortality to nine, the principle would be established; and the question in subsequent centuries would be only, how far this knowlege and obedience could be carried.

In point of fact, the records of mortality *prove* that the view now stated, correctly represents the principle on which the continuance of life is administered by the Divine Ruler of the world. When read in connection with history, these records shew that if the intelligence, morality, industry, cleanliness, and orderly habits of a community be improved, there will be an increase in the duration of life in that people. Thus, in 1786, the yearly rate of mortality for the whole of England and Wales was 1 in 42; or, in other words, 1 out of every 42 of the whole inhabitants died annually. In the Seventh Annual Report of the Registrar-General (p. 19), it is stated that the rate of mortality for the whole of England, on an average of 7 years, ending in 1844, was 1 in 46. In the Registrar-General's Report for 1854 (p. 16), it is stated that "in round numbers 24 in 1000, or 1 in 43 of the people died in that year. This is greatly in excess of the average rate, which in the last 17 years was 2·245; that is, nearly 22 in 1000, or in 1 in 45 of the population. The excess in the mortality was produced by an epidemic of cholera." This I shall shew subsequently was an avoidable evil. Allowing for some errors in the earlier reports and tables, the substantial fact remains incontestible, that the average duration of human life is increasing in England and Wales, and from the causes here assigned.

Moreover, Professor Simpson, in a pamphlet on the value and necessity of the statistical method of inquiry as applied to various questions in operative surgery, presents direct evidence in support of the proposition which I am now maintaining.

The following table, he says, calculated from the bills of mortality of London, demonstrates statistically that, in consequence of improvements in the practice of midwifery (and I should say also, in consequence of the improved habits and condition of the people), the number of deaths in childbed in that city in the nineteenth century was less by one-half than that which occurred in the seventeenth century. The table is the following:—

Average number of Mothers dying in childbed in London from 1660 to 1820.

YEARS.	PROPORTION OF MOTHERS.
For 20 years ending in......1680......1	in every 44 delivered.
For 20 years ending in......1700......1	... 56 ...
For 20 years ending in......1720......1	... 69 ...
For 20 years ending in......1740......1	... 71 ...
For 20 years ending in......1760......1	... 77 ...
For 20 years ending in......1780......1	... 82 ...
For 20 years ending in......1800......1	... 110 ...
For 20 years ending in......1820......1	... 107 ...

It is probable that in the earlier years included in this table the records were more imperfect than they were in the later years, and that the difference of the mortality is in consequence exaggerated; but, again making every reasonable allowance for errors and omissions, the grand result is still the same, a diminution of deaths from a more rigid conformity to the conditions according to which the Ruler of the world dispenses the boon of life.

Further,—the records of mortality, when arranged according to the different classes of society, and different localities of the same country, indicate the soundness of the same principle. The following results are presented by a report of the mortality in Edinburgh and Leith for the year 1846:—

The mean age at death of the 1st class, composed of gentry and professional men, was . . . . . . 43½ years.
The mean age at death of the 2d class, composed of merchants, master-tradesmen, clerks, &c., was . . . 36½ years.
The mean age at death of the 3d class, composed of artizans, labourers, servants, &c., was . . . . 27½ years.

It is a reasonable inference from, although not necessarily implied in, this table, that the third class furnished a larger proportion of the ten deaths in the thousand persons between the ages of 20 and 30 than the 2d, and this class a larger proportion of them than the 1st; and, as God is no respecter of artificial rank, that the differences in the proportions were the result of the individuals of the 1st and 2d classes having fulfilled more perfectly than those in the 3d, the conditions on which He proffers to continue with them His boon of life.

One of the conditions of health is, that we shall breathe the atmosphere in that state in which God has prepared it and adapted it to the lungs and blood. A combination of oxygen, nitrogen, and carbonic acid gas, in definite proportions, exists in the air, and is exquisitely adapted to our frame. A great increase or diminution of the proportion of any one of these, or the introduction of certain other gases, is fatal to health, and eventually to life itself.

Regardless, however, of this Divine arrangement, the inhabitants of Exeter, Liverpool, and many other towns, have, through ignorance and indolence, allowed the exhalations of decaying animal and vegetable matter to mingle with that compound atmosphere adapted by nature to their lungs and blood, and the consequence has been that many of them have suffered from disease, and prematurely died. On the 8th of December 1846, a public meeting was held at Exeter, " to consider the sanitary condition of that city." The Mayor was in the chair, and among the persons present were Viscount Ebrington, Sir J. Duckworth, M.P., Edwin Chadwick, Esq., Dr Southwood Smith, &c. A report was read by Mr Terrell, which " analysed the mortality of Exeter, and shewed that, while the deaths in those parts of the city where there was good sewerage and an ample supply of water were from 1·83 to 1·93 per cent. (per annum), in other parts, where the drainage was deficient, the mortality was 5 to 7 per cent." Mr Chadwick observed, that in infancy, " life is more susceptible than at any other period—infants, as it were live more on air." " Now, what is the mortality at Exeter compared with Tiverton? I find that, while one child out of every ten born at Tiverton dies within the year,—and one-tenth is the average of the county,—one in five dies at Exeter. And then, after its escape of the first year's mortality, it has not gone through all its chances. I find, farther, that while, in Tiverton, *twenty-six* per cent. die under the age of five years, in Exeter no less than *forty-five* per cent. die under the age of five years."

When we trace these effects to their causes, is it not clear that that purity of the atmosphere which, by the appointment of the Author of Nature, is necessary to the support of life, had been destroyed by foul exhalations; that the human intellect was capable of discovering and removing the sources of that corruption; and that it was a duty which the inhabitants of Exeter owed equally to God and to themselves, to apply the whole powers of their understandings and will to comply with the conditions of life? Can there be a more becoming theme for the combined exercise of the intellect and religious sentiments than that which is presented by such occurrences as these, in which the voice of nature calls aloud on parents to save their children by yielding obedience to the Creator's laws? Yet what occurs? Mr Chadwick informs us. " Well," says he, " here, in this city, in one of the healthiest counties of the kingdom, with an admirable site, and with all favourable circumstances, you have an infantile mortality and slaughter that very nearly follows—very closely indeed—upon the infantile slaughter of Spitalfields, &c."

The same gentleman mentioned that, "about three years ago, an epidemic raged in Glasgow, and there was scarcely a family, high or low, who escaped attacks from it. But at Glasgow they have an exceedingly well-appointed, well-ventilated prison; and in that prison there was not a single case of epidemic; and, in consequence of the overcrowding of the hospitals which killed some two thousand people, they took forty cases into the prison, and not one of them spread. In fact, there are so many classes of disease so completely within management, that medical men who have the care and custody of those who are in comparatively well-conditioned places, are in the habit of saying, in relation to cases in their private practice, 'Oh if I had but that case in prison, I could save it.' Now, what has your mortality to do with that disease here in Exeter? I find that in Tiverton, while 23 out of 10,000 of the population are swept off by epidemic diseases, in Exeter no less than 103 are killed."

Here, then, we see a man of science, whose understanding is enlightened by the study of chemistry and physiology, clearly unfolding to the people of Exeter certain relations established by the Author of Nature between the composition of the atmosphere and the human body, in consequence of the infringement of which thousands of their fellow-citizens have perished prematurely. Yet these infractions of the laws of nature were allowed to continue, year after year, under the eyes of the Bishop of Exeter, unheeded and unrestrained. Not only so; but while his flock was thus dying from causes that were discoverable and removable, his Lordship was engaged in warmly denouncing, as irreligious, the Irish system of National Education, because it proposed to teach, under the name of secular instruction, unmingled with the leaven of the Thirty-Nine Articles of the Church, a knowledge of these very institutions of the Creator, a due regard to which would have enabled the people to save their own lives and those of their children! I do not doubt that he and his clergy duly consoled the dying, read the burial-service over the bodies of the dead, and comforted the bereaved parents whose cherished offspring were thus prematurely snatched from them by the hand of death. But if these mournful effects followed, by God's appointment, from causes which were cognizable by human intelligence, and removable by human skill, why did they shrink from teaching the people to reverence this connection, and to avoid the evils, by acting on the lessons which it was reading to their understandings? This would have tended in some degree to restore the sacredness of this universe, and that earnestness of the human mind, the disappearance of which religious men so grievously deplore.

So far from acting in this manner, these excellent and estimable persons not only treat the order of creation and its lessons with neglect themselves, but by their cries of "infidelity" deter other men, who see and reverence its *sacredness*, from appealing to the nobler faculties of the mind with full practical effect in its behalf. What a soul-stirring theme did not the facts now detailed offer to Mr Chadwick and his brother philanthropists, for an appeal to the sentiment of Veneration of the people of Exeter, to induce them to bring these evils to a close! But no: science, divorced from religion, dared not to trespass on such a field. Unfortunately, also, in the minds of the suffering members of the Bishop's flock, there was no adequate knowledge of science on which to found an appeal to their religious sentiments. The speakers, therefore, could urge only the humbler motives of economy and prudence.

"Now," says Mr Chadwick, "while, amidst this population of the Tiverton district (32,499), in Tiverton 610 die, no less than 920 die in Exeter. That makes an excess of deaths due to Exeter of 332 deaths in the year. The *expense of a funeral* is certainly not less than L.5 on the average. Taking it at L.5, *your expenses in funerals*, for the excess of funerals compared with Tiverton during the year, are . . . L.1600 0 0

Every case of death involves at least 29 cases of sickness, which, at L.7 per case, is an annual expense of . 9265 0 0

Besides that, you have a loss of labour four years and eleven months by premature death, as compared with Tiverton, which, on the excess of this year's mortality, makes a sum, supposing wages to be 7s. 6d. weekly per adult, on the average (and a very low average), of . 39,000 0 0

Making a total charge to this city of at least . . L.49,865 0 0

Say L.50,000 a-year. And that does not take into account anything for the loss of the maintenance of the children that have been swept away, nothing for the extensive amount of premature widowhood, for the large amount of orphanage, you will find burdening your charities."

This is a *truly English* argument, employed to induce a people suffering from gross infringements of the order of nature, to remove the causes of pestilence and death from their dwellings! I greatly err in my estimate of the mental faculties of Mr Chadwick, if he is not as deeply impressed with the "sacredness of this universe, and of this human life itself," as he is obviously alive to the emotions of benevolence; and if he would not have felt his power over his audience greatly increased, if he had found their understandings so far enlightened, that he could have ventured to appeal to their religious sentiments in order to give weight and authority to his words. Not only, however, was the knowledge of nature wanting in them, but an appeal to it, in connection with the religious sentiments, might have been regarded by religious men as infidelity, while by some men of science it would probably have been ridiculed as "cant and a creed." Such is the predicament into which the teaching of the order of nature as a guide to human conduct under the sanction of the religious sentiments, has been brought by English education! No *safe* course was left to Mr Chadwick, but the one which he pursued, that of addressing the *lower faculties* of the people—their acquisitiveness and fear!

I do not question the force of the arguments addressed to these faculties;—because nature is so arranged, that when we depart from her paths in one direction, we are liable to fall into a multitude of errors, each accompanied by its own peculiar evils. Pecuniary loss is one of the natural consequences of bad health; but the consideration of that infliction is not one of the highest or most efficacious motives with which to rouse a well-educated people to remove from their hearths the causes of disease and death.

Instructive evidence of the possibility of diminishing the amount of premature deaths by compliance with the laws of health, is presented in a "Letter of the President of the General Board of Health," to the Home Secretary of State, and in a "Report" annexed to it, "from Dr Sutherland on Epidemic Cholera in the Metropolis in 1854." It is mentioned that "cholera is now (6th September 1854) very widely prevalent in London; up to the 2d September 4070 persons have died of the disease in the metropolis alone. I purpose to direct inquiries into the conditions which attend the presence of the epidemic so far as they can be gathered from meteorological, microscopical, and chemical observation:—

"The evidence on the localizing conditions of cholera given in the report of Dr Sutherland (which is, as I have stated, an abstract of the reports of the Medical Inspectors), points to the following as among the more prominent of the removable causes of zymotic* disease:—

1. Open ditches used as sewers.
2. Want of sewers.

---

* "This term includes the various epidemic, endemic, and contagious diseases, such as fever, smallpox, &c., which originate, or are supposed to originate, from a morbid poison being introduced into, and gradually extending itself throughout the system."— *Dr Spencer Thomson's Dictionary of Domestic Medicine.*

3. Badly constructed sewers, accumulating deposits and generating sewer gases.
4. The pollution of the atmosphere in streets and within houses, from untrapped gulleys and drains, and from sewer-ventilating openings in streets.
5. Cesspools accumulating and retaining excrementitious matters close to and under dwelling-houses, whereby the air is contaminated and the subsoil saturated with filth.
6. Want of house drainage.
7. Improperly constructed house drainage.
8. Defective paving in alleys, courts, and back yards.
9. The absence of any organized daily system of cleansing, and the consequent retention of house refuse in and near dwellings.
10. Bad water, badly distributed.
11. Recurring nuisances.
12. Unwholesome trades, such as private slaughter-houses in crowded localities, bone-boiling and crushing, manure making, and other trades evolving vapours containing organic and other noxious matters.
13. Unwholesome vapours exhaled from the Thames, in consequence of the water being polluted by the sewage of the metropolis.
14. Structural defects of dwelling houses, such as houses built in rows, back to back. Cellar habitations. Neighbourhoods the houses of which are closely packed together, with narrow overcrowded streets, alleys, and courts, so constructed as to prevent ventilation. Houses absolutely unfit for human habitation. Filthy, unventilated, and overcrowded houses, let to tenants by the week, or for other periods less than a year.

Lastly, and applying to all these,
15. Multiplicity of local authorities, and the want of sufficient powers in such authorities to deal with these evils.

"Great as these evils are in London, they are not greater, in comparison to the extent of the metropolis, than in other large cities and towns, and there is not one among them that cannot be remedied if proper steps be taken."

Dr Sutherland, in Table I. in the Appendix, gives the weekly statistics from the beginning of 1854 till the decline of cholera. "Assuming the 1st of July as the commencement of the epidemic, and the 16th December as its termination, the following table will represent the total mortality from cholera, diarrhœa, typhus, and other zymotic diseases, as contrasted with the mortality from all causes.*

DEATHS.

Cholera,	10,675
Diarrhœa,	2,601
Typhus,	1,347
All Zymotic Diseases,	19,413
All Causes,	40,599

"Although there were deaths from cholera over the whole of the metropolis, the mortality was very unequally distributed.

"On the north side of the Thames, among a population of 1,745,701 (at the last census) it was 4948, or one death from cholera to 353 inhabitants; while on the south side of the river the deaths, out of a population of 616,635, amounted to 5729, or in the proportion of one death to every 108 inhabitants. The mortality on the south side was thus above threefold, in proportion to the population, what it was on the north side of the river.

"The mortality in the districts north of the Thames was by no means equally distributed, but was, generally speaking, greatest on the lowest levels, with one marked exception, namely, the virulent outbreak of cholera in part of the parish of St James, Westminster, which I shall make the subject of a separate report."

Dr Sutherland illustrates the beneficial effects of sanitary improvements in the following words:—

"In the newly-constructed model dwellings and lodging-houses, all the evils and neglects existing in the same class of dwellings in other parts of the metropolis are as far as possible avoided.

"There are neither cesspools, ashpits, nor nuisances; all the houses have waterclosets; and there is an abundant water supply, and suitable means of ventilation are provided.

"The same improvements have been extended to the altered houses as far as it was practicable, and the results as regards the late epidemic cholera, for the seven establishments belonging to the Society for the Improvement of the Dwellings of the Labouring Classes, are thus stated in a communication received from the secretary:

"1st, Model houses for families, Streatham Street, Bloomsbury, 53 families, numbering 306 inmates, amongst whom six cases of diarrhœa have occurred, all of which speedily yielded to medical treatment.

---

* Besides the deaths from cholera given in the table there were 3 deaths registered on the week ending December 23d, and 2 deaths on the week ending the 30th. The total mortality from cholera during the year 1854 was therefore 10,696.

"2d, Thanksgiving model-buildings, Portpool Lane, Gray's Inn Lane, 26 families, and 66 females, or 166 inmates. Not a single case of sickness.

"3d, Model-buildings, Bagnigge Wells, 23 families and 30 aged females, or 175 inmates. Not one case of sickness.

"4th, Model lodging-house, George Street, St Giles', 104 inmates, without a case of either disease.

"5th, Model lodging-house, Charles Street, Drury Lane, 82 inmates, five cases of diarrhœa, very slight, and these were confined to men employed in the neighbourhood of the Tower and docks, and returned unwell. One case of cholera occurred, which can hardly be said to have been contracted in the house, as the individual had suffered from 19 days' neglected diarrhœa, and was in a state of great destitution. He died at King's College Hospital.

"6th, Model lodging-house, King Street, Drury Lane, 25 inmates, not a case of either disease.

"7th, Hatton Garden Chambers, Hatton Garden, 28 inmates, but having accommodation for 58. No sickness whatever.

"The houses numbered 4, 5, 6, and 7, are for single men.

"Mr George Glover, who was requested by the President of the General Board of Health to inspect the model lodging-houses of the metropolis after the decline of the epidemic, has reported in regard to the buildings belonging to the Metropolitan Association, that in the Old Pancras Road buildings, containing a population of 693 persons, there was no cholera, but a few slight cases of diarrhœa, only four of which required medical treatment.

"In the Soho Chambers, with an average nightly population of 88, there was no cholera during the epidemic, and only seven cases of diarrhœa. This house is situated in the immediate vicinity of the houses so frightfully visited by cholera in the parish of St James, Westminster.

"In the premises in Pelham Street and Pleasant Row, with an average population of 120, there have been no deaths either from cholera or diarrhœa.

"In the Albert Street Chambers, Spitalfields, a lodging-house, with an average population of 200, there were three cases of diarrhœa and two cases of cholera. One of the cases, however, was taken ill in Smithfield market and was removed to the London Hospital, where he recovered.

"The other case, which proved fatal, took place in a man lodger who ate stale crab, offensive to the smell, for supper and breakfast, and fell a victim to an error of diet which no improved sanitary condition could neutralize.

"In Albert Street dwellings for families, containing 354

inhabitants, there were three slight cases of diarrhœa, but there were four deaths from cholera, all confined to one family, which shews that there must have been some peculiar cause at work in that one case.

"This family consisted of a man, his wife, and eight children, who occupied a house of three small rooms, which allowed only 276½ cubic feet of sleeping space for each individual. Now experience has shewn that during cholera epidemics, about 500 cubic feet are required for safety. Mr Glover considers it probable that insufficient nourishment had also much to do with the attack.

"Besides the model dwellings belonging to the two societies, there is a street of 80 tenements, in St George's in the East, built on the plan proposed by His Royal Highness Prince Albert, and shewn in Hyde Park, at the Great Exhibition of 1851. They occupy the site of some property the inhabitants of which suffered most severely from cholera in 1849. These dwellings contain a population of about 450, and they all escaped the epidemic.

"The experience so far as concerns the results of sanitary improvements is most satisfactory, although it also shews that other things require to be attended to in order to ensure security from epidemic disease."

Dr Southwood Smith, in his instructive work on "The Philosophy of Health," shews the connection between longevity and happiness. "By a certain amount and intensity of misery," says he, "life may be suddenly destroyed; by a smaller amount and intensity, it may be slowly worn out and exhausted. The state of the mind affects the physical condition; but the continuance of life is wholly dependent on the physical condition: it follows that in the degree in which the state of the mind is capable of affecting the physical condition, it is capable of influencing the duration of life.

"Were the physical condition always perfect, and the mental state always that of enjoyment, the duration of life would always be extended to the utmost limit compatible with that of the organization of the body. But as this fortunate concurrence seldom or never happens, human life seldom or never numbers the full measure of its days. Uniform experience shews, however, that, provided no accident occur to interrupt the usual course, in proportion as body and mind approximate to this state, life is long; and as they recede from it, it is short. Improvement of the physical condition affords a foundation for the improvement of the mental state; improvement of the mental state improves, up to a certain point, the physical condition; and in the ratio in which this twofold improvement is effected, the duration of life increases.

" Longevity, then, is a good, in the first place, because it is a sign and a consequence of the possession of a certain amount of enjoyment; and, in the second place, because this being the case, of course in proportion as the term of life is extended, the sum of enjoyment must be augmented. And this view of longevity assigns the cause, and shews the reasonableness of that desire for long life which is so universal and constant as to be commonly considered instinctive. Longevity and happiness, if not invariably, are generally, coincident.

" If there may be happiness without longevity, the converse is not possible: there cannot be longevity without happiness. Unless the state of the body be that of tolerable health, and the state of the mind that of tolerable enjoyment, long life is unattainable: these physical and mental conditions no longer existing, nor capable of existing, the desire of life and the power of retaining it cease together."

The same conclusion follows from these facts—that life is administered according to regular laws, which some persons obey to a greater extent than others; and that a knowledge of the causes which favour the endurance of life, and of those which produce disease and death, is an acquaintance with the order of God's providence in this grand department of the government of the world. If this be the case, can we doubt that the relations of cause and effect, in virtue of which life is preserved, and death ensues, have been rendered by God cognisable by the human understanding, with the design of serving as guides to human conduct?*

SECTION IV.—OF THE DIVINE GOVERNMENT OF HUMAN ACTIONS.

The idea here presents itself, that, as an intimate knowledge of the structure, functions, and laws of the vital organs of the body, is apparently the true key to the right understanding of the order of God's secular providence in dispensing health

---

* While this sheet is in the press, a friend has sent me the following publications, lately issued by the " Secretary to the Glasgow City Missions," and I cannot sufficiently commend this Institution for the sound principle displayed in their circulation of these tracts, and for the practical character of the works themselves. If the precepts which they teach had been presented to the people as religious truths, founded on the laws of God embodied in their constitutions, and if obedience to these laws had been enforced *directly* as religious duties, the City Mission would have made a still greater step in advance of the general practice of missionary societies. The tracts are,—" Fever Poisons in our Streets and Homes, by Robert Pairman, Surgeon;" " Friendly Hints to the Working Classes;" and " Sanitary Reform."

and life, and disease and death, to individuals,—it is possible that, in like manner, an intimate acquaintance with the functions, relations, and laws of the organs of the mind, will open the path to the discovery of the mode in which the Divine government of human conduct is maintained.

CRIME.

One of the most striking anomalies in the moral government of the world consists in the wide-spreading magnitude and frequency of crime. Is it possible to discover whence it arises? Is it a direct result of the institutions of the Creator, or does it spring from abuses of faculties that are in themselves good? Statistical inquiries into human conduct present the same striking indications of uniformity in results as do those into the endurance of life. Mons. Quetelet furnishes us with the following table relative to crime in France :—

Years.	Accused and brought personally before the Tribunals.	Condemned.	Number of Inhabitants for each person accused.	Number condemned out of each 100 accused.	Accused of Crime		Proportion between these classes.
					Against the person.	Against Property.	
1826	6,988	4,348	4457	62	1,907	5,081	2·7
1827	6,929	4,236	4593	61	1,911	5,018	2·6
1828	7,396	4,551	4307	61	1,844	5,552	3·0
1829	7,373	4,475	4321	61	1,791	5,582	3·1
Total	28,686	17,610	4463	61	7,453	21,233	...

"Thus," says Mons. Quetelet, "although we do not yet possess the statistical returns for 1830, it is highly probable that we shall find, for that year also, 1 person accused out of every 4463 inhabitants, and 61 condemned out of each 100 accused. The probability becomes less for 1831, and less for the succeeding years. We are in the same condition for estimating, by the results of the past, the facts which we shall see realised in the future. This possibility of assigning beforehand the number of the accused and condemned which should occur in a country, is calculated to lead to serious reflections, since it involves the fate of several thousands of human beings, who are impelled, as it were, by an irresistible necessity, to the bars of the tribunals, and towards the sentences of condemnation which there await them. These conclusions flow directly from the principle, already so often stated in this work, that effects are in proportion to their causes, and that the effects remain the same if the causes which have produced them do not vary."*

The same uniformity is observable in Great Britain. A return to the House of Commons, dated 22d May 1846, shews the number of persons committed to prison for each of seventeen different denominations of offences, including robbery, housebreaking, arson, forgery, rape, and so forth, for two different periods of five years each, one while the offences were capital, and one after they had ceased to be so punished. The result is the following:—

Number of persons committed for the foregoing crimes during the five years immediately preceding the abolition of the punishment of death, ... 7276
Number of ditto during the five years immediately succeeding the abolition of the punishment of death, ... 7120

The first aspect of these facts suggests the idea that fatalism is the principle of government in the moral world also; and the questions must again be solved—Whether the causes which produce these constant results are scrutable by man? and if so, whether he is capable of modifying them; if not, whether he is capable of adapting his conduct to their action in such a manner as beneficially to vary their results? It is remarkable that in all ages, lawgivers have acted on the principle that human volitions are absolutely free; for they have directly forbidden certain actions, and enacted punishments against those who committed them, without making any inquiry into the power of their subjects to obey the law. Even in modern times, and in the face of statistical returns such as those now quoted, shewing a constant succession of crimes only partially influenced in amount by the punishments inflicted, and proclaiming, with trumpet tongue, the existence of causes lying deeper than mere punishments can reach, the rulers of nations proceed in their course of assuming absolute freedom. They proclaim the law, and inflict punishment for disobedience, irrespective of the mental condition and physical circumstances of their subjects. They have partially succeeded

* Sur L'Homme, &c., tome ii. p. 168.
The author of "Vestiges of the Natural History of Creation," edition 1844, p. 328, gives the number who commit a crime in France as 1 in 650 of the French people per annum.
And Joseph Fletcher, in "Moral Statistics in England and Wales" (population when he wrote about 16,500,000) printed for private distribution, and in possession of a friend, gives the number of persons committed annually, in these two departments of the United Kingdom, at 23,280, or about 1 in 700 inhabitants.
In September 1856, I waited on Mons. Quetelet in Brussels, and asked him if he could throw any light on the discrepancies between these statements and his own; when he informed me that his facts and figures were taken from official returns of crime in France (which he offered to shew me), and that he had the fullest confidence in their accuracy. I consider his authority, therefore, as the most to be relied on.

in checking crime, but they must confess also to much failure and disappointment. What, however, is the sound conclusion to be drawn from the facts before us?

The regularity observable in the numbers of criminals indicates the existence of regularly operating causes of crime. The first step in the investigation, therefore, must be to discover these. Several causes are generally recognised by reflecting men; such as, want of education, bad example, destitution, and so forth. These, however, do not serve to account satisfactorily for the phenomena; for out of a thousand persons all equally deficient in education, equally exposed to bad example, and equally destitute, only a definite and constant number (say ten) will become criminals in any one year in which the external circumstances of all continue unchanged. This fact shews that the primary causes of crime, be they what they may, affect some and not other individuals; and until we discover what these are, we shall never understand whether crime is a direct or a contingent result of the Divine institutions; or whether human intelligence is capable of modifying human conduct in reference to these institutions so as to diminish or remove it. Moreover, until we make this discovery, these causes, although removable, must and will produce unvarying and constant results, as if they were the mere instruments of an overwhelming fatalism.*

The solution of this problem extends far beyond the department of mere criminal legislation. It involves the whole question of God's government of the moral world; of man's freedom, and of the nature of his responsibility in this world. If the common assumption, that the will of man is *absolutely* free, were founded in fact, then God could exercise no direct control over the moral world; for the control of a superior necessarily implies limitation of freedom in the servient agent. If, on the other hand, He exercises an inscrutable and irresistible sway, dooming thousands to commit crime, and to become the victims of the tribunals erected and administered by their more favoured brethren, every notion of a moral government of the world must be abandoned. On such a supposition man could enjoy no freedom, and his only duty would be that of submission in despair.

I have already hinted at the causes why this branch of knowledge is involved in such apparently hopeless obscurity. The means by which the moral administration of the world is conducted have been unknown, and hence the scheme of government could not be comprehended. If there be any part

---

* The causes of crime are investigated in my work on "The Principles of Criminal Legislation and Prison Discipline."

of the human system by means of which all the desires, emotions, and intellectual powers of man act, and are acted upon by external objects and beings, it appears to follow, that by studying its constitution, functions, laws, and relations, in the same spirit and manner as we do those of the ear, or the eyes, or the lungs, and with analogous objects in view, we may be able to discover the mode in which it has pleased God to govern the world of mind; and that then also we may be in a condition to judge whether the causes of moral actions in general are subjected to any natural laws, and whether the moral being himself can exercise any control over those laws, or modify their results by accommodating his conduct to their sway.

If, subject to natural laws, there be organs which subserve the action of all the mental powers of man, the Divine government may have its foundation in, and maintain its authority by means of, those organs and their relations, just as that government is maintained over health and life through the medium of the laws to which the vital organs have been subjected. If man be capable of discovering those organs, of modifying them, or of accommodating his conduct to their action, so as to vary their results, then will he, within certain limits, be a free and intelligent agent; and his responsibility will be established by the fact, that while over the constitution, relations, and laws of the organs and faculties themselves, and the consequences of good and evil attached to the use and abuse of them, he will have no command; yet, by choosing between obedience and disobedience, he will enjoy that kind of freedom which consists in selecting results. It may be objected that, in this world, there is no mind distinct from the cerebral organs: But even assuming this to be the case, the thinking and feeling power embodied in these organs is endowed with self-consciousness, perception, judgment, and will, and, within certain limits, is capable of self-modification, and of acting on external objects so as to produce, with forethought and design, good or evil effects: The conclusions now stated, therefore, are not affected by this assumption.

Consciousness reveals to us our own mental powers, but it does not inform us of the existence and influence of their organs. By *observing* the organs, however, in connection with mental action, we discover that their size and condition determine the energy and activity of the faculties, and the faculties produce the moral phenomena of the world. A knowledge of the functions of the brain, then, appears to me to be an important key to the method of the moral government of man. *Moreover, each mental force has a sphere of action as certainly regulated as are the spheres of action of the physical forces, and its action produces good or evil to man, according as it operates in conformity or in opposition to the natural qualities of other beings and objects.*

A mother, for example, will love her offspring strongly or weakly, according to the size and activity of the organ of Philoprogenitiveness. The size of the organ, therefore, is, *cæteris paribus*, an index to the strength of that affection in the mother. But the well-being of the child does not depend on parental love alone. This affection is hedged in by external objects, and it must act in accordance with their qualities. Air, food, temperature, ignorantly or wisely administered, will kill or invigorate the child. Thus the physical and mental constitution of the child, the relations of that constitution to physical objects, and also to the mental forces manifested by other beings, will, *cæteris paribus*, determine the duration of its life, the character and extent of its natural capacities and dispositions, and the degree of happiness or suffering which it will experience in this world. When the mental forces are very great, they, within certain limits, control and triumph over external circumstances. Napoleon Buonaparte, by the force of a large and very active brain, rose from a private station to the command of an empire. Louis-Philippe, by an ill-balanced and partially defective brain, fell from the throne to which he had been raised by the spontaneous act of the French people.

Until physical evidence of mental qualities, and of the conditions under which they act, was reached, it was impossible to discover a solid basis either for mental philosophy or natural religion. In mental philosophy one investigator denied the existence of one faculty, and another that of another, influenced apparently by the condition of the organ in his own brain. The extent of the natural differences in the faculties of different individuals, and the effects of these on their emotional and intellectual capacities and experiences, were inappreciable ; and, moreover, the objects and relations of each faculty, and the conditions under which its permanent gratification is possible or impossible, could not be traced : How, then, could such a philosophy acquire a precise and practical character ? Again, while the means by which God governs the world of mind—the causes, for example, which render one man naturally vigorous, and another weak, in intellect, one naturally beneficent, another mischievous, one naturally pious, and another incapable of feeling a religious emotion, and so forth—were unknown, human sagacity could not unravel the principles of the Divine government in this department of nature. Moreover, in such a state of ignorance, a religion consistent with that government could not be evolved.

The reader is respectfully reminded, that I am here endeavouring to unfold only a general idea of the means by which the method of the Divine government may be most successfully investigated, and that I put forth no pretensions to a full and systematic exposition of that government. This must be the work of ages. But if we try the philosophy and natural religion of Socrates and Plato, and those of Paley and Dr Thomas Brown, by their fitness for guiding us in the practical affairs of individual and social life; and if, in the latter, we perceive no superiority corresponding to the lapse of the period of two thousand years which intervened between them, we may be permitted to suspect some deficiency in the means of investigation hitherto pursued. However imperfect, therefore, the results of the new method may now appear, the equitable test of its merits would be, to pursue it for two thousand years more, and then to compare the personal and social improvements which it had enabled mankind to reach, with those which the existing methods have been able to produce.

Let us now proceed to consider more closely the instruments by means of which the moral government of the world appears to be conducted.

As the brain and nervous system seem to be important instruments, by means of which this government is maintained, we may inquire first into THE EFFECTS OF SIZE IN THE BRAIN. An eloquent writer in the 94th number of the Edinburgh Review, has observed, that "It is in the nervous system alone that we can trace a gradual progress in the provision for the subordination of one (animal) to another, and of all to man; and are enabled to associate every faculty which gives superiority, with some addition to the nervous mass, even from the smallest indications of sensation and will up to the highest degree of sensibility, judgment, and expression." "The brain is observed progressively to be improved in its structure, and, with reference to the spinal marrow and nerves, augmented in volume more and more, until we reach the human brain—each addition being marked by some addition to, or amplification of, the powers of the animal—until in man we behold it possessing some parts of which animals are destitute, and wanting none which theirs possess." There is an assent to these propositions by scientific physiologists in general, and the facts embodied in them lay the foundation of our present inquiries. The influence of size in the brain of man is easily ascertained. If it be under thirteen inches in horizontal circumference, although the functions of animal life may be maintained, moral and intellectual imbecility, amounting to idiotcy more or less complete, will be an invariable accompaniment. Idiotcy may arise from diseases or injuries of the brain, which do not affect its size; but great deficiency of size is one and an invariable cause of idiotcy.

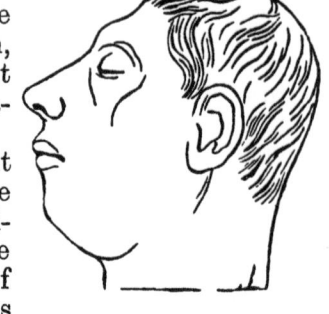

Here, then, is one most important fact in the moral government of the world. The power of mental manifestation is extremely defective where the brain is very small. The law of organization unfolded in this fact does not stop here; but the proposition may be extended to the affirmation that mental power in general bears a relation to the size of the brain, and that, *cæteris paribus*, the larger the brain, within the limits of health, the greater will be the aggregate mental power.

Highly important consequences in the moral government of the world follow from this fact. In private and in public life, other conditions being equal, the large brain will act with more energy, clear away more successfully obstacles that impede its path, exert a more powerful influence in society, and rise to greater eminence, than the small brain. This fact will be found one means of explaining the conquests of nations. The brain of the Peruvian Indian is greatly smaller than the Spanish brain, the Hindoo brain is smaller than the Anglo-Saxon; and hence one great cause of the facility with which the inferior races were overcome by the larger-headed races. The Araucanians, with brains more nearly equal to those of the Spaniards, successfully resisted them. (See *Phren. Jour.*, vol. iii. p. 432.) In revolutions, and in political action under free governments, large size of brain is, *cæteris paribus*, a highly important element of social influence, and in the ordinary business of life the same fact holds good.

The female brain is less than the male brain, besides being more delicate in structure. Sir William Hamilton states the average weight of the Scotch male brain to be 3 lb. 8 oz. troy, and of the female 3 lb. 4 oz. troy. In the superior size of the male brain we perceive the instrumentality by means of which the female has been rendered subordinate to the male in the moral government of the world. The other portions of the organisms of the two sexes are constituted in relation to the mental capacities and dispositions bestowed on each through the medium of the brain.

There are various causes which modify the influence of size in the brain: The temperaments, the effects of which are described in the standard works on Phrenology; also a feeble structure inherited from progenitors in whom the brain has been diseased, or of defective constitution; diseases of the lungs or organs of nutrition, which impair the quality of the blood that supplies the brain; impure air habitually breathed; low, damp localities; excessively severe climates, as in the narrow valleys of the Alps; excessive bodily or mental exertion; intemperance in food or drink; absence of education, and moral and intellectual training, and so forth ;— all these tend to diminish the influence of size, and their opposites to increase it. Therefore, these also must be studied as portions of the means by which the moral government of the world is conducted.

I have seen men, born to wealth, squander it through sheer inability to retain it, resulting from a small or ill-constituted brain; others sink in death under exertions which exceeded the powers of their brains; others fail in their professional pursuits, and die in poverty and obscurity; others, when raised to places of political or social trust and power, greatly disappoint expectations; all through deficiency of size in the brain.

Is not this, then, a chapter of revelation offered by God to the human understanding, regarding the means by which He conducts the moral government of the world? The causes of these occurrences have hitherto been unknown, and hence the events have been regarded as inscrutable. Religious men have met them by prayer and resignation, and looked, through faith, to heaven as the scene where the sufferers should be rewarded, and what they regarded as justice be finally dispensed. Philosophers have borne the evils with courage and resignation, as inevitable and inscrutable. If we have abandoned belief in the miraculous interference, in modern times, of Divine power in the moral world, these phenomena will apparently remain for ever inexplicable, until we shall approach them in some such manner as we are now doing. Regarded as results of the condition of the brain, they become intelligible, and indicate to us a practical line of conduct in dealing with them. We may then hope for better success than has attended our past administration of our worldly well-being.

Another important inquiry presents itself—whether man is capable of exerting any influence over the size and condition of the brain? Here the answer must be in the affirmative. Our power in this department will be found equal to, probably greater than, our influence over inorganic substances and agencies. "If," says Dr Combe, "two persons, each naturally of an excitable and delicate nervous temperament, choose to unite for life, and especially if they marry at a very early age, when the natural excitability of the system is at the highest, it will be almost impossible to prevent the concentrated influence of these peculiarities from destroying the health of their offspring, and subjecting them to all the miseries of nervous disease, madness, or melancholy. Even where no hereditary defect exists, the state of the mother during pregnancy has an influence on the mental character and health of the offspring of which few parents have any adequate conception, but with which every mother ought to be familiar."*

It is foreign to the object of the present work to describe in detail the means by which the size and condition of the brain of man may be improved. The ordinary treatises on Physiology and Hygiene throw some light on the subject; but, correctly speaking, this is still a grand *terra incognita*, on which few competently qualified explorers have entered. The cause of this backward state of things is easily discerned. Physiologists, and, still more, the public, are not aware of the influence of the size and condition of the brain in producing moral phenomena; and therefore neglect the study of it. Divines in general also have not a notion of the fact that the brain is the instrument through which God conducts the moral government of the world, and that the mental phenomena with which they professionally deal, are dependent on its condition; and hence they neglect the study of the brain. A few more generations, therefore, must pass away, and new minds must be gradually indoctrinated in these views before a serious investigation of them will be commenced. Results will then probably be discerned to be placed within human control, which, if here predicated, would appear to the present generation as pure extravagance.

These observations apply to the brain considered as a whole; let us next advert to its individual parts as the organs of moral forces.

SECTION V.—MEANS BY WHICH THE INDIVIDUAL HUMAN FACULTIES, AS MORAL FORCES, ARE REGULATED IN THEIR ACTION.

In a state of gross intellectual ignorance, human beings in some degree resemble the condition in which the lower animals would find themselves, if endowed with their present desires, without instinctive guidance how to gratify them. Suppose a brace of birds attached to each other by Amativeness and Adhesiveness, and desirous of rearing young; but

* Physiology applied to Health and Education, 14th Edition, pp. 256-7.

deprived of the instincts which now guide them, and destitute of all knowledge of a nest, and of the materials and method of constructing one, the results would be disastrous. The female would be forced to lay her eggs unprotected upon the ground, many of them would probably be destroyed, and she would not know how to hatch those that remained. In regard to many things essential to his well-being, the native New Hollander, through deficiency in certain cerebral organs, stands in a somewhat similar predicament. The bird is directed, by a wisdom superior to its own, what it should do to hatch its eggs, and *how* to do it. In place of this guidance, man has received observing and reflecting faculties to enable him to find out the means of promoting his own welfare; but wherever he has not systematically and fully applied these powers to this end, he suffers evils and deprivations. A single example will suffice to illustrate this proposition.

The vibratory powers of physical objects act in a fixed and regular manner; the air receives impulses from these and transmits them according to fixed laws; the auditory apparatus in man has received a definite structure and functions, related to those vibrations; and the organs of Time and Tune also have received a constitution related to the impressions which they make on that apparatus. Melody, harmony, and discord are the results of the action and relations of these various objects. The more perfect the development of these organs, and the greater the knowledge possessed by a composer, of the laws which the objects, in their modes of action, obey, the greater will be the range and precision of action of his organs of Time and Tune, and the more perfect his productions. Animated by the intuitive activity of these organs, and an empirical experience, he may go a certain length in composing music without scientific knowledge; but even in this case he can do so only by fulfilling the laws of melody and harmony so far as he knows them; and by no efforts could he succeed if he infringed them.

Similar propositions may be stated of all the internal faculties. The structure, functions, sphere of action, and relations to other faculties and to external objects, of every internal mental organ, are subjected to definite laws as certainly as are those of hearing. For example, through the feeling of Benevolence we may desire to heal a patient, but we cannot succeed in doing so without complying with the laws of the animal economy related to his restoration. We have long endeavoured, through humane feelings, to put an end to pauperism; but as we have failed to ascertain and remove the causes of it, we have not succeeded.

We have already considered the means by which life, health, disease, and death, are dispensed to individuals, and have seen that in the organism, its inherent qualities, and its relations and adaptations, the order of the Divine government in this department is unfolded for our guidance. However ignorant an individual may be, however savage his dispositions and limited his intellectual capacities, there are bounds set to his physical, moral, and intellectual aberrations. However eagerly he may strive to attain prosperity and happiness, if he take the wrong course he will invariably fail, and only by pursuing other modes of action will he be successful. Here, then, are indications of a controlling power or government over him. Let us consider the means by which his condition is determined while his life endures.

We must begin with the constitutional qualities of the stock from which he is descended, and with the condition and conduct of his parents. If the organism was feeble and unhealthy in the stock, or in the parents, at the period of his production, or if the whole, or a certain number, of the cerebral organs of the latter were then in a state of excitement or apathy, he may, throughout his life, be an invalid, or an incapable idiot, or a man of erratic genius, and in consequence a sufferer from his cradle to his grave: if these circumstances were reversed, his condition would be reversed. After he is born, also, and while yet incapable of influencing his own wellbeing, the treatment he receives may determine his health, morality, and intellectual capacity, and in consequence his happiness or misery during life.*

I do not wish, however, to underrate the great complication of causes, consisting of hereditary tendencies, acquired habits, temporary mental and physical conditions, and meteorological influences, which may affect the constitution of children during utero-gestation, and render it difficult to unravel this intricate web of causation, and to acquire control over its separate threads. But this problem is presented to us for our solution, and the richest rewards are promised to our efforts if successful. Dr Spurzheim, in his work on the Elementary Principles of Education, observes that "He who can convince the world of the importance of the laws of propagation, and induce mankind to conduct themselves accordingly, will do more good to them, and contribute more to their improvement, than institutions and all systems of education," (p. 74). I coincide in this opinion, and consider that human happiness and misery depend more upon the constitutions of body and brain com-

---

* See Dr Combe's Physiology applied to Health and Education, 14th edition, pp. 219, 255, 294, and also his Treatise on the Management of Infancy, 8th edition.

municated prior to birth than upon all other causes put together. Where these are radically defective and unsound, physical pain, mental imbecility, impulsive and irresistible desires, torpid inactivity, or insanity with all its deep afflictions, are the unhappy characteristics of the individual. Where, on the other hand, the whole organism is sound, well-proportioned, and normally active, there are few conditions in life to which the individual may not adapt himself, or which he may not control so as to ward off suffering and secure a measure of enjoyment. The causes, however hidden and complicated, are certain in their operation, and we may rest assured that in every instance in which we shall discover the real agencies, mystery will disappear, and order stand forth revealed.

After birth the happiness or misery of the individual is governed by the organism which he has inherited and the circumstances in which he is placed; including in the last—country, climate, instruction, training, example, and all other external influences. A few examples may be given in illustration of the mode in which the Divine government appears to be exercised on the individual after he has fairly become a denizen of this world. It is still conducted through the medium of the cerebral organs, and the relations which external objects bear to them.

The human organism undergoes waste by action, and requires a regular supply of food to maintain it in vigour. Organs of digestion, assimilation, and circulation are bestowed to enable us to supply waste, and a mental impulse is added to prompt us to make the efforts necessary to procure food. Its cerebral organ is named ALIMENTIVENESS, and its size in each individual determines, *cæteris paribus*, the strength of his appetite for nutritious substances. With a small development he will be too indifferent to the pleasures of the table, and suffer from weak digestion, and a low degree of physical vigour. If the organ be too large, he may be the slave of his appetite, and become a gourmand or drunkard. A medium-development, combined with well-proportioned lungs and abdominal viscera, will give him the best basis of health and longevity, in so far as these depend on nutrition. But the action of the nutritive functions is not arbitrary: it is regulated and intelligible, and on our observance of its laws expounded in Physiology, depend our life and health. Moreover, to procure the means of gratifying this appetite we must possess and apply knowledge. Food and all beverages, except water, require care and skill for their production; and descriptions of the modes in which they may be most successfully called into existence constitute sciences: Agriculture is the science of the production of food; Political Economy the science of its distribution; and Chemistry the science of the forms and combinations in which it may be rendered most nutritive and savoury to the human organism. In these sciences, then, we find the instruments and agencies by which God governs our conduct in regard to nutrition, and the conditions on which He proffers to supply our wants. We may pray, "Give us this day our daily bread," but unless these conditions are complied with, our daily bread will not be forthcoming; and if we do comply with them, it will rarely fail.

AMATIVENESS, of which the cerebellum is the organ, may be next noticed. There may be other functions connected with the cerebellum, but to my judgment the evidence is irresistible - that the sexual propensity is manifested by the chief portion of it. The strength of the feeling depends, *cæteris paribus*, on the size of the organ. If too small, indifference to the most endearing union in nature is the consequence; and if excessive, it becomes a source of insatiable desire, rendering life restless, immoral, and miserable. Physiology unfolds the unspeakable devastations made in the organism by its abuses, and the beneficial consequences which follow from its normal gratification; and in this science we find the laws to which its action has been subjected. These laws, by being combined with the moral and religious emotions, may be formed into moral and religious guides for its proper regulation. Yet this truth is ignored in our early training.

The question, Whom is it lawful to marry? is generally answered from Scripture, and in some instances the reply is in opposition to nature. Unions of persons within certain degrees of consanguinity, also under and beyond certain ages, or possessing constitutions seriously impaired by disease, or in whom the organs of the animal propensities greatly predominate over those of the moral and intellectual faculties, inevitably lead to suffering, and are therefore forbidden by Him who instituted these consequences. On the contrary, every union which produces healthy bodies and well-constituted active brains in the children, is permitted by the same authority. But under what system of religion or education is science brought to bear on the propensity, as an exposition of the laws under which it has been placed by the Divine Intelligence? Yet, until this shall be done, this tremendous fountain of good or evil will be allowed to flow with only such guidance as the knowledge and experience of each individual may supply.

The joys which spring from the legitimate action of this propensity, constitute the themes of the poet and the novelist, but love, and the consequences of its abuses, might also, if viewed under the lights of science and religion, find legitimate expositors in the moralist and divine. As religion and science stand at present, the feeling is allowed to run riot in the youth of the one sex, and to stimulate with a restless curiosity the other; and both are left to act under its influence with a degree of reckless levity, as if there were no Divine government whatever in this department of nature.

PHILOPROGENITIVENESS also is placed under Divine regulation. If the organ is small, children are regarded by their parents as a heavy burden. A young couple were mentioned to me who sent their first-born and only child to a stranger to be reared and educated, that they might pursue their career of fashionable gaiety unincumbered by its claims on their affections and attention. When the organ is excessively large, children are liable to be pampered and spoiled; and these different courses of action yield results corresponding to their nature. In both instances the child will suffer, and sooner or later the abuse of the faculty will react and produce misery to the erring parent. The laws of Physiology should constitute one important element in the instruction of parents, to enable them to practise a system of treatment that shall confer the greatest benefits on their children, as organized, moral, religious, and intellectual beings. And we must teach the child also WHAT IT IS, WHERE IT IS, WHAT IT OUGHT TO DO, and HOW IT SHOULD DO IT,* in order best to fulfil the objects of its existence. That such instruction and a corresponding training are commanded by the Divine Ruler appears to be indisputable, because He has so framed the organism of man, and its relations, that well-being and moral advancement can be reached only by complying with the conditions described by the sciences as records of His institutions and His Will.

COMBATIVENESS and DESTRUCTIVENESS may be selected as our next examples. The same remarks as to the influence of size in the organ on the propensity, formerly made in regard to other organs and other conditions, apply also to these. It is the province of the intellectual, moral, and religious faculties to dictate the occasions, circumstances, and extent to which those propensities may legitimately be employed.

Supposing a case to occur calling for their legitimate exercise, they are still under Divine government as to the means of their successfully accomplishing their objects. This has been so strongly felt in modern times, that the modes of their employment have been reduced to rules founded on the con-

---

* This has been attempted by Mr William Ellis, in his work, entitled " What am I? Where am I? What ought I to do?" &c. London: Smith, Elder, & Co. 1852.

stitution of physical and organized matter, and war boasts of being guided by science. Scientific instruction is now given in its various branches, from humble boxing, fencing, and shooting, to gigantic national contests, in which mathematical and algebraic calculations are employed to direct projectiles and guide the movements of armies. The results which civilized nations have been able to command by calling in the aid of science, and scientific combinations, to give efficacy through the medium of their fleets and armies to Combativeness and Destructiveness, are astounding exhibitions of human power, and should present us with motives and a lesson how to turn our other emotional faculties to good account by placing them under similar guidance.

When the organ of ACQUISITIVENESS is small, little interest is felt in property, and the individual thus organized often allows the fortune bequeathed him by his sire to melt away without leaving a trace behind; or he misses wealth through sheer indifference, when placed in the most favourable circumstances for acquiring it. Great suffering often follows from such a disposition, and in scrutinizing the ways of God, the key to the cause of the evil may probably be found, *cæteris paribus*, in the deficient size of this organ. If, again, it be excessively developed, and not guided by high moral and intellectual powers, it gives an insatiable craving for property, that knows no bounds. The ruined speculator and gamester, the grasping trader who, in hastening to be rich, overshoots his capital and credit, and falls a victim to his greed, will find one source of their calamities in the excessive development of Acquisitiveness. These dispositions, too, send forth copious streams of misery, and in the organism we must look for the fountain. When normally developed and wisely directed, the faculty becomes the stimulus to industry, economy, and accumulation, and the parent of all the enjoyments which flow from wealth honestly acquired and discreetly applied. Physical nature is constituted in direct relation to it, and to the wants of our bodies, which it prompts us to supply. Again we see, that the blessings which follow from such a course of conduct are dispensed through the medium of the organism.

But in the pursuit of its objects ACQUISITIVENESS is still subject to strict natural control. Wealth cannot be produced without labour, aided by skill, nor can it be accumulated without economy. When produced, its distribution is not a matter of chance, but is governed by laws as certain in their operation as those which regulate the evolutions of matter. Robbery, cheating, and gambling, may appear short roads to riches; but being immoral they are not only condemned by conscience, but by the order of nature they lead inevitably to ruin if persevered in and followed till they reach their natural results. The science which treats of the production and distribution of wealth is political economy, and it stands in the same relation to Acquisitiveness that the science of war bears to Combativeness and Destructiveness. Comparatively few persons know that Acquisitiveness is subjected to natural laws, fewer still what these are, and very few act steadily and consistently on them as the basis of their pursuit of gain. I have known some men who did so, and they were successful in attaining their object. One friend who has managed millions a-year informed me that he had early in life been imbued with the truth and practical character of political economy as taught by Mr James Mill, and had in business steadily acted on its rules. It did not absolve him from the consequences of floods, famines, shipwrecks, and the follies of men; but it taught him how to calculate the frequency and force of these, and to provide against them; and, taking averages of years, he found his industry and skill as certainly and as liberally rewarded in trade as if he had drawn from a regulated fountain opened by the bounty of a superior Being. In point of fact he *was* drawing from such a fountain, viz., the storehouse of the world; and his brain, knowledge, and morality were the keys by which access to it was given him. These rules appear to be inefficacious in individual instances; but in the persons who are unsuccessful in the pursuit of wealth, the cause will be found in the deficient or excessive development of the organ, the want of adequate moral and intellectual organs to guide it, or defective knowledge of the natural laws to which it has been subjected.

The sentiment of BENEVOLENCE may be next considered. The degree in which it also is experienced depends, *cæteris paribus*, on the size of its organ. When it is small, indifference or even insensibility to the welfare of other beings is the result; and when it is large, a deep interest in the happiness of every living creature is experienced, which renders the foot swift and the head active to confer enjoyment or to remove pain. These differences make the individuals in whom they occur widely different as moral agents. Place them at the head of a nation, a province, a city, a family, a school, a charitable institution for relief of the destitute, or of an army, and their measures, conduct, influence, and principles of action will be found, in the qualities of active goodness, generosity, and mercy, to bear a relation to the size of the organ in their brain. It cannot, therefore, be a matter of indifference to mankind to discover the means by which good or evil to multitudes of sentient beings are dispensed by the order of nature; and in the size of this organ the means stand, to some extent, revealed to our senses.

Moreover, great pleasure accompanies the activity of Benevolence. All nature seems to reflect the kind affection, love, and good-will which reign within the mind of him in whom the organ is large and active; while, on the other hand, the world seems cold and heartless to him in whom it is small. The one is instinctively disposed to believe in the Divine benevolence; the other experiences doubts and perplexities in arriving at the same conclusion.

In the external world, Benevolence is subjected to restraint and direction by the qualities and modes of action of other objects and beings. The intellect must study these, and guide Benevolence to a course consistent with their nature and its own relations to them, otherwise it will not succeed in conferring enjoyment, and in securing its own gratification by promoting happiness. The records of public charities afford incontrovertible evidence of this fact. "About a hundred years ago," says Dr Combe,* "when the pauper infants of London were brought up in the workhouses, amidst impure air, crowding, and want of proper food, out of 2800 received into them annually, the frightful proportion of 2690 died within the year! When this murderous mortality at length attracted the notice of Parliament, an act was passed obliging the parish officers to send the infants to nurse in the country. Under this more humane treatment the mortality speedily fell to 450, being a diminution of 2240 annually." Benevolence prompted men to make provision for rearing these children, but their intellect being uninstructed in some of the conditions indispensable to the maintenance of life, these conditions were neglected, and the children perished in the frightful numbers now mentioned.

Benevolence combined with Philoprogenitiveness, and acting without intellectual knowledge, induced some individuals to found institutions for receiving and rearing foundling children. The result was the encouragement of licentiousness, recklessness, and indifference in the parents, accompanied by deprivation to the children of all the tender cares flowing from parental love. Experience soon shewed that there was not only a waste of capital and labour in such establishments, but that they directly fostered vice, and added to infantile death and misery. When intellect had penetrated to these consequences, the institutions were suppressed, and the emotions

---

* Physiology applied to Health and Education, 14th edition, p. 207.

which had produced them were directed into better channels. This, therefore, is another example of the modes in which the emotional faculties miss their objects and afflict their possessors with disappointment, when not guided by knowledge of the order of nature.

In the same category stand most of our endowed schools, universities, and churches. They owed their origin to Benevolence, Veneration, Conscientiousness, and perhaps Love of Approbation, acting according to the lights of the times. The founders of them ordered such things to be taught as then appeared to be most conducive to human welfare; but, as new and more practical views of the order of God's providence have evolved themselves through a more profound perusal of the Book of Nature, the instruction which is now given in these seminaries, by imbuing young minds with the errors of the sixteenth and seventeenth centuries, and training them to oppose the diffusion of the knowledge of the nineteenth, operates in obstructing human well-being. These institutions were called into existence by the activity of the highest faculties, and their founders aimed at the most beneficent objects. In themselves, therefore, they are excellent, and it is only their abuses that require reformation. Under the views advocated in this work, every school, college, church and chapel, now existing in the world, is accepted as a practical manifestation of Benevolence, Veneration, Conscientiousness, and intellect, alloyed, perhaps, in some cases, by an intermingling of the lower feelings. But, notwithstanding all their defects, the preservation of these institutions is earnestly desired, because the day may come when each may act as a radiating centre of knowledge, tending to raise man to the dignity and happiness of a really moral administrator of the world. I repeat, however, that before they can be so applied, a generation must arise which shall not hesitate to employ its intellect in examining how far the things taught in them are in conformity with the order of God's secular providence.

In the Westminster Review for January 1853, there is an interesting and instructive article on "Charity, noxious and beneficent;" in which many of the evils that have arisen from the action of Benevolence, unguided by knowledge of the order of nature, are exposed, and remedies are suggested. "We find," says the reviewer, "from Mr Sampson Low's book, which we have placed at the head of this article, that the charitable institutions of London are 491 in number, and that their annual income amounts to not less than £1,765,000, of which £742,000 is derived from endowments, and £1,023,000 from voluntary contributions. Other cities and districts are not far behind; but of these we can offer no summary. Certainly, however, there are means here amply adequate to the relief of all misery that ought to exist and would naturally exist. Yet we do not find that destitution or suffering has been either eradicated or provided for: we do not feel clear that it has been *met:* we are by no means certain that it has not *increased.* There can be no doubt at least that it still prevails to a most alarming extent,—to an extent scarcely equalled in any fully civilized country; and that it prevails most in our great towns,—precisely, that is, in the very quarters where most has been done to relieve it. What, then, is the inevitable conclusion?—a conclusion not only flowing out of these premises, but confirmed by the testimony of every man of practical experience and observation,—that such charity creates more distress than it relieves.*"

How is this waste of charity to be prevented, and how are the objects of the benevolent donors of such large amounts of property to be realized? Nothing can shew more clearly than the narratives of the special evils produced by particular abuses of charity given in the Review, that *there is order* in the government of the world, and that men must condescend to comply with it before they can accomplish good. According to the views of this treatise, the first object of these charities should be to convey to the young whom they are intended to benefit, a practical knowledge of the structure and functions of their own bodies and minds, and the relations of these to God and to the world in which they are placed, and to train them to work out their own well-being, by complying with the conditions dictated by these for their guidance. If this instruction be omitted, it is impossible to render them virtuous, prosperous, and happy. The second object should be to feed, clothe, and lodge gratuitously those individuals only, who through bodily or mental infirmity are naturally incapable of being taught and trained to maintain themselves. Thirdly, It will only be when public opinion and social institutions have been brought into harmony with the order of nature, that individual charity, even when thus enlightened, will be capable of realizing its own desires. At present, the founders and administrators of many public charities, by neglecting the lessons of Political Economy and Physiology, waste the wealth with which they desire to benefit their destitute brethren.

The faculty of CONSTRUCTIVENESS may be next adverted to. It gives a desire and an aptitude for combining the elements

---

* " Charity " (said one witness), " creates the necessity it relieves; but it cannot relieve all the necessity it creates."

of nature into artificial forms for its own gratification, and that of the other faculties. This desire and aptitude are strong or weak, in proportion, *cæteris paribus*, to the size of the organ; but it does not discover the qualities of the materials which it must use, or their adaptations to accomplish its ends. This knowledge must be acquired by the intellect, and Constructiveness must act under its guidance or fail. No extent of intellect without Constructiveness will suffice to form a work of art, whether a statue, ship, or steam-engine; but neither will Constructiveness without intellect be capable of producing such combinations. In physics, science has conquered a wide domain; and in forming machinery, bridges, rail-roads, ships, houses, and innumerable other artificial compound objects, Constructiveness is aided by scientific knowledge, and its success is proportionately great. But in the department of mind, science fails, and Constructiveness works empirically. The painter and sculptor have still to learn the influence of the brain on the forms and expressions which they represent. Instances in point will be found in my work on " Phrenology applied to Painting and Sculpture."

The order of Providence is here again conspicuous. A mental force giving a desire and aptitude for realizing certain physical combinations is conferred on man; it is rendered strong or weak according to the size of its organ, and within certain limits he is capable of influencing its size: for example, I have seen the organ transmitted of large size to a child whose parent was actively engaged in a constructive enterprise at the time of the child's production. The mental force is furnished with a world-wide storehouse of materials, which it may employ for accomplishing its own gratification, and that of the other faculties; but these materials are endowed with unchanging qualities and modes of action, in conformity with which they must be used, otherwise successful employment of them is impossible. To enable us to discover these qualities and modes of action, intellect has been bestowed on us, and we must use it in observing and studying them, or fail. This exercise of our faculties is spontaneous and pleasurable, but it is regulated and controlled by the Author of nature. By acting, therefore, morally, religiously, and intellectually in the spirit of His arrangements, we improve and elevate our own nature, increase our own happiness, and thus, in theological language, promote the glory of God.

All our other faculties might be treated in a similar way, but the foregoing instances will suffice to point out the general idea of the mode in which each is provided with a special sphere of action, but in which it is controlled by its own constitution and its relations to other objects and beings, and thereby subjected to the Divine government. Until all our faculties shall have been investigated in this manner, and the results of their different modes of action discovered and generally taught, we shall not possess either a sound and practical philosophy or religion. When this task shall have been accomplished, the meagreness and imperfections of our present systems, contrasted with the pertinacity with which we resist the improvement of them, will excite the wonder of posterity.

SECTION VI.—EFFECTS OF THE PREDOMINANCE OF PARTICULAR GROUPS OF ORGANS IN INDIVIDUALS IN DETERMINING THEIR QUALITIES AS MORAL AGENTS.

I have stated that each mental faculty is a moral force, the amount of which is indicated, *cæteris paribus*, by the size of its organ. In the compound power called mind, each separate faculty holds a place analogous to that held by a simple chemical element in a vegetable compound. "The ultimate constituents of plants," says Professor Liebig,* "are those which form organic matter in general, namely, carbon, hydrogen, nitrogen, and oxygen. These elements are always present in plants, and produce by their union the various proximate principles of which they consist. It is, therefore, necessary to be acquainted with their individual characters; for it is only by a correct appreciation of these that we are enabled to explain the functions which they perform in the vegetable organisation." * * * "Such are the principal characters of the elements which constitute organic matter; but it remains for us to consider in what form they are united in plants.

"The substances which constitute the principal mass of every vegetable are compounds of carbon with oxygen and hydrogen, in the proper relative proportions for forming water. Woody fibre, starch, sugar, and gum, for example, are such compounds of carbon with the elements of water. In another class of substances, containing carbon as an element, oxygen and hydrogen are again present; but the proportion of oxygen is greater than would be required for producing water by union with hydrogen. The numerous organic acids met with in plants belong, with few exceptions, to this class. A third class of vegetable compounds contains carbon and hydrogen, but no oxygen, or less of that element than would be required to convert all the hydrogen into water. These may be regarded as compounds of carbon with the elements of water, and an excess of hydrogen. Such are the volatile and fixed

* Chemistry in its Application to Agriculture and Physiology, Chap. I.

oils, wax, and the resins. Many of them have acid characters."

The moral forces and their organs are never found, like chemical elements, existing singly, but always in combination with each other. The combination is not that of blending, as in chemistry, but of juxtaposition: but as, *cœteris paribus*, each is strong or weak in proportion to the size of its organ, the combinations of moral forces, in different degrees of relative strength, produce effects analogous to those which result from the combination of the same chemical elements in different proportions. By increasing the quantity of oxygen in a chemical combination, nature produces an acid substance; by diminishing the oxygen, the other elements remaining the same, it produces sugar. In an analogous way by diminishing the moral and increasing the animal organs, nature renders an individual selfish and low in his desires. By diminishing the intellectual organs, he is made stupid; and *vice versa*. Each human being, therefore, is a compound moral force, somewhat analogous to what a piece of sugar or wormwood is in chemical science. The human compound will act differently in its own sphere, affect other human beings differently, and produce different moral results, individual, domestic, and social, according to the predominance of certain of its elementary faculties over the others. We proceed, then, to consider the effects of the predominance of particular groups of organs in individuals, in determining their qualities as compound moral forces, or moral agents.

The brain, as the seat of a compound mental power, may be divided into three regions. Of these the base, with the posterior and the lower lateral parts, manifests the propensities common to man with the lower animals; the coronal region manifests the moral emotions; and the anterior lobe the intellectual faculties. Now, as the mental faculties are truly the forces which produce the moral phenomena of the world, and as each acts with a vigour, and embraces a sphere of desire, emotion, or knowledge, corresponding, *cœteris paribus*, to its size, we shall probably find that the preponderance in size of some portions of the brain over others is the key to varieties of talents and dispositions, which appear so conspicuously in practical life, and constitute compound moral forces. In the common phrenological works, the effects of size in the organs have been stated and illustrated, but their relations to the moral government of the world and to religion have not been fully examined; and yet this appears to me to be one of their most important aspects. In the following pages I shall introduce no new illustrations, but I shall endeavour to draw from familiar facts some inferences that appear to me to be important, and not hitherto to have received, even from Phrenologists, that serious consideration which they deserve.

The skull represented in Fig. 1 is that of an executed murderer of a low character. Fig. 2 represents a Swiss skull in which the moral and intellectual organs are largely developed, while the animal organs are of normal size.

THE EFFECTS OF PREDOMINANCE IN THE ANIMAL REGION.

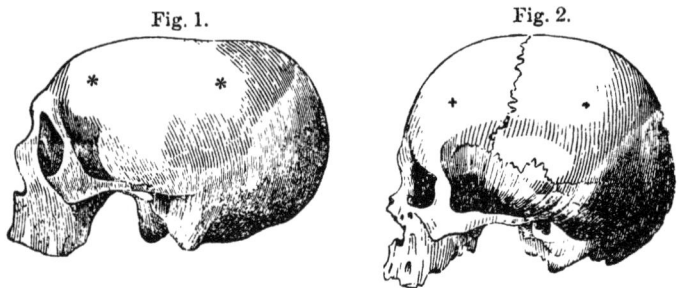

Fig. 1.   Fig. 2.

All above the asterisks belongs to the moral, and all below and behind to the animal faculties. The intellectual organs lie in the forehead.

In this world moral evil arises from abuse of some one or more of the faculties. Each has a legitimate sphere of action, within which it produces results necessary or good; but each has also a wide field in which, when unguided, it may give rise to vice, crime, and misery. The natural guiding powers are the moral sentiments and intellectual faculties; but to qualify them thoroughly for this office, they must be cultivated and instructed. We must learn the nature of the faculties themselves, their spheres of action, their relations to each other and to external objects, and the laws to which themselves and all other objects have been subjected, and on their conformity to which happiness depends. When the organs of the animal propensities are large and active, they vehemently desire gratification, and find it in sensual indulgence, intemperance, aggressive inroads on the property, persons, feelings, and rights of other men; in selfish ambition, in domineering exercises of power; and so forth. If the moral organs are deficient, men thus constituted are to a corresponding extent wanting in the natural qualities of benevolence and justice, and of respect for God and their fellow-men; and, in consequence, their lower propensities act without the control of these moral powers. If the intellectual organs are deficient, the individual is, to a corresponding extent, wanting in the power of comprehending the nature of his own mental impulses, and that of external objects; and he is blind to the relations established between them, and to the inevitable results of their action. In consequence, he approaches to the condition of an inferior animal, and yields to the urgent cravings of his propensities, regardless of consequences, and unmoved by the dictates of conscience, which in him scarcely exists.

To guide the propensities to virtue, *both* the moral and intellectual organs must be largely developed in relation to those of the propensities. If the intellectual organs be large and well cultivated, but the moral deficient, and those of the propensities large, the individual may be intellectually powerful, but unprincipled and profligate. If the moral organs be well developed, but those of the intellect deficient, and those of the propensities large, he will be constantly sinning and repenting, blundering and trying to do better, but will rarely, if left to his own guidance, be able to move steadily in the paths of wisdom and virtue.

It is an old saying, "*Video meliora proboque, deteriora sequor.*" The state of mind which it describes arises from a certain degree of deficiency of the moral and intellectual organs in relation to those of the propensities. The first and second are large enough to give a perception of the abuses of the last, but are not sufficiently developed to arrest them in their career of wickedness. Deficient Causality allows the propensities to act without restraint when the moral organs are deficient; for this faculty enables us to perceive results, and the inevitable link between the antecedent and the consequent. Aided by Cautiousness, it prompts us to bring the future vividly and strongly before us, as if it were present, and to feel and act as we should do if it were. When the organ is very deficient, there is no such power of perception of the future. The individual lives only in the present; results that are distant appear purely contingent; and hence the future is either not discerned, or seen only in a feeble and flickering light, which has little effect on the conduct. This defect is very little understood by those who have never studied Phrenology, yet it is the source of innumerable failures of men engaged in both public and private enterprises.

Here, then, is a glimpse of another important fact in the moral government of the world. We see unfolded some important primary causes of vice, crime, and misery; and in the operation of these causes we see order, fixed relations, and regular sequence,—all indications of divine appointment, and presented to us as means of instruction for the guidance of our conduct. Through ignorance of the functions of the brain, this chapter of the government of the world has hitherto remained a profound mystery. The evils referred to have been ascribed to the fall of man and the temptations of the devil; and we have been taught that God sent a series of inspired prophets to Judea to teach the remedy for them: But in these teachings there is no practical exposition of the physiological causes which are the grand roots of vice and crime, or of any physiological means for diminishing them, by improvement in the production of future human brains. In concomitance with this omission, we find these scourges of humanity everywhere abounding, and baffling the applications of clerical teaching to eradicate them. Not only so, but the doctrine that Christ endured in his own person the punishment held to be due to the possessors of these ill-balanced organs, for the abuses flowing from them, appears destitute of logical relation to the natural causes of their crimes. Gross and habitual evil-doers stand in the category of the idiotic or insane. They are the victims of an imperfectly-constituted, an ill-balanced, or an over-excited organism, placed in circumstances which appeal to its vicious proclivities; and they stand in need of guidance or humane restraint from the better constituted members of society, rather than of vindictive punishment.

During the last thirty years my attention has been directed to this subject, and I have observed the criminal brain in the prisons of most of the countries of Europe and of the United States of North America; and everywhere the type was the same. Several of the governors of the prisons had become aware of the fact, and had arrived at conclusions similar to those now stated; and in the Appendix to my System of Phrenology (vol. ii., fifth edition), I have produced evidence from a large number of highly intelligent observers to the same effect. Moreover, I have, in private life, seen ill-constituted brains work out their unhappy destiny in the present state of knowledge; and the conviction has been forced on me, that great evils and sufferings might have been avoided by recognising the hand of God in the formation of that organ. With such experience and convictions pressing on my understanding and conscience, I should not be justifiable in withholding the foregoing statements, although they may offend some readers who are not convinced of their truth.

This view of the constitution of criminals does not affect the distinction between right and wrong, which is founded on the inherent constitution of the moral and intellectual faculties. These, when strong, active, and instructed in the natural consequences of actions, intuitively condemn licentiousness, intemperance, dishonesty, arrogance, and all other abuses of the faculties; and the fact that the perpetrators of crime have ill-balanced or morbid brains, affords no reason for permitting them to continue in a career of vice and crime unchecked. On the contrary, while a knowledge of it does not diminish the desire of men with well-constituted brains to prevent and repress crime, it greatly adds to their power of doing so successfully. The great difference which a knowledge of the real causes of the evil will make, will be found in our selection of the best means to remove it. In ignorance of the causes, men have imprisoned, scourged, hanged, and decapitated evil-doers in this world, and assured them, that unless they repent, and believe that Jesus Christ died to save them from punishment in the world to come, they will be eternally miserable there. Under this mode of treatment, vice and crime have continued to afflict society. When the true causes of crime shall have been discerned by the public mind, and when the moral and religious sentiments shall have been trained to sanction the dictates of the intellect, in regard to the practical means of diminishing them, it is reasonable to hope that our posterity will act differently. Let us trust that they will also endeavour to supply, by external physical or moral restraint, that want of internal guiding power which is thus revealed to them as characterising these individuals; and also that they will try to discover, by observation and reflection, the causes which lead to the production of these ill-conditioned brains, and endeavour to induce posterity to avoid them. Indeed, until our wealth and intelligence shall be applied in conformity with the real order of God's government on earth, we shall make small progress in diminishing misery and crime; whereas, if society, penetrated with this conviction, were to concentrate its powers in effecting physical, intellectual, moral, and religious improvements in the people, as energetically as it has done in spreading desolation by war, the condition of the world might be changed to an extent at present unascertainable.

When the government of the moral world is regarded in this light, the fact of a steady reappearance of nearly the same number of offenders before the judicial tribunals every year is easily accounted for. The causes which lead to the formation of brains disposed to crime being unknown and unattended to, they continue in steady operation, and regular successions of abnormal brains are in consequence born into the world. These, not being recognised as abnormal, are permitted to develop themselves in action according to their inherent tendencies, which are towards evil; and hence, as the same number of causes are regularly acting in circumstances nearly the same, a corresponding succession of effects or offences appears to be an inevitable result.

As the object of the present work is to develop merely a general idea of the plan and means by which the moral government of the world appears to be conducted, I do not enter into farther details. In "The Constitution of Man," "Lectures on Moral Philosophy," and "Criminal Legislation," I have presented some views of the mode of treatment of criminals to which a knowledge of their nature would, in my opinion, lead; and to these I beg leave to refer.

EFFECTS WHEN BOTH THE ANIMAL AND INTELLECTUAL ORGANS ARE LARGE, AND THE MORAL ORGANS ARE SMALL.

An individual thus constituted is a compound moral power of a low, and often of a dangerous character. He is conscious of strong selfish desires, the direction of which will depend, *cæteris paribus*, on the particular organs which are largest, in relation to the others in his brain. In some individuals it may be towards sensual pleasure; in others to the accumulation, *per fas aut nefas*, of wealth; in others to achieving, by any means, social distinction and power; and each will believe the generality of mankind to be constituted like himself. He will be an unbeliever in the disinterested love of good, and view the profession of it as a mere blazon, by which to deceive. He will be ignorant of the influence of the moral emotions as social forces. His intellect will view justice as the creature of the law, and the law as founded only on expediency. He will view religion as the offspring of fear or cunning, but, nevertheless, as a useful invention to control the ignorant. He will regard charity as a virtue to be practised as much as possible in subserviency to self-interest. Persons of this class are disbelievers in the actual moral government of the world, and consider individual and national prosperity to be attainable only through the instrumentality of selfishness. If their brains are large and their temperaments active, and if, by education and social position, they attain to stations of influence and authority, they become scourges of mankind, and constitute the worst advisers of kings and the most disastrous rulers of nations. Corruption and intimidation are the forces best known to them. They plan some great scheme of aggrandisement, ostensibly for the benefit of their country, or their king, but really of themselves; and bribe individuals by money, places, and honours, to work it out by force or fraud. They crush opposition by the strong arm of power; involve their country in war, or their sovereign in contests with his subjects, and obstruct the well-being of the whole society over which their malign influence extends; and all in profound ignorance of the real character and inevitable results of the course of action they pursue. The moral as well as the selfish faculties existing in other men are outraged by the obstructions to their legitimate action, which are heaped up around them by immoral laws and unwise public measures.

At last these rulers are dethroned, displaced, or removed by death; but nations ignorant of the nature of the moral fountain from which those bitter waters have flowed, are ever ready to open a new source of suffering in a new tyrant or minister as unfavourably organised as the former. They are ignorant of the means by which God governs the moral world, are blind to the palpable characters in which He has indicated, for our guidance, the real nature of these individuals as compound moral forces; and therefore, they apply them, or allow them to apply themselves, to pursuits for which they are altogether unfit. To give authority to such instruments, in expectation that they will lead a nation through virtue to prosperity, is as preposterous as it would be to construct a smelting furnace of ice.

In a narrower field, the same results ensue from placing men with deficient moral organs, although gifted in intellect, at the head of joint-stock commercial companies. Strangers to moral principle, they pursue wealth through what appear to them to be shorter roads than honesty and industry. Some of them, through blindness to moral causation, involve their constituents in ruin without intending to do so; while others plunder them for their own advantage, without scruple or remorse. During forty years' experience and observation in active life I have never seen a sane individual in whom both the moral and intellectual organs were largely developed, devote himself to fraud.

We have lately heard many demands made, that in the public service the right men should be put in the right places; but nobody is able to indicate a sure method of discovering the right men. Lord Palmerston truly remarked in Parliament that the only criterion of *merit* is one man's opinion of another, which is often very fallacious; and he was right. But in the quality, form, and size of the brain, nature has laid the foundations of different natural dispositions and capacities; and when these are thoroughly understood, and practically attended to as fundamental elements of fitness, and when instruction and experience in the special duty to be performed, are also ascertained, it may become possible to solve the problem. The public are not yet aware of the necessity of the moral organs to the comprehension of the moral order of Providence. They believe in intellect as all-sufficient for successful public conduct: if they find a man able intellectually, they, full of hope and confidence, invest him with authority; and although disappointed, they repeat the same experiment again and again, in helpless incapacity to discover any reliable indication of natural integrity. They will be forced, in time, by sheer suffering, to look on the brain with more respect than now.

In barbarous states of society, that is, states in which the animal propensities exist in a state of habitual excitement in the majority of the community, in which the intellect and moral sentiments are less active, and still unenlightened concerning the moral relations of things, and in consequence are unable to control the propensities, an individual possessing a large brain of the form now under consideration, and an active temperament, constitutes the conqueror, tyrant, rebel, or usurper. The emperor Baber seems to have been such a man. In more civilised ages, the intellect must play a higher, and the propensities a less conspicuous part; but in this class of men, there is still the absence of moral aim. In the semi-civilised state of society, the tyrant, despot, or conqueror, no longer orders individuals obnoxious to his sway to be put summarily to death: but he brings them to trial before judges whom he bribes or forces to condemn them to capital punishment. In an enemy's country, he does not send forth his victorious legions to plunder private dwellings, murder the males and ravish the females, and to lay the fields waste; but he exhausts the substance of the conquered by enormous forced contributions, with which he maintains his army and enriches himself. In such practices, the selfish and injurious action of the propensities is clearly distinguishable as the moving power, the moral sentiments being in a state of abeyance. Men thus constituted, having a very feeble consciousness of the influence of the superior sentiments as moral forces in social life, are blind to the execration and repugnance which their conduct is exciting in the best-constituted minds, and to the fierce animal resentment which it is calling forth in men of inferior natures. They do not perceive that they are sapping the foundations of their own authority, and that sooner or later reaction will ensue. They trust in the omnipotence of force and fraud, wielded by superior intellect, and they succeed, but only for a time.

The main cause of their success, while it lasts, is the ignorance of the society which they oppress, of the nature of the moral forces by which the world is governed. Ignorant of the nature of the tyrant, of their own nature, and of the laws to which the mental faculties, as social forces, have been subjected, average men are incapable of united action from possessing no commonly recognised principles; and are trampled on singly, and suffer. The men endowed with large moral and intellectual organs, who perceive and feel the real character of the oppressing power, having no external sign by which to recognise each other, remain isolated and ignorant of their own numbers and power. They being, also, unprovided with any common theory of the human faculties, and with the means of discriminating the nature of individuals as compound moral forces,—and ignorant of the natural laws by which social and political well-being can be reached,—are incapable of forming combinations founded on moral impressions and intellectual convictions. They are, therefore, powerless; and, conscious of their feebleness, they quietly yield to the oppressing force.

In the North American Revolution, there were many individuals possessing the higher class of brains, who, having been trained to political action under British institutions, practically acquired considerable knowledge of the moral forces; and after encountering innumerable obstructions from inferior minds, they succeeded in establishing a moral national power. I speak of the cerebral organisation of these distinguished men, from observations made on original portraits and busts of them, during my visit to the United States in 1838-39-40. Had they themselves been greatly deficient in the moral organs, or had they not been trained in an arena in which these had been brought into play, they might have succeeded in achieving the *independence*, but they would not have established the civil liberty of their country. Distrust of human nature, and ignorance of the influence of the moral powers, would have led them to invent safeguards for order, which would have laid the foundations of despotism or oligarchy.

EFFECTS OF THE COMBINATION IN WHICH THE ANIMAL, MORAL, AND INTELLECTUAL REGIONS OF THE BRAIN ARE ALL LARGE AND NEARLY EQUALLY BALANCED.

In brains thus proportioned we have the three classes of mental forces all energetic: strong animal propensities, craving vehemently for indulgence; powerful moral sentiments applying restraint; and intellectual faculties capable of apprehending and acting upon the relations of things. The practical results will depend on two circumstances: 1st, Instruction and training; and, 2dly, Habitual association. As explained in the works on Phrenology, the affective faculties, whether propensities or sentiments, do not discern intellectually; they produce merely desires and emotions. Knowledge of the things related to them is acquired by the intellect, which studies both the emotional qualities and the things. If the intellect, therefore, has not been instructed and disciplined to apply its knowledge of the relations of the propensities and sentiments to outward objects, as its guide in restraining and directing them, endless aberrations from the standard of duty may ensue. In such circumstances the emotional or affective faculties will act at one time according to their internal impulses; at another, according to the solicitations presented to them by external circumstances; and at another, according to the views entertained by the intellectual faculties of what is right or wrong, expedient or inexpedient. In short, life will be a chaos of contradictory impulses and actions.

This is a very common combination of faculties, and while the individual and his instructors possess little knowledge of the functions, spheres of action, and relative strength in him of the mental faculties, and of their relations to the external world, it appears impossible for him to comprehend either the principles of God's moral government, or his own relations to it. On this class, good or evil example, and favourable or unfavourable external circumstances, produce the greatest influence, leading them to vice or virtue according to the groups of faculties which these excite. On them also the prevalent system of criminal legislation and prison discipline produces the greatest effects. The punishments inflicted by these act as deterring motives from crime, which their organism enables them to feel and appreciate; a result which is not reached in cases of the lowest grade of cerebral development. If religiously educated, they are most deeply impressed by what is called evangelical Christianity. In point of fact, that form of religion has emanated from brains like theirs; and I have observed that it is professed and upheld most earnestly and sincerely by persons whose brains belong to this class. They feel the solicitations of the propensities strongly, and also the dictates of the moral and religious sentiments, or conscience, condemning their aberrations; they are conscious of inability always to guide themselves aright, and suffer from remorse when they err; and amidst this internal darkness and confusion they find consolation in prayer, and in belief in the atonement by Jesus Christ for their sins. Some of these individuals, when ignorant, and endowed with active temperaments which give vivid spontaneous activity to the cerebral organs, mistake the solicitations of their propensities for temptations of the Devil, and emotions naturally arising from the action of the moral and religious faculties for the influence of the Holy Spirit. The cases described on pages 40, 41, 42, are merely morbid states which occur in minor degrees in many persons not insane.

Individuals possessing this equally-balanced combination of organs, when their temperament is active, and their intellectual faculties are uninstructed, constitute what, in despotic countries, are called the dangerous classes. They are conscious of mental power, and feel trammelled and degraded; but having no faith in moral force, and no knowledge of the laws of the moral government of the world, they conspire, arm, and rebel. Occasionally, when the oppressor and his instruments are weak, they succeed in overthrowing an actual government, as has happened again and again in France; but after having acquired political influence, they, through defect of moral power in themselves, and through intellectual ignorance of the natural conditions of social well-being, are incapable of wielding it beneficially. They proclaim liberty, and immediately proceed to banish, imprison, or kill those who use that liberty in opposing them. If they rule over a people who also are unacquainted with the moral forces, and ignorant of their laws, and who in consequence have no faith in them, a despotic government is inevitable; because, in such a state of things, public safety is incompatible with allowing every man to follow the dictates of his own desires and understanding. In ignorant men thus organised, the propensities are the most active powers, and these all aim at selfish objects. If every man were to pursue his own selfish gratification, irrespective of the rights and interests of his neighbours, collision would be inevitable; and in the collision of animal forces the strongest would conquer. There must therefore be provided, from some quarter or another, a guiding and restraining power. In the first French Revolution, some of the leaders appear, from their portraits published in Lamartine's History of the Girondists, to have had equally-balanced brains, while others belonged to the lowest class, and all were uninstructed in the natural conditions of social well-being. Anarchy was the speedy result of their sway, and it was speedily followed by an iron despotism.

The ruler in whose brain the moral and intellectual organs are inferior in size to those of the propensities, be he in name a republican president, a constitutional monarch, or a despotic emperor, will, if left to his own guidance, resort to force and fear as his means of government. He will address himself at once to the animal propensities of his subjects. He will gratify them to gain ends, and threaten them with pains and penalties in case of resistance to his will. Any people, therefore, which places in power over them, without restraint, brains of inferior combinations, or even brains of a medium order if ignorant of the nature of the moral forces through which the world is governed, will unquestionably reap tyranny as their reward. In rare emergencies, however, a high organisation, full of energy and confidence in itself, may exercise great moral control, for a limited time, even over an ignorant people.

In the French Revolution of 1848, Lamartine, by the fervour of his benevolent emotions and poetical eloquence, saved France and Europe from great calamities. He induced the republican government to remain at peace with foreign nations, and to abrogate the punishment of death for political offences. The large organs of Benevolence, Veneration, and Ideality, and the relatively moderate size of Combativeness and Destructiveness, combined with a considerable degree of intellect and the poetical temperament, gave Lamartine the consciousness of that moral power, and of its influence, on which he acted: and the feelings of the French people responded to it. Apparently, the organs of Conscientiousness are less developed in his brain than those now mentioned; and through this defect, and also because he was ignorant of the natural laws by which the social forces are governed, he was incapable of proceeding in the course which alone could have led to permanent success. By sanctioning acts of benevolence disowned by intellect and conscientiousness, and therefore opposed to the social laws of nature, he lost his influence and his power. He is blamed by some politicians for having disowned, on the part of France, the intention of interfering with the governments of foreign nations; and it is said that it was this announcement that gave so many of the sovereigns of Europe courage to break their solemn oaths, to recal their concessions of freedom, to re-establish despotism, and to employ religion to rivet its chains round the necks of their subjects. The experience of the bad effects which followed from an opposite course of action in the first French Revolution is the best answer to this charge. In every case sovereigns and their subjects should be left to adjust their own differences, uninfluenced by foreign interference; and then that party which possesses the greatest amount of wealth, intelligence, morality, and energy, will prevail.

Without knowledge of the nature of man, and of the natural

laws to which he is subjected, even those who possess the best form and constitution of brain are incapable of instituting and maintaining a moral government—*i. e.*, a government so free that the subjects of it shall, by the force of their own moral and intellectual faculties, aided by adequate instruction and training, be capable of restraining their own selfish propensities, and desire to pursue only such public objects as are compatible with the welfare of all. The incapacity shews itself in a distrust of moral power. They are conscious of a love of good, but they do not know *how* to pursue it, so as to rely with confidence on its being attained. Again, through the want of an index to discover the existence of the predominant qualities of other men, they find a difficulty in selecting efficient co-operators in good. In proposing reforms, therefore, they are afraid to go the whole length in trusting to the action of moral power; and in consequence, mar their best efforts by large infusions of precautionary elements addressed to the animal faculties, and calculated, as they believe, to steady political action and to secure order. In England they limit the franchise with a view to exclude the ignorant from political power, and at the same time they refuse to educate the people in order to remove this ignorance. In France, the leaders of the Revolution in 1848 enacted universal suffrage, which is the highest recognition of moral power, but without enquiring whether the people possessed knowledge and moral and religious training to fit them to exercise this power beneficially for themselves. The consequence was, that no sooner was an Assembly chosen under this suffrage, than certain portions of it commenced to act in diametrical opposition to the principle of the supremacy of moral right; and the remainder, with the nation at their back, had neither knowledge enough of the nature of that power, nor confidence enough in it, to enable them to wield it and rely on its efficacy as a safeguard to society: anarchy was avoided only by usurpation; and the usurpation was sanctioned by the majority of the people whose liberty it annihilated!

Such occurrences will continue to present themselves until the people shall be instructed in the fact, that the brain is an index of the animal, moral, and intellectual forces of men; and that it is through it chiefly that the moral government of the world is conducted. This knowledge will lead them to prepare themselves by self-improvement for freedom, and enable them to choose as their rulers men who are naturally capable of guiding them through virtue to social well-being. These rulers also must learn that the results of the action of these forces in private and social life are all regulated by divinely appointed laws, which must be studied and obeyed before individual and social prosperity and happiness can be securely reached.

EFFECTS OF THE COMBINATION IN WHICH THE MORAL AND INTELLECTUAL ORGANS ARE LARGE IN PROPORTION TO THOSE OF THE PROPENSITIES.

The effect of this combination, *cæteris paribus*, is to produce moderate impulses in the animal propensities, strong moral and religious emotions, and good intellectual powers. When aided by an active temperament, it produces the ardent practical reformer. The moral and intellectual organs are then spontaneously active, and crave for gratification, which can be found only in doing good in the fields of private and social life. Individuals thus constituted are keenly alive to the causes of evil, and desire to remove them. They are disposed to believe in a moral order of the world, and in the capability of mankind to advance in the career of virtue and happiness. They labour to remove obstacles, and to bring into action all influences that will hasten progress in well-being, virtue, and holiness. Men possessing the lowest, and also many having the middle form of brain, are disbelievers in the capacity of mankind for great improvement. They expect the future to present merely an endless recurrence of the past; and sneer at the more hopeful as enthusiasts and utopian schemers.

When a low temperament predominates, or a feeble constitution occurs in concomitance with the highest form of brain, conservative tendencies are produced. Such individuals having honestly and religiously imbibed the moral, religious, and political opinions taught to them in their youth, by authorities whom they reverenced, have little inclination, when they are old, to depart from them. The inactivity of their brains renders them incapable of forming new ideas. They love good, and fear to lose that which they possess. They, therefore, form the *vis inertiæ* of established social institutions; they cling to all that has been tried and found even tolerable, and to much that is felt to be intolerable by others, provided that it does not very painfully affect themselves. Their moral worth, sincerity and piety, give them great weight in social life and also in the councils of the nation, and it forms no small portion of the duty and labour of more active men to urge them forward. When once inured to improved institutions, they adhere to their forms and substance with equal pertinacity, and form buttresses of strength around them, until time shall have consolidated and hallowed the fabric.

As this class feels intuitively the paramount authority of the moral and religious faculties over the propensities, and desires to control and direct them to good, it becomes conscious of its need of information how to accomplish this end. In countries which profess to have received a special divine revelation, and do not recognise God's will in the constitution of nature, it betakes itself to the study of the books presented to it as sacred, and of the accredited commentaries on them, and yields itself to the guidance of the authorised expounders of these with a meek and holy reverence.

Men possessing this higher combination, however, if their brains be large and active, have the tendency to form interpretations of their sacred books which harmonise with their own mental constitution ; and when bold, energetic, and enlightened, they demur to doctrines which violently contradict their emotions and intuitive convictions. Rammohun Roy, a Brahmin of Bengal, may be cited as an example. His brain was large, even tried by the European average size, and the moral and intellectual organs predominated over those of the animal propensities. The organs of Veneration, Hope, and Wonder, however, were smaller than those of Conscientiousness and Benevolence. He was skilled in the Bengalee, Persian, Arabic, Sanscrit, Greek, Hebrew, and English languages and literature. He died at Bristol on the 27th September 1833, and the following cuts represent a cast of his head.

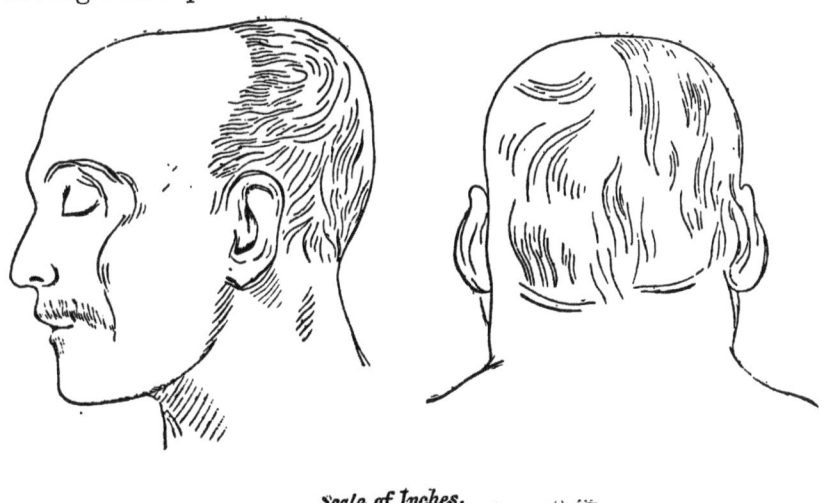

An account of his life, character, and writings, is given in the Phrenological Journal, vol. viii. p. 577, from which the following extracts are made as an example of the manner in which a person with a powerful development of the moral and intellectual organs, and only a moderate degree of Veneration, is able to surmount the prejudices of education, caste, and country, and pursue truth at the hazard of all that is dear to him. If Veneration and Wonder had predominated over Conscientiousness and Benevolence, he would have had a feeble love of truth and goodness, and been disposed to conform to his own religion, irrespective of its merits.

"The body of Hindoo theology is comprised in the Veds, which are writings of very high antiquity. On account of their great bulk, and the obscurity of the style in which they are composed, Vyas, a person of great celebrity in Hindoo literature, was induced, about 2000 years ago, to draw up a compendious abstract of the whole, accompanied with explanations of the more difficult passages. This digest he called the Vedant, or the Resolution of all the Veds. One portion of it respects the ritual, and another the principles of religion. It is written in the Sanscrit language. Rammohun Roy translated it into the Bengalee and Hindoostanee languages, for the benefit of his countrymen; and afterwards published an abridgment of it, for gratuitous and extensive distribution. Of this abridgment he published an English translation in 1816, the title of which represents the Vedant as 'the most celebrated and revered work of Brahminical theology, establishing the unity of the Supreme Being, and that he alone is the object of propitiation and worship.' Towards the close of his preface he thus writes—' My constant reflections on the inconvenient, or rather, injurious rites introduced by the peculiar practice of Hindoo idolatry, which, more than any other Pagan worship, destroys the texture of society—together with compassion for my countrymen—have compelled me to use every possible effort to awaken them from their dream of error; and by making them acquainted with the [their] scriptures, enable them to contemplate, with true devotion, the unity and omnipresence of nature's God.' * * *

"After the publication of the Vedant, Rammohun Roy printed, in Bengalee and in English, some of the principal chapters of the Veds. The first of the series was published in 1816, and is entitled 'A Translation of the Cena Upanishad, one of the Chapters of the Sama Veda, according to the gloss of the celebrated Shancaracharya; establishing the Unity and sole Omnipotence of the Supreme Being, and that He alone is the object of worship.' This was prefixed to a reprint of the Abridgment of the Vedant, published in London in 1817, by Mr Digby. The English preface contains a letter from Rammohun Roy to this gentleman, in which he says—' The consesequence of my long and uninterrupted researches into religious truth, has been, that I have found the doctrines of Christ more conducive to moral principles, and better adapted for the use of rational beings, than any other which have come to my knowledge; and have also found Hindoos in general more superstitious and miserable, both in performance of their religious rites, and in their domestic concerns, than the rest of the known nations of the earth.' He then proceeds to state what he had done in order to render them 'more happy and comfortable both here and hereafter;' and adds, 'I, however, in the beginning of my pursuits, met with great opposition from their self-interested leaders the Brahmins, and was deserted by my nearest relations; and I consequently felt extremely melancholy. In that critical situation, the only comfort that I had, was the consoling and rational conversation of my European friends, especially those of Scotland and England.'"

"His head and history concur in shewing, that intellect, justice, and independence, had with him complete control over the sentiment of Veneration. As soon as he began to think, he intuitively perceived the absurdity of the dogmas taught by the Brahmin priests. He seems never to have venerated except in accordance with Intellect and Conscientiousness. The whole tendency of his mind was opposite to superstition. Wonder, the feeling which, when excessive, leads mankind to gloat upon, and swallow with peculiar avidity, the marvellous, the occult, the supernatural, and the astonishing,—and so tends to produce credulity,—had here but little sway. The mysterious and unintelligible had no charms for him: he submitted everything to the test of consistency and reason. His great aim was to deliver his countrymen from the degrading idolatry in which they were engulphed, and to establish among them the belief of a Great Supreme. He was no friend of ceremonies in the worship of God. With him, adoration implied only 'the elevation of the mind to the conviction of the existence of the Omnipotent Deity, as testified by His wise and wonderful works, and continual contemplation of His power as so displayed; together with a constant sense of the gratitude which we naturally owe Him, for our existence, sensation, and comfort.' He had no tendency to believe in miraculous interpositions of the Deity, where his judgment did not perceive sufficient occasion for them; and it even appears that he did not credit the miraculous origin of Christianity. His views respecting miracles are pretty obvious from a passage in the Second Appeal (p. 225). 'If all assertions,' he says, 'were to be indiscriminately admitted as facts, merely because they are testified by numbers, how can we dispute the truth of those miracles which are said to have been performed by persons esteemed holy among natives of this country (India) ? The very same argument, pursued by the Editor (of the 'Friend of India'), would equally avail the Hindoos. Have they not accounts and records handed down to them, relating to the wonderful miracles stated to have been performed by their saints, such as Ugustyu, Vushistu, and Gotum ; and their gods incarnate, such as Ram, Krishnu, and Nursingh ; in presence of their contemporary friends and enemies, the wise and the ignorant, the select and the multitude ? Could not the Hindoos quote, in support of tneir narrated miracles, authorities from the histories of their most inveterate enemies the Jeins, who join the Hindoos entirely in acknowledging the truth and credibility of their miraculous accounts ?' 'Moosulmans, on the other hand, can produce records written and testified by contemporaries of Mohummed, both friends and enemies, who are represented as eye-witnesses of the miracles ascribed to him ; such as his dividing the moon into two parts, and walking in sunshine without casting a shadow. They assert, too, that several of those witnesses suffered the greatest calamities, and some even death, in defence of that religion ; some before the attempts of Mohummed at conquest, others after his commencing such attempts, and others after his death.'" * * *

"The Rajah's published works," it is remarked, "state not what be believed, but what he considered the sacred books of different persuasions to inculcate ; for example, he maintained that the most ancient Hindoo works taught pure theism ; and that the Christian Scriptures, both Old and New Testament, taught the leading doctrines of the Unitarians." It is proper to mention, however, that two conflicting accounts were given of his latest opinions (expressed when in bad health at Bristol, and shortly before his death), on the Divine authority of Christ and the reality of his miracles—the one reporting that he acknowledged, and the other that he denied these; but it does not conclusively appear which was correct. See *Phrenological Journal*, vol. viii. p. 594, and vol. ix. pp. 96, 232.

As already mentioned, the sterner views of God's character and government, which prevail in the standards of certain sects, emanated from the lower propensities acting in combination with Veneration and Intellect ; while from the higher class of brains spring Unitarianism, Universalism, and all other doctrines in which the attempt is made to embody the dictates of Benevolence, Veneration, Conscientiousness, Comparison, and Causality, in forms of religious belief. We have observed, that in Rammohun Roy's brain, the organs of Benevolence and Conscientiousness were larger than those of Veneration; and "it was with him a favourite maxim, and one which he wished to be inscribed on his tomb, that 'THE TRUE WAY OF SERVING GOD IS TO DO GOOD TO MAN.'"

Hitherto, however, even the highest class has laboured under the disadvantage of ignorance of the means by which God conducts the moral government of the world. It entertains an intuitive impression, rather than a clear intellectual conviction, that He does govern it; but *how*, is to it a mystery. In consequence, numerous, and often contradictory, schemes for improving the world, are constantly emanating from it. None of these meet with general approval; but some are supported by so large and influential a body of the rich as to obtain a trial. Partial good is achieved, but there are many short-comings from what was expected, and many disappointments. Missionary labours, Church-extension Schemes, Bible Societies, Temperance Societies, Sabbath-observance Societies, Prison Discipline Societies, Industrial School Societies, and innumerable charitable institutions for alleviating human suffering, are the offspring of the high moral and religious aspirations of this class, and of many individuals of the second class whom they induce by precept and example to join them. Their guides are their sacred books and common sense, which last means the dictates of their own faculties, illuminated by such knowledge and experience as they have reached. From this class also emanate those political reformers who are sincere lovers of their country, and not mere partisans trading in politics for the sake of power and profit.

The grand step which this class require to take to become capable of realizing their own aspirations, is to open their eyes to the order of God's Providence as revealed in organic beings and inorganic objects, and their mutual relations. They must view the brain as a congeries of moral forces, the action of which constitutes individual and social mental life. They must learn that each of these stands in definite relations to the others and to external objects, and that the good or evil which each is capable of performing is limited by the size and condition of its own organ, and by these relations. They must undertake the serious study of these moral forces, and the laws which determine the results of their action, whether for good or evil; and form their own arrangements upon this knowledge. Then they may expect to perceive that order in the moral world which actually exists, but which cannot be discerned until its elements be comprehended. At present, not only are schemes for human improvement devised by this class in comparative ignorance of the order of the physical and moral worlds, but individuals are frequently selected to execute them, who, from some peculiarity of cerebral combination, or defective or false information, are incapable of doing them justice. If they were instructed in these points, their powers of combination and action for beneficent objects would be greatly increased. In the first place, they would know and recognise each other, and escape the evil of admitting to their counsels men of inferior organization, who are often fertile in schemes, confident in their own wisdom, and ardent in action, but, nevertheless, morally and intellectually incapable of discerning the line of conduct which the Ruler of the world has prescribed as that alone by which well-being can be reached. Secondly, they would have a stable basis in nature on which to ground their practical schemes. This would greatly promote agreement in the pursuit, and success in the results of their beneficent objects. Thirdly, their principles and action being supported by the order of nature, the class would exert a moral power of arresting evil and achieving good, of which—while their minds continue in a state of comparative moral and religious chaos—no adequate conception can be formed.

We have hitherto considered compound mental forces in classes, and adverted to general results. Let us now select individual instances, and trace the effects of special combinations of these forces as they occur in individuals.

EFFECTS OF SPECIAL COMBINATIONS OF THE MENTAL FORCES AS THEY OCCUR IN INDIVIDUALS.

In Mr Samuel Bailey's "Essays on the Formation and Publication of Opinions, and other Subjects," the second edition of which was published in 1826, there is one, the Sixth, "On some of the Causes and Consequences of Individual Character," in which the author (apparently not altogether unacquainted with the functions of the brain) anticipates to some extent the views presented in this work, but without attempting to solve any of the problems which he states.

He observes, that "Whatever subsequent circumstances may effect, it can scarcely be questioned that all human beings come into the world with the germs of peculiar mental as well as physical qualities. Attempts, indeed, have been made to resolve all mental varieties into the effects of dissimilar external circumstances, but with too little success to require any formal refutation. We are, then, naturally led to inquire, how are these original peculiarities occasioned? whence arise those qualities of mind which constitute the individuality of men? There must be causes why the mind as well as the body of one man differs constitutionally from that of another: what are they? Perhaps all that can be said in reply to these inquiries is, that the mental, like the bodily constitution of every individual, depends, in some inexplicable way, on the conjoint qualities of his parents. It depends, evidently, not on the qualities of one of the parents only, but on those of both. A moment's reflection will teach us, that the individuality of any human being that ever existed was absolutely dependent on the union of one particular man with one particular woman. If either the husband or the wife had been different, a different being would have come into the world. For the production of the individual called Shakespeare, it was necessary that his father should marry the identical woman whom he did marry. Had he selected any other wife, the world would have had no Shakespeare. He might have had a son, but that son would have been an essentially different individual; he would have been the same neither in mental nor physical qualities; he would have been placed in a different position amongst mankind, and subject to the operation of different circumstances. It seems highly probable also, that if a marriage had taken place between the same male and female, either at an earlier or a later period of their lives, the age at which they came together would have affected the identity of the progeny. If they had been married, for instance, in the year 1810, their eldest son would not be the same being as if they had been married ten years sooner. It may be remarked, too, that not only the time at which persons are married, but their mode of living, and their habits generally, as they have the power to affect the physical constitution of their progeny, may also affect the constitution of their minds, and occasion beings to be brought into the world absolutely different from those who would have seen the light under other circumstances.

" With regard to physical conformation, every one knows that the face and figure are frequently transmitted from parents to their offspring. Sometimes the father's form and lineaments seem to predominate, sometimes the mother's, and sometimes there is a variety produced unlike either of the parents; but by what principles these proportions and modifications are regulated, it is impossible to ascertain. The transmission of mental qualities is not, perhaps, equally apparent, but it is equally capricious. In some cases we see the characteristics of the parents perpetuated in their offspring, and in other cases no resemblance is to be discovered."

Mr Bailey continues: "We have already intimated, that both the mental and physical constitution seem to depend on the united qualities of both the parents; not solely, however, for we every day see phenomena, both of mind and body, which we can refer only to inexplicable accidents. Such are idiotism and malorganization."

* * * * * * *

These anomalies are apparent only, and seem such owing to our ignorance of the causes which produce the phenomena. Several of the causes have been discovered, more or less completely, since Mr Bailey wrote.*

"These cursory observations naturally lead us to reflect on the long chain of consequences of which the marriage of two persons may be the first link, and what an important influence such an union may have on human affairs. If two men and two women founded a colony, by removing to some uninhabited district or island, where they were cut off from all intercourse with the rest of their species, the whole train of subsequent events in that colony to the end of time would depend on the manner in which they paired. If the older man married the older woman, a different train of affairs, it is manifest, would ensue from that which would take place if the older man married the younger woman. In the first case the offspring of the marriage would be totally different individuals from those which would have been brought into the world in the second case. They would think, feel, and act in a widely different manner, and not a single event depending on human action would be precisely the same as any event in the other case.

"As a farther illustration, it may not be devoid of amusement to trace the consequences which would have ensued, or rather, which would have been prevented, had the father of some eminent character formed a different matrimonial connection. Suppose the father of Bonaparte had married any other lady than the one who was actually destined to become his mother. Agreeably to the tenor of the preceding observations, it is obvious that Bonaparte himself would not have appeared in the world. The affairs of France would have fallen into different hands, and have been conducted in another manner. The measures of the British cabinet,—the debates in Parliament,—the subsidies to foreign powers,—the battles by sea and land,—the marches and countermarches,—the

---

* Several years ago, Dr Howe and other Commissioners presented to the Legislature of Massachusetts an instructive Report on the Causes of Idiotism, on which the Legislature acted; and in *Fraser's Magazine* for August and September 1856, two articles appeared, attempting to elucidate the physiological conditions of the human **organism** in which Dwarfs and Giants are produced. They shew talent, observation, and a just appreciation of the relation of physiology to the solution of such questions.

wounds, deaths, and promotions,—the fears, and hopes, and anxieties of a thousand individuals,—would all have been different. The speculations of those writers and speakers who employed themselves in discussing these various subjects, and canvassing the conduct of this celebrated man, would not have been called forth. The train of ideas in every mind interested in public affairs would not have been the same. Pitt would not have made the same speeches, nor Fox the same replies. Lord Byron's poetry would have wanted some splendid passages. The Duke of Wellington might have still been plain Arthur Wellesley. Mr Warden would not have written his book, nor the Edinburgh critic his review of it; nor could the author of this essay have availed himself of his present illustration. The imagination of the reader will easily carry him through all the various consequences to soldiers and sailors, tradesmen and artisans, printers and booksellers, downward through every gradation of society. In a word, when we take into account these various consequences, and the thousand ways in which the mere intelligence of Bonaparte's proceedings, and of the measures pursued to counteract them, influenced the feelings, the speech, and the actions of mankind, it is scarcely too much to say, that the single circumstance of Bonaparte's father marrying as he did has more or less affected almost every individual in Europe, as well as a numerous multitude in the other quarters of the globe.

"We see from the preceding glance what an important share an individual may have in modifying the course of events, and how his influence may extend, in some way or other, through the minutest ramifications of society. Yet amidst all this influence we may also perceive the operation of general causes; of those principles of the mind common to all individuals, and of the physical circumstances by which they are surrounded. The individual character itself, indeed, partly receives its tone and properties from general causes, and much of the reaction which it exerts may be, in an indirect sense, ascribed to them." * * *

"The remark may be extended, with still more certainty, to almost all the arts and sciences. Composed as their history necessarily is of the achievements of individuals, their advancement is the result of general causes, and independent, in a certain sense, on individual character. The inventions of printing and gunpowder, the discovery of the virtues of the loadstone, and even the inductive logic of Bacon, were sure to mark the progress of human affairs, and were not owing to the mere personal qualities, nor necessarily bound to the destiny, of those who promulgated them to the world. The discoveries of modern astronomy would, doubtless, have been ultimately attained, although such a person as Sir Isaac Newton had never seen the light; but they would not have been attained in the same way, nor, perhaps, at the same period. The science, it is probable, would have been extremely dissimilar in the detail, in the rapidity of its progress, and the order of its discoveries, while there is every reason to think it would have been much the same in its final result."

These observations have been published for thirty years, and contain the elements of important practical truths; yet none of the existing systems of Psychology enables us to explain the phenomena described, or to modify them to any useful purpose. And why is this the case? Because they all depend on physiological causes, and these have never been investigated with a view to the solution of such problems. It appears to me that physiology, and particularly that of the brain, may in time enable us to render specific the ideas which are here so distinctly stated as general propositions, and that, by this means, we may become capable also of rendering them practical. If, through physiology, we shall attain correct knowledge of the specific mental forces with which any individual is endowed, we shall be qualified to judge what duties he is capable of discharging, and what place in society he is calculated to fill with the greatest success. For example:—In the Phrenological Museum there is a cast of the face and forehead of Napoleon Bonaparte, taken after death; and it indicates the greatest length in the anterior lobe of the brain which I have seen, with considerable height and breadth—a combination conferring great intellectual power. If the cast had embraced the whole head, knowing his temperament, and education, and circumstances as we do, we should have been able to discover the extent and relative proportions of his extraordinary powers, and also of those moral defects which constituted him such a stupendous, yet unsuccessful, actor in European history. Let us take another example, and see whether we can throw any light on the character of

ROBERT BURNS.

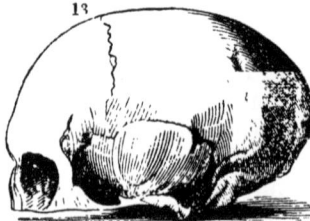

There is an authentic cast of the skull of Robert Burns in the Phrenological Museum. The region of the propensities is large, particularly in Amativeness, Philoprogenitiveness, Combativeness, and Destructiveness. The moral region, including Ideality, is large, and the Intellectual region is large;

but although Causality is not deficient, the knowing organs, with those of Eventuality and Comparison, predominate over it. The temperament was bilious-nervous, and extremely active. Burns was educated in Calvinistic theology, in reading, writing, and accounts, and bred to the plough. He had no index to his own nature except his own consciousness, and none to that of other men except his powers of observation. He had no instruction in the laws of the moral government of the world, beyond those which he could deduce from experience, from empirical observations of human conduct, and from the Bible and other books. When we know the elements of his mental character; and their relative strength, and his external circumstances, the forces which impelled him to action stand revealed before us. The same intensity of cerebral activity which, when pervading the observing intellectual organs, gave rise to his exquisite descriptions of men and things, and which, when pervading Ideality, Benevolence, Amativeness, Philoprogenitiveness, Adhesiveness, and Conscientiousness, sent forth those thrilling strains of love, tenderness, and attachment, which have stirred so many readers with a kindred sympathy, pervaded the organs of all his animal propensities. From Amativeness, thus excited, when uncontrolled by the moral organs, proceeded the licentiousness which stained his conduct; and from Combativeness and Destructiveness, similarly affected, flowed that coarseness and fierceness which occasionally break forth in his strains. When better directed, this combination gave him his satirical power. His comparatively moderate Causality set limits to his intellectual grasp, and he never executed comprehensive works like that of Dante or Milton.

Men possessing only ordinary cerebral activity, experience great difficulty in comprehending how, with so much truth, beauty, true affection, and high-toned principle in his mind, Burns could be licentious, intemperate and coarse, as he occasionally was. But such persons do not understand the nature of men like him. Genius is the result of fine quality and intense activity in the brain. The size of this organ determines its vigour, and the predominance of particular parts gives its peculiar sphere of action. In the case of Burns, large size in the organs of the propensities, combined with an intensely active temperament, solves the problem of the contradictions in his character. The quality which constituted his genius, pervaded the organs of the propensities, and they, too, from their great size, acted with the energy and intensity of genius. His inherited religious creed grated against his moral sentiments; his intellect in vain laboured to reconcile them to it. This discord roused his propensities, and under the impulse of both his higher and his lower emotions he cast it aside, and fell back upon natural religion, the power of which he strongly felt. His aspirations after a better order of things were strong and ardent; but his knowledge of *how* it could be attained being defective, he could contribute little practically towards introducing it. If there be any truth in the views which I am now endeavouring to unfold, and he had been trained to understand them, and the natural laws to which he was subjected, and also of the effects of the circumstances in which he was placed, all before his propensities had been kindled into a devouring flame, he might have enjoyed a greater command over his own nature. Even in this case, however, he would still have had their fierce internal solicitations to contend with; but it is probable that, especially if aided by friendly restraint and social opinion, his genius might have penetrated into the order of Providence, followed it in action, and consecrated it in eloquence and song. In such circumstances, his course of action might have been widely different from what it actually was. Not only so, but had Dugald Stewart and the other benevolent and influential men, who for a brief space caressed Burns at the commencement of his career, comprehended his nature as we now do, and viewed the effect of circumstances upon it, how differently might not their kind feelings towards him have been directed! Burns, in his Bard's Epitaph, has left behind him a remarkably correct and touching appreciation of his own character, learned by himself, however, only after a career of blended sin and suffering, and of virtue and enjoyment. But Dugald Stewart had not even a glimpse of what genius is. He informs us that "what we call the power of Imagination, is *not the gift of nature*, but the result of acquired habits, aided by favourable circumstances." Common observation informs us, that musical talent, and a genius for poetry and painting, are gifts of nature, bestowed only on a few; but Mr Stewart, by dint of his philosophy, discovered that these powers, and also a genius for mathematics, "are gradually formed by particular habits of study or of business." How could a mind entertaining such views comprehend Burns? Assuredly, knowledge of the functions of the brain will expunge such notions from philosophy, and enable future leaders of public opinion better to appreciate the young.*

---

* Lord Cockburn's Memorials of his Own Times shew how great an influence Dugald Stewart exercised over the students who subsequently became the leading men of the last generation in Edinburgh; and the omission from his lectures and publications on Mental Philosophy of all practical reference to the connection of the organism with the

Brains like those of Burns, become fountains of emotions and ideas which they impress on other men, and as such they constitute a part of the machinery by means of which the moral government of the world is conducted. In this view sound knowledge of the real qualities of such men, and of the natural laws to which their action is subject, and of the consequences which they are capable of producing, becomes important. As they are self-acting conscious forces, it is desirable also that they should be instructed and trained to direct and regulate their own powers. By delivering them from empirical views of themselves and the world, and the dominion of unregulated impulses, and by enlightening their whole minds with a knowledge of God's laws and their consequences, their beneficial influence might be greatly augmented.

Sir Walter Scott was another important mental phenomenon; and yet so inveterate, in his circle, was the prejudice against Phrenology, that, so far as is generally known, no authentic cast of his head, skull, or brain was taken. His brain was examined after death, but no scientific report on it was published. Sir John Watson Gordon, however, told me that his head was three-quarters of an inch higher than any head he had ever painted. Is such a fact of no importance, if the brain be the medium through which God governs the world of mind?

[NOTE.—While this work is in the press, an event has occurred near Edinburgh which has excited deep regret and sympathy in the public mind; namely, THE DEATH OF MR HUGH MILLER. The circumstances in which it occurred afford such a striking illustration of the practical bearing of the principles expounded in these pages, that I am induced briefly to advert to them.

Mr Hugh Miller, originally an operative mason, educated himself, acquired an admirable command of the English language, distinguished himself as a scientific geologist, and became the Editor of the *Witness* Newspaper, published in Edinburgh as the organ of the Free Church. The details which follow appeared in that paper of the 27th of December 1856, in an article avowedly from the pen of the biographer of the late Dr Chalmers. This writer expresses it as " his own judgment, and the judgment of the vast body of his Church, that, next to the writings and actings of Dr Chalmers, the leading articles of Mr Miller in this journal [the *Witness*] did more

mental faculties, helps to account for their blindness and aversion to Gall's discovery of the functions of the brain.

than any thing else to give the Free Church the place it holds in the affections of so many of our fellow countrymen."

For some time Mr Miller had ceased to take any active part in ecclesiastical affairs. " The great work, as it now seems to us, which it was given him on earth to do,"—was—" to illustrate the perfect harmony of all that science tells us of the physical history and structure of our globe, with all that the Bible tells us of the creation *and government of this earth* by and through Jesus Christ our Lord."

We are told, "that he wrought at a work, entitled *The Testimony of the Rocks*, too eagerly. Hours after midnight the light was seen to glimmer through the window of that room which, within the same eventful week, was to witness the close of the volume, and the close of the writer's life. This overworking of the brain began to tell upon his mental health." He said to his medical adviser, " My brain is giving way; I cannot put two thoughts together to-day : I have had a dreadful night of it."—" On rising, I felt as if a stiletto was suddenly, and as quickly as an electric shock, passed through my brain from front to back, and left a burning sensation on the top of the brain, just below the bone."

He wrote this most touching valedictory letter to his wife, and then shot himself dead:—" Dearest Lydia,—My brain burns. I *must* have *walked ;* and a fearful dream arises upon me. I cannot bear the horrible thought. God and Father of the Lord Jesus Christ have mercy upon me. Dearest Lydia, dear children, farewell. My brain burns as the recollection grows. My dear, dear wife, farewell. HUGH MILLER."

Four medical men examined the body, and their report bears: " The cause of death we found to be a pistol-shot through the left side of the chest ; and this, we are satisfied, was inflicted by his own hand. From the diseased appearances found in the brain, taken in connection with the history of the case, we have no doubt that the act was suicidal, under the impulse of insanity."

The " diseased appearances found in the brain" could not arise in a day—they must have been the result of long-continued disregard of the conditions of health, established by the laws of Divine Wisdom. "Miller," says a writer in the *Spectator* of 3d Jan. 1857, " broke down because he was disobeying the laws of the creation in which he lived. He was concentrating the whole force of his nature in one pursuit, and suffering himself to be carried away by the excitement into which he had worked himself. He was necessarily arrested. It is imperative that the laws of the creation be obeyed ; it is *not* imperative that they be 'understood.' Man, indeed, may, for his own benefit, work out a better intellectual comprehension of the laws under which he lives, but he must do it consistently with obedience. He cannot snatch a further revelation, nor will Nature permit excess, even when the object of the excess is laudable or pious. Whether understood or not in the critical sense, the law goes on relentless, and all who stand across its path are mowed down." In this respect, Nature makes no distinction between those who are ignorant, even though not culpably so, and a man such as this—of earnest and undoubted piety, great intellect, and high scientific and literary acquirements, devoted to what he and his Church considered to be an exposition of one department of the Divine " government of this earth." Of the soundness of his belief in the dogmas of the Calvinistic faith there cannot be a question, for he spent his vigour in defending them; but, apparently, his religious emotions had not been trained to recognise *nature as sacred*—that very nature which he explored with a view to maintain the authority of the Bible: and especially he appears to have had no perception that the human organism is sacred; that in the " government of this earth," its laws are the laws of God; that ignorance of them in a man of his talent, and with his opportunities of instruction, was culpable; or that, if he knew them, disregard of them was practical irreverence towards their Divine Author. Is it probable that a man of Hugh Miller's deep religious feeling, large intellect, and powerful will, could have persevered for years in such a course of action, if he had been trained to regard it as an open violation of the will of God, fraught with destruction to his own life, and with such a legacy of sorrow to his wife and children? It is difficult to believe it; and I can account for his conduct only by the fact, that in the religious education of our youth nature is *not represented as sacred*, and we are not taught to obey its requirements as religious duties.

This case affords a striking and painful illustration of the remarks made on page 91.

His reverend biographer sums up the account of his life and death in the following words:—" His very intellect, his reason, —God's most precious gift,—a gift dearer than life,—perished in the great endeavour to harmonize the works and word of the Eternal. *A most inscrutable event, that such an intellect should have been suffered to go to wreck through too eager a prosecution of such a work!*" Does this mean " suffered" by God? And if so, are we to regard it *as a mystery*, why, because God did not interfere specially to avert the consequences which HE had appointed to follow from overaction of the brain? Hugh Miller was engaged in an attempt to reconcile the records of nature with the Calvinistic interpretations of Scripture. Surely, our religious men stand in need of more light than such writing indicates, to enable them to interpret correctly the ways of Providence, and to lead their flocks to reverence the Divine Institutions.]

SECTION VII.—OF NATIONS CONSIDERED AS MORAL FORCES.*

A nation is composed of individuals, each of whom, in all circumstances, preserves his personality; yet they are capable of feeling, thinking, and acting, as an aggregate power, and the history of the human race is chiefly a narrative of their evolutions. When we regard the different quarters of the globe, we are struck with the extreme dissimilarity in the attainments of the varieties of men who inhabit them. In the history of Europe, Asia, Africa, and America, we shall find distinct and permanent features of mental character, which strongly indicate natural differences. The inhabitants of Europe, belonging to the Caucasian variety of mankind, have manifested, in all ages, a tendency towards moral and intellectual improvement. As far back as history reaches, we find society instituted, arts practised, and literature taking root, not only in intervals of tranquillity, but amidst the alarms of war. When, on the other hand, we turn our attention to Asia, we perceive manners and institutions which belong to a period too remote to be ascertained, yet far inferior to the European. The people of Asia early arrived at a point comparatively low in the scale of improvement, beyond which they have never passed.

The history of Africa, so far as Africa can be said to have a history, presents similar phenomena. The annals of the races who have inhabited that continent, with few exceptions, exhibit one unbroken scene of moral and intellectual desolation. Dr Fergusson has recently described a superior variety of negroes inhabiting the interior of Africa, hitherto unknown to Europeans, but even they are still far below the European standard of civilisation.

The aspect of America is still more deplorable than that of Africa. Surrounded for centuries by European knowledge, enterprise, and energy, and incited to improvement by the example of European institutions, many of the natives of that continent remain, at the present time, the same miserable,

* I beg to refer the reader to the System of Phrenology, vol ii. p. 327, "On the coincidence between the natural talents and dispositions of Nations, and the development of their Brains," and to the works there cited.

wandering, houseless, and lawless savages as their ancestors were, when Columbus first set foot upon their soil. Partial exceptions to this description may be found in some of the southern districts of North America; but the numbers who have adopted the modes of civilised life are so small, and the progress made by them is so limited, that, speaking of the race, we do not exaggerate in saying, that they remain to the present hour enveloped in all their primitive barbarity, and that they have profited little by the introduction into the new continent, of arts, sciences, and philosophy. Nay, they have to a great extent perished, and are now melting away under the influence of the vices which they have adopted, although they have rarely imbibed the virtues of their European invaders.

The theory usually advanced to account for these differences of national character is, that they are produced by diversities of soil and climate. But, although these may reasonably be supposed to exert a certain influence, they are altogether inadequate to explain the whole phenomena. If we survey the world, we shall find nations whose soil is fertile and climate temperate, in a lower degree of improvement than others who are less favoured. In Van Diemen's Land and New South Wales a few natives have existed in the most wretched poverty, ignorance, and degradation, in a country which enriches Europeans as fast as they subject it to cultivation. In America, too, Europeans and native Indians have lived for centuries under the influence of the same physical causes; the former have kept pace in their advances with their brethren in the Old Continent, while the latter, as we have seen, remain stationary in savage ignorance and indolence.

These differences between nations living under similar climates, are commonly attributed to differences in their religious and political institutions. Presbytery and parish schools, for example, are supposed to have rendered the Scotchman habitually attentive to his own interest, but cautious, thoughtful, and honest ; while Popery and Catholic priests have made the Irishman free and generous, but precipitate and unreflecting withal,—ready in the gust of passion to sacrifice his friend, and in the glow of friendship to immolate himself. It is forgotten that there were ages in which Popery and priests had equal ascendency in both of the British isles, and that then the Englishman, Irishman, and Scotchman, were as specifically different as at present : Besides, the more correct, as well as the profounder view, is to regard religious and political institutions, when not forced upon a people by external conquest, as the spontaneous growth of their natural

L

propensities, sentiments, and intellectual faculties ; for hierarchies and constitutions do not spring from the ground, but from the minds of men.

The phrenologist is not satisfied with these common theories of national character : he has observed that a particular form of brain is the invariable concomitant of particular dispositions and talents, and that this fact holds good in the case of nations as well as of individuals. If the fact be so, a knowledge of the size of the brain and of its different parts, in the varieties of the human race, will be the key to a correct appreciation of the differences in their natural mental endowments, on which external circumstances act only as modifying influences. " In order," says Dr Gall, " to discover the general character, it is necessary to study a great number of individuals,—entire regiments,—the whole nation so far as possible. With such facilities, it will be easy for the organologist to discover in the structure of the head, the material cause of the peculiar character of the people."

Theological authors have dwelt largely on the agency of Divine Providence as manifested in historical events ; but one and all of them have written in ignorance of the influence of the brain in conferring particular mental dispositions and capacities on the individuals whose aggregate numbers constituted nations, and consequently in ignorance of the chief instrumentality through which the events contemplated were produced. In this department, the order of Providence appears to them almost inexplicable. Whole races of men seem to have inhabited fertile regions of the earth from time immemorial, without developing even the rudiments of civilisation, and have disappeared and become extinct before other races endowed with higher energies and capacities. The size and form of the brain in the contrasted races, shew at least the instrumentality by means of which these results have been brought to pass. Of the origin of the lower and higher races, or, if both proceeded from one stock, of the causes which produced the differences of cerebral size and form, by means of which their fate was accomplished, we possess no certain knowledge ; but the great fact stands revealed before us, that in the action of Providence the condition of the brain, *cæteris paribus*, determines the condition of nations as of individuals. This assertion will be found to be supported by irrefragable evidence, whenever the crania of the native New Hollanders, North American Indians, and other tribes which have perished, or are receding before the European races, are compared with the crania of their invaders.

The power which different races of men possess of working

out political institutions, and of reaching social results, is bounded by the limits of their development of brain. Within these boundaries, important improvements, by education and training, and by political institutions, may be practicable; but before proper means of advancement can be judiciously introduced, it is as necessary to discover the qualities of the men with whom we are dealing, as it is to know the nature of the soil which we mean to cultivate, or of the horses which we mean to train and employ in agricultural undertakings.

Where the development and condition of the brain is highest, there *natural* moral and intellectual capacity is greatest for receiving training and instruction, and also for originating or adopting such moral and political institutions as will produce the greatest amount of individual and social elevation and prosperity. The rulers of nations, and political writers in general, have hitherto *ignored* this fact. In Europe they have legislated and created institutions as if all the races were alike in their native capacities. They have recognised differences in degrees of cultivation, but not differences in capacity for receiving and applying knowledge. The individuals who have led the French nation after each successive revolution, have signally disregarded equally the native capacities and the acquired attainments of the people. The first revolutionists assumed the existence of morality and intelligence in the whole body of the people, sufficient to lead them to freedom, virtue, and prosperity, by the exercise of their own inclinations and judgment. Anarchy and material ruin were the results. Napoleon, Louis XVIII., Charles X., and Louis-Philippe, treated them in some degree as overgrown children, incapable of self-government, and ruled them,—Napoleon with a rod of iron, Louis XVIII. and Charles X. by force and superstition, and Louis-Philippe by corruption; and all failed. Once more the leaders of the Revolution of 1848 assumed the masses of the French people to be the wisest and the best of men; and placed the lives, property, religion, and liberty of the entire nation at their disposal by universal suffrage. Ledru Rollin actually recommended ignorance as a qualification, and relied on native sense and practical experience as all-sufficient qualifications for legislators. How signally this mode of government failed, and what has followed it, need not here be told.

England boasts of its practical character; but here the French far surpass us. They try practical experiments of the most gigantic magnitude. But why are their schemes so diverse in character, and so uniform in failure? The phenomena must result from *causes* which the leaders of the French people have never stopped to investigate, or been capable of comprehending. The fact is, that their political action has been purely empirical; but empirical practice leads to truth only by one process,—that of exhausting errors. As it is based on no adequate consideration of causes, it is constantly leading to disappointment in its anticipated results. When experiments of this nature are tried with the lives and property of thirty-five millions of people, the game becomes appalling. Yet this is the age of empiricism, especially in moral and political movements. It is voted to be an abstraction, a dream, and a bore, to inquire into the natural qualities and aptitude of men to wield institutions, or to act out particular duties imposed on them by legislation. But, nevertheless, the native qualities exist, whether we ignore them or not; they are the real causes which determine the results of the institutions and legislation, however firmly we may close our eyes to their influence; and it is only by knowing them that our experience can become instructive and profitable for our future guidance.*

Napoleon, Duclos, and other able men, have correctly discri-

* I have presented, in the System of Phrenology, vol. ii. p. 327, 5th Edition, remarks on the development of the brain, and the characteristic mental qualities which occur in several of the best known varieties of mankind, to which I beg leave to refer. The skulls are open to public inspection in the Phrenological Museum, Edinburgh. The facts adduced have hitherto excited no general interest, and they will continue to be neglected or undervalued until the public mind shall awaken to a conviction that God instituted the brain and its functions, and that in its varieties of size and form, His wisdom is addressing us for our instruction regarding the order of His moral government of the world. I have assisted in digging up the skulls of North American Indians, buried before an Englishman had set his foot on the Western Continent; I have examined the large collection of native American skulls, specimens of which are represented with exquisite fidelity in Dr Morton's *Crania Americana*, and I was present at many deliberations and experiments instituted by him and Mr Phillips how best to measure the relative proportions of their different regions; I have repeatedly visited the three home divisions of the British Empire; also France, Belgium, Holland, Germany, Switzerland, Bohemia, and Italy, and observed the development of brain in the different nations, and compared it with all I could learn of their mental characteristics; and what I have recorded is neither fancy nor fiction, but what appeared to me to be truth, open of course to correction, but I firmly believe not to be set aside by the most rigid investigations. I am led to make these observations by the pertinacity with which the appeals made by phrenologists to nature are disregarded, even by men professedly treating scientifically of human crania, such as the late Dr Prichard, and more recently by Mr J. Barnard Davis and Dr John Thurnam, in the 1st Decade of their *Crania Britannica*. There they give no distinct account of Dr Gall's method of discovering the connection between particular forms and sizes of crania and peculiar qualities of mind; and especially, while reporting the opinions of other investigators, they do not mention the facts stated by phrenologists, that, *cæteris paribus*, the vigour of the intellectual faculties is in proportion to the size of the anterior lobe, that of the moral and religious sentiments to the coronal region, and that of the animal propensities to the other and lower regions of the brain. Although assuredly one object of Ethnology, especially that part of it which treats of the cranium, is to discover whether civilisation has any influence in increasing the moral and intellectual regions, and diminishing that of the animal propensities in the human brain, the readers of their works who have not studied Phrenology, are furnished with no directions how to draw conclusions on this point from the crania delineated in their plates. Whether the phrenologists be right or wrong in maintaining that the size of those regions is an indication of corresponding power in these different mental qualities, is an open question; but, in my opinion, the means of judging of it is a desideratum in this work, and I hope the omission may yet be supplied.

minated and described the natural qualities of the French people without reference to the character of their brains. "The nation," said Napoleon, "in its character and tastes is provisional and lavish;—every thing for the moment and caprice—nothing for endurance! such are the motto and manners of France. Every one passes his life in doing and undoing; nothing remains." (Las Cases—*Memoires de Sainte Helene.*) " The great defect of the French character," says Duclos, " is to be always young; by which circumstance it is often amiable, but rarely steady. It has almost no ripe manhood, but passes from youth directly to old age. Our talents of every description appear early. We neglect them for a long time by dissipation, and scarcely do we commence to turn them to account before their time is past." (*Considerations on Manners.*) But have the means enjoyed by such describers, of conveying their own convictions to men less acute in observation and less profound in mental analysis than themselves, been equal to those of the phrenologist? It appears evident that several, and probably the whole, members of the late Provisional Government of France did not believe in the views of the French character and capabilities given by Napoleon and Duclos. They formed a far higher estimate of them, and acted on their own convictions. Who, then, shall decide between the conflicting authorities? If such men as Napoleon and Duclos perceive and proclaim certain great and palpable deficiencies in the French national character which seem to unfit them for self-government, while Lamartine, Arago, and Louis Blanc, also men of talent and honourable purpose, have been blind to the existence of these defects, or at least have not recognised them as presenting serious obstacles to their own schemes of social and political regeneration, is it not clear that some *element of evidence* on this fundamental point must be wanting?

While the knowledge of national character continues purely empirical, rulers will be liable to judge of it by the standard of their own feelings and perceptions. If they be shallow and ill-instructed, they will act irrespective of causes, and be blind to consequences. Unless such rulers stumble by accident upon the right path, they will advance the sciences of government and social economy chiefly by exhausting errors. If they lead a shallow and excitable people, the whole will go to destruction together. Meantime, they will play this game with the fortunes, perhaps the lives, of millions of men, and the well-being of unborn generations. Again, therefore, I hazard the opinion that the question of mental capabilities in different races is one of momentous practical importance, and as such merits the serious consideration of statesmen and legislators.

If, as phrenologists maintain, the size and proportions of the different regions of the brain constitute Nature's tangible and visible indications of mental qualities, the question of evidence, with a view to practice, will be considerably simplified. Thousands of individuals who might be incapable of analysing intellectual phenomena, and drawing sound inferences from them, might be capable of discerning a low and narrow forehead, and recognising in it the natural sign of defective reasoning powers ; and might see in a flat and narrow coronal region of the brain the indication of deficiency in the powers of moral susceptibility and appreciation.* If they believed in the reality of these forms and proportions as Nature's indications of the degrees of these mental qualities, they might be disposed to modify their conduct by this knowledge.

To judge of the importance of a physical sign of mental qualities, we must assume it, for the moment, to be real. If, then, for the sake of argument, we hold Dr Vimont's descriptions to be founded in fact, and the organisation which he delineates to be tangible and visible, the question of the degrees in which particular mental qualities are possessed by different races of men, passes from the debateable ground of psychology to the more definite region of organic structure. When the evidence by which degrees of qualities are proved becomes palpable, the doctrine itself will become practical. The science of chemistry created no new elements of fertility ; but, by presenting correct physical indications of the qualities of soils, which men of average intellect could comprehend, it rendered this class of persons not only equal, but superior, in discriminative power and practical judgment, to individuals of the highest capacities under the old empirical system. Besides, it unfolded more correctly and completely than mere experience had ever done, the relations of these qualities to different kinds of manures, and to different modes of treatment ; and then, but then only, agriculture made rapid progress, and assumed the character of a scientific pursuit.

If physical signs of degrees of mental capacities exist, will not the introduction of the knowledge of them into the domain of moral and intellectual science, produce an effect analogous to that of the introduction of chemistry into practical agriculture ? It appears calculated to give to average minds that clear insight into natural capabilities which is at present possessed, and possessed imperfectly, by men of the highest endowments and cultivation ; and only when this shall be accomplished, will this species of knowledge become practically useful.

* See Dr Vimont's comparison of the French head and mental character, and also of those of other nations, in his *Traité de Phrénologie*, Paris, 1831, vol. ii. p. 470.

Numerous temporary and adventitious circumstances have been mentioned by political writers as accounting for the phenomena of French history above noticed; but unless there had been in the French people the mental qualities which Napoleon and others describe, the circumstances, in my opinion, could not have occurred : Even assuming some of them, in some inexplicable way, to have arisen, the general results could not have been such as we have seen them to be. These events constitute important epochs in the history of Europe, and affect the well-being of millions of men, and yet to the philosophers and statesmen of the age which beheld them, they were mere occurrences. The natural mental forces of the French people are assumed, contrary to the fact, to be the same with those of the German, English, and all other European nations. Their primitive faculties are the same, but the strength of each of these in proportion to that of the others is different in them and in the Teutonic and Anglo-Saxon races. As the mental forces of the people constitute the fundamental causes of their social action, until these be understood, science cannot explain the events, or draw from them practical instruction for the future, nor can religious men comprehend the principles of the Divine government under which they have occurred.

Moreover, the aim of the French people has been to reach material well-being and mental freedom. But material prosperity can be attained only by acting in conformity with the natural laws which govern the production and distribution of wealth; yet these have never been taught to the people, and none of their various rulers have recognised the necessity of studying and enforcing them as preliminary and indispensable conditions to the accomplishment of this object. Political economists, and men of practical philosophical understandings, have long urged the practical importance of this knowledge equally to legislators and people, but their counsels have not been followed.

Again : mental freedom cannot exist in a community unless the great majority of the individuals composing it understand the natural *moral* conditions of social well-being, and are capable of fulfilling them. These consist in controlling the animal propensities, which are all selfish, by means of the moral faculties, which are social, and directing both classes of powers into legitimate courses of action by enlightened intellect. While the majority of a nation desire material well-being and mental liberty, and yet continue ignorant of the natural conditions on which these may be obtained, every revolution is a step in the dark: The people may institute any form of government they please; but as water cannot flow higher than

its fountain, so will uninstructed rulers never succeed in realising the moral and material prosperity of their subjects.
These remarks apply to all the governments of the world. It signifies little by what name they are called, for they will produce well-being only in proportion to their fulfilment of the natural conditions on which it depends. It is the object of science to unfold these for the instruction equally of rulers and people. Until, therefore, nations shall choose for their governors and legislators men possessing the most favourably-constituted brains and best-instructed faculties, and induce them to study and act in conformity to the laws of the Divine government, and until the people themselves shall manifest the same spirit in their public conduct—only partial, uncertain, and, to some extent, ephemeral success will attend their efforts to attain public prosperity. So far are even some British statesmen from acknowledging such principles of action as wise and practical, that, a few years ago, Lord Stanley, now Lord Derby, presented, in a public document on convict-treatment, a distinct expression of his conviction, that it is *not lawful* for man to adopt the order of nature as a guide to his conduct. Captain Maconochie had urged on his Lordship that "we cannot err in taking that model (viz., ' the discipline to which we are all subjected by Divine providence') for our guidance in our attempts to elevate the characters of our guilty, but yet more unhappy brethren." To which his Lordship answered: " I do not understand that it is permitted to us thus to constitute ourselves imitators of the Divine government under which we live; or that, in this respect, the march of infinite wisdom is to be followed by beings of so contracted a range of knowledge and foresight as we are."* Such a sentence as this appears to amount to a denial that the constitution and order of nature are presented to man as indications of the principles of the Divine government on earth for the guidance of his own conduct. However unintentionally, it is practically an announcement of atheism.†

Schiller, in his essay entitled " Die Gesetzgebung des Lycurgus und Solon," remarks, that the *State* itself is not an end; it is " important only as a condition under which the object of man's existence may be accomplished; and this object is no other than the development and improvement of all the powers of his nature. If the constitution of a state prevents the

* Parliamentary Paper on " Van Diemen's Land," ordered by the House of Commons to be printed, 9th February 1846, p. 11.
† The Earl of Derby's son, Lord Stanley, appears to entertain sounder views of the order of nature. In his recent speeches at public meetings he has evinced great intellectual powers, enlightened by knowledge of science, which give promise of a highly honourable and useful practical career in the service of his country.

faculties of the human being from unfolding themselves, and if it obstructs the advance of mind, it is exceptionable and injurious, however profoundly it may have been conceived, and however perfectly it may have been framed in relation to other objects. Its durability is then an objection, and not a commendable quality; it constitutes it an abiding evil; for the longer it is capable of maintaining itself, it is only the more baneful." " In judging of political institutions especially, we may assume it as a fixed rule, that they are beneficial and praiseworthy, only in so far as they bring into active operation all the powers with which human nature is endowed, and in so far as they promote, or at least do not impede, mental cultivation." These remarks are worthy of the great mind from which they proceeded; but a *method* of discovering " the conditions under which the objects of man's existence may be accomplished," is a *desideratum* which must be supplied before scientific progress can be made towards that end. When the method is discovered and applied, it will be seen that different nations will prefer different political institutions as the means of enabling each, according to its particular combination of cerebral organs, to work out its own well-being.

Rulers and people are both subjected to an actual Divine government which controls their actions and determines the results, although, at present, unknown to themselves. In my works on "The Constitution of Man" and "Moral Philosophy," I have endeavoured to shew that this government is moral, and that the farther nations advance in the practice of moral and economical science, the nearer approaches they will make to material and social prosperity. If these views shall ever be recognised as practical truths, government and legislation will proceed on principles widely different from those which now prevail. In despotic countries the sovereigns preserve order by armed force, and their chief anxiety is to maintain their authority over their subjects, and to defend themselves against their neighbours, who generally are employed in a similar manner. Few of them aim at introducing the knowledge and practice of the natural conditions of well-being among their people, as a leading object of their sway. In countries which enjoy representative legislatures, we see each member of the legislative assembly propounding such methods of attaining general prosperity, as he has been enabled, by his peculiar form of brain and opportunities of instruction, to comprehend. If he is deficient in the reflecting organs, causation is omitted in his schemes; if he is deficient in the moral organs, his measures spring from and are addressed to the selfish desires. If he has large organs of Acquisitiveness, Self-Esteem, Combativeness, and Destructiveness, he grasps, and brags, and bullies. If his moral organs are very large, and the base of his brain moderate, he is the advocate of moral force, as superior in efficacy to physical coercion; but he may lack the vigorous urgency which large Combativeness communicates when directed by the higher faculties. When a scheme is brought forward for consideration, the speakers seldom think of inquiring how far it is in accordance with the constitution of human nature, and the laws which govern the moral and physical worlds. The discussion is essentially empirical. Only a very few superior minds penetrate to first principles, and they are generally treated as abstract and unpractical men. Weeks, months, and years are wasted in wordy debate, and at last legislation is accomplished by party combinations, and not in obedience to the dictates of reason and morality.

When science shall take the place of empiricism, improvement will follow in its train. Men on whom nature has placed the stamp of moral and intellectual capacity will then be chosen as legislators, and they will inquire only which is the way appointed by the Author of nature to lead to prosperity; and having found it, or come as near to it as possible, they will follow it, and trust in God for the results. Sovereigns will then cease to fear their subjects, and subjects will act in harmony with their rulers; all being conscious of their practical subjection to the sway of God, through his natural institutions.

Schiller's propositions before stated hold good in regard to religious as well as to civil laws. "Both," says he, "are exceptionable when they chain up any power of the human mind, and enjoin it to stand still. A law, for instance, by which a nation is compelled to retain for ever a certain scheme of religious belief, merely because at a certain epoch it had appeared to be the truest and the best, is practically an attack against humanity itself, and no pretence of other advantages attending it, however plausible, can justify it. It is unquestionably directed against the greatest public good, and against the highest object of human society,"—the development of its whole faculties in conformity with the principles of the Divine government.

In this chapter I have treated chiefly of the effects of Size in the cerebral organs on the force of mental action, because Size is the fundamental element of power. The influences which modify the effects of Size, such as age, temperament, health, training, hereditary descent, and others, are treated of in the works on Phrenology, to which I beg leave to refer.

CHAPTER VII.

HISTORICAL EVIDENCE THAT THE DIVINE GOVERNMENT OF NATIONS IS MORAL.

IN the Bible we are told "to do justly, to love mercy, and to walk humbly with our God;" that is, to obey His commandments. We are desired also to love our neighbours as ourselves, and to do unto them as we should wish that they should do unto us. Are these precepts *practical* in this world, or are they not? and what is implied in their being practical? Before they can become practical, it must be shown that they are in harmony with, and supported by, the order of nature; that is to say, that nature is so constituted and arranged, that all the real interests of individuals and nations are compatible with each other, and that it is not necessary to rob and impoverish one, whether individual or nation, in order to enrich another. Not only so, but that all injustice, oppression, and spoliation, being in opposition to the order of nature, must ultimately lead to evil and suffering to the perpetrator, or to those to whom he leaves the legacy of his spoils and his crimes. If such be the constitution of nature, then these precepts *are* practical. If, on the other hand, the order of Providence admits of individuals and nations profiting by injustice and oppression, and reaching and continuing to enjoy real prosperity and happiness through the systematic practice of crimes and violence, then are these precepts *not* practical in this world.

The history of all Christian nations shews that while they professed to believe in the divine authority of the Scriptures, they were in a great measure sceptics as to the Scriptural precepts being supported and enforced by the order of nature. In their conduct towards each other, they have too often set them at defiance; nay, each has striven to depress, spoil, and ruin its neighbour, as the most effectual means of raising itself to independence and prosperity. But not one of the nations has succeeded in attaining its ends by these means. The history of the treatment of Ireland by England affords an instructive lesson on this topic.

Six centuries ago, in the reign of Henry the Second, England conquered the sister isle, and ever since has continued to sway her destinies. From the first day of her conquest to very recent times, English statesmen have acted towards Ireland on principles diametrically opposed to the injunctions of the New Testament. They insulted the feelings of the Irish, placed shackles on their industry, excluded them from many of the most valuable rights of British subjects, placed the religion of the majority out of the pale of the constitution, prohibited its professors, under pain of banishment for the first offence, and of death for the second, to act as schoolmasters or tutors in the instruction of their own people; and when at last Ireland, in a moment of her strength, and of England's weakness, asserted her independence, and achieved a native legislature, English statesmen, in 1783, converted that legislature, by means of systematic corruption, into a new instrument of injustice and oppression. England pursued this course notoriously with the view of providing for her own safety, prosperity, and power. Has she succeeded? No. A calm survey of her history will shew that from the first day of her oppression to the present time, every injury inflicted on Ireland has recoiled on her own head; and that Ireland continued to be the source of her greatest weakness, anxiety, and suffering, until she amended her line of conduct. She has paid eight millions sterling to save from starvation the victims of the system which she had pursued, but she does not yet discern the end of the retribution which she has drawn upon her head.

During the whole period of this long crusade against the course of Providence and the precepts of Christianity, the rulers and people of England professed to believe in the Divine authority of the Scripture injunctions which they were trampling under foot. They had the Bible in their hands, they had catechisms, a liturgy, clergymen, and bishops; in short, all the means of learning their duty to God and to their fellowmen; but all did not suffice to lead them into the practice of benevolence and justice. What did they lack? They did not believe in the reality of a Divine government on earth; and if they even imagined such a thing, they did not perceive that it was moral. Their religious emotions were entwined with dogmas which represented this world as the wreck of a better system, and the heart of man as "deceitful above all things and desperately wicked." They believed in a day of judgment and in future reward and punishment; but this belief did not affect their conduct so as to lead them to practise what they professed to believe. If they had believed in an actual moral government of the world, their conduct would have been as insane as that of men who should sow corn in snow, and expect to reap a harvest from it in winter. Cromwell, and the religious men of his age, did not recognise the order of nature as supporting Christianity. On the contrary, they not only believed in a special supernatural providence, but when they were gratifying their own misguided passions, they complacently viewed themselves as the chosen instruments of God's vengeance for punishing His enemies. Statesmen who were not religious, either formed no deliberate opinion of any kind regarding the course of Providence on earth, or considered it as arbitrary or mysterious; not cognisable by man, and not available as a guide to human conduct. Indeed, the great majority of Christian statesmen and people, while they are disposed to acknowledge the existence of physical laws of nature, still show a practical disbelief in the government of the world by *moral* laws.

Another example of unbelief in the action of a moral providence in nature is afforded by the author of an able and eloquent pamphlet,—" The Case of Ireland stated, by Robert Holmes, Esq." After detailing the wrongs of Ireland, he speaks of the proposal to employ " moral force" as a means of her deliverance, in the following terms:—" Moral force is a power, by the mere operation of reason, to convince the understanding and satisfy the consciences of those on whom the effect is to be wrought, that there is some particular moral act, within their ability to perform, which ought to be performed, and which it is their duty to perform; and, also, by the operation of the same divine principle only, making those free moral agents do the very thing required. The intended effect must be produced, and must be moral—the efficient cause must be moral, purely moral, unmixed, unadulterated by any mean or sordid views; reason, heavenly reason, applied with eloquence divine; no threat, no intimidation, no cold iron, no ' vile guns,' no ' villanous saltpetre digged out of the bowels of the harmless earth,' nothing but the radiant illuminations of moral truth." Mr Holmes regards this as a mere " evaporation plan," adopted as a safety-valve to Irish discontent. " It seemed," says he, " to be considered by the expediency men of the day as a first-rate contrivance;" but he regards it as pure " fudge," and seems to prefer " monster meetings," and displays of physical force, which may be used in case of need, as better calculated to accomplish " repeal of the Union," and the redress of Ireland's wrongs.—But Ireland had frequently tried to right herself by means of " cold iron," " vile guns," and " villanous saltpetre," and with what success her present condition shews.* It is obvious that Mr Holmes

* I am no advocate of the doctrine of non-resistance. Organs of Combativeness and

does not comprehend the lessons contained in his own pamphlet, and is an unbeliever in the moral government of the world. He does not see that the advocates of justice to Ireland are backed not only by the "moral" but by the "physical force" of God's providence, in virtue of which they are able to demonstrate to England, that every sordid act which she has committed against Ireland has redounded in evil to herself, and that the Divine Government is so thoroughly moral, so skilfully combined, and so unbendingly enforced, that the wisdom of all her statesmen, and the counsels of all her bishops, have not sufficed to turn aside the stream of suffering which she has drawn, and will continue to draw, upon herself, from every fountain of injustice which she has opened, or may hereafter open, in Ireland. What are the disappointments to avarice, the humiliations of baffled bigotry, the incessant consciousness of insecurity and weakness, and the lavish waste of treasure, which England so long experienced from her injustice to Ireland, but the sanctions of Nature's moral laws, and the punishments which give reality and efficacy to the doctrine of "moral force?" One gigantic wrong to Ireland remains unredressed—the seizure of the property of her Roman Catholic Church, and the application of it to maintain a Protestant ecclesiastical establishment disowned by the great majority of the people. If not relinquished, this enormity will lead to the downfall of the Church of England itself. The transfer is grossly immoral, because the Church of England's creed is sacred only to the individuals whose religious emotions have been trained to reverence it, and the faith of the Roman Catholic is equally sacred in his estimation. (See page 20.) The conveyance of the property from the one Church to the other, therefore, was an act of pure oppression, perpetrated by the strong against the weak; and when the moral and religious emotions of the British people are emancipated from their present errors, they will discover the magnitude of this injustice, and ask if the faith of that Church *can be pure* which permitted its votaries to commit, and for so many centuries to maintain, such a spoliation, accompanied by

---

Destructiveness exist in man, and they have legitimate spheres of activity, one of which appears to be to repel, by physical force, aggression which we cannot overcome by moral means. Armed resistance is one of the natural checks to injustice; but it is attended by a great disadvantage. The contests of force are governed by the laws of force. The most numerous, best appointed, best disciplined, and most ably commanded army, will gain the victory, irrespective of the moral merits of the cause for which it fights. High moral motives animating it will, no doubt, add to its discipline, its patience, and its devotion, and thus indirectly contribute to success; but they will not, in any other respect, supply the place of the ordinary sinews of war. Nature, however, has other modes of arresting injustice; and violence should never be resorted to until all better means have been tried without success.

all the demoralising influences on both Catholics and Protestants which have flowed from its polluted fountains? When this question shall be answered, a new Reformation will not be far distant.

Mr Cobden and his coadjutors carried repeal of the corn-laws by the use of moral force alone; but they understood its nature and sanctions: that is to say, they demonstrated to the religious public that free trade is implied in the Scripture precepts before quoted—to the moral public, that free trade is prescribed by the dictates of the sentiment of justice inherent in the human mind—to the merchant, manufacturer, and husbandman, not only that free trade is compatible with, and calculated to promote, their worldly interests, but that these cannot be permanently and systematically advanced by any other means. In short, they shewed that every attempt of every class to benefit itself by unjust monopolies and restrictions had not merely failed, but actually obstructed the attainment, through other and moral means, of the very objects which the monopolies were introduced to promote.

Unless all this be actually true, free trade cannot maintain itself even now when it is established; and it was the moral conviction that these views *are* true, that first inspired Mr Cobden with full confidence in the success of his agitation. Already we have evidence in the results, that the principles of free trade are supported by the order of nature.

The advocates of "moral force," therefore, who see a moral government of the world established and enforced by God, wield not only "reason, heavenly reason," as an instrument for attaining justice, but "threats" and "intimidation;"—not the threats of "cold iron" and "vile guns," which may be employed in support of oppression and wrong as successfully as in vindication of right, but "threats" of evil from a Power which no human sagacity can baffle, and no might withstand. Yet if the threats *be* real, and if the inflictions be as certain as fate, what a strange condition of mind must Christian men be in, when they imagine moral force to be a mere "evaporation plan," altogether unsupported when not backed by "vile guns and villanous saltpetre!" Before, however, they can wield moral force with effect, they must be converted to a belief in the real, actual, and efficient government of the world by God's secular providence; they must understand the scheme, and search for the evidence of this government, and teach it to their countrymen. The creeds and confessions of churches must be revised and new-modelled into accordance with the order of Nature, and the Christian precepts must be allowed the benefit of Nature's support to give efficacy to their injunctions.

If the liberal members of the European community who desire to accomplish moral, religious, and political reforms, could be convinced of the reality of the moral government of the world, and take up this doctrine as the basis of their operations, no political tyranny, and no erroneous creed, could withstand their assaults. While they rely on guns and bayonets as their means of resisting misrule, they stand at a disadvantage, for these are equally available to defend error as to maintain truth; but when, abjuring these, they shall employ their higher faculties in discovering and demonstrating the combination of causes and effects, by means of which that moral government is actually carried into operation, they will become conscious of a strength before which error in every form will ultimately succumb.

Mr Holmes' blindness to the moral order of creation is evinced by another proposal which he advocates. While he admits that, during all the period of England's oppression, Irishmen were, in general, so destitute of moral principle, patriotism, and mutual confidence, that England, at all times, found among them willing tools to perpetrate her deeds of injustice, and Ireland never (except for a few months in 1782) found in her own population moral, intellectual, and physical resources sufficient to oppose or arrest them,—he looks to repeal of the Union, and the delivery of Irish affairs into Irish hands, as the only panacea for her sufferings and her wrongs. But if the view which I am now expounding is not a dream, the wrongs of Ireland will never be righted until her destinies are swayed by a moral and enlightened legislature: and whether this shall hold its sittings on the one side of St George's Channel or the other, will matter little to either country; for, as God's providence embraces both, and has rendered beneficence and justice the only road to permanent happiness and prosperity for either, that legislature will first redress her wrongs which shall first bow before the power of God, and enforce His laws as superior in wisdom and efficacy to any which their own selfishness and prejudices can substitute in their place.*

Another striking example of a people professing Christianity being utter unbelievers in the Divine moral government of the world is afforded by the legal enactment of slavery as a "domestic institution" in the Southern States of the American Union. Every principle of natural humanity and justice condemns the gross selfishness of converting men into "chattels,"

---

* These observations were written and first published in 1847. England has since partially changed her course of action towards Ireland, and already blessed fruits are visible in Ireland's peace and prosperity, and England's tranquillity.

compelling them to labour for the profit of others, and buying and selling them, irrespectively of all ties of kindred, place, and custom ; and if there be a moral Providence at all ruling in the world, this " Institution," being founded in iniquity, and a flagrant and presumptuous defiance of the Divine laws, can lead sooner or later to no result but terrible disaster to all who participate in it. Nevertheless, it is a melancholy spectacle to see ministers of the Christian religion, after being driven from every position of reason and morality in attempting to defend this institution, falling back on the authority of Scripture, as the last and strongest tower of strength by which to maintain its odious existence.

The advocates of the inherent moral disorder of the world, however, will probably point to history and to the actual condition of the human race in every country of the globe, as affording demonstrative evidence that this supposed moral government is a dream. The past and present sufferings of mankind cannot be disputed ; but in what age, and in what nation, have the religious instructors of the people been believers in an actual practical moral government of the world by God ? Where and when have they expounded the natural arrangements by means of which this government is accomplished ? And when and where have they directed the religious sentiments of the people to reverence and obey the natural laws as the roads that lead to virtue and prosperity ? Ever since the promulgation of Christianity, has any nation discovered, and practically fulfilled, the natural conditions by which the precepts of this religion may be supported and enforced ? Not one example is known of such conduct :—need we, therefore, be surprised at the results being such as history discloses and we perceive ? The evidence of past and present experience certainly demonstrates that mankind, by shutting their eyes to the order of Providence in the world, by trampling the dictates of morality and religion under foot, and by seeking prosperity and happiness under the guidance of unsound religious dogmas, and of their selfish animal propensities, have never realized the objects of their desires ; but it does not prove that no scheme of moral government adapted to their nature exists. It shows that they have not discovered such a scheme ; but neither had they discovered the steam-engine, railroads, or the effects of chloroform, until a very recent date. They have been, and generally speaking continue to be, ignorant of their own nature ; of the adaptations of the external world to its constitution ; of the principles on which the order of nature is framed ; and of their own capabilities of conforming to it ; and hence many of their sufferings may be

M

accounted for: but the requisite discoveries may be made, and indeed have been partially made, and all experience shews that human happiness has increased in proportion to obedience to the natural laws. The most intelligent, moral, and industrious nations are the most prosperous and happy; the most ignorant, idle, self-seeking, turbulent, and aggressive, are the most miserable and poor. These undeniable facts afford strong indications that a moral government of the world by natural laws exists; and if it does so, is not the discovery of its scheme an important study claiming the serious attention of man? I cannot too often repeat that unless the Christian morality be sustained and enforced by the order of nature, it is in vain to teach it as a rule of conduct in secular affairs. And how can this study be commenced and prosecuted, how can new truths be turned to practical account, except by reverencing Nature and her adaptations as Divine institutions—teaching them to the young—and enforcing them by the authority of the moral and religious sentiments? If man is a moral and intellectual being, it appears not to be inconsistent with this character to have constituted his mind and body and external nature in harmony with each other, and to have left him, in the exercise of his discretion, to work out, to a considerable extent, his own weal or woe. The fact that he, through ignorance and the misapplication of his powers, has hitherto experienced much misery, affords no conclusive evidence that by more extensive knowledge, and stricter obedience to the laws of his nature, he may not greatly improve his condition.

CHAPTER VIII.

IS THIS WORLD, SUCH AS IT NOW EXISTS, AN INSTITUTION?—OR IS IT THE WRECK OF A BETTER SYSTEM?

SECTION I.—IS THIS WORLD AN INSTITUTION?

By an Institution, I mean an object formed apparently according to a plan, and designed for a purpose. By the wreck of a better system is meant a state of things in which order and design may be inferred to have once existed, but no longer appear. In it dislocation of parts has destroyed consistency of plan, and abortive results indicate defeated design. To which category does this world, such as it now exists, belong?

In attempting to answer this question we may begin with the Planetary System. Apparently *it* is an *Institution*; for, so far as has yet been discovered, its parts are systematically arranged, and design is discernible in its objects. Our Earth is a member of this system; and the place it holds in it is therefore systematic and designed. One feature of its position, is the inclination of its axis at an angle of 23 degrees to the plane of the ecliptic; and among its phenomena is its annual revolution round the sun. These, therefore, are portions of the plan of the solar system, and the effects which they produce must be regarded as designed.

One of these effects is the production of Summer and Winter, with arctic, temperate, and torrid zones; and all the enjoyments and sufferings arising from them. Surveying these regions, we discover men and animals constituted with qualities adapted to each of them: the reindeer and the walrus are adapted to regions of ice and snow, and could not live within the tropics; while the camel and the dolphin flourish in heat, but would perish in the arctic zone. The Hindoo and Negro would become extinct in Lapland, and the Laplander on the plains of Bengal, or in the interior of Africa.

Pursuing our observations, we might at first imagine the vast expanse of ocean, in which none of the higher forms of vegetable or animal life can exist, to be the result of some hideous catastrophe which has befallen our planet, and defaced its originally fairer features. But if we investigated the constitution and relations of the ocean more closely, we should probably be led to view it in a different light. Experience, for example, shews that the soil requires water to render it fertile, and that the higher forms of animal and vegetable life are absolutely dependent on its fertility for their existence. Although man has discovered that water can be produced by combining oxygen and hydrogen gases, no process has yet been observed in active operation in nature for providing a constant supply of water by this method. Indeed, such a process could not be permanently continued in operation without sooner or later producing a deluge, unless a counteracting process for resolving the water back into its elements were also provided; and such processes, continued on the gigantic scale necessary to irrigate the whole earth, would have produced continual changes in the proportions of the gases which constitute our atmosphere, and on the permanence of whose proportions animal and vegetable life absolutely depends.

The actual order of Nature has been to form water sufficient for supplying moisture for the land, to collect it in huge basins, and to endow the air with sponge-like properties for absorbing it, carrying it to great distances, and depositing it in the form of dew and rain where it is wanted. In process of time, after having fertilized the ground, and helped to nourish animal and vegetable life, it finds its way back by rivers into its original ocean bed, whence it is again absorbed, again travels on the wings of the wind, again fertilizes the plains, the valleys, and the mountains, and thus continues to perform an endless series of beneficent revolutions, without increasing or decreasing in quantity, and without deranging any other part or process of nature.

Moreover, we find the ocean replete with animal life, and the forms in which it exists adapted not only to the watery element itself, but to the temperature which pervades the ocean in the different zones.

Viewed in this light, then, does the ocean present itself to our minds as the result of a catastrophe, or as an Institution formed on a plan, and designed for a purpose?—To me the latter appears the rational inference: yet, while these arrangements are the sources of innumerable enjoyments, it is undeniable that they are also accompanied by contingent evils.

Natural History also shews that unity of plan is discernible in the formation of the organisms of man and the lower animals. Göthe, in his theories on the morphology of plants, Oken, a German physiologist, and Geoffroy St Hilaire, a celebrated French writer on the same science, are considered to have demonstrated this proposition. Structures so various, so extensive, and adapted to such different *habitats* as earth, ocean, and air, all characterized by similarity of plan, seem to proclaim design, and not the wreck of a higher system.

Geological investigations, again, have demonstrated that the order of Nature instead of retrograding has been advancing. Lower conditions of physical, vegetable, and animal existence, have passed away and been succeeded by higher states; and there is no reason to suppose that the limit of improvement has been attained. But in all the changes, we perceive the organic adaptation to the inorganic conditions of the earth. At present, we are capable of penetrating fully into neither the plan nor the design of the constitution of the earth and its occupants, but wherever our knowledge of nature is exact and tolerably complete, we are led to the conclusion that, with all its unexplained anomalies and apparent imperfections, it is not only an Institution, *but an advancing Institution*, rather than the wreck of a higher order of things. The work of Paley on Natural Theology, and the Bridgewater Treatises,* afford strong evidence in support of this proposition; and in " The Constitution of Man," I have endeavoured to shew that the chief object of all the well-known arrangements of Nature is beneficent.

Extending our inquiries to the human constitution and its adaptations, we discover that man is composed of chemical elements, and is brought into existence as a sentient, intelligent, moral, and religious being, according to fixed laws, and endowed with organs and faculties adapted in the most striking manner to the condition in which the earth now exists;

* The authors of the Bridgewater Treatises do not attempt to render the admirable and beneficent structures, agencies, and adaptations of Nature which they so eloquently unfold, *religious truths,* by entwining them with the religious emotions; nor do they draw from them, for the guidance of human conduct, rules invested with the authority of Divine wisdom and power. These omissions apparently had their source in the fact that the writers were restrained by the existing dogmas of religious faith from proceeding to such applications of the truths which they unfolded. The consequence, however, has been, that their works remain barren of practical fruits. They are read and admired, and help to elevate and liberalize the minds of their readers in a general way, but here their influence ends. Nobody acts on them. The authors of " Typical Forms and Special Ends in Creation," appear also to have laboured under a similar restraint; for while they have brought into a focus a mass of interesting elucidations of the prevalence of design and adaptation in Nature, they do not venture on the application of the grand truths which they exhibit to practical religion. Bishop Butler, too, appears, in his Sermons on " Human Nature," and " Upon the Love of our Neighbour," to have made such a near approach 'to the practical doctrine of the present work, that I am led to think that the dogmas of his creed also restrained the full and free exercise of his profound upright, and comprehensive understanding, in pursuing the subject to its legitimate conclusions.

If some future patron of human progress should offer a premium for a work carrying forward, by correcting and enlarging, the views which I am now feebly presenting in general outline, truths might be elicited which would prove eminently practical, and, by being entwined with the religious emotions, become highly influential in action.

his muscles to the force of gravitation, which is a planetary force; his eye and faculty of Colouring to the sun's rays; his lungs to the air, his stomach to the vegetable and animal productions of the soil and sea; his skin and sensitive nerves to the actual temperature of the earth and air, and his mental faculties to the whole objects of the arena in which he is destined to live and act. The preceding pages are devoted to expositions and proofs of these propositions, and it is unnecessary to recapitulate them in detail. The facts appear to indicate that man, such as he now exists, is a part of an Institution. One remark, however, remains, to be added.

In "The Constitution of Man," I have attempted to shew, not only that the world has been instituted for benevolent purposes, but that even the contingent evil of pain has beneficent objects. When that work appeared, it was objected that pain is obviously the punishment of sin, inflicted in consequence of Adam's first transgression; and the statement of the contrary was represented as an infidel denial of the authority of Scripture, in which the pains of child-birth are inflicted in express terms on Eve and all her sex, as a retribution for her share in that unfortunate transaction. The argument, that as those pains are not suffered by all women, and are not equally severe in all whom they visit,* they could not justly be regarded as an essential portion of the order of nature, was urged in vain. In the course of time, however, sulphuric ether and chloroform, and more recently a new substance named amelyne, have been discovered, all of which have the power of suspending sensibility to pain, while they leave the muscular system unaffected. The consequence is, that child-birth and severe surgical operations are now accomplished without suffering.

The inference to be drawn from such facts is well stated by Dr Symonds, Physician to the Bristol Infirmary, in a letter published by him in the British and Foreign Medical Review for 1846. "*Art*, after all," says he, "is but Nature in a new form—*a fresh arrangement of the forces of Nature, compelling them to work under new conditions.*" He adds, "I am not fond of arguments from final causes; *but can it be doubted that the various medicines we possess, were, as such, a part of the plan of the universe designed to have a relation to morbid states of living organisms*, as much as esculent matters to healthy conditions?" On page 28, I have adverted to the fact that the organism of man and animals possesses, up to a certain point, the power of repairing injuries which it may sustain; and that this power remains latent until called into action by the wants

* See evidence of this fact in No. III. of the Appendix to "The Constitution of Man," post 8vo edition, 1847.

of the lacerated parts. If esculent matters have been adapted by God to the healthy condition of the human organism, does not this indicate that our digestive and assimilating organs, and their relations to those substances, are Institutions? But if that organism itself possesses a power of repairing injuries which are only prospective and contingent, and if there are also substances in nature adapted to remove its morbid states when they occur, is it not a just inference that *liability* to disease also is a part of this Institution, but that pain and disease are *not* direct—essential—designed—and therefore inevitable elements of it?

The adaptations of one portion of physical nature to another, by which man is benefited, also proclaim that this world, such as it now exists, is an Institution. Coal and mineral beds are familiar examples; and Dr Lyon Playfair presents another which is not so generally known. "In 1842," says he, "I had the pleasure of travelling with the Dean of Westminster and Liebig over different parts of England. Among other places we visited a limestone in the neighbourhood of Clifton, where in former times saurian reptiles had been the pirates of the sea. There, along with the relics of the fishes on which they had preyed, were their own animal remains. Coprolites existed in great abundance, and proved the extraordinary number of the reptiles which must have existed. The interesting question arose as to whether these excretions of extinct animals contained the mineral ingredients of so much value in animal manure. The question was in fact not yet solved by the chemist, and we took specimens, in order to confirm by chemical analysis the views of the geologist. After Liebig had completed their analysis, he saw that they might be made applicable to practical purposes. 'What a curious and interesting subject for contemplation! In the remains of an extinct *animal* world England is to find the means of increasing her wealth in agricultural produce, as she has already found the great support of her manufacturing industry in fossil fuel—the preserved matter of primeval forests—the remains of a vegetable world! May this expectation be realised! and may her excellent population be thus redeemed from poverty and misery!' I well recollect the storm of ridicule raised by these expressions of the German philosopher, and yet truth has triumphed over scepticism, and thousands of tons of similar animal remains are now used in promoting the fertility of our fields. The geological observer, in his search after evidences of ancient life, aided by the chemist, excavated extinct remains which produce new life to future generations."—*Records of the School of Mines,* 1852.

In regarding this world as an Institution I do not pretend to solve all the difficulties which this view of it presents. Man, apparently, is only in the beginning of his career of study and discovery, and also probably far from the highest attainable improvement in his own physical and mental endowments. All that I aim at, therefore, is to direct, if possible, future inquiries into the right road of investigation, and to animate them with faith in a rich harvest of beneficial results, as the reward of studying Nature in the spirit of religion and truth. Some of the objections to the views now maintained are well stated and candidly discussed in a letter addressed to me by an esteemed scientific friend, and published in 1847 in the Appendix, No. IX., to the post 8vo edition of "The Constitution of Man." The following extract from it is instructive :—

"Our concern is with the one species man. With other organic beings, the course of nature has been to sacrifice the inferior for the benefit of the superior. Species have been (perhaps still are) sacrificed for other species more favoured. Individuals have been and are sacrificed in countless numbers for other individuals more favoured, that is, superior in some mode. The history of mankind shews, that individuals of the human species have constantly been sacrificed or injured, for the advantage of other individuals. Notwithstanding many apparent anomalies, nature has kept on the same course here, namely, that of sacrificing the inferior to the superior, the weak to the strong. The red and black races are sacrificed to the white; the feebler or inferior whites to the stronger or superior. And it is an undeniable fact, that individuals are now daily suffering, even unto death, while other individuals are benefited by the warnings and instruction thus furnished to them.

"There is, then, nothing at variance with the usual course of natural events, in a belief that the sufferings of some are actually intended to instruct, even though the instruction (that is, the benefit) falls chiefly or solely to the lot of other individuals of the human species.

"But is this always to continue until the human species, in its turn, gives place to some other species? The one peculiarity which distinguishes man, as a species, from all other species, viz., the mental power of funding his experience into capital, available to all succeeding individuals, arrests the analogy here. As the experiential capital accumulates, there may be (there must be?) less and less necessity of sacrificing individuals for the benefit (instruction) of other individuals; while the interest which any shareholder may draw from the joint-stock capital of experience will enable him so much the more easily and certainly to preserve himself from being made into a sacrifice. Moreover, part of the experiential capital will probably be that physiological knowledge which may enable parents to improve the organic development of their offspring, so as to keep raising individuals up towards the highest possible type, and thus decreasing the inferior specimens of the race, until no very bad ones remain.

" Under this view, there is no need to distort or explain away the facts of nature. They fully harmonize with your creed about the mode of instructing the human race by individual suffering and destruction. But the one difficulty will still remain, namely, that as man is the only species instructed thereby, 'What is the ultimate purpose of all the sufferings and destruction of all other organized individuals, for time unreckonable?' The analogy is too close to warrant the assumption of two different purposes, one applicable only to man, and one only to other species. Are there two purposes? one applicable to the progressive species man, the other applicable to the non-progressive species, and to man so far as he is analogous with them? If so, What *is* the latter purpose?"

It is obvious that other objects than human instruction must have been contemplated by the great Author of the universe when He subjected animals to pain and death before man existed, and when He continues the same system in regions beyond the reach of man's intelligence and control. In the work referred to, I have endeavoured to show, that, in regard to man, suffering is chiefly incidental, that it is not the *object* of any portion of his organization, and that, by obedience to the natural laws, it may, in a great degree, be avoided. In regard to the lower animals also, it appears to me that the state of suffering is not the normal but the incidental and exceptional condition of their being, and that destruction of individual life, which forms such an important element in the system of nature, opens the way on the whole, directly and indirectly, to enjoyments which more than compensate the evils attending it.

SECTION II.—IS THIS WORLD THE WRECK OF A BETTER SYSTEM?

The dogmas of the most numerous and influential sects of Christians represent man's condition in this world as the wreck of a better system, and many of them consider physical and animal nature also to have been involved in the catastrophe which befell him.

The following description of the nature of man, and of his

relations to God, is given in the Larger Catechism of the Church of Scotland, which was ratified and established by *Act of Parliament,* dated 7th February 1649,—which the great majority of Scotch children are taught to venerate as an unquestionably just and correct interpretation of Scripture,—and which, being thus entwined with their religious emotions, constitutes the basis of their religion :—

" *Q.* 13. What hath God especially decreed concerning angels and men ?

" *A.* God, by an eternal and immutable decree, out of his mere love, for the praise of his glorious grace, to be manifested in due time, hath selected some angels to glory; and, in Christ, hath chosen some men to eternal life, and the means thereof: and also, according to his sovereign power, and the unsearchable counsel of his own will (whereby he extendeth or withholdeth favour as he pleaseth), hath passed by and foreordained the rest to dishonour and wrath, to be for their sin inflicted, to the praise of the glory of his justice.

" *Q.* 14. How doth God execute his decrees?

" *A.* God executeth his decrees in the works of creation and providence, according to his infallible foreknowledge, and the free and immutable counsel of his own will.

" *Q.* 15. What is the work of creation ?

" *A.* The work of creation is that wherein God did in the beginning, by the word of his power, make of nothing the world, and all things therein, for himself, within the space of six days, and all very good.

" *Q.* 16. How did God create angels ?

" *A.* God created all the angels spirits, immortal, holy, excelling in knowledge, mighty in power, to execute his commandments, and to praise his name, yet subject to change.

" *Q.* 17. How did God create man ?

" *A.* After God had made all other creatures he created man male and female ; formed the body of the man of the dust of the ground, and the woman of the rib of the man ; endued them with living, reasonable, and immortal souls ; made them after his own image, in knowledge, righteousness, and holiness, having the law of God written in their hearts, and power to fulfil it, with dominion over the creatures ; yet subject to fall.

" *Q.* 18. What are God's works of providence ?

" *A.* God's works of providence are his most holy, wise, and powerful preserving and governing all his creatures ; ordering them, and all their actions, to his own glory.

" *Q.* 19. What is God's providence towards the angels ?

" *A.* God by his providence permitted some of the angels, wilfully and irrecoverably, to fall into sin and damnation, limiting and ordering that, and all their sins, to his own glory, and established the rest in holiness and happiness; employing them all, at his pleasure, in the administration of his power, mercy, and justice.

"*Q.* 20. What was the providence of God toward man in the estate in which he was created?

"*A.* The providence of God toward man in the estate in which he was created, was the placing him in paradise, appointing him to dress it, giving him liberty to eat of the fruit of the earth; putting the creatures under his dominion, and ordaining marriage for his help; affording him communion with Himself; instituting the Sabbath; entering into a covenant of life with him, upon condition of personal, perfect, and perpetual obedience, of which the tree of life was a pledge; and forbidding to eat of the tree of the knowledge of good and evil upon the pain of death.

"*Q.* 21. Did man continue in that estate wherein God at first created him?

"*A.* Our first parents being left to the freedom of their own will, through the temptation of Satan, transgressed the commandment of God in eating the forbidden fruit; and thereby fell from the estate of innocency wherein they were created.

"*Q.* 22. Did all mankind fall in that first transgression?

"*A.* The covenant being made with Adam as a public person, not for himself only, but for his posterity, all mankind descending from him by ordinary generation sinned in him, and fell with him, in that first transgression.

"*Q.* 23. Into what estate did the fall bring mankind?

"*A.* The fall brought mankind into an estate of sin and misery.

"*Q.* 24. What is sin?

"*A.* Sin is any want of conformity unto, or transgression of, any law of God, given as a rule to the reasonable creature.

"*Q.* 25. Wherein consisteth the sinfulness of that estate whereinto man fell?

"*A.* The sinfulness of that estate whereinto man fell, consisteth in the guilt of Adam's first sin, the want of that righteousness wherein he was created, and the corruption of his nature, whereby he is utterly indisposed, disabled, and made opposite unto all that is spiritually good, and wholly inclined to all evil, and that continually; which is commonly called original sin, and from which do proceed all actual transgressions.

"*Q.* 26. How is original sin conveyed from our first parents unto their posterity?

"*A.* Original sin is conveyed from our first parents unto their posterity by natural generation, so as all that proceed from them in that way are conceived and born in sin.

"*Q.* 27. What misery did the fall bring upon mankind?

"*A.* The fall brought upon mankind the loss of communion with God, his displeasure and curse; so as we are by nature children of wrath, bond slaves to Satan, and justly liable to all punishments in this world, and that which is to come.

"*Q.* 28. What are the punishments of sin in this world?

"*A.* The punishments of sin in this world are either inward, as blindness of mind, a reprobate sense, strong delusions, hardness of heart, horror of conscience, and vile affections; or outward, as the curse of God upon the creatures for our sakes, and all other evils that befall us in our bodies, names, estates, relations, and employments; together with death itself.

"*Q.* 29. What are the punishments of sin in the world to come?

"*A.* The punishments of sin in the world to come are everlasting separation from the comfortable presence of God, and most grievous torments in soul and body, without intermission, in hell-fire for ever."

"Of old," says a writer in the North British Review, "the earth was regarded as itself the centre of a system, and the heavenly bodies as moving round it. Even when there was no direct reference to this erroneous theory of the nature of celestial objects, it imparted a false light or colouring to every idea of terrestrial things." (Vol. xvii., p. 68.) This correctly expresses what appears to me to be the inevitable effect of the doctrine that this world, such as it now exists, is not an Institution, but a wreck. "It imparts a false light or colouring to every idea of terrestrial things."

In the Catechism, then, there is a direct contradiction to the notion that this world, such as it now exists, is an Institution. If the evidence before adduced is sufficient to support the latter hypothesis, then the hypothesis of a wreck is necessarily excluded; if not, we must embrace *it* with all its consequences. The solution of the question is of momentous importance. Before the religious sentiments and the reflecting intellect of the people can be induced to reverence and obey the precepts of God addressed to them in the order of nature, they must be taught that nature is still such as God made it, and that wherever it has been thoroughly understood, it appears to reflect wisdom and goodness. There *can be no sacredness* in nature, if it be intrinsically disordered. In studying it, we cannot come into communion with God, if, through either its inherent derangement or our own natural obliquity of mind, His wisdom and goodness are *not* discernible in it; while, if they *are* discernible, it cannot be justly said that man has lost communion with his Maker. If the Divine Institutions and adaptations in nature are calculated to promote the enjoyment of man, and to instruct, improve, guide, and elevate him as a moral, religious, and intellectual administrator of this world, he cannot be truly said to be under God's "wrath and curse."

Farther, if the practical efficacy of religion in guiding human conduct, depends on its harmony with the order of nature,—then this representation of the world and its relations to God, is not only speculatively erroneous, but constitutes a positive and important obstacle to the progress of Divine truth. It tends to blind the intellect, and mislead the moral and religious sentiments of the people, and thereby to retard their advance in practical religion, virtue, and civilization.

Incredible as it may appear, there are millions of excellent persons whose religious emotions have been so interwoven with the doctrines of this and similar Catechisms that they are painfully affected when they hear the doctrines called in question. When we point out to them that the facts brought to light by geological researches and comparative anatomy, contradict the dogma that the present constitution and condition of the lower animals are the consequence of " the curse of God upon the creatures for our sakes;" that chemical, anatomical, and physiological facts shew that the ground and the human organism are adapted to each other in beneficent relationship, and contradict the text, " Cursed is the ground for thy sake," as it has been generally interpreted ; and that the physiology of the brain, and the adaptation of the external world to its functions, contradict the dogma that man's whole nature is corrupt—in other words, that the mental faculties are naturally incapable of legitimate action—and when we assure them that the authority on which they believe the contrary doctrine is only that of a Church, and of a Catechism compiled by fallible men, all of whom were ignorant of the sciences of Geology, Chemistry, Comparative and Human Anatomy and Physiology, and the physiology of the brain, and many of whom were unacquainted with any other natural science, we only give them pain and provoke their anger. Did not evil consequences to society flow from this belief, it might be unjustifiable to assail it; but persons thus trained fear science, from the suspicion that it is at variance with their creed, and openly or covertly resist its introduction into schools. In Scotland, they insist that their Catechism shall form the basis of instruction in national schools; and as they would be affronted were we to assert that they deliberately intend to teach contradictions, they must mean to twist all natural science into apparent accordance with its doctrines, or exclude scientific instruction altogether. The latter is the course hitherto generally pursued. Nevertheless, the dogma that human nature is wholly corrupt, contradicts the facts that every faculty has a legitimate sphere of action, and that vice and crime are only abuses which, to an extent at present unascertained, may be prevented by an improved development of the cerebral organs and more thorough and practical instruction and training. Being opposed to a natural fact, it forces the individual who embraces it, either to shut his eyes against the true order of nature, and thus to mistake at once his duty to himself and to society, or to attempt to believe in contradictions, a process which perverts the moral faculties, paralyses the intellect, and renders consistent action impossible. By giving a false direction to our intellectual faculties in searching for the path of duty, by maintaining our feelings, opinions, and practical habits either dissociated from our religious emotions, or, if joined with them, then in some degree at war with God's natural institutions, it brings upon us many of the miseries which it describes—viz., the natural penalties of error,—and by this means supports its own authority and prolongs our degradation.

CHAPTER IX.

PRACTICAL CONSIDERATIONS.

SECTION I.—HOW SHOULD WE ACT, IF THE WORLD IS AN INSTITUTION?

IF this world is an *Institution*, and if God is its Author and Governor, it appears to be the duty and interest of man to regard it with reverence, to study its arrangements, and, as far as possible, to act in accordance with the rules which it indicates for the guidance of his conduct. We must cease to be affronted with it because it and our own organism are material; to revolt from it because our bodies and those of the lower animals appear to be constructed on one plan, to run similar courses on earth, and to be adapted by surpassing wisdom, each species to its circumstances, and all to the general laws of Nature. In particular, we must cease to treat with ridicule, contempt, or indifference, the influence of the size and condition of the brain in determining, in this life, the amount and condition of the mental power of individuals; and no longer recoil from the proposition that this organ is the grand instrument by means of which God conducts the moral government of the world. We must approach Nature in the spirit of little children, humble, eager for instruction, and willing to obey. To reach this state of mind, we must lay aside that practical atheism which blinds us to the laws of God's Providence, manifested in Nature, and devote our best energies to discover the Divine Will revealed in that record. Having discovered that Will, we must entwine it with our religious emotions, constitute it our religion, and make obedience to it the business of our lives.

If we approach the consideration of the world in this spirit, we shall find that every organ, bodily and mental, stands in admirable adaptation to external nature, to the other organs, and to God; and that enjoyment, improvement, and elevation of character, are the objects of the whole, while pain, sorrow, and premature death, are only contingent consequences of abnormal conditions.

Man is ushered into life not only naked, but with an organism that imperatively demands clothing and shelter; with digestive organs that constantly require new supplies of food;

and with faculties that desire property, social consideration, and multifarious productions of skill and industry, for their gratification. The dogmas represent this state of things as a "curse" inflicted in consequence of Adam's first transgression. Viewed as a designed Institution, it wears a widely different aspect. The earth is endowed with properties calculated to yield products which man may call forth by the application of his skill and labour, and which he may fashion into food, clothing, houses, ships, and innumerable articles of utility and ornament, for his own gratification. God has bestowed on him bones, muscles, and a nervous system which generate strength within him, and rendered labour agreeable. He has given him pleasure, recurring several times a day, in repairing, by the use of wholesome food, the waste of organic substance occasioned by the exertions of labour. He has given him cerebral organs and intellectual faculties which enable him to acquire knowledge and skill, and also moral and religious emotions to refine, elevate, and direct him in fulfilling the duties which he is appointed to perform on earth. Among these are faculties of Ideality, Wonder, Veneration and Hope, Causality and Comparison, which, carrying him beyond this earthly sphere, enable him to penetrate to some extent into the regions of boundless space and endless time, there to trace the power and wisdom of God, and to expand his own nature by intercommunion with the greatness and glories of the universe.

Man's faculties enable him also to explore the depths of the earth and sea, the summits of the mountains, and the recesses of rocks; and there, in the minutest as in the grandest forms of Nature, he discovers design, order, beauty, and adaptation. When properly trained and directed, his religious emotions are capable of investing all these minute and stupendous objects, their properties and modes of action, with a holy reverence, as manifestations of Divine power, wisdom, and goodness ; and when things are so viewed, the inherent adaptation of his faculties to them all, renders it a gratification of the highest order to enter into this temple of the most High, to act as ministering servants in fulfilling the Divine designs, and to reap the joys which have been connected with obedience to the Divine laws.

When viewed in this light, labour ceases to be regarded as a "curse," and becomes holy and honourable, a privilege and a boon. The understanding then willingly tries to discover the *conditions* which must be observed to invest it with its pleasing and beneficial qualities, and how to avoid the course which renders it painful or abortive. If the world is an Institution, if physical nature is benevolently and wisely adapted to man's bodily and mental qualities, and these to it, then when labour is attended with suffering, aberration from the proper conditions of that relationship may be safely predicated, and we should be taught, trained, and encouraged, in reliance on Divine Wisdom and Goodness, to search out the sources of our errors, and, if possible, to dry them up.

To turn our thoughts in disgust from labour as a "curse;" to regard its inconveniences as a punishment, and to leap at once in imagination into another sphere of existence in which there shall be neither toil nor sorrow, as a refuge from the evils which our unskilful arrangements produce in this life, is not religion, nor doing honour to God, but is really indulging in a maudlin sentimental egotism.

If labour is not a curse but a boon, all our necessary duties and occupations, when fulfilled in conformity with the Divine law, become not only useful and pleasurable, but morally right and religious, and the whole aspect of the world is changed from one of gloom and misery to one of hope and encouragement to virtuous exertion. The grand objection to the proposition that this world is an Institution, is founded on the sufferings which have afflicted humanity in all ages and conditions of life. It is said that the individual is racked with pain, or becomes the victim of sorrow; that the young, loving, and happy husband and wife are engulphed in irremediable poverty, or separated by death; or their hearts are wrung with anguish by the death of their beloved offspring; that ruin's stern ploughshare often levels in the dust the fortunes that should have been the reward of the toils of life and the comfort of declining years; that friends forsake us, scoundrels betray us, fire consumes our property, and floods extinguish our lives; and that hence all is vanity and vexation of spirit. We are told that all this misery has only one great object—to wean our affections from the earth, and to concentrate them on God and Heaven.

As declamation, this objection appears formidable; but when the facts on which it is reared, are more closely investigated, their weight is greatly diminished. In surveying the phenomena of life, it is difficult to forget the observation of Mr Robert Forsyth in his work on Moral Science, that as this world is the only one of which we have experience, it is illogical to infer from *its disorders*, that God has made *a better world* in which to compensate us for the evils which He has appointed us to endure in this. It appears more respectful to our Maker to doubt whether we are rightly understanding His institutions, and acting properly our own part under them, before we condemn them in this querulous tone and fly to heaven as a refuge from the alleged imperfections of earth. I beg leave, therefore, to direct the attention of the reader to the exposition of the sources of some of our chief sufferings given in the preceding pages, and to solicit his serious consideration of the question, whether it is within the power of man, in any degree, to mitigate or avoid them—and if so, to what extent they are the results of our own imperfect knowledge and erroneous modes of action, or of inherent imperfections in the constitution of Nature?

1st, Our sufferings from the operations of physical nature, and how to mitigate them, are treated of in Chap. VI. sec. i. p. 82.

2d, Our sufferings from disease and death are considered in sec. ii. p. 89, and an attempt is made to estimate their true character as parts of the order of nature.

3d, The sufferings that arise from misdirection of our emotional faculties, and from failure in our plans of life, and the ruin and destitution thence arising, and how to lessen them, are treated of in sec. v. from p. 118 to p. 130.

4th, The evils that arise from placing individuals in situations for which their natural qualities do not fit them, and how these may be avoided, are considered in sec. vi. p. 130; and in "The Constitution of Man," also, I have endeavoured to throw light on these and similar objections to the doctrine of Divine benevolence pervading the order of Nature.

This work is not designed as a full investigation of these and the other difficult and important questions which present themselves to a reflecting mind on surveying the phenomena of life; but merely as an exposition of a useful method according to which, in my opinion, this enquiry should be conducted. I shall here add only a few observations on the provisions made by Nature for the mitigation of some of the sufferings before mentioned when they have actually, and from whatever cause, overtaken us.

I have adverted to a process which an injury to our bones or muscles calls into play in our organism, in order to repair the wounded tissues and restore the part to health and strength. An analogous provision is instituted in the case of our mental afflictions. Every faculty receives pleasure from the presence of its objects, and suffers pain on their removal. No one objects to the first alternative, but many to the second; yet, it is difficult to imagine how the first could exist without liability to the second. The effect of this order of things is to bind us to the objects of our desires by a double tie, the pleasure of enjoyment, and the pain of deprivation. The mother's joy in her healthy, beautiful, virtuous, and intelligent child is intense; but her grief in losing it is commensurately great. Her affection is ardent in proportion to the size of the organ of Philoprogenitiveness and those of the moral emotions in her brain. This fact is positively demonstrable, and the phenomena of life confirm it, for there are mothers who are indifferent to their children, and some who when under destructive excitement even kill them as troublesome encumbrances. Lately, in Chester, a father was executed for having led his two children into a garden and given them deadly stabs with a knife in the throat, as he had done with pigs when he assisted a butcher. There he dug a hole and buried them. Our philosophy and religion must embrace all the phenomena of nature, and not shrink from investigating their causes. In the first of these cases, the death of offspring by disease or accident is a dire calamity; in the second, it would have been secretly felt as a pleasure. It is differences in the organisms of the individuals, influenced by their circumstances, that give rise to these differences in feeling; and there is reason to believe that by attention to the laws of reproduction, the brain may be greatly improved.

Moreover, there is a condition of each organ corresponding to its state of gratification, and another corresponding to its state of pain, and we are so constituted that in process of time both conditions will abate, and in many instances cease by the mere action of the organism itself; in each case to the advantage of the individual.

This proposition is strikingly illustrated in the case of the lower animals. Among these some are more and others less ardently attached to their young; and those most attached suffer severe distress when they are removed. I have heard a cow utter heart-rending lamentations for days when her calf was led to the slaughter; and who has not felt pained by the sufferings of the domestic cat when her kittens were taken from her and drowned? Yet in a few months, in the ordinary course of nature, these mothers would have become indifferent to their offspring, and driven them from their presence. An explanation of these phenomena is found in processes established by Nature in the organisms of the animals, and destined to come into action and cease when circumstances require them. Can we doubt that it is an organic impulse implanted and directed by the Author of Nature that incites the young bird to build her first nest, before she has either seen such a process performed or produced eggs to deposit in it?

Let us not shrink from applying the light afforded by these examples to our own species. In the human mother in whom the organ of Philoprogenitiveness is very large and the organs of the moral sentiments are deficient, there is an intense love of her children while they are young, but it decreases as they grow older, and almost entirely ceases when they become men and women. At that age they become the objects of the moral affections, which in her are feeble, and hence her indifference. This is no theory, but the statement of a fact which I have repeatedly observed. It shows that by the order of nature parental love decreases in women, and finally disappears when the object of it no longer requires its exercise, very much as occurs in the case of the lower creatures; in other words, the organ being no longer stimulated by its object, which is a child and not a man or woman, ceases to act, and then indifference ensues. If the child, even of such a mother, should die prematurely, the organ being deprived of its object in the full blaze of its intensity, and before the period had arrived when its action would have naturally diminished, great anguish would be experienced. The removal of the object is the removal of the stimulus which maintains it in action, and we have seen that in her case the normal order of Nature diminishes her interest as her children grow up, until at last it ceases altogether. Now, even when the object is removed suddenly and prematurely, a similar process ensues. A gradual diminution of the action of the organ, attended by a corresponding diminution of the sense of deprivation takes place, until, in a healthy organism, by the mere lapse of time the painful emotion ceases. If the organ be very large and the brain feeble in constitution, a permanent morbid action may be established, which will produce inconsolable grief; but this is disease, and forms an exception to the general rule.

Here, then, is one proof of benevolent natural provision for the removal of mental anguish. Other laws of our constitution conduce to the same effect. When one organ is in circumstances which give rise to suffering, its action may be mitigated by rousing others into play. It is in virtue of this law that religion consoles us in our afflictions. If we have large organs of Hope and Veneration, and believe in God, the activity of these organs manifested in submission to His will and reliance on His goodness, introduces pure, calm, and holy emotions into our consciousness, and by diminishing the circulation of the blood in the excited organs, it mitigates and assuages the intensity of our suffering. Our grief, however, is not *instantly* removed; because cerebral action when strongly excited does not suddenly cease, and the brain reaches the normal state of repose only by degrees.

The principles involved in these illustrations apply to all our faculties. I had a friend in whom the organs of the domestic affections and of the moral sentiments were large, and he was ardently attached to his wife. She died when he was yet in the vigour of life, and his sufferings were intense. Dr Andrew Combe was his physician, and so inconsolable was the patient, that for six months after her death he was in much anxiety lest a permanent morbid action of the brain should ensue. At length, however, our friend was accidentally thrown from his horse, and fell on his back on a newly-made road. He was severely bruised, and suffered great pain, but no bone and no vital organ were injured. Dr Combe, in mentioning the accident to me, said, " It relieves me from much anxiety, for it is not in itself attended with danger, and the pain will excite a new action in the brain, which will relieve the organs that are suffering so severely through the loss of his wife; and on his restoration to health, his mental tranquillity will be re-established." The result coincided in every respect with that prediction. Although he lived many years after his loss he never married again.

Similar phenomena occur in the case of widows. A sagacious woman who had long been employed as a sick-nurse, remarked, on being asked how a lady was, whose husband she had recently attended on his death-bed, " Oh, she is suffering very severely ; I fear this will be a two years' case." " What do you mean by a two years' case ?" " There are great differences in women ; some seem scarcely to feel at all when their husbands die ; others suffer for three or four months—some for a year—and a few, who are very sensitive and have been greatly attached, will be inconsolable even for two years, but the suffering rarely goes beyond that time. After two years, tranquillity returns, and the usual habits of life are resumed." Be it observed that these remarks are equally applicable to men and women of all countries and religions, and therefore indicate that this recuperative process is really an institution of Nature, and not an accidental occurrence, and that it is through the laws of the organism that it takes place.

As a contrast to the friend before mentioned, I may notice the case of an evangelical clergyman well known in Edinburgh forty years ago. He was married four times, and the bridal day of each new wife was separated by only six or eight weeks from that of the funeral of her predecessor. What consolation did he require on losing his bosom friend ? Could he have looked to the pleasure of meeting her in heaven ? One would think that he should have blushed at the thought of seeing her there, considering the indecent haste with which he had provided her successor. The development of his brain was widely different from that of my friend; and he acted according to his impulses. I have heard some of his clerical brethren charitably and truly ascribe his conduct to peculiarity of disposition; but it was in the disproportionate size of particular cerebral organs that the peculiarity had its rise, and such different mental results from the same calamity render it necessary to find a consistent explanation of them, otherwise the moral government of the world remains an enigma.

It is in virtue of the same benevolent arrangement of Nature for relieving one organ by exciting others, that active and laborious individuals suffer less from mental afflictions than the luxurious and the idle. The mother whose duties call on her for constant exertion of muscular strength and intellectual thought, is sooner relieved from the pain that attends the loss of her child than another who, nursed in the lap of luxury, has no imperative calls to excite the other organs into action for her relief.

By the decay of power and activity in the brain and nervous system as age advances, Nature diminishes our attachment to the objects which we shall soon be called on to leave. From year to year the circle of our interests contracts: in reading the newspapers, for example, we first pass over scientific and abstract discussions; next we omit the foreign intelligence; by and by we care little about distant occurrences even in our own country, and we end by confining our attention chiefly to the incidents of our neighbourhood, and of our private sphere.

The same benevolent preparation of our feelings to meet our destiny is apparent in the case even of premature death. I have heard physicians who had passed forty years in practice remark, that they had rarely met with patients who were unwilling to die. The changes which take place in the organism and which end in death, are attended by a corresponding influence on the brain. Its energy is weakened, interest in its objects diminishes with its decay, and thus we become prepared to die. Many years ago I asked one of the gentlemen who accompanied Sir John Franklin in his first expedition to the arctic regions, how he felt when strength for farther exertions had failed, and when the party were seated before what appeared to be their last fire: " Did you think painfully of the friends whom you expected never to meet again, of the home which you had left, and which contrasted so strongly with the frozen wilderness in which you were perishing? What sustained you in that hour of trial?" His reply was: " Home and the moon possessed equal interest in my feelings. We were so completely exhausted in mind and body by cold, starvation, and fatigue, that our whole interests were concentrated in the fire. My chief distress arose when it came to my turn to rise and place fresh timber on it to support the combustion. We knew that a party of Indians had been sent from the nearest settlement to search for and succour us, and that on their finding us before our fire was extinguished depended our only chance of life. This, although nearly a forlorn hope, was still possible, but, nevertheless, the pain attending the effort to rise and move the timber extinguished all other considerations." A narrative closely similar was given by the captain of the American ship "Oswego," which was stranded on the coast of Africa. He was made captive by the natives, stript naked, placed on the back of a camel, and taken across the desert under a burning sun. For three or four days his misery was so intense that he searched for the means of committing suicide, but could not find them. After that time, a stupor came over him; and during three months' travelling and living in the same circumstances, he had consciousness only of existence and of passing scenes, but little suffering. He was at length given up at an English settlement on the coast, and many months elapsed before his brain and nervous system fully recovered their usual powers of thought and sensation.

These instances show that Nature sets a limit to our sufferings, whether the causes of them have been avoidable or unavoidable, and does not leave us in hopeless misery when no farther sources of enjoyment are open to us.

In the prevailing religious creeds little or no notice is taken of these benevolent provisions of Divine wisdom and goodness, and in consequence the benefits of a religious reliance on the prospective mitigation of our sufferings which they are calculated to afford, are to a great extent lost.

We need a new Reformation; and if the views before presented have to any reasonable extent a foundation in nature, Natural Religion may now assume a new form, and come forth with a degree of beneficence and power which it has never hitherto possessed.

The views stated in Chap. III. sec. iv. p. 34, that man is *naturally a religious being*, are not speculative propositions, but rest on positive evidence of the existence of tangible and visible cerebral organs, endowed with functions producing religious emotions. Readers who doubt the existence of such emotions will perhaps find an explanation of their differing in this respect so widely from general opinion, in a deficient development of the organs in their own brains; for it is certain that in all ages the great majority of mankind have given expression to these emotions in religious observances and dogmas of one character or another.

Again, the reader is referred to the elucidation given in Chap. II. p. 15 of the complex character of Religion ; and to the evidence there adduced, that it is constituted by entwining intellectual ideas with the religious emotions, and that these ideas may possess almost any character, provided they are not in flagrant discord with the predominant mental condition of the people.

If these two propositions are sound, it appears to follow that instead of the Mahometan, Hindoo, and other false religions resting on the sacred books which are represented as their foundations, they repose on the basis of the natural religious faculties of man ; and that the books are the mere embodiments of the views of God and man and the world, entertained by certain individuals who aspired to give specific forms and directions to the religious emotions of these nations. The soundness and usefulness of the intellectual ideas which by this means they formed into religious dogmas, will be correctly measured by the extent to which they embody or harmonize with the institutions and laws of God in Nature. Wherever the founders of these religions have converted false views of God, or erroneous interpretations of the course of His administration in Nature, into religious dogmas, and thereby constituted them sacred articles of faith and rules of conduct, to be believed and followed, but never questioned, or tried by any appeal except to the sacred books themselves, they have misdirected the understandings and corrupted the principles of action of the people whom they professed to guide and instruct.

Before sound, useful, and practical intellectual ideas can be associated with the religious emotions, so as to constitute a really true religion, we must possess correct notions of what we are capable of understanding concerning God, and His mode of governing the world ; and also sound views of our own nature, and of our relations to Him and His Institutions. This knowledge being entwined with the religious emotions becomes sacred and religious ; and from being thus a hallowed embodiment of the real order of Nature it is highly practical. It enlarges and improves as knowledge of God's laws advances ; it harmonizes with all truth ; and if God be the Author at once of Nature, and of the human body and mind, such a religion must be wisely adapted to the wants, wishes, and welfare of man.

The knowledge now alluded to must rest on evidence that is open to observation. At present, mental science as generally taught is a chaos, and cannot be used with advantage in religious investigations. The reader is referred to Chap. III. p. 23, in which I have considered the physical elements and mental faculties of man: the chief value of the observations there brought forward, consists in their forming an example of the kind of knowledge which, in my opinion, should form an element in a true religion.

Another important, indeed a fundamental portion of such a faith, is a correct notion of what our minds are capable of conceiving concerning God. I have treated of this subject in Chap. V. p. 66. If we form erroneous notions on this point, and embody them as dogmas in our religion, we confound, bewilder, and mislead the weak in mind, and outrage and repel the strong. Lately, a highly gifted and educated friend, with whom I was conversing on religion, said, "Please, define God." My reply was, " Ask that intelligent dog which you are so fond of, to define Man." "Impossible," was the reply, " he has not our faculties and cannot comprehend us." "But surely," I rejoined, " he is nearer your level than you are to that of the Deity; and how can you expect man to define a Being who so unspeakably transcends all that he is capable of conceiving?" "Well, then, tell me what you mean by 'religious emotions?' I never in my life felt such emotions; religion has always appeared to me to consist in the desire to get to heaven and the fear of going to hell, and I never had any other feeling on the subject." I perceived a palpable deficiency in the organs of the religious emotions in the head of my friend, and had no difficulty in believing this statement to be true. It embodied, however, only an individual, and not a general truth; for the experience of the majority of mankind is widely different.

If we were permitted to discover the intimate consciousness even of excellent, sincere, and intelligent persons, we should find that extraordinary discrepancies of views and feelings exist in their minds on the subject of God and religion, and that an elucidation of the range of the human faculties in this and all other departments of knowledge, is as indispensable to a sound religion as to a true and useful philosophy.

I have already remarked that the Bible does not *reveal* God, but commences by *assuming* His existence. " In the beginning God created the heavens and the earth." Subsequently, several descriptions are given of Him and His attributes; but none of these do more than ascribe to Him human qualities, enlarged, purified, and exalted to the utmost stretch of our imaginations. Thus, man exists in time, and God exists in endless time, *i.e.*, He is everlasting. Man possesses some power, God unlimited power—He is Almighty; man exists in limited space, God in unlimited space—He is everywhere present; man knows some things, God knows all things; man is benevolent, God is long-suffering and merciful; man has a sentiment of truth and justice—God is perfect truth and perfect justice. In the Old Testament, human passions even are ascribed to God; He is jealous, angry, placable, and so forth. It is in vain to condemn descriptions of the Divine Being ascribing to Him human qualities, for we cannot conceive any object or being that does not lie within the limits of cognition of our faculties. The enquiry, therefore, which I have attempted to institute—" What is man capable of discovering and comprehending concerning God?"—is not a barren speculation, but one of a practical and important nature.

Dr Johnson defines the substantive "*Worship*" to mean "Adoration; religious act of reverence;" "to *worship*" is "to adore; to honour or venerate with religious rites." Again, ".to *adore*" is "to worship with external homage." Now, the external rites in which we embody our "worship," "reverence," or "homage," will obviously bear a relation to our motives in worshipping; and these will be influenced by our opinions of the character of the Being whom we adore. Tribes who ascribe the lower passions to their Deities institute immoral rites and ceremonies in honour of them. Those nations who regard God as cruel and revengeful, sacrifice animals and some of them men, to appease Him. Others, who ascribe to Him self-esteem and love of approbation, (their own predominant qualities,) offer him praise and glorification, and try to please him by expressing their own consciousness, (generally with much exaggeration,) of abject meanness and unworthiness.

If I am right in saying that although God has not given us faculties fitted to comprehend Himself, yet He has given us powers which enable us *to understand His will in relation to ourselves and other beings over whom He has given us some degree of influence and control*, and that in the order of nature, He has revealed duties which we are capable of performing, then we may reasonably consider whether the rites of our religious worship should partake of the character of attempts to please God as a Being possessing human qualities, or be directed to do Him honour, reverence, and homage, by studying, expounding, and obeying His will as thus revealed to us. All existing forms of worship should be tried by their relation to what we can comprehend of the nature of God, and of His will. If without irreverence I might borrow an illustration from the relation between man and the lower animals, I should remark that it appears possible for one being to comprehend portions of the will of another, although he cannot conceive adequately the nature of that other. The dog, for instance, cannot comprehend the nature of the shepherd, but he can learn the shepherd's will to be, that he, the dog, should tend the sheep;

and the dog, without attempting to know more of the shepherd's nature than this portion of his will, may obey it and preserve the flock. The horses which in our circuses are trained to dance, to fire pistols, to fetch tea-kettles, and to perform other surprising feats, do not comprehend the nature of the men who teach them to do these things, nor apparently do they understand the object or design of the actions themselves ; but they seem to understand the will of the men, so far as it relates to the actions required of them, for they do the things they are taught. We should all agree that the dog sadly mistook his own capacities and his relations to man, if instead of hearkening to the shepherd's voice, obeying his will, and guarding the flock, he turned a deaf ear to the one and set the other at defiance, and commenced a grand speculation on the *nature* of his master, and his *attributes*. We should be still more astonished at the want of a due sense of his own deficiencies and position, if the dog, in the midst of his speculation on this, to him, incomprehensible subject, and of his neglect of duty, ever and anon turned up his eyes and raised his fore-paws to his master, and uttered indications of intense admiration and veneration for him, calling him a being possessed of every faculty of canine consciousness in the highest state of perfection and in unlimited degree. And yet, ignorant and superstitious men do something analogous to this, when, instead of " walking humbly" with God, studying His Institutions and obeying His will, they ascribe to Him their own qualities, praise Him, and implore Him to protect them as His devoted worshippers ; they all the while violating His laws. In the words of Dr Fellowes, " The only use which some religionists make of their understanding is to perplex it by inquiring into the nature of God. They leave the easy and feasible to attempt the impossible. They forsake the clear and the simple to lose themselves in a region of clouds and darkness. For how can the finite hope to comprehend the infinite, the material the spiritual, the temporal the eternal ? God can be known only in His works. THERE His agency is seen. THERE His will may be traced ; there His laws be developed. But, what His nature is, or how He exists, must ever be past finding out. It is enough for us to know that He exists ; but *how* He exists, it is vain, and indeed presumptuous to inquire."*

Christian believers institute forms of worship in honour of God, corresponding to their peculiar notions of His character derived from the Bible. In 1839 I visited, on a Sunday, the establishment of Shaking Quakers at Niskayŭna, near Albany,

---

* *The Religion of the Universe, &c.*, by ROBERT FELLOWES, LL.D. London, 1836.

in the United States of North America. Visitors were freely admitted as spectators of their worship.

The service began by one of the men delivering some sensible moral precepts; after which, as the day was warm, the men stripped off their coats and laid aside their hats; while the women took off their shawls and bonnets. They then commenced singing and dancing; at the same time waving their hands, which they held in the attitude of the fore-feet of the kangaroo. While singing, they knelt occasionally; and, at other times, several of them took their station in the middle of the floor and sang, while the rest danced round them. Their tunes were merry measures, with strongly marked time, such as are played in farces and pantomimes. By and by some of them began to bend their bodies forwards, to shake from side to side, and to whirl round. A favourite motion was to let the trunk of the body drop downwards, with a sudden jerk, to one side, care being always taken to recover the perpendicular before the equilibrium was lost. The head and trunk were drawn up with another jerk. In all their shakings and contortions they never lost the step in their dance, nor ran against each other.

During these gesticulations some of the strangers laughed. One of the male Shakers, singling out a young lady whom he had observed committing this breach of decorum, addressed her thus: "Young woman, you laugh too much. We are a-worshippin' God: we want you to be quiet; that's all we desire." (*Notes on America*, Vol. II. p. 302, and Appendix, No. V.)

This, then, was worship calculated to do honour to God and benefit to man, according to the notions which these people had formed of the Supreme Being. It will be observed that there is no *natural* relation between these ceremonies and the religious emotions of man; and that their sacred character as acts of worship was only communicated to them by artificially associating them with the natural emotions. Do I greatly err in supposing that had their leaders expounded to them the order of God's government on earth, and enforced obedience to His laws as rules of conduct revealed in His works, and thereby called forth in their minds, holy, reverential, and grateful emotions towards God, and more earnest desires to discharge their own duties, the worship would probably have been not less acceptable to God, and perhaps more edifying and beneficial to themselves? In St Peter's magnificent cathedral in Rome, and in splendid churches in other cities, I have often been a spectator of the celebration of High Mass and other gorgeous ceremonies of the Roman Catholic religion. These, too, were acts of Divine worship, intended to do honour to God and to lead the people to holy living. But here also the sacred character as worship was not inherent in the ceremonies, but was communicated to them by training.

Were I to ask a sound Scotch Presbyterian, whether, in his opinion, such a substitute as I have supposed to be made for the worship of the Shaking Quakers, would be admissible in their case, he probably would not be greatly shocked, but would calmly consider the merits of the question. If, however, I were to hint that his own worship consists in the expression, in prayers, psalms, and sermons, of the dogmas quoted on p. 186, and other similar notions of God and man; to suggest that there is no inherent sacredness in them, and to ask whether they so completely accord with the highest views attainable of the character of God's administration on earth, and are so perfectly calculated to do honour to Him, and to direct the moral, religious, and intellectual faculties of the people towards holy, pure, and beneficent conduct, that such a substitution would in this case also be admissible—I should probably be accused of profanity, and call forth a storm of indignation. And why so? Because in youth these dogmas and forms of worship had been entwined with the religious emotions of the Presbyterian, had become sacred in his mind, and now constitute his mode of expressing love, reverence, gratitude, obedience, and every other holy emotion towards God. Why does not the same feelings arise in his mind when it is suggested that the substitute proposed might be an improvement on the worship of the Shakers or Roman Catholics? Simply because *his* religious emotions have never been entwined with *their* ceremonies, and he is able to judge *of them* by his unbiassed reason. In point of fact all forms of divine worship derive their existence and efficacy from their being expressions of the longings and aspirations of the religious emotions inherent in the human mind; and their power over the devotee depends not on their conformity to absolute truth, but on the size and activity of the organs of these emotions in his brain, and on the degree in which his intellect is satisfied with the dogmas, forms, or ceremonies, through which this activity finds expression.

If this view be correct, it will be as impossible to extinguish religion, as to supersede music, painting, sculpture, dress, or any other thing which is desired in consequence of wants, and supplied by the activity of faculties inherent in the human constitution; and the only important consideration is—What kind of worship stands in the truest and most direct relationship to the whole faculties of man, in their most cultivated and enlightened condition? Is it such dogmas and ceremonies as have just been mentioned? or a service based on the laws of God and our relationship to Him and them as revealed in Nature?

Mr Angus Macpherson, in an excellent little work on "English Education,"* asks "those who maintain the *indispensability* of the Greek and Roman classics in education:" "Is it not *more probable* that the proper and legitimate means for training the intellect coexisted with the intellect itself, not since the period of the rise and fall of the Greek and Roman empires, *but since the beginning of the world?*" In like manner I ask whether, if there is a God, and if He has conferred religious emotions on man, as maintained in Chap. III. p. 34, it is not probable that He has constituted the order of this world in harmony with these emotions, and fitted His natural Institutions, and the lessons which they teach, when regarded as manifestations of His will, to become objects of reverential respect and obedience, and thus to constitute elements in divine worship? It would be felt as a strange contradiction equally to our moral, religious, and intellectual emotions and perceptions, if the case were otherwise, and if such ceremonies as I have described were sacred, and God's will revealed in Nature were profane; nevertheless the religious dogmas of all nations repudiate this view! The only explanation of this rejection that I can conjecture is—that until the order of external Nature and the functions of the brain, by means of which the adaptation of the world to our faculties becomes manifest, were discovered, the relationship of Nature to our religious emotions, although in all ages felt and recognised as existing, could not become the foundation of a practical religion.

It is objected, however, that if we adopt rules of conduct founded on the order of nature, God and religion become equally unnecessary; and that knowledge of these rules and obedience to them, for the sake of the good consequent on obedience, is all-sufficient for our welfare. In answer, I remark—1st, That men in whom the organs of the religious emotions and those of the intellectual faculties are developed to an average extent, believe intuitively in the existence of a Power and Intelligence above and beyond nature (see p. 66); and 2d, That there is abundant evidence in nature that this Being has constituted the human faculties in relationship to Himself and His works; among which faculties are religious emotions. This will be regarded by some readers as begging the whole question; but as I have already stated the grounds on which these views are entertained, I shall here only apply them in answering the foregoing objection. The objectors, although they dispense with a God and religion, will probably admit that we are placed in this world to discharge duties to ourselves and our

---

* Glasgow: David Robertson, 1854.

fellow-men. Well, then, the *more* and the *higher* the motives which can be supplied to induce us to discharge these duties, the greater will be the probability of their being *well discharged.* It is the duty of a soldier, for example, when commanded, to storm a fortress, at the peril of life and limb. He is under military discipline which provides that if he refuse he shall be shot. This is one motive, and it might be supposed to include all others. But if we add to it the desire of the applause of his officers, his comrades, and his country, constituting together the love of glory, we raise and strengthen his resolution by another and higher motive. Add a sense of moral duty to his country and his king, and a third and a still higher motive comes into play. And those who believe in God say, Add the religious emotions, which infuse new fire into the other faculties, and elevate and render them holy, and you will then kindle in the soldier a great moral and religious excitement before which death and danger will lose all their terrors. An army composed of men in this condition of mind, if equally numerous, and as well fed, equipped, drilled, and commanded, as an opposing force animated by no motive but the fear of the Provost-Marshal, would sweep it from the field like a whirlwind. In the late war, the Emperor of Russia appealed strongly to the religious emotions of his people, and in the Ironsides of Cromwell's army we may see the effects of such an influence on the soldier's courage.

The foregoing illustration is applicable to all the duties and trials of life. The religious emotions appear to me to have been bestowed to sanctify, elevate, invigorate, and ennoble every act of our other faculties; and although hitherto they have never been so applied with due intelligence, and therefore have not been applied successfully, I can discover no adequate reason for despairing that this will yet be accomplished. The grand obstacle in the way is the existence and deep-rooted influence of the prevailing dogmas; but, if the views now advanced are founded in truth, these will be gradually superseded by sounder and more practical interpretations of Scripture.

It is farther objected, that if we should base religion upon the will of God manifested in nature, there could be no general agreement in doctrine and practice, because every one sees nature through the medium of his own faculties, and these differ in relative power and cultivation in different individuals. This objection is to some extent well founded; but it is equally applicable to religion founded on a supernatural revelation, as is demonstrated by the different interpretations put upon the Bible by the different Christian sects. The subject is considered on pages 48 and 49, to which I beg leave to refer, and particularly to the answer given to this objection on p. 49.

It is certain that the impressions which each individual receives from the external world, are modified by the condition of his own organism. Light does not exist to a man born blind, nor melody to one in whom the organs of Tune are very deficient; colour is not fully and accurately perceived by one in whom the organs of Colouring are small, nor is the beauty of nature discernible by an individual in whom Ideality is very imperfectly developed. Neither does one in whom the organs of the moral and religious emotions are small, but in whom those of the animal propensities and intellectual faculties are large, on surveying external nature, receive strong impressions of benevolence and goodness as characteristics pervading it; on the contrary, the representations of it and of man's condition embodied in the Catechism quoted on p. 186, appear to him to be nearer the truth. The only answer that can be given to the objections against nature, urged by persons thus organized, is, that men with better developments of brain and more cultivation, receive higher impressions from it, and that the presumption is stronger in favour of its being really such as these perceive it, than of its being defective, and such as it appears to individuals with defective brains. There *is* a Sun, although the man born blind does not see it.

If, then, the qualities of things, and their relations, modes of action, and results, are real, and bear evidence of design in the intelligent and moral Power which instituted and upholds them; and if our intellect perceives the design, and also forms rules of action from the perception of it; then we need only to train the sentiments of Veneration and Wonder to hallow these as rules revealed through nature to our understandings by God, and they will become *religious*,—and to train the sentiments of Benevolence and Conscientiousness to recognise them as embodying duties prescribed by God, and they will become moral; and thus the laws of nature will furnish us with a basis of religion and morality. I cannot overstate the importance of our keeping in view, that all existing religions have been formed by associating intellectual ideas about God and His will, in some instances drawn from polluted sources, with the religious emotions; and that there is no natural obstacle to our associating with these emotions, the conceptions of God and His will which we derive from the study of his works, and thus constituting a religion in harmony with our knowledge of existing things and their relations. It is presumable that such a religion would excite, gratify, cherish, and improve all the faculties of our mind. It would necessarily also embrace a code of systematic morality.

Another advantage which would follow from acknowledging

Nature to be sacred, would be the introduction of an efficient religious discipline into life. Discipline consists in prescribing rules of action and enforcing observance of them by motives that strongly influence the Will. The soldier, as I have said, affords a striking example of its efficacy. I knew a dirty, slovenly, ill-conditioned lad, who used to drive coal-carts, and who in a fit of drunkenness enlisted as a soldier. Three months afterwards I saw him again, and scarcely recognised his identity. He was then clean in person and attire, walked erect, and his manner was decided yet respectful. Discipline,—in other words, commands strictly enforced, but accompanied by instruction how to obey them, and the example of obedience in others,—had produced the change. In the case of the soldier, discipline accomplishes much more than this. It renders the individual alert, obedient, resolute, and all-enduring, in the discharge of his duties; still the mainspring of its influence is Command strictly enforced. Now, we have a discipline of this sort in Nature, if we only open our minds to understand it. If we know the structure, functions, and laws of health, of the digestive and respiratory organs, we shall perceive that temperance, cleanliness, exercise, breathing pure air, and other observances, are prescribed to us by a command that is absolute in authority, that of God Himself, and enforced by a discipline that is irresistible. On the one hand, we have health, enjoyment, efficiency, abundance, and length of days, as the rewards of observance; and disease, pain, incapacity, mental misery, physical destitution, and premature death, as the consequences of disobedience. Every organ and faculty, bodily and mental, acts under similar conditions; and a work which should elucidate each organ, in its structure, functions, and modes of action, and the natural and inevitable consequences of its use and abuse, would reveal a system of philosophy, morality, and practical wisdom, which might be indissolubly combined with religion, for it would proceed from, and be enforced by a discipline instituted by, God. All these advantages are lost by our obstinate refusal to regard Nature as sacred, and by the exclusion of her authority and teaching as practical rules from our literature, our schools, our pulpits, and our legislative assemblies, either ignorantly, or out of deference to the dogmas of a dark and semi-barbarous age.

It is only by regarding Nature as an Institution, and its ruler as God, that religion can be successfully introduced as a sanctifying influence and an element of discipline into daily life; and this is not only possible, but is so obviously practicable when earnestly and intelligently attempted, that only the misdirection of our faculties by the dogmas can account for its being so long neglected and resisted. I have been favoured with the perusal of the manuscript outlines of a series of lessons on Social Economy given privately by my friend Mr William Ellis of Lancaster Terrace, London, to several young pupils, in which he demonstrated that by the order of Nature every line of conduct—in the pursuit whether of wealth by farming, manufacturing, navigation, commerce, or by the practice of professions,—in order to be successful must be moral; and that success follows skill, industry, and morality; as failure follows ignorance, sloth, and immorality, with the same certainty that a rich crop of corn follows from skilful ploughing, manuring, sowing, tending, and reaping.

The dogmas, on the contrary, represent a state of war as existing between God and Mammon; but Mr Ellis shews that when this is understood to be a condemnation of the pursuit of wealth, it must be a mistake; because, as the production of wealth is indispensable to human wellbeing, and also to the practice of morality and religion, there must be modes of pursuing it which are in harmony with morality and religion. Now, surveying in detail all trades and professions, and the specific acts by means of which their objects,—namely, the acquisition of wealth, social distinction, power, influence, and other enjoyments,—are most successfully attained, he shews that morality must pervade and form the basis of them all. For example—The commercial maxim to buy in the cheapest and sell in the dearest market, is generally held to breathe the concentrated spirit of selfishness or Mammonism. But let us try this condemnation by the rules of reason and morality before we acquiesce in its justice. In Odessa, for instance, after a period of peace and a good harvest, there is a superabundance of wheat, more than its inhabitants can consume; in consequence of which its price is very low. In the same city, however, there is a scarcity of cotton and woollen cloths and cutlery; in consequence of which the prices of these necessaries of life are very high. The people of Odessa would feel greatly relieved if some benevolent person would bring them a supply of these articles and take in return a portion of their superabundant corn. But in Liverpool, in consequence of a bad harvest, there is a great scarcity of wheat; while, owing to the untiring industry of Manchester, Leeds, and Sheffield, there is a superabundance of woollens, calicos, and broad cloths, which lie unsold, because the people are forced to lay out their money in large amounts in buying the scarce, and therefore high-priced corn. The people of these towns desire, above all things, that some kind friend would bring them wheat and exchange it for these goods that are lumbering their warehouses.

Now, a merchant who owns a ship and has abundance of capital, buys in Liverpool the manufactured articles at the prices at which their owners are anxious to sell them:—they are cheap, because they are superabundant, and the English people are too poor to buy them. He fills his ship with them, sends it to Odessa, sells them there at the price which the inhabitants offer to give him for them; and with that money he buys the wheat with which they are encumbered, and pays them the price they ask; it is a low price, because they have more wheat than they can consume or sell. The ship carries this cargo to Liverpool, and there it is eagerly purchased, because it lessens the scarcity of food, one of the greatest evils with which human beings can be afflicted. But on counting the results of these transactions, the merchant finds that he has gained a considerable addition to his capital. This stimulates him and others to repeat the same course of transactions. And what is the ultimate effect? The inhabitants of Odessa are at length relieved of much of their superfluous wheat, and the price of it has risen, to their great contentment; while the supply of the manufactured articles has become so abundant that the prices of these have fallen, also to their great advantage. Turning to England, again, what has ensued? Wheat has been imported so largely that it has fallen in price, and the poor rejoice; while hardware, woollens, and calicos have been purchased, paid for, and exported to so great an extent, that the warehouses are empty, prices have risen, and the manufacturers are again in full employment at remunerating prices.

These results are all the direct consequences of Divine Institutions, which give differences of climates and products to different parts of the globe; and the gains of the merchant are the rewards furnished by divine wisdom and goodness to those who intelligently, honestly, and diligently, apply their knowledge, skill, and capital, in removing the wants and increasing the enjoyments of their fellow-men. Viewed in this light, as the fulfilment of a divine appointment, buying in the cheapest and selling in the dearest market passes from the dominion of Mammon into that of God, and becomes not merely a moral but a religious act. Similar observations will be found to hold good in regard to all the other necessary acts and duties of life, whenever we shall consent to view this world as a Divine Institution, and turn our whole faculties to discover its laws and to act conformably to them. It is from the *pursuit of wealth by immoral means*, and the *application* of it to immoral or useless purposes, that the evils erroneously ascribed to it arise. As, by the fiat of Nature, wealth is indispensable to human welfare, the sin even of the miser, who makes his property his god, consists not in accumulating and investing, but in something else. The wealth he has saved is so much capital gained to the society in which he lives, and when he invests it on good securities, he lends it to men of skill, enterprise, and industry, who apply it in still farther augmenting the capital of their country, by which all are benefited; for capital is an indispensable element in the production of the necessaries and comforts, as well as the luxuries of life. The miser's sin lies in his neglect of all the personal, domestic, and social duties which are incumbent on him as the possessor of riches. It is by such conduct that he becomes the slave of Mammon and the contemner of God. The profligate spendthrift who dissipates an inherited fortune in immoral indulgences cannot be called a worshipper, but a contemner of Mammon, yet he is equally a contemner of God; for, so far as lies in his power, he wastes the products of the skill and industry of his more virtuous predecessors, deprives himself of the means of discharging his personal and social duties, and impedes the progress of his country by destroying the fund for promoting the industry and rewarding the skill and intelligence of his fellow-men.*

Mr Williams and I taught the laws of health and social economy on these principles, in a school kept by him in Edinburgh, for the children of the working-classes; and while we were calumniated by excellent evangelical persons, as inculcators of infidelity, the more intelligent children understood, rejoiced in, and profited by the lessons, and even the less gifted were interested, so that no blows or chastisements were needed, exclusion from the lessons being felt to be the severest punishment that could be inflicted.†

It has been objected to these views that they omit altogether the higher or spiritual life—the grand aspirations of the soul after eternity and universal knowledge, its longing after the everlasting progress of our spiritual being, its desire of a more intimate communion with God, and so forth: But what really is this higher life? In St Peter's Cathedral in Rome, I have seen the most ignorant of men and women kneeling before the images of the Virgin Mary and the saints, and in the outpouring of their devotional emotions towards them enjoying the higher life. It was unmistakeably expressed in their eyes, features, and attitudes. I have observed the widow and the

---

* These principles are successfully expounded in several works on Social Economy, by Mr William Ellis, published by Smith, Elder, & Co., of London. The latest is entitled, "Where must we look for the further prevention of Crime?" and is both interesting and instructive. 8vo, pp. 100, price 1s. 1857.

† See Reports of Mr Williams' School, sold by the publishers of this work.

mother, broken down with sorrow for the loss of a beloved husband or child, there unburden their souls of grief, and depart relieved and comforted. I have seen a Swedenborgian congregation in possession of the higher life as the religious emotions soared through their spiritual world, and drew joy and hope, peace and consolation, from the communications which they thence received. The congregation of Shaking Quakers, before described, were seen rising into ecstasies, and almost sinking into convulsions, under the influence of their higher life, elicited by their chants, their songs, and their dances. I have listened to the Calvinist describing his higher life, unfolding its glories, its consolations, its inspiring hopes, and its strengthening grace, all elicited by his contemplation of the length and breadth, the height and depth of the love of Christ, in giving himself up as a sacrifice for sin. I have heard the Unitarian pour forth his vivid experience of the higher life, founded on his deep apprehension of the all-embracing benevolence, wisdom, and justice of God, on his perceptions of God's overflowing love, pervading all beings, time, and space. And were we to visit Turkey, Persia, and Hindostan, there also should we find thousands of ardent worshippers, each in the blaze of enjoyment of his own higher life. Now, what is the true meaning and explanation of these phenomena? One circumstance characterises them all,—the organs of Veneration, Wonder, and Hope, are intensely active, although directed differently in each devotee. The emotions and the pleasure accompanying their activity are natural, and constitute the higher life; but their direction to particular objects is accidental, and depends on what they have been trained to venerate. Morbid excitement in the cerebral organs is also by some individuals mistaken for experience of the higher life. See pp. 41, 42.

It thus appears that it is not the *absolute truth* of religion, *i.e.* its truth in the sight of God, that gives it the power of producing in believers what is called the higher life, with all the hopes, joys, consolations, and feelings of resignation and endurance, which accompany it; but that these depend primarily on the force with which the faith stimulates the religious faculties of the devotee. To do this effectually, the faith and ritual used as exciting instruments must be in harmony with, or at least not violently in contradiction to, the state of enlightenment of his other faculties. Hence, the lower the moral and intellectual development and instruction of the worshipper, the farther may his creed and ritual deviate from reason, and from the dictates of benevolence and justice, without impairing their emotional influence on him. But conversely, the more powerful the intellect, and the higher its instruction, the larger the moral organs, and the more extensive and beneficial the sphere in which they have been trained to act in any individual, the more pure, rational, beneficent, and self-consistent, must a creed and ritual become, before they will be capable of satisfying the demands of his faculties, and of eliciting in him that fervid action of the religious emotions which constitutes the higher life. If the view stated in Chap. V. be correct, that man cannot comprehend the nature and mode of being of God, because the finite cannot comprehend the Infinite, it follows that the only rational conception we can form of the Divine Being consists of a concentration and personification by our own minds in Him, of all the power, wisdom, and goodness discernible in nature; and if so, then the more we know of the manifestations of these qualities, the higher must our conceptions of the attributes of that Being become. And if the "highest" life consists in the highest exercise and condition of our faculties, it follows, that in proportion to the enlargement of our knowledge we shall augment the means of vivifying our emotional faculties, and of bringing them into harmony with the institutions of God, and thereby approach the highest point of improvement permitted to man.

It is often stated as a reproach to science, that it makes men infidels. The real fact is, that by carrying their intellectual and moral faculties to a higher state of development and cultivation, by giving them larger and truer views of God and His works, it renders the creeds and rituals of a less enlightened age, with their barbarous dogmas and conflicting propositions, repugnant to their minds, and incapable of exciting and satisfying their religious emotions. The greater the number of other faculties in addition to the religious, which any faith and worship are able to excite and satisfy, the greater will be their influence over practical conduct; and their power of leading to beneficial results will diminish, and ultimately cease, in proportion to the extent to which they become isolated from the other powers. This will hold good whether the discrepancy between the faith and ritual and other faculties, arises from the improvement or degradation of the latter. The creeds of the sixteenth century do not now exercise the same influence over men's minds which they did when, through a corresponding ignorance and barbarism, the whole faculties were in harmony with them. This point has been considered in Chap. I., to which I beg to refer.

The longing after the infinite, which is at present regarded by many persons as the grand foundation of religious life, when traced to its source, does not appear to merit this distinction.

Each propensity and sentiment, from producing a mere desire or emotion, is constitutionally indefinite in its longings and aspirations. It needs the intellect to limit and guide it. If the organs be large, active, and unrestrained by enlightened intellect, there is no boundary to the desire of Acquisitiveness for property, of Self-Esteem for dominion, of Secretiveness for the mysterious, of Ideality for the beautiful and perfect, of Benevolence for universal good, of Conscientiousness for all-pervading justice, of Veneration for devotion and worship, of the Love of Life for eternal existence, of Wonder for the new, the grand, the spiritual, the supernatural, and so forth. If we ask the most exalted devotees of every religion and of every sect to define their higher life, and if we analyse their definition, we shall find that indulgence in boundless aspirations proceeding from the religious emotions, constitute its essential element.

The higher emotional faculties are the sources not only of religious devotion, but of pure morality and the sublimest poetry. In the present state of human knowledge, however, when the moral, religious, and political opinions of most men rest on a confused basis of the natural, founded on experience, and the supernatural drawn from Scripture, the preacher, author, poet, orator, and political agitator, who is capable of strongly exciting not them chiefly, but the lower propensities also, wields a stupendous power over his fellow-men. The emotions yield to his passionate and thrilling calls; intellect stands aside; and his hearers glow with his fervour, give up their souls to his impulsive guidance, and embrace his propositions. But because the means of attaining the real, permanent, and only desirable gratification of the emotional faculties, are fixed and regulated by a power which does not yield to human impulses; and because these means can be discovered and employed only by the intellect enlightened by observation and experience; the schemes of even the most eloquent orators, whenever they partake of the vagueness of the emotional faculties, or are based on erroneous or imperfect views of the natural means of achieving good, fail and end in disappointment.

What, then, should constitute the higher life in natural religion? The vivid action of the religious emotions, combined with that of the moral sentiments and of the intellect, enlightened by the highest attainable knowledge of God's will manifested in nature, and all directed to the attainment of a pure, holy, and beneficent state of being. The ecstatic delights of fervid devotion and undoubting faith; hope, joy, and resignation; consolation in affliction, and strength to endure and persevere in the dark hours of life, may all be drawn from these sources at least as copiously and certainly as from the fountains from which, in many countries, they are now sought to be derived. According to this system, God's institutions are the basis of our judgments, and His will the rule and standard of our actions. The framework of our bodies and the endowments of our minds are ascribed to Him. Every relation in which we stand is viewed as of His appointment. In the language of Scripture, therefore, " Whether we eat or drink, or whatsoever we do, we do all to the glory of God," when we apply every function of mind and body to its legitimate uses, from deference to His will, as well as in the conviction that by this means alone can we reach our own happiness.

In reference to personal and social improvement, religion severed from the laws of nature stands in the same predicament as pure mathematics do when they are unapplied to practical objects. Ask the profoundest mathematician who had never studied navigation or served on board a ship, to steer a vessel to China, and his mathematics would be perfectly inadequate to enable him to execute the task. To that abstract science, he must add a practical knowledge of ships, and of the mode of applying mathematics to direct their course at sea. Ask a pure mathematician to construct a railroad or a steam-driven spinning-mill, and he would be equally helpless; because his science needs to be embodied in practical forms before it can become useful. In like manner, religion, which, in itself, is a sentiment or emotion, must condescend to borrow aid from nature, before it can accomplish any practical earthly purpose whatever. All personal and social improvements have been made by the Ruler of this world to depend on physical and physiological conditions. Health and life depend on them, wealth and destitution depend on them, mental vigour, even the ability to pray, depends on them; for when the brain is incapable of action, the religious emotions vanish. I repeat, therefore, that before religion can accomplish its highest objects, —the glory of God and the wellbeing of man,—it must include an embodiment of the will of the Infinite, as manifested in His institutions.

Tracing the condition of the religious emotions through the savage, barbarous, and modern stages of society, we perceive that the higher the enlightenment of the intellect, and the more perfect the cultivation of the moral sentiments, the more pure and beneficent has religion become, and the more effectually has it operated on the minds of its votaries as a stimulus to social improvement. The same results will probably distinguish its future course. The present prevalent creeds of Europe appear to be at war with its science, and in consequence to be retarding its progress. Religion is employed as the instrument of priests and sovereigns to maintain themselves in authority, and to repress the moral and intellectual life of nations. In our own dominions the conflict of clerical leaders for power over the laity distracts the public mind, and obstructs many enlightened measures of improvement. It seems incredible, however, that when the religious emotions, freed from the trammels of barbarous ages, shall in future centuries ally themselves with the knowledge and morality of an advanced civilization, a richer harvest of individual enjoyment and social happiness will not be reaped from their action. The connection of our mental powers with cerebral organs gives a substantive basis to our moral, religious, and intellectual perceptions, and enables us to demonstrate their foundation in nature, which it is extremely difficult to do when each person judges only by his individual consciousness, illuminated by his own experience. In this state of things, many men deny the existence of emotions and perceptions which they cannot themselves reach, and pursue phantoms under the unsuspected influence of peculiar states of their own organisms. But this state of things must pass away, and the sphere and influence of natural religion must necessarily enlarge and rise in proportion to our knowledge of the qualities, modes of action, and relations of things. The discovery of the functions of the brain will supply an indispensable element towards the foundation of a progressive code of religion and morality, ever enlarging, and becoming more pure and exalted as the human faculties and knowledge advance. Mr John Stuart Mill, in the Sixth Book of his Logic, states, in his own language, that our desires of improvement proceed from the propensities and sentiments, but that these give mere desires, and cannot tell us *how* to satisfy them. This depends on knowledge, and knowledge on intellect. The intellectual state of any nation is, therefore, says he, the best index of its real civilization; and in the history of the world, every great intellectual discovery was the precursor, and the indispensable precursor, of a great stride in material civilization. "Every considerable change, historically known to us, in the condition of any portion of mankind," continues Mr Mill, "has been preceded by a change of proportional extent in the state of their knowledge, or in their prevalent beliefs. From this accumulated evidence, we are justified in concluding, that the order of human progression in all respects will be a corollary deducible from the order of progression in the intellectual convictions of mankind, that is, from the law of the successive transformations of religion and science." These remarks are equally profound and true; yet how far is the world from believing that the discovery of the physiology of the brain,—in other words, of the substantive basis of our mental faculties, and of the means by which they act, and their relations to external objects,—will lead to important reformations in religion and moral science !*

SEC. 2. THE CONSEQUENCES WHICH HAVE FOLLOWED FROM THE PREVAILING RELIGIOUS DOGMAS.

The bearing of the views of the Divine government before stated on Christianity, is an important consideration, but I do not enter into it in detail, because Christians are divided into so many different sects, each of which maintains its own views to constitute the true religion of Jesus Christ, while it denounces those entertained by other sects as "soul-destroying errors," that it is difficult for a layman to select a view of it which will not be widely disputed. The evangelical Protestants, for example, often apply these words to the Roman Catholic Faith; while at the same time they denounce Unitarians as infidels. Their own doctrines, on the other hand, are described by some of their opponents in terms not less reproachful: by John Wesley, for example, the doctrine of election is described in the following terms:—" The sum of all this is: One in twenty (suppose) of mankind are elected, nineteen in twenty are reprobated ! The elect shall be saved, *do what they will ;* the reprobate shall be damned, *do what they can.* This is the doctrine of Calvinism, for which Diabolism would be a better name, and in the worst and bloodiest idolatry that ever defiled the earth, there is nothing so horrid, so monstrous, so impious as this."† (*Southey's Life of Wesley*, 3d edit., vol. i. p. 321.)

If a majority is entitled to decide, then the Roman Catholic Faith has the best claim to be considered as the true exposition of the religion of the New Testament; but in religious questions we cannot admit numbers as decisive of truth.

I confine myself, therefore, to the dogmas taught in the standards of the prevailing churches of Christendom, and I use the expression "doctrinal *interpretations,*" because nearly all

---

* The views entertained by eminent divines on the authority of the law of nature in reference to morals and religion, have been collected and published in a learned and instructive work by Robert Cox, entitled " Sabbath Laws and Sabbath Duties considered in relation to their Natural and Scriptural Grounds," &c. (Edinburgh, Maclachlan and Stewart; London, Simpkin, Marshall, and Co., 1853), pages 202-7, to which I beg leave to refer. The chief error of the writers there cited, lies in their ascribing *to men in general,* moral, religious, and intellectual emotions and perceptions which arise naturally only in men having well-developed and active brains. And being unacquainted with the functions of the brain, they could not render natural religion so practicable as it now is.

† See other striking examples of the way in which the adherents of the different sects speak of each other's views of Christian doctrine, in Mr Cox's " Sabbath Laws and Sabbath Duties," before referred to, pp. 54, 55, 127-9.

that passes in the world for Christian faith, really consists of systems of doctrine founded upon particular texts, interpreted in a particular manner by particular individuals or conclaves of men; and in point of fact, the Bible contains no systematic exposition of religious doctrine which all men must necessarily acknowledge as Divine revelation. It is chiefly as expounded in catechisms and creeds that the Christian religion is now practically operating on social well being; yet were a dozen men, possessed of the highest order of brains (the best natural foundation for the ability to judge soundly), and thoroughly instructed in the ancient languages, and in the modern sciences (cerebral physiology included), to read the Bible, without previous bias, and were they commissioned to produce an authoritative interpretation of it, I doubt very much if they would present to the world a *facsimile* of any existing creed or articles of faith. Miss Joanna Baillie, in her "*View of the general tenor of the New Testament regarding the nature and dignity of Jesus Christ*,"* remarks that the three leading systems of doctrine on this subject "stand far and far apart;" and if besides these, there are very many minor doctrinal interpretations of Scripture embraced by large and intelligent bodies of men, it is clear that none of these can, on the ground of their perfect infallibility, be logically accepted as Divine revelation, calculated to guide the faith and practice of all mankind in reference to time and eternity. Instead of progress being made towards unity of belief, the process is the reverse. During the last fifteen years, I have resided for periods of greater or less duration, in the United States of North America, Germany, and Italy, have visited France, and been a good deal in England; and from the nature of my published works, I have been brought into familiar and confidential communication with many able and highly instructed individuals of all faiths and sects: and my conclusion is, that Christianity, as taught in the prevailing creeds, is already undermined in the convictions of very many men and women of great capacity and attainments, and unexceptionable moral character. Archbishop Whately remarks, that "Force, together with fraud, the two great engines for the support of the Papal dominion, have almost annihilated sincere belief in Christianity among the educated classes, throughout a great portion of Europe." According to my observation, the obstinate and arrogant adherence of the clergy to Protestant articles of faith, at variance with the science of the age, has to some extent produced a similar effect in countries that are not Roman Catholic. Indeed, I have found that even where belief in some form of doctrine is still professed, the

* Longman and Co. 1831.

greatest liberties are often taken with it, one individual rejecting one point of faith, and another another; so much so, that had I written down the views of some dozens of professed believers and published them, they would have presented a spectacle of extraordinary conflict and inconsistency. This statement, I am convinced, will be confirmed by most persons who have enjoyed similar means of observation both at home and abroad. Those, on the other hand, who travel wrapped up in an impenetrable conviction of the infallibility of their own opinions, will rarely find other men inclined to disclose to them their true sentiments on religious subjects.

There are indeed liberal sects, and many high-minded individuals, who reject the extreme doctrines of Church standards, and see in Christianity only a religion of love to God and good will to man, and who regard its founder as a sublime instructor, teaching us by precept and example how to live and how to die. To their views of Christianity my objections do not apply. But these sects and individuals are still so few in number, and so feeble in social influence, and many of them so deficient in courage to proclaim their convictions, and to support them by open and active efforts, that practically, their interpretations of Christianity exert little influence on society. The views embodied in the standards of the predominant churches, appear to me to be now acting as great obstacles to social progress and civilization. The grand principles there represented are all supernatural; and the revelations of the Divine will in nature, as a basis of morals and religion, are excluded from schools, colleges, churches, and social consideration; and thus these interpretations are chaining up the moral, intellectual, and religious faculties of many superior minds. The earnestly religious are truly the salt of the earth; their aspirations are high, their motives pure, and the objects at which they aim transcendently important. It is grievous therefore to see so many of them trammelled by the fetters of narrow sectarian creeds, wasting their lives and their substance in wars with each other; opposing now one alleged error of doctrine or form, and now another; clearly observing the mote in their neighbour's eye, but never discerning the beam in their own; while God's fair world of mind and matter lies before them, inviting in vain their highest efforts to improve it, and to render it a scene of greater goodness, more fervent piety, and purer happiness than it now exhibits. The Divine laws of religion, morality, and practical conduct revealed in Nature are nearly banished from the pulpit, and few attempts are made to harmonize them with Christianity. In England, disquisitions about the real presence, prevenient grace, the efficacy of baptism, the communication of the Holy Spirit by Ordination, and so forth, usurp the place of God's revelations in Nature; while in Scotland the dogmas cited on pages 186-7 are made to play a similar part.

The prevailing dogmas rest on the Fall of Man as their basis. The religion of nature appears to contradict this assumption; for if the human constitution, bodily and mental, has been adapted to external nature such as it now exists, and nature to it, then apparently man never was essentially different from what he now is.

The next dogma is that the Fall brought sin into the world, and all its woes; and that the Second Person of the Trinity, himself God, assumed the form of man, suffered the penalty of that sin, atoned for it, and thereby restored the human race to the favour of God. And as a corollary, it is said that it is only through faith in that atonement, and through the influence of the Holy Spirit, that the moral taint introduced into man's nature by the Fall can be removed, and the punishment due for it and for each individual's actual transgressions can be averted.

The doctrines of the Fall and the Atonement are rejected by some sects as unsupported by sound interpretation of Scripture; and they are entertained by other sects and individuals under various modifications. Into these questions it is not my province to enter, and therefore I confine myself to observing, that according to the views before expounded, moral evil arises from abuse of our bodily and mental functions, and the natural mode of averting it is to give to all the organs of body and mind the best possible constitution and a proportionate development, and then, by instruction in the laws to which God has subjected them, and which are real indications of His Will in regard to their uses, to direct the whole to their highest objects. If this be the true view of man's nature and relations, the dogmas must be tried by this new standard, and the remedies proposed by them for human evils must be reconsidered in reference to this exposition of their causes. Modern science and the physiological constitution of man, and the consequences which flow from them, were undoubtedly unknown to the earnest but ignorant men who compiled the dogmas from Scripture.

Lastly, the dogmas represent the Gospel to have brought " life and immortality to light," and to teach a resurrection of the body from the dead, a Divine judgment, and the final consignment of all human beings either to heaven or hell—that is, to an eternity of happiness or misery—according to their good or bad conduct in this world, or, as is the doctrine of many sects, according to their having believed soundly or unsoundly in points of faith, or even according to an eternal decree consigning them to the one or other of these destinations, passed on them before they came into existence.

Those doctrines lie beyond the limits of science, and I shall, therefore, confine my remarks to what appear to me to be serious abuses of them. In regard to heaven: It is generally allotted to the true believer, who shews the soundness of his faith by his good works; but some sects maintain that faith alone suffices to ensure salvation. Now, the capacity of an individual to believe anything and to do any works, depends on the development and condition of his brain, and the training and instruction he has received. The higher his moral and physiological endowments, the better is he qualified to believe and act rightly, and the lower, the less so. These conditions are determined chiefly for the individual, and little by him. Moreover, by the order of God's moral government, as before explained, highly-endowed individuals have the fewest temptations to resist, and struggles to maintain, in this life; and as a general rule they enjoy the greatest share of happiness allotted to humanity. These are great and precious boons conferred on them by their bountiful Father; but the best use which they can make of such gifts appears to me to give them *no claim* to heaven—their trust for it should rest exclusively on the will of God. Farther, they are called on by their gifts, to use all the means in their power to raise themselves and their less-favoured brethren higher in the scale of improvement, by seeking truth, abandoning error, and removing personal and social evils, and in all things endeavouring to conform to the Divine laws. Instead of doing so, many highly endowed persons teach only catechisms and dogmas in schools and from the pulpit, and too generally leave the people the prey of bad habits, foul air, intemperance, and destitution, without instructing them how to make adequate efforts to remove the natural causes of these evils. Crime is frequently the result of a low development of brain placed in adverse circumstances, yet when an offence has been proved to the satisfaction of a jury, the accused is condemned to punishment without reference to these causes. No spectacle is more common than to see an unhappy individual, after a life of immorality, which society regards as so flagrant that his existence can no longer be tolerated on earth, assured by his spiritual guides that his repentance in prison, accompanied by unhesitating faith in the atonement of Jesus Christ, will prove sufficient to transmit his soul from the gallows to heaven, where he will enjoy through eternity the society of God, angels, and just men made perfect.

The felon who throughly believes this, declares, and apparently with good reason, that the day of his ignominious death is the happiest of his life: but surely this is an abuse of the Scripture doctrine.

In reference to hell: It is generally assigned to unbelievers, to misbelievers, and to evil-doers. But erroneous belief and evil deeds arise chiefly from a deficient or an ill-proportioned development, or an unfavourable constitution, of the brain, or from these combined with deficient training and instruction. These evils are generally inherited, and not voluntarily selected by individuals. According to this view, the tendency to vice, crime, and sin, appears to be a misfortune, and the remedy for it seems to be removal of its natural causes. To consign individuals thus constituted and placed, to eternal misery for conduct which is mainly the natural result of their faculties and circumstances, appears at variance with benevolence and justice; while to assure them of heaven as the result of a prison-inspired repentance and belief, seems to be equally opposed to all sound views of a moral government of the world here or hereafter.

The abuses of the doctrine of heaven and hell appear to me to be subversive of all efficacious discipline over the human mind. For example. A banker passes a long period of his life in genteel society, making great professions of evangelical religion, and abounding in prayers. At length he is discovered to have been all the while robbing his customers, feloniously selling their securities, and applying the price to his own uses. By this conduct he plunges many honest and industrious families into irretrievable ruin, and casts a deep shade of suffering over their remaining days. Under the dogmas, the sufferers, in their ire, thank God that there is a day of future judgment and final retribution, in which canting, hypocritical scoundrels who make a cloak of religion to cover their crimes, and who embitter the lives of the honest and the good, will receive their reward in condemnation to eternal misery. The prospect of future punishment is thus believed to exercise a grand protecting influence to save society from such catastrophes. But let us turn to the prison cell. There the condemned felon finds consolation in the dogmas which teach that "the human heart is deceitful above all things and desperately wicked;" and that he has been left to feel the truth of this representation, and to act it out in deeds in order to subdue his obdurate heart and bring him into a state of grace. Thanks to the mercy of God, he now looks "to the rock that is higher than I," believes in the' atonement; finds all his iniquities forgiven; the gates of heaven thrown open to him, and the angels singing songs of joy over the great sinner who has repented! The dogmas, when thus applied, be it observed, not only lead to these inconsistent consequences, but blind men's understandings to the real order of the Divine Government on earth. I venture to say, after forty years' observation and experience, that the development of the moral and intellectual organs in individuals who are not insane, affords an indication of their natural proclivity to dishonesty, or natural strength of virtuous resolution; and that while society spurns and neglects this great fact in the Divine Government of the world, these substitutes for it are feeble as gossamer webs, to protect us against the crimes of ill-constituted brains placed in unfavourable circumstances. On the other hand, such individuals themselves, if placed in favourable situations in which scope would be afforded for all the talents and moral qualities they possess, and no strain, in the form of temptation or opportunity, be applied to overpower their weaker faculties, would find this discipline more effective than that now applied,— namely, leaving them at liberty, in ignorance of their own deficiencies and amidst severe temptations, to follow the dictates of their own ill-balanced desires; restrained only by the criminal law on earth, and the prospect of a final judgment in the world to come. The former, they hope by dexterity to evade; while they are taught that a condemnatory sentence in the latter may at all times be avoided by means of repentance and faith.

But the abuses of this doctrine reach their acme in obstructing the social improvement of man. In almost all the kingdoms of Christendom, the governments have allied themselves with the Priesthood to prevent the people from the pursuing their own happiness by the development and free exercise of their mental faculties. The government of the Pope is highly injurious to his subjects. He excludes the study of natural science, and of all moral, religious, and political subjects that might by any possibility conflict with the dogmas of which he is the fountain, or teach his people to scrutinize the uses he makes of his temporal and spiritual power. He places works suspected of such tendencies on his *Index expurgatorius*, and prohibits his people, under the peril of future condemnation, and also of temporal punishment, from reading them. It is the belief in the mass of his subjects that he and his church actually hold the keys of heaven and hell that gives him his tremendous power; while it is the consciousness on his part, that the knowledge of the real order of God's government on earth, if attained by his people, would blow his dogmas to the winds, and hurl him from his throne, that prompts him to repel this information as his most formidable enemy. The temporal interests of the subjects of the Pope are sacrificed with the most unhesitating alacrity to the interests of his spiritual authority, and a degree of physical and moral degradation reigns in his territories unexampled in the worst parts of Europe. Next to him stands the King of Naples, who rules on the same principles, and with the same results. Austria follows a similar course. Her Emperor has recently concluded a concordat with the Pope, the object of which is to place all moral and religious training and social action under the trammels of the Priesthood of that country; they are the tools of the secular government, which again seeks to maintain its own power and permanency by using them as instruments for suppressing moral and intellectual enlightenment, and free thought and action in the people. Nor is this abuse of spiritual power confined to Roman Catholic Sovereigns. The King of Prussia is labouring to circumscribe the illuminating and improving influence of the public schools of his kingdom, established by his more enlightened predecessors, because their tendency has been to foster the desire for political freedom and social improvement. He is doing all that lies in his power to diminish the amount of instruction in natural science in the schools, and to augment belief in the dogmas of the Calvinist sect, there called "Pietism."

The clergy of our own country may be divided into two classes—men of high moral, religious, and intellectual endowments, imbued with the pure and benign spirit of Christianity, who preach it from the pulpit, and exhibit it in their lives—and persons who have chosen the clerical profession from inferior motives, and never rise to a full comprehension and experience of the sources and nature of its vital power. These latter take Catechisms, Confessions, and Liturgies for their rules of faith, preach the letter of them, and employ them as ladders of ambition, or as engines of war with which to assail other sects. It is of this class that I here write. Many of them are the determined opponents of the introduction of science into schools, while they maintain that the catechism and other expositions of the dogmas form the only safe basis for education. It is their influence that prevents the legislature from giving pecuniary assistance to schools in which the order of Nature is taught as a revelation of the will of God to man, in regard to his terrestrial conduct. It is they who lead the people's religious emotions away from the recognition of Nature as sacred, and of its Divine laws as worthy of reverence. They too have their *Index expurgatorius*, their list of *dangerous books*, not to be read without peril to the soul, and displeasure from the pastor. Their object is the same as that of the Pope, Emperor, and King—to retain the people in subjection to the spiritual power of which they are the depositaries on earth; and it is the promise of heaven and threat of hell which enable them to succeed in these unholy and most injurious schemes.

The countries in which political freedom shows its most benign influences are those in which the government rests on the power of the people, and its administrators are purely secular. England, Switzerland, and the United States of North America are examples in point.

Most English Protestant readers will acknowledge the evils here described to be true results of Papal ascendency; but I beg to remark that the Pope, Emperors, and Kings, and all their clergy, who thus abuse religion, hold the Bible in their hands all the while that they are thus perverting it. The Bible, therefore, when unsupported by knowledge of the laws of God's government on earth, has not proved sufficient to conduct even educated and talented men to a sincere practice of its principles. They have so interpreted it as to convert it,— by the prospect which it holds forth of future rewards and punishments not exclusively for good and bad actions, but *for belief*, belief in their dogmas and in their infallibility, or superior wisdom, as guides to heaven,—into a tremendous instrument for degrading the people and obstructing their social improvement. It appears to me, therefore, in vain, after eighteen hundred years' experience of the insufficiency of the Bible to protect itself from abuse, when unaided by knowledge of the order of God's providence in nature, to hope to prevent men from turning it into an instrument for gratifying their own lust of power, to the injury of the world. Something obviously is wanted to render it incapable of being thus misapplied; and it is worthy of consideration whether an interpretation of it in harmony with nature may have this effect.

The way in which the dogmas act in supporting despotism is not generally understood. By excluding secular knowledge they render men timid and incapable as children.

Tyranny, for example, is the direct result of a low moral and intellectual condition of the people. A kingly tyrant has the strength only of one man, and cannot imprison and torture his liberal subjects by his personal strength. He is served by ministers whose moral condition is so low that they voluntarily lend him their aid in wickedness for the sake of honours and pay. They, however, do not personally execute his decrees. They find police-officers whose morality is such, that for pay they voluntarily arrest, imprison, chain, and degrade whomsoever the king and cabinet desire them so to treat. Even these men are not sufficient to do these disgraceful deeds with their unaided strength. Officers and soldiers are found so destitute of patriotism and all high principle, that they lend them the aid of their physical force and discipline to support and protect them in the exercise of their odious vocation. The kingly power thus obviously rests on the low moral condition of the subjects. Why cannot Queen Victoria order a liberal to be imprisoned and chained? Because the moral and intellectual condition of her people is such, that if she had the inclination (which we know is the reverse of the fact), her subjects would not lend her their moral and physical power to gratify malignant propensities. No officer of the law would voluntarily execute her warrant without the signature of a secretary of state; and no secretary would, to gratify her, risk his neck by impeachment, and encounter a fearful storm of public indignation and resistance by subscribing such a document;—hence tyranny, like that recently ascribed to the King of Naples, is morally impossible in England. But the cause why it is so, lies in the moral and intellectual condition of the people. The United States of North America, and Switzerland, afford similar examples. Let the President of the one, or the federal chief officer of the other, issue warrants of his own authority to apprehend, and, without trial, to imprison, chain, and torment any citizen of these countries for political offences, and let him even find a secretary of state to countersign them, the moral energy of the people would hurl both tyrants and secretaries to destruction.

The Divine law, therefore, is, that social well-being is the direct result of wide-spread individual intelligence, morality and religion reduced to practice, and it has no other substantial basis. The dogmas, by holding out Heaven as the reward to despots for maintaining the true faith, and through it, social order; and by giving the people the solace of revenge in their sufferings, by the thought that there is a day of future retribution awaiting their oppressors; distract the minds of both parties from perceiving the fundamental truth that knowledge of, and conformity to, God's laws in nature, afford the only secure basis for individual and social prosperity; that these laws are moral and may be rendered religious by training; and that, if honestly acted on, they will conduct both kings and subjects to the highest state of improvement attainable on earth. Nature, however, will proceed in her course whether we ignore, or study and reverence her ways. The only difference will be in our course of action. If we regard the principles advocated in this work as having any pretensions to truth, we shall reform our religious creeds, our criminal laws, and our treatment of all individuals who labour under cerebral deficiency; and apply the true principles of the moral government of the world to the regulation of individual and social conduct. If we regard them as false, we shall adhere to our present opinions and line of action. In religion, we shall continue to view the order of God's providence in relation to mankind in general, in the light in which it is represented in the dogmas, and which continues to be earnestly inculcated by men of great talent and influence; of which the following extract from an exposition of the Book of Genesis, by Dr Candlish, is an example. He has been speaking of the fate of Sodom, and, referring to Luke xvii. 28-30, he continues :—

" What will all their vain expedients for dissipating thought and pacifying conscience avail the unjust then? They have lived in pleasure on the earth, and been wanton; they have nourished their hearts as in a day of slaughter. They have been reserved unto that day; shut up, so that none could escape.

" Thus viewed, what a spectacle does the world, lying in wickedness, present! A pen, in which sheep are making themselves fat for slaughter; a place of confinement; a condemned cell, in which sentenced prisoners are shut up; sinners held fast in the hands of an angry God!

" Yes, you may run and riot as you choose; you may drown thought in drunkenness, and lull conscience asleep; hand may join in hand, and you may say, one to another,—a confederacy —let us shake off superstitious fear—let us dispel gloomy forebodings—let us eat, drink, and be merry. You may struggle as you can, and strive to get rid of God; but here you are in his keeping—under lock and key. He has you safe, reserved unto the day of judgment; and you cannot escape—no, not though you call on the rocks and mountains to fall on you, and cover you from the wrath of the Lamb.

" Have you no knowledge, ye workers of iniquity? no consideration, no sense or feeling? What hollow mockery of laughter is that which rings through the vaults of the dungeon? Prisoners at their sports! men doomed to die, taking their ease, and making merry! What infatuation, what madness is this! Will none of you be sober for a moment? Will none of you—inclosed, shut in, reserved as you are for judgment, so that you cannot escape—will none of you, ere the fatal day dawns, and its sun rises on the earth, pause, and be persuaded to relent, to submit, to sue out the freely-offered pardon, to believe and be saved,—saved now,—saved in that day,—saved for ever?"—(Pages 95–96.)

To an individual who regards human transgressions as having their origin in abuses of the functions of the brain which may best be prevented by restraint, instruction, and training, such sentiments as the foregoing appear more like the emanations of a fervid Destructiveness in the preacher, than as oracles of divine wisdom. The spirit of them contrasts strongly with the prayer, " Father, forgive them, for they know not what they do." The governments of Europe rely on such teaching as the sheet-anchor of social order, and prevent higher and more efficacious natural means from being applied to improve our habits and to preserve the people from crime. Yet it is a fact that these doctrines rarely reach the class of offenders whom they are designed to terrify, for they do not generally frequent churches, and least of all churches in which such doctrines as these are preached; and if they did, the denunciations would fall powerless on their defective brains. An example of the incapacity of very inferior brains, even when under sentence of death, to comprehend or feel the terrors of eternity, may be read in the Transactions of the Phrenological Society, p. 370. The statement there given rests on the authority of the late Rev. Dr Andrew Thomson of Edinburgh. On the other hand, criminals having large brains, with deficient moral and religious organs, such as the Mannings, set them at defiance.

In future times, when society shall recognise the true causes and preventives of criminal action,* in all classes of men, they will discover that the denunciations and promises of the dogmas are slender and inefficacious substitutes for the true means of dealing with evil which God has presented to them in nature, but from the use of which these erroneous opinions at present induce them to shrink with aversion. This doctrine does not affect the distinction between right and wrong.

Farther, the life and immortality which Christianity, as generally interpreted, has brought to light, is the eternal enjoyment of the few, and the endless misery of the many. If Natural religion throws us exclusively on the bounty of God for our hopes of a future life, it delivers us from the horrors of hell ; for no traces of hell or the devil are to be found in Nature. The Divine practice in Nature is to bring suffer-

* See Criminal Jurisprudence considered in relation to the Physiology of the Brain, by Marmaduke B. Sampson. 3d Edition, revised. London, Highley and Son. Price 2d. ; —Lectures on Moral Philosophy, by George Combe, Lectures XII., XIII., XIV. ;—and " The Principles of Criminal Legislation and the Practice of Prison Discipline Investigated," by Geo. Combe.

ing to a close, after all possibility of its benefiting the sufferer ceases. And this is no small advantage, for, as already mentioned, while the fear of hell does not appal men with a low development of brain, I know from confidential communications with many persons, that when the organs of Causality, Comparison, Cautiousness, Conscientiousness, and Benevolence are large, and those of Hope, Wonder, and Self-Esteem, are only moderately developed; and still more when these are deficient, and when the temperament is nervous and bilious; there is a constant trouble in the mind in consequence of the uncertainty of salvation. The individual cannot feel secure that if *any* are to be passed over to the left hand in the day of judgment, *he* shall belong to the favoured class on the right. On the contrary, when the temperament is sanguine, and the organs of Cautiousness and Conscientiousness are small, and those of Self-Esteem, Veneration, Hope, and Wonder, are large, the self-complacent possessor never entertains a doubt that *he* will be found among the faithful, and enjoy eternal felicity in heaven. The prospect of future reward and punishment exercises a restraining effect chiefly on individuals in whom the three regions of the brain, animal, moral, and intellectual, are pretty equally developed.

The prevalent interpretation of the doctrine of heaven and hell, if not supported by nature, must be fraught with tremendous evils to mankind. It is the grand instrument by means of which the clergy hold sway over the laity, and have acquired a temporal power which enables them in many instances to control or embarrass the legislature ;—to substitute their own interpretations not only for the Bible itself, but for the order of Nature, in the instruction of the people ;—and to prevent the public mind from entering honestly and independently into the consideration of many departments of natural science, and from drawing unbiassed conclusions from them. A writer in the *Edinburgh Review*, after making some observations on conventional hypocrisy, proceeds as follows :—" Then there are the deliberate dishonesties of the learned, imposing upon the people what they do not believe themselves, for the sake of the end it is supposed to answer. Sir Charles Lyell [in his *Second Visit to the United States of North America,* vol. i. p. 222] adduces at length the text of the three heavenly witnesses, which no scholar, since Porson's investigation of it, professes to believe genuine, but which is still nevertheless retained in our Bibles, and also in those of the Episcopal Church of America, notwithstanding their opportunity of expunging it when the American Episcopalians revised the liturgy and struck out the Athanasian creed. This disingenuous timidity has long been a reflection upon all our religious teachers. It is now becoming extremely dangerous to their influence and authority. There is no meeting an age of inquiry except in the spirit of perfect candour. The question which lies at the root of all dogmatic Christianity, is the authority of the letter of Scripture; yet, strange to say, that question is neither a settled nor an open one even among Protestants. All the clergy of almost all sects are afraid of it; and the students of Nature, intent only upon facts that God has revealed to our senses, have to fight their way against the self-same religious prejudice which consigned Galileo to his dungeon. The geologists, following in the track of the astronomers, have made good some very important positions, and number among them many eminent churchmen of unquestioned fidelity to their ordination vows. It is now, therefore, admitted that the text is not conclusive against physical demonstration. Is the text conclusive against moral induction and metaphysical inquiry? Let a layman put that question, and an awful silence is the least forbidding answer he will receive. No minister of a parish, no master of a school, no father of a family in England feels himself free to pursue any train of instruction that seems in conflict with a familiar text or a dogmatic formula, excepting only the subject of the opening verses of Genesis. He is either fearful of the ground himself, or he cannot clear his own path for others without opening a discussion, which is discountenanced on all sides and branded with reproachful names. He, in spite of himself, must take refuge in evasions and reserve, and close a subject of perhaps the liveliest interest to the most reverential minds, lest the works of God should *seem* to be at variance with His word. Here is the dilemma which will be found at the bottom of the education question in England. This is what is consciously or unconsciously meant in many important quarters, by the cry against secular instruction. This is why the natural sciences were so long frowned upon in our grammar schools and colleges, and ancient knowledge preferred to modern as sounder and a holier lore. The theology of the Vatican was at home among the Pagan mythologies, the Aristotelian physics, and the Hebrew cosmogonies; yet stood in awe of 'the Tuscan artist's optic glass;' and the spirit of the ancient Church has ever since been true to that instinct. But Protestantism, we say again, and printing, have admitted the light of nature into the schools; and, in the unlimited ecclesiastical freedom of the United States, religion and education go hand in hand."

Few persons conversant with the state of religious opinion in Great Britain will question the correctness of this representation; especially of that part of it which follows the question,

"Is the text conclusive against moral induction and metaphysical inquiry?" Let us look, then, into the cause of this humiliating and injurious condition of things.

There is a distinction between "conviction" and "belief." To "convince" a person, is to lead his intellect by evidence and logical induction to acknowledge a truth previously unknown, or to admit a contested proposition. By teaching him Astronomy, we may convince him of the rotation and revolution of the globe. By shewing him the facts of Geology, and the logical deductions from them, we may convince him that the earth has existed for a longer period than six thousand years; and so forth. In these and similar instances, we present facts to the observing faculties, and employ the reflecting powers to judge of them; and as, when the organs of these faculties are normally developed, active, and cultivated, they act with precision and uniformity, the results which they reach are not voluntary, but the natural consequences of their action. In other words, conviction depends on evidence presented to the observing and intellectual faculties, and is involuntary.

On the other hand, there are two sources of "belief." By the constitution of our minds, we believe, *intuitively*, in the existence and qualities of certain things, when they are presented to our observation (see pages 54, 55). And we "believe" also on credit or persuasion. To "believe" is to "credit upon the authority of another;" to "put confidence in the veracity of any one;" to "have a firm persuasion of any thing." In attaining this kind of belief, the intellect does not come directly into contact with the thing believed, but reaches it through the medium of testimony. The tendency to credit testimony depends primarily on the emotional faculties. A person endowed with a large organ of Wonder feels pleasure in believing in marvellous incidents and narratives; one endowed with large organs of Hope and small organs of Cautiousness, is predisposed to believe in a happy state, here or hereafter; one possessing large organs of Cautiousness combined with deficient organs of Hope, is constitutionally prone to believe in a disastrous future. In these instances, the emotional faculties appear to lead the intellect to embrace whatever views are most consonant to their likings, and to believe in them. Thus, we had believers in witchcraft; and now we see many believers in ghosts, clairvoyance, spirit-rapping, and other mysterious phenomena. The causes of these phenomena are not cognisable by the intellectual faculties; and hence, in common language, we call those who embrace them, "believers" in them. Among the definitions of "belief" given by Dr Johnson is this: "The theological virtue of faith; firm confidence of the truths of religion." But in Chap. II., p. 15, I have endeavoured to shew that "belief" may be formed by associating, in childhood, almost any form of religious doctrines or opinions with the emotional faculties of Veneration and Wonder (see Appendix, No. III.); and that this process is actually carried on with great success, by the priests of many religions acknowledged by us to be false. The rise and establishment of Mormonism, in our own day, is an example in point.

Keeping this distinction in view, let us next remark that the rigid dogmatists of nearly every Christian sect attach the stupendous reward of heaven to "belief," and the awful punishment of hell, not to conviction, but to "unbelief," in man-concocted articles of faith. (See Appendix, No. IV.) The promise of heaven is a lure to all the animal, moral, and religious faculties, while the threat of hell is an appalling appeal to our selfish feelings. They are, therefore, engines of tremendous power for forming and maintaining belief. I have used the expression "man-concocted articles," because history tells us that the Roman Catholic, and the Protestant, and almost all other sectarian articles of faith, were drawn up by councils or assemblies of fallible men, who interpreted Scripture with their human faculties, and with such human lights as their own ages afforded, which we know were scanty enough, compared with the duty they had upon hand, viz., to fix the articles which they themselves and all their posterity should believe as their passport to heaven and protection from hell. Not only so, but we know that many of these articles were the subjects of vehement dispute among the members of these councils and assemblies, and that several of them were admitted into the code of Divine truths by narrow majorities! Nevertheless, it is to belief in articles of faith thus enacted, that strict dogmatists of every sect assign heaven, and to unbelief in them, hell! The Protestants may be heard vehemently denouncing the Roman Catholic faith as "soul-destroying error," while the Pope prohibits, under the severest penalties, every one from teaching his subjects Protestant Christianity, and for the same reason. In his opinion, *it* is "soul-destroying error." Moreover, every sect, when it sends forth its missionaries to convert the heathen, gives them a commission to teach its own doctrines as "the only certain way of salvation."

Few sects assign salvation to those who conscientiously study the Scriptures and interpret and believe them as their own unbiassed understandings dictate, whether the results be orthodox or not; and fewer of them still, allow an entrance into heaven to conscientious men who cannot believe in any recognised form of Christianity! The Protestants profess to grant freedom of inquiry; but how, if they sincerely did so, could they consistently proclaim the conscientious interpretations of any human being to be " soul-destroying errors?" When we contemplate a body of intelligent men, who are cognisant not only of these facts, but of the great difficulties attending the questions of the authenticity and inspiration of the books of the Old and New Testaments, and of the inroads which science is making on the established interpretations of them*—I say, when we contemplate men in such circumstances, day by day, and with unhesitating confidence threatening hell as the punishment of unbelief, and promising heaven as the reward of belief in their own peculiar doctrines, we are astounded at their boldness, and thrown back upon a variety of hypotheses to account for the spectacle. These threats and promises, too, be it observed, are publicly addressed to many laymen who are perfectly cognisant of all that is here stated. If the clergy could only hear the comments which such hearers make on their discourses, they would pause in their career. Some individuals may be heard remarking that the preacher is only discharging a professional duty, like a lawyer pleading a cause ; and that his own convictions going beyond the narrow boundaries of his creed, he has no liberty of independent thought and action, and where there is no freedom there can be no responsibility. But what an appalling supposition, to imagine a human being, who believes in a God at all, consciously investing doctrines with Divine authority, and enforcing belief in them on others by means of heaven and hell, merely as a professional exercise, regardless alike of their human origin, and of the uncertainty which he knows to exist as to their absolute truth ! Another supposition, frequently hazarded, is, that the preacher employs these portentous engines of belief from habit, without much consideration of their import. This I can readily admit, for few men could indulge in proclamations of eternal misery if they formed an adequate conception of all that it implies. During the French

* Astronomy has overturned the belief of educated men in Joshua's commanding the Sun and Moon to stand still, and in God's fearing that men should reach heaven by building a high tower, the tower of Babel. Geology has shaken the credibility of the Hebrew account of the creation and also of the Deluge. Natural history has demonstrated that the Ark could not contain all the animals of the world ; for many of them did not exist in the region where Noah embarked, and others could not live in an Ark. These sciences, combined with Physiology, have shaken the doctrine that death was introduced in consequence of Adam and Eve eating the forbidden fruit. And Phrenology, by establishing the fact that ill-formed brains, placed in unfavourable circumstances, are the grand sources of vice, crime, and misery ; while favourably constituted brains, placed in opposite circumstances, are the natural fountains of virtue, and of individual and social happiness; militates against the belief that the doctrines of the dogmas are logically related to these causes of good and bad conduct on earth.

war, a near relation of mine happened to go with a friend into Edinburgh Castle on some business, when they observed a regiment forming in a circle within the walls. They stopped to see what the movement meant. It was preparatory to a military punishment. The two civilians were led, by an irresistible curiosity, to watch the subsequent proceedings. It happened that, before this occurred, my relative had frequently discussed the subject of the eternity of future punishment with his friend, who maintained sternly the orthodox opinions on this point. They saw the culprit tied up; the lashing commenced; the blood flowed, and they heard acute cries of agony. They became sick, and left the scene in disgust. As they retired, my relative said to his friend, " What amount of sin, in your opinion, would justify that infliction continued through eternity?" The reply was, "Good God! no human being could, in a whole lifetime, incur guilt that would justify that torture for a week!" This individual never afterwards believed in the eternity of hell torments. He had here the means of comprehending what human torture really is, and his whole being revolted from the idea of its endless duration. Previously, hell was to him little more than a word, but now he could form some definite notion of the horrors implied in it.

The grand cause, however, of the prevalent use of future reward and punishment to support belief in man-concocted articles of faith, appears to me to be this. By laying down the corruption of human nature as a fundamental proposition in religion, and founding on it the doctrine of man's natural aversion to holiness and virtue, and his natural incapacity to discern Divine truth, the dogmatists deprive themselves of a secure resting-place in science and in human nature for religion and morality. Some time ago, I heard a sermon preached by an able divine, on the text, " Thou shalt love thy neighbour as thyself." In answer to the inquiry, *How* shall we be able to love our neighbours as ourselves? he said that the philosophers present us only with motives of prudence or selfishness, which can never produce disinterested goodness; and that the only means of becoming capable of fulfilling the precept, is to obtain the influence of the Holy Spirit, in answer to prayer. " Ask and it shall be given to you." The Holy Spirit alone, said he, can plant in the human mind true Christian charity and brotherly love: secondary means may cultivate it after it is so planted, but can do nothing to produce it.—But I ask, If God instituted the world, and endowed man with all his functions, may we not truly say that all our gifts proceed from Him, and that secondary means can only cultivate, improve, and direct them? Farther—If the feeling of pure disinterested goodness, prompting us to love our neighbour as ourselves for the sake of making him happy, without any selfish object of our own, is communicated to us, when a large and active organ of Benevolence is bestowed on us, is not this an example of God's grace producing the emotion in a way which those misinterpreters of Scripture and repudiators of nature erroneously deny?

According to the doctrine now referred to, all religious attainments and hopes rest on belief in doctrines of which the clergy are virtually the interpreters. The original records are not directly accessible to the laity, and hence it is impossible for them, generally speaking, to reach CONVICTION in regard to the basis on which morality, religion, and salvation, are said to rest. *Belief*, therefore, is the only alternative left to them; and belief being, in the dogmatical view, indispensable to salvation, and salvation being transcendently important, some of the clergy act as if they thought all appliances to produce belief justifiable. If any inquirer desires to reach *conviction* rather than to rest satisfied with *belief*, he is not referred to nature and to legitimate inductions from it, but to books written in dead languages, and to volumes of disputation concerning the authors of these books, the genuineness of the text, the degree in which the text is inspired, and, finally, the soundness of discordant interpretations of it, on belief in which salvation is said to depend. On all these points, the difficulties are increasing instead of diminishing with the advances of scholarship and science.* If personal and social wellbeing depend on the fulfilment of *natural* conditions instituted by God, then no religion resting exclusively on belief in dogmas which ignore these conditions, *can* be thoroughly practical. Moreover, I have attempted to shew that the order of the Divine administration of this world is unfolded to man by means of the instruments through which it is conducted; that it is addressed equally to the *intellectual* as to the emotional faculties; and that, therefore, before a religion of *conviction*,—*i.e.*, a religion based on discernible manifestations of Divine wisdom, goodness, and power, cognisable by the intellect, gratifying to the moral and religious emotions, and conducing, practically, to the wellbeing of the race,—can be attained, we must resort to the records of these manifestations in the book of Nature, and from them extract elements for the formation of our faith.

In every religion, we shall find, that, in proportion to the

---

* See "*An Inquiry concerning the origin of Christianity,*" by C. HENNELL. *Second Edition.* "*The Creed of Christendom,*" by W. RATHBONE GREG. "*The Essence of Christianity,*" by LUDWIG FEUERBACH, 1854. *Prize Essay,*—"*Christianity and Infidelity,*" by S. S. HENNELL. London: Hall, Virtue, and Co., 1857.

importance attached to pure *belief*, is the extent of superstition in its followers, and of domination in its clergy. The Hindoo, Mahometan, Roman Catholic, and Protestant religions, may be selected as examples. The priests of the first and second exact belief without a shadow of free investigation, and their flocks are their blind fanatical puppets, and also the recipients of every degrading superstition they choose to teach them. The Roman Catholic priesthood, also, require unreasoning belief, and their power is proportionally great, and their peculiar doctrines proportionally distant from reason. The Protestant laity are nominally allowed freedom of inquiry, and in proportion to the use they have made of this privilege is their religion rational, and their subjection to clerical dominion mitigated. It is necessary only to refer to the sects which have renounced the most appalling of the dogmas cited on pages 186-7, as containing the most independent thinkers, and least priest-ridden portion of the Christian laity. The clergy of those sects having lost their priestly power, appeal to reason, and to man's moral and religious emotions, as the means of guiding their flocks: They substitute *conviction* for *belief*, a certain mode of training the laity to mental independence; and to become the sincere friends of human progress.

The practice of founding religion on dogmas which cannot bear the investigation of reason, is attended with another great evil. It is the cause why the Christian clergy, like the Levites among the Jews, and the Priests in idolatrous countries, constitute a class apart from the laity. The Scotch advocate formerly mentioned, who had been educated as a clergyman in the Church of Scotland, but subsequently embraced the legal profession, mentioned to me that so completely are the clergy a separate class, that were two of them, one from John-o'-Groat's House, and another from Gretna Green, to meet for the first time in their lives, even in an inn, they would in a short time enter upon an interchange of opinions upon religion and church government, and church politics, far more confidential than either of them would venture to indulge in with his own lay father or brother. The same reserve infects the laity in their communications with their spiritual guides. When I visited Boston in the United States of North America, I happened to mention to the Rev. Dr Channing some opinions which I had heard discussed the previous day at a dinner party consisting of lawyers, physicians, and merchants; when he observed, "This is very interesting to me. But for you, a stranger, I should never have learned that such views are entertained; and yet it is of great importance to clergymen to know the real sentiments of the laity on religious doctrines. I have often told my lay friends that I desire nothing more ardently than to hear their true convictions; and I have assured them that whatever these may be, if I am satisfied that they are honestly entertained, the holders of them shall not forfeit my esteem. But," he added, "it has been all in vain. They fear to hurt my feelings by contesting my opinions: they erect a barrier of good breeding between themselves and their clergy, which no skill of mine has been able to break through."

This is a grave charge against the laity, and, in my opinion, it is well-founded. By concealing their real opinions concerning the doctrines and worship sanctioned by the standards of their churches, they render it impossible for the most upright and enlightened members of the clerical profession to move a step towards reformation. No clergyman *can* proclaim doubts in the soundness of the dogmas which, probably in the immaturity of his understanding and absence of experience, he has vowed to preach, while the laity continue ostensibly to uphold them. The movement towards reformation *must commence with the laity.* By expressing openly and honestly their dissatisfaction with things as they stand, they will afford the clergy, many of whom are groaning in creed-imposed fetters, encouragement and opportunity to declare whatever changes the increase of learning and the evolution of scientific truths may have produced in their convictions. The laity act an unmanly and dishonourable part, in secretly condemning what they publicly support.

How strongly do such cases indicate unsoundness in the creeds which lead to such reserve; yet it arises exclusively from the dogmatic elements introduced into our religion. As before mentioned, Christian theology is to the laity an occult science, resting on interpretations of Hebrew and Greek records; and *belief* in certain doctrines is the foundation of all their hopes. There is no common ground, therefore, on which the ordinary layman and his pastor can meet to discuss the merits of their faith. It stands apart from nature and secular experience; unbelief and misbelief involve eternal perdition; and there is thus no alternative left to the layman but to surrender his conscience and understanding to his spiritual master, or encounter (as he thinks) the risk of losing his soul. The Pope and his clergy proclaim this as the natural result of their faith, and they act consistently in doing so. The Protestant clergy, on the other hand, *de facto* exercise the same authority over the unlearned laity, while they profess to acknowledge the right of individual judgment.

These considerations are urged with no hostile design against religion. They are presented with an earnest desire to strengthen its foundations and extend its usefulness. The Edinburgh Review for October 1840 expresses wonder that there should be so small a proportion of sermons destined to live; that, out of the *million* and upwards preached annually throughout the empire there should be a very few that are remembered *three whole days after they are delivered,*—fewer still that are committed to the press, scarcely one that is not in a few years absolutely forgotten. One explanation may be given of these facts. As the sermons are preached by the best educated men in the country, and by men of at least average abilities, the subjects of them must be such that they do not stand in a natural relation to the human faculties, and therefore, even when supported by the religious emotions, do not permanently interest or edify their hearers. How then, it may be asked, do the sermons continue to be listened to, with even the appearance of devotion? The answer is, the dogmas having been entwined with the religious emotions of the people from infancy, are regarded as divine truths, and by repeating them, the preachers excite the emotions, and thus listening becomes an act of divine worship. But in this monotonous practice there is no progress towards a higher development of human intelligence, virtue, and happiness. In consequence, the Christian religion, as now interpreted, actually stands still; nay, it is the boast of the adherents of the dogmas that it must necessarily do so, until it shall bring all opinions under its sway. But this standing still in the midst of a host of assailants striving, and not altogether without success, to undermine its very foundations,—and of a rapidly-advancing stream of scientific knowledge at variance with its dogmas, cannot fail to sap its strength. In page 66 it is stated that when the intellectual faculties furnish the emotional faculties of Wonder and Veneration with knowledge of the qualities and phenomena of Nature, the two sets of faculties acting together generate an intuitive belief in the existence of a supernatural power and intelligence. We can give no account of the origin of this belief, except that the faculties of normal men are so constituted in relation to Nature that it excites it in them. But we learn by observation, that where knowledge of Nature is so deficient that the mind cannot comprehend the order and lessons of nature, the religious emotions, in seeking for the supernatural, are liable to go astray into gross superstitions, and that the intellect then invents idols, demons, witches, and other monstrous objects or imaginary beings to which the emotions cling. The *supernatural,* therefore, in one form or other, appears to be indispensable to their satisfaction. Accordingly, we find that the founders of the Hindoo and Mahometan religions, based them on alleged supernatural communications. Belief in their sacred books was not produced by reason and evidence, but by the aid of authority, the promise of reward and threat of punishment. The assurance of a Divine origin was accepted by the people, because, in the actual condition of their intelligence, it satisfied their love of the supernatural. Being communicated to the young, from generation to generation, and supported by public opinion and many social advantages, these religions have had an abiding endurance.

Both natural and communicated religions, therefore, appear to rest on the basis of the *supernatural*, real or pretended; for although it may appear paradoxical, it seems nevertheless true, that it is the intuitive belief that all the qualities and phenomena of Nature manifest a Supernatural Power that fits the rules which they reveal for human guidance, to become religious laws. If this view be sound, religious belief founded on the objects and phenomena of Nature cannot be shaken, because these objects and phenomena are constantly present as sources of conviction, and the human faculties are all adapted to receive as Divine the lessons logically deducible from them.

The Hindoo religion does not possess this quality of stability, and hence it requires and has received support from external motives; and these are unscrupulously applied. (See p. 47.) In consequence of this weakness, it is in constant danger of being subverted by the revelations of Divine Truth in Nature; but much less so, by another communicated Faith, however much superior it may be to itself. When the Bible is presented to its votaries, they examine it with their intellects alone, and in general it does not appear to them to possess the character of a Divine message. Their minds are preoccupied by their own supernatural communications. These not having been embraced from *reason*, but from authority and training, and being supported only by the authority of their Priests, by the law, and by public opinion, Christianity has not yet succeeded in extinguishing this faith and taking its place. Ida Pffeifer informs us that the Christian villages or communities in India are composed of orphan children left utterly destitute by visitations of the cholera, who were collected and clothed, fed, educated, and trained by Christian Missionaries; in other words, training has made them Christians as it had made their Fathers Hindoos. But generally speaking, the Hindoo people, satisfied with their own religion, continue to reject the religion of their conquerors. The missionaries find it extremely difficult to undo the connection formed in their minds between the doctrines of that faith and their religious emotions. The Rev. Dr Duff, a missionary from the Church of Scotland to Bengal, perceived the obstacles to his success presented by this state of things, and begged of the Church to send him the means of instructing the Hindoos in Natural Science, in order to prepare them to receive Christianity. In his pamphlet, entitled *The Church of Scotland's Indian Mission*, p. 3 (Edinburgh, 1835), he says of the Hindoos, that with them the argument for Christianity from miracles is utterly powerless. " They retort, that they themselves have miracles far more stupendous. And doubtless if mere *gross magnitude* is considered, they say what is true ; for in this respect *their* miracles set all comparison at defiance. Besides, with them the *original* miracles form an *inherent* part of their *theology ;* and they have no notion of what is meant by an appeal to them, in order to authenticate *a doctrine*. And *modern* miracles they have in such abundance, that they are exhibited on the most trivial occasions, and become matters of daily occurrence."

The means of teaching Natural Science have been supplied in Bengal, and have been largely taken advantage of by intelligent young Hindoos ; but, according to my information, they apply the knowledge thus acquired to refute the Bible. Be it observed that the missionaries and Christian laymen who have taught them Natural Science have abstained from investing it with a sacred character ; have not represented it as revealing rules of practical conduct which are directly related to the moral and religious faculties of man, and, therefore, calculated by teaching and training to become moral and religious truths. The consequence is the production of unbelief in all religions. Surely natural religion would be less dangerous than none.

The Greeks and Romans had no written records professing to proceed directly from their gods. Their religion was traditionary, and rested on physical representations of their deities in statuary, and on temples, rites, and ceremonies. We have seen how obstinately Christianity is resisted by the Hindoos in consequence of the preoccupation of their religious emotions by a religion which they believe to have proceeded from a supernatural source. When the Christian religion was presented to the Greeks and Romans it did not meet with any obstacle of this kind, for they had no divine records. Its success among them was, therefore, proportionately easy and great; and it spread also among all those nations whose brains were well formed, and who had no previous sacred books to preoccupy them. Among most of the tribes of the native American Indians it failed, apparently because their cerebral organs were so defective that they could not comprehend it.

These facts appear to shew that it is much more difficult to subvert a religion alleged to rest on a supernatural basis, than to infuse a new faith, claiming such an origin, into minds not preoccupied by belief in supernatural communications. Might not a religion, founded on the rules of belief and conduct revealed to us by God in the agencies and phenomena of nature, aid us in rooting out superstitions which we find it so difficult to exterminate merely by presenting another supernatural revelation, however superior in truth and practical utility? If the missionaries would teach the dictates of science for human guidance, as religious as well as intellectual truths, to the Hindoos, they might bring them at least nearer to Christianity.

In Legislation, also, the obstructive effects of the Dogmas may be observed. If this world is an Institution, it follows that personal and social prosperity can be reached only by studying the agencies of Nature, and conforming to the rules of conduct which they prescribe. In this view, the function of the human legislator is simply to discover and apply the rules of action dictated by the Divine Lawgiver. In my opinion, science has already made such progress that valuable rules have been demonstrated, conformity to which will aid us in securing healthy constitutions at birth, and preserving them unimpaired by disease throughout life; also in the production and distribution of wealth; in the elevation and refinement of our mental faculties; in the attainment of social distinction and other objects of legitimate ambition; in short, in the improvement of our minds and bodies, and the augmentation of our happiness, as individuals; and more emphatically still, in reaching national prosperity. No human legislature *can* produce any beneficial results, private or public, except by acting in conformity with the order of nature; while it may, and often does, call forth floods of suffering and disappointment by enacting and enforcing laws in opposition to it. Yet the mere suggestion of such an idea in the British Parliament would probably call forth shouts of laughter and derision. There is no more recognition of a Divine government of the world in our legislature than in that of Greece and Rome; and religion is never heard of, as a basis of legislation, except when some miserable sectarian interest demands the aid of Parliament for its aggrandisement or protection. And what is the cause of this untoward state of things? The interpretations of Scripture embodied in our prevailing dogmas, which have usurped the place of Christianity, represent this world as a wreck, and incapable of improvement, except by supernatural means, which can be evoked only by conduct in conformity with the dictates of church standards and catechisms!

The national mind discerns no actual intelligible Divine Government in the world, and practical men find the principles laid down as Divine in the Dogmas little applicable to secular affairs; hence comes the exclusion of the recognition of God's government of the world from our legislature, and also of all religion whatever! Hence, also, the exclusion of instruction in the rules of this government from schools, colleges, churches, and literature! What are the substitutes in Parliament for knowledge of these rules? In all but a few great minds, we have only crude and conflicting notions about the laws of commerce, health, crime, education, and all the natural agencies which are producing the weal or woe of mankind. Hence, finally, government by party combinations, in supporting which, men of honourable character do not hesitate, when in opposition, to maintain in debate that a principle or measure is wholly wrong, which, when in power, they defended as entirely sound and beneficial, or *vice versa!* When a Divine Government shall be recognised, such conduct will become indicative only of intellectual weakness or moral dishonesty, and this stigma on our national reputation will cease.

In the legislation of the despotic countries of Europe, the effects of ignoring a Divine Government of the world are still more disastrous. The Sovereign claims to reign by Divine right, and uses the Dogmas to banish from the minds of his subjects every notion that he exercises only a delegated power, and that he and they live under laws enacted by an Authority which controls every act of his legislation, and produces good or evil from it, irrespective of his intentions or wishes. The Emperor of Russia, for example, appears not to perceive that by the order of Nature an Empire can attain the necessaries, comforts, and luxuries of life, which are indispensable to the enjoyment of the people as individuals, and to their strength as a nation, only by employing labour and skill in the development of their natural resources; and that knowledge, morality, and economy are necessary to their success. Apparently he does not believe that national greatness does not consist in mere length and breadth of territory and numbers of subjects; or that the extension of his sovereignty over comparatively barren regions and barbarous men, has the natural tendency to distract his attention from raising the physical and moral condition of his people, also to weaken the central power, by stretching it over too wide a space, and thereby to lead to feeble and corrupt government, thence to anarchy, and finally to dissolution of his Empire. His religious dogmas have taught him that he is the vicegerent of God in his own dominions; but apparently he does not perceive that Divine rules of conduct are prescribed by the order of Nature, and he acts as if they had no existence. Hence, he desires to augment his dominions by absorbing into them, Circassia, Turkey, Persia, and other barbarous countries, wholly blind to the inevitable exhaustion of the wealth, and destruction of the welfare, of the most civilized and industrious, and, therefore, the most estimable and valuable portion of his subjects, in gratifying this unwise ambition. From not perceiving that these projects are immoral, and that, by the law of Nature, nothing that is immoral is permanent and strong, he does not discern the certain disastrous future which he is now providing for his empire. By a patient exposition of the modes of action of the natural forces, physical and moral, which determine human wellbeing or suffering, these results, in my opinion, might be demonstrated; and yet religious dogmas exclude even the attempt to investigate the rules of conduct which they dictate, and discountenance their application to practical purposes!

Another disastrous effect of the Dogmas is seen in their influence in obstructing the education of the people. Many religious men denounce the teaching of science as "godless education." While they are thus nearly unanimous in practically rejecting the course of Providence in Nature as a source of instruction, each places in the hands of the young its own Catechism of doctrines, its Liturgy, its Confession of Faith, or its other articles of belief; and with the most pertinacious assiduity labours to imprint these indelibly on the memory, and to imbed them in the affections of its pupils. Meanwhile many of the sects denounce the catechisms, liturgies, and confessions of certain others as unsound, unscriptural, and dangerous to the eternal welfare of the people. Here, then, is a record unquestionably Divine, in so far as we read it rightly, superseded and set aside for books of human compilation, denounced as unsound by large masses of the community.

The effect of this on education is described by Mr Horace Mann* in the following words:—" After the particular attention which I gave to this subject (religious instruction) both in England and Scotland, I can say, without any exception, that, in those schools where religious creeds and forms of faith, and modes of worship, were directly taught, I found the common doctrines and injunctions of morality, and the meaning of the preceptive parts of the Gospel, to be much less taught and

* Report of an Educational Tour in Germany and Parts of Great Britain and Ireland, by Horace Mann, Esq., Secretary of the Board of Education, Massachusetts, U. S. With Preface and Notes, by W. B. Hodgson. London: Simpkin, Marshall, and Co. 1846.

much less understood by the pupils, than in the same grade of schools, and by the same classes of pupils with us," in Massachusetts, where the teaching of all sectarian doctrines in common schools is prohibited by law. Is not this sacrificing Christianity itself at the shrine of Sectarianism?

The elements of which a sect is composed, are the points in which it differs from other sects; and its existence depends on the success and assiduity with which it infuses a knowledge of and reverence for these into the minds of the young. It represents them as subjects of the utmost importance to their temporal and eternal welfare. In the estimation of its zealous leaders, they greatly surpass in practical as well as religious importance, the order of Nature. If any sect were to cease investing its points of difference with the highest reverence in the estimation of its pupils, and begin to magnify the truth and utility of the doctrines in which all are agreed, it would commit *felo de se*. Its dissolution and fusion into the general body of Christian believers would be inevitable and speedy. The more completely, therefore, the different sects obtain the command of education, the greater will be the obstacles to the introduction of the order of Nature into schools.

The points in which all Christian sects are agreed *must* constitute the essential substance of Christianity; because it is on these that Christian men of all denominations act in the business and relations of life. Pious, honest, and benevolent men, abound in them all; and this common excellence must spring from a common source. The points on which they differ, although forming the life-blood and bonds of union of sects, cannot constitute Christianity; because if they did, the Christian religion would really have scarcely any practical form or substance. It would consist of abstract disquisitions, discernible only by microscopic eyes, and inapplicable to all beneficent ends. Who will say that the points of faith in which the Church of England differs from the Congregationalists, or the views of church government in which the Free Church differs from the Established Church of Scotland—or the Secession Church from the Free Church—or the Scotch Episcopalian Church from them all—are the essential elements of Christianity? And yet it is for the sake of maintaining these distinctions from generation to generation, and of transmitting to the remotest posterity the bitter contentions which have so frequently vexed the spirits and alloyed the happiness of this age, that we are called on to exclude instruction in the course of nature, as a guide to human conduct, from our schools; to reject a system of education founded on the points in which all are agreed; to prostrate the national mind beneath the car of sectarianism, and to allow it to be crushed and distorted by its unhallowed wheels!

Practical Christianity, on the other hand, and the laws of Nature, physical, organic, and moral, present the same instruction and recommend the same line of action to all, and are, therefore, destructive of sectarianism. Hence the cry of infidelity which all sects raise against them! Obedience to them is calculated to bind man to man, and nation to nation, by the ties of reciprocal interest as well as of affection and duty, and to bring all into communion with God. Our knowledge of them grows with the growth of science, and their influence increases with the augmentation of the prosperity which obedience to their dictates yields.

Every motive of duty and interest, therefore, calls on the laity and the Legislature to disenthral education from the dominion of sects, and to allow to God's providence a fair field for working out its beneficial ends. Disguise the fact as we will, the order of Nature—in other words, God's secular providence—is a power which in this world shapes our destinies for weal or woe; while the peculiar doctrines of sectarianism only exalt the consequence and power of clerical teachers, and the few zealous laymen who constitute their staff. To vote money, therefore, as is done under the Minutes of Council of August and December 1846, to every sect, to enable it to educate its own members in its own religious doctrines, is actually to endow discord. It is deserting the shrine of reason and of moral and religious principle, and bowing at that of prejudice and bigotry. It is renouncing all reverence for God's providence, as revealed in the course of nature; for every one of the sects, if it does not exclude, deny, and denounce the order of Nature as a source of practical instruction to the young, at least practically treats it as a matter of small importance compared with its own peculiar dogmas. To give them the public money to enable them to pursue this course of instruction more effectually, is to encourage them in placing their own wisdom high above that of the Creator. Nor is this the worst feature of the case. To make the teaching of God's order of Providence in nature *as religious truth*, if the Dogmas are not taught along with it, an unsurmountable objection to granting public aid to secular schools, is actually treating the Divine laws as dangerous, and, however, unintentionally, with contumely; yet this is the rule of the Committee of Council on Education! See Appendix, No. IX.

Truth alone can benefit a nation, and the doctrines of *every sect* cannot possibly be true: to give each of them public money, therefore, to teach its own tenets, is to endow equally truth and error. It is tantamount in physics to setting in motion antagonistic forces; in cookery, to paying one man to pour wormwood, and another sugar, into the cup of which the nation is to drink. By all means allow the men who prefer wormwood to fill their own bowl with it; and those who prefer sugar to fill theirs with sugar; but let not the Government, which superintends the cup out of which all must drink, pay men with national money to destroy the contents of that cup, and render them a potion which no human palate can endure. To pay all sects, who are teaching solemn contradictions, implies an utter disbelief in any intelligible order of God's providence on earth. It deliberately supersedes the teaching of it, and plants conflicting catechisms, liturgies, and confessions, in its place. If the heads of the Government cannot discern in science an exposition of the order of Nature, or, in other words, of the course of God's providence on earth, they may at least so far defer to Divine wisdom and intelligence, as to believe that God's providence, however dark, must be self-consistent, and that it does not promise to prosper contradictions!

Will not the men of intellect and science who see this to be the case assume courage, speak out, and help to stem the torrent of sectarianism which overflows the land? They have it in their power at this moment to do their country an invaluable service, for which she would one day rear monuments of gratitude to their names. Will they, through fear of a little temporary obloquy, desert the standard of truth, of God, and of the people? Let their own consciences answer the appeal, and let them act as their consciences dictate. Will no teachers arise, embued with knowledge of the order of Nature, as unfolded in science, and, with faith in its adaptation to the human faculties, communicate it, under the sanction of the religious sentiments, to the young, as a help to guide them through the thorny paths of life? Yes! Such teachers exist, and they lack only the countenance of the enlightened laity to follow the strong impulses of their affections and understandings, and accomplish this great improvement in secular instruction.

Moreover, under the sectarian system, not only is the advancing intelligence of the people shackled by the consecrated errors of the dark ages, but the most vigorous and profound thinkers among the clergy of all denominations are subdued and held in thraldom by their feebler brethren. The men of inferior endowments and intelligence take their stand on the accredited dogmas, which they cherish because they are in accordance with their own narrow and prejudiced perceptions; and they resist every liberal idea and study that has the most remote appearance of conflicting with their preconceived ideas. As they exert a great influence over a half-educated people, trained to regard their doctrines with holy reverence, the more powerful minds too generally retire from the field, and leave to them an undisputed sway.

The best interests of society suffer from this unhappy state of things; whereas if Nature were taught, as the harmonious ally of a sounder interpretation of Christianity, the men endowed with the profoundest intellects, and the purest and most elevated emotions, would lead the general mind, and we should constantly advance. In the present time, the leaders of the Calvinistic sects are strenuously exerting themselves to bring back the public sentiment to the opinions of the middle of the seventeenth century; and if they do not succeed, it is science alone which prevents this consummation of their labours.

From the neglect of Nature by the sects, and the paramount importance which they attach to their own peculiar doctrines, they languish when not excited by contention among themselves. Dr Candlish illustrated this fact lately, when he called on the Free Church to renew and proclaim its "testimony;" in other words, constantly to obtrude on public attention the peculiar views which distinguish it from all other sects. He assigned, as the motive for doing so, the danger of decay, with which it appears already to be threatened, from its distinctive characteristics being forgotten, seeing that its standards, doctrines, and discipline, are identical with those of the Established Church of Scotland. There is no perennial source of activity and progress in any doctrine that is not in harmony with and supported by the course of nature. A scheme, on the contrary, founded on Christianity interpreted in conformity with God's natural laws, will enjoy an inherent vitality, and a self-rectifying energy, that will cause it constantly to flourish and advance. It will in time root out sectarian errors, and unite all classes in the bonds of harmonious truth.

In advocating a non-sectarian system of national education, I do not propose to deliver over scholars and teachers to government officers, with power to mould their minds into whatever forms our rulers may prefer, as some advocates of sectarian instruction pretend. The United States of North America have set us a bright example in this enterprise. They have divided their country into convenient spaces, and designated them as school-districts. The existing law of Massachusetts (Revised Statutes, 1835, title x., chap. 23), ordains that districts containing fifty families shall maintain one school—districts containing one hundred and fifty families shall provide two schools; and so forth,—" in which children shall be instructed in reading, writing, geography, arithmetic, and good behaviour, by teachers of competent ability and good morals." Larger districts, again, are required to maintain a school, " in which the history of the United States, book-keeping, surveying, geometry, and algebra, shall be taught." And if the locality shall contain four thousand inhabitants, the teacher shall—" in addition to all the branches above enumerated, be competent to instruct in the Latin and Greek languages, general history, rhetoric, and logic." The law requires the inhabitants to raise money by taxing themselves for supporting these schools, and ordains them to appoint committees annually for managing them.*

We are told, however, by some able opponents of the educational scheme introduced by the orders of Council, that Government has no right to interfere with the secular instruction of the people, and that voluntary effort is adequate to accomplish all that is needed for the public welfare. In my late " Remarks on National Education," I endeavoured to shew that Government is not only entitled, but bound, to enable the people, by legislative aid, to organize their own wealth and intelligence for the establishment and maintenance of schools for universal instruction; and I now beg to add, that experience shews that legislative aid far excels voluntary effort in this good work. England has been left to voluntary effort for the education of her people from the foundation of her institutions, and what has been the result: Mr Horace Mann, in his Educational Tour, says: " England is the only one among the nations of Europe, conspicuous for its civilization and resources, which has not, and never has had, any system for the education of its people. *And it is the country where, incomparably beyond any other, the greatest and most appalling social contrast exists; where, in comparison with the intelligence, wealth, and refinement of what are called the higher classes, there is the most ignorance, poverty, and crime among the lower!* Owing to the inherent vice and selfishness of their system, or their no-system, there is no country in which so little is effected, compared with their expenditure of means; and what is done only tends to separate the different classes of society more and more widely from each other."

There is a great difference between the influence of the voluntary principle when applied to the support of churches, and of schools for the poor. The main object of the church is to provide means for securing the eternal salvation of the contributor and his family—a most momentous consideration to every

* Farther details concerning the machinery by which the schools are managed, and the taxes levied, in Massachusetts, will be found in an article in the *Edinburgh Review* for July 1841, under the title of " Education in America."

reflecting man. It involves the selfish principles of his nature, as well as his affections and his sense of religious duty. The school for the poor, on the other hand, addresses chiefly his moral and religious sentiments, leaving his self-interest far in the rear. Experience shews that these emotions do not suffice to induce the rich to provide sufficiently for the physical wants of the poor, and in consequence, Parliament has enacted poor-laws. Why, then, should we rely on them for providing for a less clamant mental destitution?

The dogmas are obstructing educational progress in still another direction. They are depriving society of the full beneficial use of the Sunday. Their adherents insist that that day shall be devoted exclusively to hearing the dogmas preached, and to practising the solemnities they inculcate. One whole day of rest in seven is, to a toil-worn people, an inestimable boon, the necessity of which is clearly proclaimed by the constitution of our organism; and if judiciously employed, it may be rendered a grand instrument of civilization. If nature is a Divine Institution, and if it teaches rules of practical conduct to men, what a precious day may Sunday become when it shall be devoted in an adequate measure to the exposition of these rules and of the wonderful structures and estrangements of Nature on which they are founded! How gratifying to all our faculties, to the wants of which they are adapted by Divine wisdom and goodness! And how fruitful in benefits to the mind and body of man! But under the thraldom of the Dogmas, all this instruction, if given on Sundays, is regarded as sin, and society is excluded from the advantages of receiving it on that day—the only one set apart for mental improvement. The laborious inhabitants of our large towns who cannot travel in quest of the elements of this instruction and enjoyment, have had these brought to them by the philanthropy of a few enlightened men, in the form of parks, museums, and collections of works of art, all calculated not only to recreate a wearied body and brain, but to furnish captivating texts from which the most salutary and elevating practical lessons may be drawn. God has bestowed on us faculties of Melody and Time; endowed timber, steel, brass, and the air with qualities exquisitely fitting them to minister to their gratification, and given us constructive talents enabling us to combine and apply these materials to the production of sounds capable of soothing us in sorrow, inspiring us with gay and cheerful emotions, rousing us to fervid action, or lifting up our whole being in wrapt devotion to Him the Giver of all Good. If benevolent design can be proved to human apprehension, here is evidence of it in abundance. Yet the adherents of the Dogmas petition the Legislature, and successfully too, to shut up all these museums and collections of works of art, and to withdraw musical performances from the public parks on Sundays! They claim the whole of that day to themselves. But under their teaching and preaching there is scarcely any social progress. Their dogmas are stereotyped, and ever the same; and I can bear testimony, that for fifty years I attended churches, and after the first four or five, when everything was new, I rarely received any addition to my knowledge; and it is to maintain the interminable repetition of such doctrines that God, His works, His wisdom, and His lessons, so prolifically abounding in nature, must be thrust aside as profane, unprofitable, and unfitted for the day set apart by society for rest, devotion, recreation, and instruction in things that are Divine! If the Dogmas were removed, or modified, and a more rational interpretation of the Bible introduced, and the elements of science and the practical rules of conduct they dictate were taught in schools as God's revelations for our guidance, we should come prepared to hear the same sublime and soul-elevating instruction extended and enforced every Sunday from the pulpit; and it appears to me that the beneficial consequences to society would be incalculably great. Progress would never cease; monotony would be the fault of sloth and incapacity alone; and no man of average mental endowments could truly say at the close of fifty years of such preaching, I " am no wiser and little better than I was at the beginning."

The unreasonableness of the oppression exercised by the adherents of the Dogmas over society in regard to the enjoyment of these sources of improvement and happiness on Sundays, is the more striking when we consider on what it is founded. From infancy, certain interpretations of the Fourth Commandment have been entwined in their minds with their religious emotions, and have become sacred in their estimation. They are unconscious that the sacred and religious character of the notions *has been given to them by training*, and regard them as infallible Divine truths. The inhabitants of Continental Europe, on the other hand, holding the same Commandment in their hands, put a different interpretation on the words, and, under the influence of *their training*, regarding *that interpretation* as the sound one, act on it. Nevertheless our dogmatists seem incapable of conceiving that these other opinions can possibly be true; and not satisfied with unbounded liberty to act on their own impressions, they insist on *forcing* these on their countrymen! They not only refuse to listen on Sundays to God's teaching in Nature, but prohibit their equals from enjoying this unspeakable pleasure and advantage.

Finally,—In all ages and countries, religious teachers have succeeded in persuading their own flocks that only *their doctrines* constitute true religion, are capable of supporting the mind in affliction, and are certain to lead to salvation; and laymen, when trained from infancy under such impressions, really feel no religion in their souls, and cannot, even by their understandings, conceive any to exist that is calculated to produce these effects, except that which is embodied in their own tenets. When, therefore, a doctrine, be it that of election or the fall of man, or any other (however uncertain in its foundation, and vehemently disputed by other sects), which has been woven into the mind of an individual as the only foundation of *his* hopes and consolations, happens to be subverted, *he* is really deprived, *pro tempore*, of his *religion*, and all its accompanying advantages and enjoyments; for *he* has *no religion* unconnected with belief in the dogmas which have perished. Such believers are as sensitive to every doubt thrown on their faith as they would be to an attack on their lives; and if they are not strong-minded, or are past the middle period of life, they only obey the law of their nature in feeling and thinking in this manner. Were it likely that any of them would peruse these pages, I should be most unwilling to disturb their tranquillity. On the contrary, I should refer them to the case of Rammohun Roy's mother, and encourage them to hold fast by the faith which gives them support and consolation. Though convinced that his Christian doctrines were true, she could not throw off the shackles of idolatrous customs. "Rammohun," she said to him before she set out on her last pilgrimage to the Temple of Juggernaut, "you are right, but I am a weak woman, and am grown too old to give up these observances, which are a comfort to me." She maintained them with the most self-denying devotion. She would not allow a female servant to accompany her; or any other provision to be made for her comfort, or even support on her journey: and when at Juggernaut, she engaged in sweeping the temple of the idol. There she spent the remainder of her life—nearly a year, if not more; and there she died.* When Melancthon paid a visit to his mother in her old age, she asked "What am I to believe amidst so many different opinions of the present day?" To which he answered,—"Go on, believe and pray as you now do and have done before, and do not disturb yourself about the disputes and controversies of the times." —(*Life of Melancthon*, by Francis Augustus Cox, A.M., 2d edit., p. 281.)

* Review of the Labours, Opinions, and Character of Rajah Rammohun Roy, by Lant Carpenter, LL.D. London, 1833.

CHAPTER X.

CONCLUSION.

IN reference to the present condition and future prospects of the Religion of Christendom, the fundamental point to be determined appears to me to be—Whether the world, as it now exists, is merely the wreck of a better system,—or an Institution? If it is the former, I leave to other hands, the task of mending its disjointed parts, and educing from them whatever good they can be made to yield. If it is an Institution,—then, as before remarked, it will be our duty and our interest to regard it with respect as the design of its Author, to try to discover its plan, and to conform to its laws. With this view we may approach the study of it in the following order:—

Human nature will constitute the central point of our investigations; because the adaptations of the world to our capacities, wants, and desires cannot be understood while the latter are unknown. If the views of man's nature, stated in Chapter III., §§ 1 and 2, and elucidated in the Appendix, No. II., be well founded, physiology will form one grand source from which this information will be derived.

If we find evidence, as maintained in Chapter III., § 4, that man is constitutionally a religious being—then we shall see a firm foundation in nature for religion; and if, as stated in § 5, we discover in him organs of the moral emotions, we shall perceive also an indestructible basis for morality.

These two points being fixed, the next question will be—Whether nature is constituted in such a relationship to our religious faculties as to inspire us intuitively with belief in the existence of a supernatural Power and Intelligence—whom we call God? The affirmative of this question is maintained in Chapter V., p. 66. If this conclusion is well founded, we shall then be led to view our own constitution and that of the external world, as institutions proceeding from this supernatural Power, and under this conviction our duties will become obvious.

If we desire to be healthy and to live long, we shall enquire *into the conditions* on which He has been pleased to dispense these advantages. If we desire to possess the necessaries, elegancies, and beneficial luxuries that contribute, by His appointment, to the enjoyment of life, we shall try to discover and to fulfil *the conditions* on which He offers to us these advantages. If we wish to live in the society of intelligent, moral, religious, industrious, and happy men—we shall enquire into and fulfil the social duties on which He has made these boons to depend. Finally, if we desire to improve our whole being to its highest attainable point of perfection, and to raise our souls to communion with their Divine Author, we shall acquire and carry into practice the kind of knowledge, the morality, and the religion which He has rendered indispensable to our highest state of existence on earth.

These are not Utopian and impracticable ideas; for, be it observed, if the world *is* an Institution and man's faculties are adapted to it, *there must be* divinely appointed ways of gratifying these powers, and the corollary seems evident that man must be capable of finding them out and complying with their requirements, when he shall seriously apply his endowments to this end.

Our next aim should be to discover the qualities, agencies, and relations of natural objects. These exist and act under divinely imposed laws; which we call the Laws of Nature. As we cannot alter the qualities, suspend their action, or prevent the consequences which have been attached to it, our chief duty in regard to them will be to investigate them and to discover everything that can be known regarding them. This is the aim of scientific enquiry as now conducted; and the expiscation of the qualities and agencies of natural objects should continue to be conducted on purely scientific principles, for the sake of the knowledge which it affords, without, in the first instance, attempting to apply it to moral and religious purposes. But the Divine origin of Nature should be constantly inculcated, and all our investigations should be conducted in a reverential spirit.

In the next place, all the thoroughly ascertained facts concerning the qualities and agencies of nature should be surveyed in their relations to man. When they are compared with his position, structure, wants, capacities, and desires, it will be seen that highly instructive rules of conduct are dictated to his understanding by Divine wisdom in these qualities, agencies, and relations. Examples of this fact are given in Chapter VI. Now, I respectfully maintain that these rules, when correctly inferred, *are Divine Laws*, because the things from which they are deduced are Divine Institutions, and obedience to them *is enforced* by *the consequences* attached to them, which man can neither alter nor evade. Here, then, we have Divine Law and Divine discipline combined. To render these rules moral in our minds, we require only to entwine them from infancy with our natural moral emotions; and to render them religious, to present them habitually to our religious emotions as Divine, and train our whole faculties to reverence and obey them.

If, by training, the doctrines of Calvinism quoted on pages 186-7, and the dancing evolutions of the Shakers described on page 204, and in the Appendix, No. VI., have been invested with sacred qualities, become religious truths, and solemn ceremonies of Divine worship in the minds of large classes of good and intelligent people, why should we doubt that rules which can be demonstrated to be Divine, may be made to assume a moral and religious character, when proper means shall be used to communicate to them in our apprehension that sanctity which they inherently possess? The low estimate which is now formed of them, as rules of prudence, but not of moral or religious obligation, appears to me to arise solely from the misdirection of our moral and religious emotions to other objects, and to the false light in which we have been taught to view man and the world.

In the reformed faith, a distinction will be made between religion and theology. RELIGION will rest on the sentiments of Veneration, Hope, and Wonder, as its basis, and be recognised as emotional in its nature; its elements being reverence, admiration, and faith. It will be seen that, by training, these emotions may be directed to almost any objects or doctrines; which, by being closely associated with them, assume a sacred or religious character. Hence, by such training, all truth conducive to human happiness may be rendered religious.

THEOLOGY will be referred to the intellectual faculties and their organs as its basis; and these will not permit any objects or doctrines to be associated with the religious emotions which they cannot comprehend and trace to Divine authority. The intellect will not pretend to comprehend the *nature* of God, but will recognise His existence, such of His attributes as it sees manifested, and also His Will, as revealed in His works; and it will compose a theology out of these elements, associate them with the religious emotions, and thus constitute a religion. Forms will be invented to give expression to this religion, and in which to teach it to the people.

MORALITY will be recognised as resting on the sentiments of Benevolence and Conscientiousness, as its peculiar basis, using the intellect to give it form in precepts and laws, and to direct us in its practical applications. It will include the proper use of all the other faculties. It will not be viewed as *dependent* on religion for its foundation, but be regarded as a co-ordinate supreme tribunal, having authority in co-operation with the intellect and religious emotions, to direct all the faculties towards their proper objects,—itself receiving from the latter a sacred and religious character. There will then be no accepted religious duty at variance with morality, and no morality that is discordant with religion.

The DESIRE OF PERFECTION will be recognised as resting on Ideality, which, combined with the intellect, will prompt to constant improvement in all arts and sciences, and, combined with the moral and religious sentiments, will give an intense pleasure in elevating human nature, and applying all its powers to their highest objects.

" The higher life," under the reformed faith, will consist in the zealous endeavour to improve every organ and faculty in ourselves and others, and to direct them to their highest uses. Intellect will investigate the means by which these ends can be accomplished, and it will recognise the order of the Divine government as its rule and guide. The moral and religious sentiments will sanctify and elevate the results of the researches of the intellect, and also the labour of the hands and the head in giving them practical effect. The grace or good will of God will be recognised as pervading all objects and beings, inviting us to study and apply their qualities to their proper uses, with unhesitating faith that increase of knowledge and obedience will be accompanied by augmentation of happiness and holiness.

It is in vain to object that hitherto natural religion has been barren. It has had no key to the real principles of the Divine government, and could not become practical. It may accomplish more when this key has been discovered.

A great revolution in human perception, judgment, and action, will follow the general diffusion of the reformed faith. The selfishness, vices, and crimes, through which individuals and nations at present too frequently seek to attain happiness, will be recognised as follies as well as offences; and every individual will find that the most effectual way to promote his own wellbeing is that which likewise advances the improvement and enjoyment of his fellows.

In regard to his future destiny; under the reformed faith he will rely with confidence and resignation on the goodness of that Divine Power which has called him into existence here, and bestowed on him so many admirable enjoyments. He will claim nothing as a right, but hope all as a boon.

Whose duty will it be to deduce, expound, render sacred, these Divine rules of conduct and apply them to the promotion of human wellbeing, morality, and religion? In my opinion, that of the clergyman, moral philosopher, and teacher.

What a glorious profession that of a clergyman will then become! With an immovable and indestructible foundation for morality and religion; with a knowledge of man's admirable capacities and high aspirations; with an understanding cleared of mists and prejudices, and alive to the perception of Divine power, wisdom, and goodness, radiating from every object; an ear open to the precepts which that wisdom is teaching; benevolent, just, and reverential emotions excited to intensity by the contemplation of this assemblage of Divine gifts, and the wide world before him in which to apply all this knowledge, and to expand these emotions in diffusing truth, happiness, and a spirit of obedience to God, he will occupy a position which even angels might envy. The priests, temples, churches, creeds, catechisms, and confessions, which fill such large and conspicuous positions in the history of all ages and nations, are the forms in which the moral and religious emotions have welled forth and embodied themselves on earth. Far, therefore, from looking on them with indifference, I see in them manifestations of the highest human endowments, in many instances straying for want of light, but still holy in their aspirations; and I rejoice in the religious fervour and agitation of our own day, as indicative of the heaving of these sublime emotions labouring to cast off the load of errors and superstitions which now oppresses them. Nor need the Bible form any obstacle to this consummation. It appears to me that with far less violence than has been done to it in framing the Westminster Confession of Faith, a new creed could be formed, every point of which would harmonize with a sound Natural Religion, adding from the Scriptures, doctrines beyond the reach of reason, but not contradicting it. From all I have learnt of the progress of opinion among thinking men who have studied the subject, the conclusion is forced on me, that within the next fifty years this must be done, otherwise Christianity, as now taught, will perish. Were this course followed, every church would become a focus of Divine light, radiating blessings on humanity, and every school a vestibule to the church.

In the school, Physiology and the Laws of Life and Health (See Appendix, No. X.), and Social Economy, or an exposition of man's position and duties as the administrator of external nature, and of the natural laws which regulate his success or failure in his trade, profession, or other employment, should form the first elements of scientific instruction. I have assisted in teaching these branches of knowledge to children from 10 to 14 years of age, and in leading their understandings to deduce from them rules of practical conduct, which they recognised as Divine injunctions or commands, and I can testify that the interest and effect of the lessons was greatly enhanced by this appeal to their moral and religious emotions.

The failure of most attempts to support continued interest in scientific lectures in Mechanics' Institutes is now generally recognised and lamented, but the cause of it has been little thought of. It appears to me discernible. Pure science addresses the intellectual faculties only. In the working classes in general these have not been cultivated, either in their school instruction or practically in their trades. They come to the lecture-room, therefore, untrained to intellectual exertions, and many of them weary with toil; and indifference to abstract science is the natural consequence of their condition. But their moral and religious emotions possess far greater power and activity than their intellectual faculties; and judging from the analogy of children, I should expect that they would listen with profound and sustained interest to courses of lectures based on clear scientific expositions of the structure, qualities, and modes of action of natural objects, accompanied by demonstrations of the rules of conduct which their Divine Author, through them, dictates to us for our guidance. By appeals to their moral and religious emotions, and a convincing elucidation of the practical bearing of these laws on their wellbeing and improvement, the lessons would probably become living fountains of instruction and enjoyment.

If all this is not a dream, the day will come when these Divine rules for the guidance of our conduct, with the basis in science on which they are founded, will be taught in every school, preached from every pulpit, promulgated by the press, enforced by the law, and supported by an overwhelming public opinion; and then the incapable, and the ill-constituted in brain and body, whose actions now form the great afflictions of society, will be protected, restrained, and guided by social power, directed by benevolence, intelligence, and justice, and their crimes and sufferings will be circumscribed. Under the illuminating influence and discipline of the Divine law, Hell will probably appear unnecessary, Heaven will be realized on earth, and Man will prove himself by his conduct to be better fitted for an immortality of glory than he has ever hitherto been. Some religious sects rely on a millennium, in which human nature will appear in the perfection of its powers and in possession of its highest enjoyments. This hope appears to me to spring from the insatiable desires of Ideality for perfection, and of Benevolence, Veneration, and Conscientiousness, for the universal prevalence of happiness, truth, piety, and justice. The aspirations may be clothed in fanciful forms, but in themselves they are real; and nature appears to me to point in a similar direction.

The opinion advocated in this work, that *a Divine government is discernible in Nature*, is gaining strength in public conviction. On page 10 I have cited a letter on this subject from Lord Palmerston to the Presbytery of Edinburgh; and in a speech delivered by his Lordship in Manchester, in November 1856, he is reported to have said:—" If a man were to enter a town of some foreign country where there were laws the violation of which was attended with pain, imprisonment, or, it may be, with death, would he not be deemed mad if he did not take the earliest opportunity to make himself acquainted with these enactments, so that he might avoid the penalties attached to their infringement? Yet there are laws of nature applicable to the daily pursuits of men, which, if not attended to, inflict bodily pain in the form of diseases, imprisonment in the shape of the loss of corporeal powers, and even death, through the neglect of those sanitary conditions on which life depends. How important, then, it is that the working-classes should be made aware of those natural laws and regulations which are indispensable to their own welfare, and to that of their families." His Royal Highness Prince Albert,* is reported to have expressed the opinion, that "Man is approaching a more complete fulfilment of that great and sacred mission which he has to perform in this world. His reason being created after the image of God, he has to use it to discover the laws by which the Almighty governs His creation, and, by making these laws his standard of action, to conquer nature to his use—himself a divine instrument. Science discovers these laws of power, motion, and transformation; industry applies them to the raw matter which the earth yields us in abundance, but which becomes valuable only by knowledge; art teaches us the immutable laws of beauty and symmetry, and gives to our productions forms in accordance with them."

Again, in a speech delivered at Birmingham in November 1855, his Royal Highness is reported to have said:—" The study of the laws by which the Almighty governs the universe is our bounden duty. Of these laws our great academies and seats of education have, rather arbitrarily, selected only two spheres or groups (as I may call them), as essential parts of our national education—the laws which regulate quantities and proportions, which form the subject of mathematics; and the laws regulating the expression of our thoughts through the

---

* At the Mansion-House, 21st March 1850.

medium of language—that is to say, grammar, which finds its purest expression in the classical languages. These laws are most important branches of knowledge; their study trains and elevates the mind. But they are not the only ones; there are others which we cannot disregard—which we cannot do without. There are, for instance, the laws governing the human mind and its relations to the Divine Spirit—the subjects of logic and metaphysics. There are those which govern our bodily nature and its connection with the soul—the subjects of physiology and psychology; those which govern human society and the relations between man and man—the subjects of politics, jurisprudence, and political economy; and many others."

In contemplating the endowments of man, the provision made in nature for his happiness, and the order of God's providence for encouraging him to work out his own improvement and elevation, the intelligent mind thrills with vivid emotions of love, gratitude, and admiration of their great Author. A "present Deity" is felt to be no longer a figure of speech or a flight of poetry, but a positive and operating reality. We not only feel that we "live, and move, and have our being" in God, but become acquainted with the means through which His power, wisdom, and goodness affect us, and discover that we are invited, as His moral and intelligent creatures, to co-operate in the fulfilment of His designs. The beautiful exclamations of King David, "If I climb up into heaven, Thou art there; if I go down to hell, Thou art there also; if I take the wings of the morning, and remain in the uttermost parts of the sea; even there also shall Thy hand lead me, and Thy right hand shall hold me," are felt to be expressions of a living truth; and man takes his true station as the interpreter and administrator of nature under the guidance of nature's God.

APPENDIX No. I. (Referred to in Text, p. 33.)

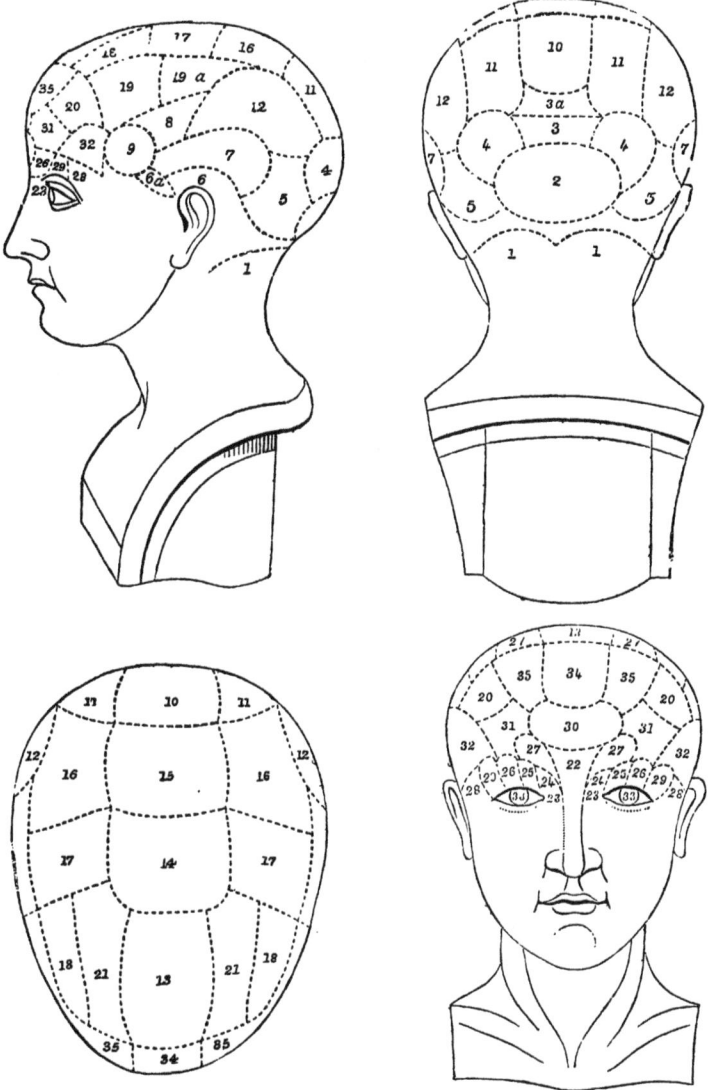

NAMES OF THE PHRENOLOGICAL ORGANS.
REFERRING TO THE FIGURES INDICATING THEIR RELATIVE POSITION.

AFFECTIVE.

I. PROPENSITIES.
1. Amativeness.
2. Philoprogenitiveness.
3. Concentrativeness.
4. Adhesiveness.
5. Combativeness.
6. Destructiveness.
6. *a.* Alimentiveness. Love of Life.
7. Secretiveness.
8. Acquisitiveness.
9. Constructiveness.

II. SENTIMENTS.
10. Self-Esteem.
11. Love of Approbation.
12. Cautiousness.
13. Benevolence.
14. Veneration.
15. Firmness.
16. Conscientiousness.
17. Hope.
18. Wonder.
19. Ideality.
19. *a* Unascertained.
20. Wit or Mirthfulness.
21. Imitation.

INTELLECTUAL.

I. PERCEPTIVE.
22. Individuality.
23. Form.
24. Size.
25. Weight.
26. Colouring.
27. Locality.
28. Number.
29. Order.
30. Eventuality.
31. Time.
32. Tune.
33. Language.

II. REFLECTIVE.
34. Comparison.
35. Causality.

No. II.—EVIDENCE OF THE INFLUENCE OF THE BRAIN ON FEELING AND THOUGHT. (Referred to on p. 28.)

The influence of the brain on the power of thinking and feeling, is elucidated by the observed effects of sleep, of stopping the flow of blood to the brain, of altering its normal state by drugs, of compressing it, and of diseases which change its condition.

If, through sudden fright, or congestion of blood in the liver or lungs, or any other cause which greatly diminishes the action of the heart, the supply of arterial blood to the brain be withheld, fainting or entire unconsciousness ensues: The manifestations of a thinking and feeling mind disappear, and are not restored till the action of the heart recommences.

Again: When we inhale carbonic acid gas, the blood ceases to be capable of stimulating the brain, and the same prostration of mental power is observed. When we breathe air impregnated with chloroform, sensation and consciousness are suspended, while the power of muscular movement partially remains.

In profound sleep also, consciousness is entirely suspended. We neither think nor feel, and to us neither time, nor the external world, nor ourselves, appear to exist. Physiologists regard these results as the effects of a certain condition of the brain. In a case which fell under the notice of the distinguished German physiologist Blumenbach, the brain was seen to sink whenever the patient was asleep, and to swell again with blood the moment he awoke.*

Another case is reported by Dr Pierquin, as having been observed by him in one of the hospitals of Montpelier, in the year 1821. The patient was a female, who had lost a large portion of her scalp, skull, and dura mater, so that a corresponding portion of the brain was subject to inspection. When she was in a dreamless sleep, her brain was motionless, and lay within the cranium. When her sleep was imperfect, and she was agitated by dreams, her brain moved, and protruded without the cranium, forming cerebral hernia. In vivid dreams, reported as such by herself, the protrusion was considerable; and when she was perfectly awake, especially if engaged in active thought or sprightly conversation, it was still greater.† A writer in the *Medico-Chirurgical Review*, after alluding to this case, mentions that many years ago he had " frequent opportunities of witnessing similar phenomena in a robust young man, who lost a considerable portion of his skull by an accident which had almost proved mortal. When excited by pain, fear, or anger, his brain protruded greatly, so as sometimes to disturb the dressings, which were necessarily applied loosely; and it throbbed tumultuously, in accordance with the arterial pulsations."‡

But cases of compression of the brain afford irrefragable evidence that in this life the exercise of the thinking power depends on the state of that organ. M. Richerand had a patient whose brain was exposed in consequence of disease of the skull. One day, in washing off the purulent matter, he chanced to press with more than usual force; and instantly the patient, who, the moment before, had answered his questions with perfect correctness, stopped short in the middle of a sentence, and became altogether in-

---

* Elliotson's " Blumenbach," 4th edition, p. 283.
† " Annals of Phrenology," No. I., Boston, U. S., Oct. 1833, p. 37.
‡ " Medico-Chirurgical Review," No. 46, p. 365, Oct. 1835.

sensible. As the pressure gave her no pain, it was repeated thrice, and always with the same result. She uniformly recovered her faculties the moment the pressure was taken off. M. Richerand mentions also the case of an individual who was trepanned for a fracture of the skull, and whose faculties and consciousness became weak in proportion as the pus so accumulated under the dressings as to occasion pressure of the brain.* A man at the battle of Waterloo had a small portion of his skull beaten in upon the brain, and became quite unconscious, and almost lifeless; but Mr Cooper having raised up the depressed portion of bone, the patient immediately arose, dressed himself, became perfectly rational, and recovered rapidly.† Professor Chapman of Philadelphia mentions in his Lectures, that he saw an individual with his skull perforated, and the brain exposed, who used to submit himself to the same experiment of pressure as that performed on Richerand's patient, and who was exhibited by the late Professor Wistar to his class. The man's intellect and emotional faculties disappeared when pressure was applied to the brain: they were literally " held under the thumb," and could be restored at pleasure to their full activity.‡ A still more remarkable case is that of a person named Jones, recorded by Sir Astley Cooper. This man was deprived of consciousness, by being wounded in the head, while on board a vessel in the Mediterranean. In this state of insensibility he remained for several months at Gibraltar, whence he was transmitted to Deptford, and subsequently to St Thomas's Hospital, London. Mr Cline, the surgeon, found a portion of the skull depressed, trepanned him, and removed the depressed part of the bone. Three hours after this operation he sat up in bed, sensation and volition returned, and in four days he was able to get up and converse. The last circumstance he remembered was the capture of a prize in the Mediterranean thirteen months before. A young man at Hartford, in the United States of America, was rendered insensible by a fall, and had every appearance of being in a dying condition. Dr Brigham removed more than a gill of clotted blood from beneath the skull; upon which " the man immediately spoke, soon recovered his mind entirely, and is now, six weeks after the accident, in good health both as to mind and body."§

The question may present itself, Why did pressure applied to only a small portion of the brain induce general insensibility, instead of disturbing only a single faculty? The answer is this:—The brain is soft and pulpy; and is very full of blood-vessels, which during life contain a large quantity of blood. It is enveloped in an unyielding air-tight case, so that it approaches very closely to the condition of a fluid mass contained within a hollow sphere. By the law which regulates the pressure of fluids, force applied to any portion of such a mass, diffuses itself equally over the whole of it; and every part is pressed with the same degree of force. This law applies to the brain; and all the faculties are suspended, because the flow of blood in all the vessels is impeded, and all the brain is compressed. If a blow cut the skull and integuments, so as to allow the blood to escape outwardly, or the brain to protrude, the pressure will cease, and general insensibility will not ensue.

When the whole brain becomes diseased, general insanity ensues, and when particular parts of it are affected, only particular mental powers suffer. These facts are so generally admitted, that it appears unnecessary

---

* " Nouveaux Elémens de Physiologie," 7th edition, ii. 195-6.
† Hennen's " Principles of Military Surgery."
‡ " Principles of Medicine," by Samuel Jackson, M.D.
§ " Remarks on the Influence of Mental Cultivation, &c., upon Health," by Amariah Brigham, M.D., 2d edition, p. 23. Boston, U. S., 1833. Several of the above cases

to adduce evidence of them here; but they are of great importance in discussing natural religion, and the inferences from them are adverted to in the body of this work.

I may remark, that consciousness localises the mind in the head, and gives us a full conviction that it acts there, although it does not reveal what substance occupies the interior of the skull, or the influence of that substance on our powers of thinking and feeling. It is worthy of observation also, that the popular notions of the independence of the mind on the body are modern, and the offspring of philosophical theories that have sprung up chiefly since the days of Locke. In Shakspeare and the older writers, the word "brains" is frequently used as implying the mental functions.

The cases which are supposed to contradict these phenomena are easily reconciled with them. It is often said of persons dying at an advanced age that their mental faculties remained entire to the last. The real meaning of this phrase is, that the patients were not deranged; that is to say, that in so far as they were capable of manifesting the mind, their faculties acted normally: but it is a complete mistake to suppose that their minds were then as capable of profound investigation, of vivid emotion, and of energetic action, as in the maturity of life. Sometimes cerebral excitement from *disease* renders the mind particularly brilliant, however weak the body at large may be. The fact of the mental powers being the last to fade, is explained by the circumstance, that the brain and nervous system suffer the least diminution of size in the general decay of the corporeal frame.*

As this treatise may be read by non-scientific readers, some of whom are influenced by authorities, I may mention that the Rev. Dr John Taylor of Norwich, in a letter to Bishop Law, quoted approvingly by the latter in his Considerations on the Theory of Religion, &c., 5th ed., p. 423, maintains that "the operations of the mind depend, constantly and invariably, upon the state of the body, of the brain in particular. If some dying persons have a lively use of their rational faculties to the very last, it is because death has invaded some other part, and the brain remains sound and vigorous." Dr Taylor was an able and learned Theologian, and a Nonconformist, who flourished in the reign of Geo. II.

No. III.—HEAVEN AND HELL. (Referred to on p. 235.)

The following descriptions of Heaven and Hell are extracted from "A First Catechism for Children, to assist Parents and Teachers. By Joseph Hay, A.M., Minister, Arbroath. New Edition. Edinburgh: William Oliphant and Sons; David Robertson, Glasgow; William Curry and Co., Dublin; and Hamilton, Adams, and Co., London. Price One Penny." It is extensively taught to the young in schools in Scotland.

HEAVEN.

Where will the righteous go after they are judged? Into life eternal.
Why is this life called eternal? Because it will last for ever.
Will they never die any more? No; "there shall be no more death."
Will they ever be sick in heaven? No; there shall be "neither sorrow, nor crying, nor any more pain." Rev. xxi. 4.

---

have already been collected by this intelligent writer, whose little volume has been reprinted here by Dr Macnish. See also "System of Phrenology," by George Combe, from p. 10 to p. 20.

* The brain and spinal cord lose only 0·019 of their original substance in a warm-blooded animal starved to death. Of the fat, 0·933 parts are lost; of the blood, 0·750; of the muscles, 0·423; of the organs of respiration, 0·222; and of the bones, 0·167

Why will there be no more sickness nor death there? Because they will have no more sin. Isaiah xxxiii. 24.

Will they ever grow old in heaven? No; they will be like the angels of God. Luke xx. 36; Mark xvi. 5.

What company will they have in heaven? The company of God, of holy angels, and of all good men. Heb. xii. 22–24.

What will they be employed in? They will serve God day and night in his temple. Rev. vii. 15.

Will they ever be wearied in his service? No; it will be rest to them. Heb. iv. 9.

Will they be very happy in heaven? Yes; they will always sing the new song. Rev. v. 9–10.

What honour will they have there? They will be kings and priests unto God.

What glory will they have? The glory of Christ. Rev. iii. 21.

What will give light to them in heaven? The glory of God and the Lamb. Rev. xxi. 23.

Will there be any night in heaven? No; "there will be no night there." Rev. xxii. 5.

HELL.

Where will the bad people go after they are judged? Into everlasting punishment.

With whom will they be punished in hell? With the devil and his angels.

What will they be tormented with? With fire and brimstone. Rev. xxi. 8.

Will they have any rest from their torments? No; they will have no rest day nor night. Rev. xvi. 10.

Will the pain of their torments be very great? Yes; they will gnaw their tongues with pain. Rev. xvi. 10.

Will they cry out under their pain? Yes; with weeping and wailing and gnashing of teeth. Matt. xiii. 50.

Will they get any relief from these torments? No; not a drop of water to cool their tongue. Luke xvi. 24–26.

Will their torments ever come to an end? No; their worm dieth not, and their fire shall never be quenched. Mark ix. 44.

Will their torments make them any better? No; they will blaspheme God because of their pains, and their sores, and not repent of their deeds. Rev. xvi. 11.

Will they have any light in hell? No; it will be the blackness of darkness for ever. Jude 13.

A girl of seven years of age, to whom this Catechism is taught, recently put this question to her mother: "Mother," said she, "the Catechism says in one place that the bad people will have no light in hell, and in another place that they will be tormented with fire and brimstone. How can there be fire and no light? I always see light where there is fire." Her mother could not account for this anomaly, and gave an evasive answer. This indicated active reflective faculties in the child, and this Catechism supplied the materials, presented by the mother, and by many other evangelical Christians to their children, on which to exercise them! The same persons denounce

Chossat, Recherches Experimentales sur l'Inanition, p. 92. Paris, 1843. See also "The Physiology of Digestion," by Andrew Combe, M.D., p. 86, edition 1849.

as infidel the proposal to instruct the young in the objects and order of God's providence in nature, which stand in the same relation to their intellects that wholesome food bears to their stomachs.

The following account of sickness and death is given in the same Catechism :—

SICKNESS AND DISEASE.

Wherefore do sickness and disease come upon both old and young? Because all have sinned. Rom. v. 12.

What is sickness to all who are not God's people? It is punishment for their sin, and a warning to them to flee from it.

What is it to God's people? It is correction, to turn them from their sins. Rev. iii. 19.

What will afflictions do to God's people? They will make them love and serve God more. Ps. cxix. 67.

What will they do to bad people? Sometimes they will turn them to God. 2 Chron. xxxiii. 12, 13.

If they do not turn them to God, what will they do to them? Make them more hardened against him. Isa. i. 5.

What should we do when we are sick? We should seek God, and cry to him for help.

What help will he give us? He will heal us of our sickness, or prepare us for death.

TEMPORAL DEATH.

How did death come into the world? By sin.

Wherefore do all men die? Because they have all sinned.

Why do even the youngest infants die? Because they sinned in Adam. Rom. v. 14.

What is death to bad people? The beginning of eternal death.

What is meant by the sting of death? Its power of destroying men. Rev. ii. 11.

What is its sting? It is sin in us, unpardoned.

To whom does death have its sting? To them who die in their sin.

What is death to good people? The beginning of eternal life. John xi. 25, 26.

Why is there such a change on it to them? Because Christ suffered it for them, and took away its sting. 1 Cor. xv. 57.

What is the death of good people like? It is like a sleep. Acts vii. 60.

Why is it called their last enemy? Because, after it, they have no more sin nor suffering.

How many of God's people have gone to heaven without dying? Two; Enoch and Elijah.

Will all who shall ever be in the world die? No; those who are on the earth when Christ comes, shall not die, but be changed. 1 Cor. xv. 51, 52.

This is called religious instruction; and for it the whole lessons for the guidance of human conduct, deducible from the Divine government of the world in nature, are thrust aside and excluded from schools!

No. IV.—MAN-CONCOCTED ARTICLES OF FAITH. (See p. 233.)

The remark in the text, that the original records of the Christian religion are sealed books to the laity, and that their Christianity is really nothing more than certain interpretations of them concocted by fallible and somewhat barbarous men in the sixteenth and seventeenth centuries, received a curious illustration at a meeting of the Synod of Lothian and Tweeddale, held in Edinburgh on 3d May 1853. The following report appeared in the *Scotsman* newspaper of 4th May :—" In the evening the Synod took up an appeal by Mr Goodsir, from the decision of the Edinburgh Presbytery, confirming a finding of the kirk-session of the High Church—of which church he is a member—with reference to an application by him for an explanation how the doctrine of Justification, as explained in the eleventh chapter of the Confession of Faith, was proved to be deducible from, and reconcilable with, the Greek New Testament. The kirk-session, having considered the petition, found that while to them belonged the duty of inquiring into the spiritual state of the members of the congregation, and of admonishing or encouraging them as they might see cause, they were bound to conduct their inquiries in accordance with the recognised standards of the Church, and they declined to go beyond their constitutional purposes—the more so as a knowledge of the Greek language, and of the principles of philological criticism, were qualifications which all the lay members of a kirk-session could not be expected to possess. The case was then carried to the Presbytery, who confirmed the finding of the kirk-session, and this decision was appealed against. Mr Goodsir was now heard in support of his appeal ; he stated that, as a lay member of the Church, he had applied to the kirk-session, as being the only body to which he could legitimately apply, for the removal of his difficulties, and because, according to the law of the Church, it was the duty of that court to inquire into the spiritual knowledge of the members of the congregation under its charge. He had proceeded with his remarks for some time, when Mr Tait of Kirkliston moved, and Mr Muir of Dalmeny seconded, a proposal, that the Synod could not competently hear him, because they could not allow any arguments which would impugn the doctrines laid down in the Confession of Faith. Mr Goodsir declared that he did not intend to impugn these doctrines : all he desired was to make out that he had certain rights which no Church Court could ignore. After some discussion, Mr Kerr of Yester and Mr Scott of Dirleton proposed that Mr Goodsir should be allowed to proceed, and, on a division, this amendment was carried by 7 against 5. Mr Goodsir accordingly went on to state that a Church Court alone could in his opinion satisfactorily give a deliverance on the point as to which he had applied for information, and that this was his reason for not acceding to an interview with the ministers of the High Church. He argued that it was the duty of the Church Courts to explain and defend her standards, while the finding of the kirk-session, referring to ' the recognised standards of the Church as compared with the authorised English version of the Scriptures,' made it appear as if there was a law debarring any reference to the real inspired Word of God—the Greek New Testament. If this were the case, it was exalting a version of the Scriptures to a position of power and authority which no mere version ever held in the Christian Church. Again, if there was such a law—and he maintained there was not—he asked how far it went, and how many courts it bound ? and whether he was to understand that even the General Assembly could not explain from the Scripture, as directly inspired, how a certain chapter in the Confession of Faith was deducible from, or reconcilable with the Word of God ? Dr Simpson of Kirknewton was then heard on behalf of the Presbytery. He urged that not only was it no part of the duty of a kirk-session to give the explanation asked for by Mr Goodsir, but that they were utterly unqualified to do so, involving as it did a minute acquaintance with the Greek language. Nine-tenths of Mr Goodsir's arguments appeared to him to be directed against Church standards altogether ; while the fact was that the Confession of Faith—their standard

—must not be impugned, and the Church could allow no discussion which seemed to call it in question. Dr Simpson also maintained that Mr Goodsir ought to have accepted the offer of the ministers of the High Church, who had declared their willingness to give him their best assistance in removing the difficulties which he felt; the more so because it was not a question of authority, and the mere decision of any Church Court could not settle the matter for the appellant. Mr Goodsir having said a few words in reply, Mr Scott of Dirleton moved that the deliverance of the Presbytery should be confirmed by the Synod, on the ground that Mr Goodsir had asked the kirk-session to do what the greater part of them were totally incapable of doing, and what it was legally incompetent for them to do. He had asked them, in fact, to reconstruct for him a new Confession of Faith, while, if he found anything in that Confession which he considered inconsistent with the Word of God, his only alternative was to cease to be a member of the Church. Dr Cook of Haddington, in supporting this motion, recommended Mr Goodsir to study carefully and thoughtfully the works of authors who had written on the subject as to which he felt a difficulty. The motion was unanimously agreed to, Mr Goodsir appealing to the General Assembly.—The Synod soon after adjourned."

If a few laymen would take courage and ask the Church Courts to justify their standards by an appeal to Scripture, their errors and imperfections would speedily become palpable to ordinary minds. If man be *by nature a progressive being*, no greater injury can be done to him than to tie up his faculties by an interpretation, virtually held to be infallible, of the Divine will. The views stated in this work appear to me to accord better with the advancement of such a being.

No. V.—Definition of the "Personality" of the Deity.

A writer in Macphail's Edinburgh Ecclesiastical Journal, said to be the organ of the Church of Scotland, in a notice of "The Constitution of Man," says:—" The error of Mr Combe goes on the assumption that either the Deity is not a person, or that, if he is a person, he does not act as a person, which virtually, so far as we are concerned with his government, amounts to the same thing. We do our author no injustice, therefore, if we at once impute to him the virtual denial of the personality of the Deity. To deny the personality of the Deity is equivalent to the denial of Deity altogether; and thus we have Mr Combe, though perhaps he did not foresee such consequences to follow from his assumptions, avowing a doctrine which, to all intents and purposes, is absolute Atheism." (No. 85, for Feb. 1853, p. 27.) The writer proceeds to remark, that "It can scarcely be said that a distinct or definite opinion exists as to what personality really is." "It is quite evident," he adds, "that Paley had not a definite notion of it in his own mind when he attempted to define it." The definition of Locke, quoted *ante*, p. 54, sect. 172, it is said, "has been deservedly rejected, as involving the most absurd and ridiculous consequences." To supply all these and other defects, the writer gives what he considers a perfect definition. "*Personality*," says he, "*consists in the Causality of Volition*. This is what constitutes the man. The man is another name for the will. The man or the will is the person. Wherever there is volition there is a person. There is volition throughout nature, inasmuch as there is power in constant exercise, a power beyond and above the power of man. This exercise of power is the volition of a person, and that person is God. This volition is his Law. And it is here that we conceive Mr Combe has gone wrong; and he has done so, because all other philosophers who have preceded him have gone wrong on the same point." (P. 29.)

It is some mitigation of this censure to find that the critic includes all other philosophers in my error, and we must acknowledge our obligations to him for at last setting us all right. His definition appears to me to coincide closely with the views which I have stated on " The Existence of God," in chap. V.; with this exception, that I have endeavoured to shew that our faculties do not enable us, as finite beings, to comprehend the *nature* of God, who is infinite, and whom we cannot define, for the simple reason that we cannot define what we cannot understand.

It would not be difficult to state objections to this writer's own definition. An acephalous infant, for example, has no "causality of volition," and, therefore, according to him, is not a person: Nevertheless, if he were deliberately to kill such a child, the law would hold it to have been a person, and would visit him with the punishment of death for murdering it. A man dead drunk has "no causality of volition," and is, therefore, by parity of reason, not a person. But, again, if the critic, suiting his actions to his words, were to rob or kill such a man, the law would recognise him to have been a person, and would sentence the critic to be punished as a robber or a murderer.

Nay, the definition presents an aspect of still stranger incongruity when applied to the cases mentioned in Appendix, No. II., p. 263. The man Jones, for example, was a "person" before he was wounded in the head. For a period of thirteen months after that event he had no consciousness, and no "causality of volition." During that time, therefore, he was not a "person." At length, Mr Cline, the surgeon, raised a portion of the bone of the skull which had been depressed, and within three hours after the operation, Jones sat up in bed, and sensation and volition returned; he then *became* a "person!"

It appears to me that the word "person," in its common acceptation, means a living human body, and that the early Jews really understood God to have a body, after the image of which the human body was formed; hence arose the notion of the personality of the Deity. Men like Locke and Paley of course did not embrace this idea, and tried to give a definition of a person irrespective of a bodily form, but with very little success. The truth seems to me to be that we cannot define what we cannot comprehend.

This writer is respectful in his tone towards me and my errors, for which I thank him; but considering the class of persons who constitute the majority of the readers of religious magazines, and the inherent difficulties of such a subject as this, would it not have been more graceful, not to say more just and modest, if he had abstained from charging me, even by implication, with " absolute atheism ;" knowing, as he well does, the effect of such a charge on vulgar minds?

No. VI.—On the Worship of the Shakers. (Referred to on pp. 204 and 213.)

As some readers may have a difficulty in believing that the dancing evolutions and singing of the Shakers, described on page 204, were really understood by themselves to constitute Divine worship, I present the following extracts from an account of their tenets, published by Seth Wells and Calvin Green, of New Lebanon, in the State of New York. It appears in " The Cyclopædia of Religious Denominations :—"

"Concerning their mode of worship. This subject is generally greatly misunderstood. The people of this Society do not believe that any external performance whatever, without the sincere devotion of the heart, with all the feelings of the soul, in devotion and praise to the Creator of all their powers and faculties, can be any acceptable worship to Him who looks at the heart. But in a united assembly, a unity of exercise in acts of devotion to God is desirable; for harmony is beautiful, and appears like the order of heaven. It will be difficult to describe all the various modes of exercise given in the worship of God at different times; because the operations of the Spirit are so various, that even the leaders are unable to tell beforehand what manner will be given by the Spirit in the next meeting. Yet, in a regular meeting, where nothing extraordinary appears, they sometimes exercise in a regular dance, while formed in straight lines, and sometimes in a regular march around the room, in harmony with regular songs sung on the occasion. Shouting and clapping of hands, and many other operations are frequently given, all which have a tendency to keep the assembly alive, with their hearts and all their senses and feelings devoted to the service of God.

"Our benevolent Creator has given us hands and feet as well as tongues, which we are able to exercise in our own services. And where a people are united in one spirit, we know of no reason why a unity of exercise in the service of God should not be attained, so as to give the devotion of every active power of soul and body as a free-will offering to the God of all goodness, who has given us these faculties. When the Israelites were delivered from their Egyptian bondage, they praised God with songs and dances. (See Exod. chap. xv.) This was figurative of the deliverance of spiritual Israel from the bondage of sin. This dancing before the Lord was predicted by the ancient prophets. (See Jer. chap. xxxi.) See also the account of David's dancing before the ark of the Lord. (See 2 Sam. vi. 14.) This is considered figurative of the spiritual ark of salvation, before which, according to the faith of God's true witnesses, thousands and millions will yet rejoice in the dance. See also the return of the prodigal son. (Luke xv. 25.) We notice these figurative representations and prophetic declarations as evidently pointing to a day of greater and more glorious light, which in those days was veiled in futurity, and if this is not the commencement of such a day, then where shall we look for it?"

This forms a striking example of the doctrine maintained in the text, that almost any ceremony may be rendered sacred and religious, by being entwined from infancy with the religious emotions.

No. VII.—LETTERS FROM THE LATE DR SAMUEL BROWN TO GEORGE COMBE, ON THE NATURAL EVIDENCE FOR THE EXISTENCE AND ATTRIBUTES OF GOD, AND OTHER TOPICS.

Dr Samuel Brown was descended from a family long distinguished in Scotland for piety and theological erudition. He inherited their spirit, but with the advantages of a scientific education, and an acute and discursive intellect, his theological studies took the range of the modern literature of Europe; and without being shaken in the basis of his faith, he rose above the narrow and sectarian views which are generally regarded as characteristic of Scotland in the present day. While the views published in the present work were dawning in my own mind, I communicated some of the most important of them to him in letters, and solicited his opinion; and he wrote to me several letters in reply, which I preserved as valuable on account of the close and vigorous thinking, the learning, and the genuine spirit of free inquiry which they displayed. On his death-bed, he mentioned these letters to his wife, and expressed a wish that she would apply to me for them on behalf of a friend to whom he was then unable to write fully on the subject. He died on the 20th of September 1856, and they were accordingly sent to her; and with her permission they are now published. An extract from one of them is given on page 78.

For several years before his death Dr Brown suffered severely from bad health, to which reference is made in this correspondence.

Letter No. I.—To George Combe, Esq.

St James' Square, Notting Hill, London, Feb. 7, 1853.

I have been long of answering your last kind and touching letter; but solely because I wished to do so at some little length, and my ailing state has forbidden that.

I heartily respond to all you say in magnification of that standing and perpetual miracle, the Order of Nature, to the disparagement of so-called special miracles, supposed to be produced by the divine or sub-divine breaking in upon that order. I, too, wish no such miracle to be performed on my behalf. I would be cured according to law or not at all. I love to be beloved of God, I seem to myself most surely to be so beloved; but God forbid I should ask anything like favouritism at his hands. I am content with, nay, like you, I exult in the blessed way of Nature; and I look for recovery from this weary malady only to my own obedience. It has been brought on me by disobedience, that of a line of ancestry stretching to Adam on one hand, and that of my proper sinful and ignorant self on the other; and if it be now incurable I shall succumb without weak complaint or insolent upbraiding. If it be curable by anything I can learn and do, I may be cured in good time; and in that case I shall bless our God for no special and private act, but for the great and public beneficence of his wide creation.

At the same time, let me add, that I think those Christian Theologians who have defined a miracle (in reference to the classical miracles narrated in the Bible) as a suspension of the common order of nature have done an injury to those very wonders. A miracle is simply a wonderful thing; and the cures wrought by Jesus and his Apostles were wonderful things enough, without being made poor and private by the invocation of a *Deus ex machinâ*. I conceive that the miracles in question (the authentic ones) were made in concert with the nature of things. Our modern cures by homœopathic quantities, by friction, by what they call Mesmerism, by the action of faith, are modern miracles in their degree; yet, in so far as they are real, they are truly according to nature.

I know both Dr M'Cosh and his big book. I confess I think the defect of his book is the want of originality. There is a heavy, Dutch, compilatory spirit all over it; it is nearly one-third part quotation: it iterates and reiterates old arguments too much. Amazingly well read, and very intelligent, he yet seems to me to be void of the genius of inquiry. Hardly any ism in the world would improve him in these respects, I fancy.

As for his Calvinism, I have not so strong objections to it as you have, you know. I certainly think Calvinism an infelicitous putting of the theory of life lower and higher; but, when it is stated philosophically (as by Jonathan Edwards, for example), it seems to me vastly ingenious, profound, and sublime—a doctrine, in short, easily made ridiculous by its friends, and easily reduced to absurdity by its enemies perhaps, but not easily surpassed in gloomy grandeur and power over the true believer in its deep and dark propositions. I enter into the feeling of Emerson when he assured a friend of yours and mine, who visited him at Concord with a letter from me, that " he regretted to see the old Calvinism dying out of New England, for he saw nothing half so good coming up to take its place."

Yet, ever since I have been convinced of the vitality of Christianity, I have refused the Calvinistic interpretation of it. I rather side with the view of Henry More, Jeremy Taylor, Robert Scougal,—having also a decided taste for the sweet poetic formalism of dear George Herbert. But "Fichte's Blessed Life" comes nearer my own doctrine, I think. Yet none of the views that I know anything of, from Augustine down to Strauss, pleases me wholly! Hence I am a member of no visible church, but simply a cool adherent of them all, with a vivid affection for the true blue of my fathers, side by side with an intellectual and æsthetical preference on the whole for that of England. In the meantime, the Bible, and especially the writings of John in the New Testament, constitute my divine classic, my *opus sine pari*, my unexhausted treasury of good things—in plain English, it seems to me to tell me infinitely more of what I want to know regarding the interior nature of myself and my relations to my God than all other books put together. The Hebrew spirit consummated in Christ and John appears to have exhausted that species of inspiration or insight, just as the Greeks seem to have begun and ended sculpture, or, as we say, Shakspeare has finished the drama. Single men, and nations of men, do tasks once for all, you see. With all my getting, therefore, I desire to get understanding from my Bible. Such is a glance at my Confession of Faith. * * * * * *

SAMUEL BROWN.

No. II.—*To George Combe, Esq.*

Edinburgh, 3d May 1847.

Allow me to thank you, not only for sending your searching pamphlet [On the Relation between Science and Religion], but also for the pamphlet itself. It does me much good; and gives me great pleasure to see the obligatoriness of the Law of Nature inculcated on the ground that it is the revealed will of God, or rather the will of God in the course of being slowly revealed by the labours of research. No other consideration will do. It makes obedience holy and beautiful, as well as necessary, to the idea of the good man. It makes nature a sublime missal,—a book of common-prayer,—an unfolding confession of faith,—and a true New Testament. If your ideas were universally believed and lived, there would then be the circumstances for a still higher life than you indicate in the present address.

I have to thank you also for deprecating the conception that the penalties of disobedience are mere punishments. They are corrections. The puritanic mind would call them, with both truth and beauty, "the chastening hand of the Lord,"—at least, when inflicted on the elect; alas that any one should have ever dared to call them the vengeance of God, when they fall upon us who are not chosen!

When you remember that I have John Brown of Haddington in my veins, you will understand the high satisfaction I experience in sacred views of the phenomena of Nature, and *practical* ones.

That you may reap the fruits of your philanthropic endeavours, both in this life and in the next—if there be another—is the sincere wish of your affectionate servant, SAMUEL BROWN.

No. III.—*To George Combe, Esq.*

Edinburgh, 13th June 1847.

Permit me to describe my views of the argument of design, in a few short propositions, which I submit to your judgment with both diffidence and consideration.

1. The argument of design is *a posteriori*. It is an argument of analogy. It ascends from the known to the unknown. The subjects of the analogy are, the works of man, a watch, a code of laws, or any other human contrivance,

on one hand, and the phenomena of Nature on the other. The former, the watch, &c., are known to have been designed by the human designer—man; the latter, the phenomena of Nature, are inferred analogically to have been designed by the unknown, but sought, designer—God. Well, it appears to me that an analogy, to be good for demonstration, must be extensible, at least in its essence, equally to both of the terms of that analogy. Now, man, the known designer, invents or designs, by discovering laws external to and independent of himself, and then applying these laws to the sure production of effects which he desiderates—Black discovers latent heat, Watt applies that discovery in a desiderated direction; and the steam-engine is brought to perfection. Therefore, the unknown designer, who is inferred by this analogy, does, for all the analogy makes good, simply discover truth external to and independent of himself, and then apply that truth to the production of effects (the phenomena of nature), which he desiderates. This is not God, the eternal, almighty, and everyway infinite one, whose existence the argument professes to demonstrate.

2. Suppose for a moment, however, that the argument of design did establish the existence of a *creative* designer, and not only a mere vastly great *modifying* one. yet since the number and kind of instances of design in nature known to man are by 'no means *infinite*, so neither is the inferred creative designer *infinite* in power, wisdom, and goodness, for all the argument goes to prove. Neither is this indefinitely great creator the God whom we seek.

The force of both these strictures your statement of the argument allows and implies; and it is consequently, to my mind, the justest, or rather the only just statement of it I have seen, although I am considerably versant in the literature of the subject. But I confess I am not content with the demiurgic God, or demigod, or principality, to use a word of St Paul's, on the mighty and beneficent arm of whom you are willing to repose. If, however, nothing more could be said concerning God, I should consider myself bound, as a man of humility and candour, not to fly into an unmitigated atheism, but to satisfy myself with the probabilities and limitation of your just and candid putting of the argument of design. But,

3. It is not things I see, but sensations of what I believe to be things. I cannot prove that they are things, I cannot disprove them to be things, yet I believe them to be things. It is a fundamental or ultimate law of my nature to believe in external nature. It is the beginning of my knowledge of Nature.

Now, I see design among these sensations (or things, as we may now call them), which I believe to be the design of God. I cannot prove it to be the design of God, I cannot disprove it to be so, yet I believe it to be so. It is a fundamental law of my nature to believe in God the designer, precisely as it is to believe in Nature the sensible. It is the beginning of my knowledge of God. All men believe in Nature, all believe in God; although a few idealists on the one hand, and a few atheists on the other, have professed to reject both of these fundamental beliefs. I suppose—only suppose—that in a typal, very complete man, the belief in God would be prior to that in Nature. This being emphatically the era of the victory of man over Nature, we Britons of the nineteenth century are certainly nearer to Nature than to God, to use a figure of speech.

4. God being recognised according to this fundamental belief (the common sense of Reid, the *faith* of St Paul, who says, " By faith we know that the worlds were made by God"), then the argument of design becomes an illuminated commentary upon the attributes of the Deity.

5. It seems to me, and it seems so truly that nothing could trouble the seeming, that to expect God to be demonstrable is to expect God to be finite; for that only can be demonstrated which is susceptible of *definition*—I mean

s

a positive definition, and not one by such words as a*l*mighty, om*ni*scient, i*n*finite, *un*changeable, and so on.

If you will favour me with your opinion of this way of putting the relation of God to Nature and man, you will much oblige yours, &c.,

SAMUEL BROWN.

No. IV.—To George Combe, Esq.

Edinburgh, 17th June 1847.

Let me add three things to my last note, in answer to your kind and just criticism of my naked and unelaborated formula. I do so without fearing to weary you; because I know that a man of science cannot fail to take some interest in seeing how anything in the universe appears to another mind, especially one which has been pastured in other fields of investigation than he himself has traversed. There is, accordingly, no need of diffidence in ingenuously showing you the very foundations of my beliefs concerning Nature and God.

I. God being by me, as has been said already, *a*pprehended, (since, according to the understood negative definition, that being cannot be *com*prehended,) in accordance with what Dugald Stewart calls a fundamental law of my nature, it seems to me that infinitude of attribute is involved in the very idea of God so apprehended. It is so, at all events, in and for myself personally, I know. It is possible that this is so in my case, simply because I may be deficient in the faculty of analysis, and because I am thereby unable to analyse my consciousness to any greater depth. Yet I know a multitude of sincere thinkers who homologate this intuition of mine, each in his own case; not to mention any particular great names,—since names go for nothing. At the same time, I must confess that this is not the universal, or even very general, testimony of humanity; for the vast majority of men, down to the present day and hour, worship (or think they worship) a very, very finite and ignoble Godhead. Hence, in fairness to your way of putting the question, we must suppose that infinitude of attribute is *not* involved in the aboriginal intuition by which you and I agree that mankind do recognise the existence of a Creator. In order that there may be no possibility of mistake regarding the phrase *aboriginal intuitions*, allow me to repeat, that I mean to designate by it the belief, according to the fundamental laws of our nature, of Stewart, the *sensus communis humanitatis* of his teacher Reid, the primary beliefs of Kant, the *primitive emotions* of Jacobi the sentimental theologian, the *faith* of St Paul. Well,

II. The idea of God, whatever it involve, being developed simultaneously with the conception of Nature, these two ideas do at once fall into true opposition to one another; not mere difference,—not contradiction,—but opposition, like that of the positive and negative poles of a magnet,—like that of motion and rest, beauty and deformity, finitude and infinitude, and so on. They are for the mind polar opposites,—the creator, the created. They therefore define one another. A positive definition of the one shall be a negative definition of the other, or, more strictly, shall be convertible into such. Now Nature is susceptible of positive investigation, and may be positively defined as finite, multiform, changing, &c.; does it not follow that God, the genuine polar opposite of nature, is infinite One, and Invariable? But,

III. Even dismissing this second putting of the question, there is another, I think. The truths of mathematics are absolute truths. They are not contingent, like the propositions of unmixed physics, which are contingent on accuracy and completeness of observation, on justness of generalization, and on the intuitive belief that the order of Nature is according to law. No god can gainsay them. They are legislative, not interpretative. In that sphere man is no longer only *minister et interpres*, he is sovereign and lawgiver. Is it not an axiom, that the faculty in man (pure reason) which *decrees*, not simply *discovers*, *absolute* truth is itself necessarily absolute? *Absolute* is another word for *infinite*, and both are other words for *Divine*.

Now the discoveries of astronomy, and all the applicate sciences, display God in the character of a geometer of indefinitely vast resources, *i.e.* as absolute and infinite in faculty, *i.e.* Divine in the sense of infinitude of attribute.

It seems to follow from this, that man too is Divine ; but this is only apparent. Man, a man, is not his body, with its wondrous complication of cerebral and other organs; but neither is he his soul; neither of them is *He ;* He is the *tertium quid*, the *resultant*, as a geometer would say, of the two. But it does follow that his soul is Divine, and I believe it to the very letter. The immaterial element of each of us is "*very God of very God*," to my sincere thinking,—not my judgment, my memory, my emotions, my anything, is Divine; but absolute Reason in me is Divine. In this sense I am the son of God. If all that is creatural, and finite, and personal in me were subordinate to the ideas of pure Reason, I should be the son of God, as Christ *is so*, for the heart and imagination of Christendom; I should be God-man; I should be the Emmanuel of old prophetic intuition; I should be the Idealreal of human nature; as it is, I am only the feeble child of circumstances, and yours most truly,

SAMUEL BROWN.

P. S.—If I were writing as a phrenologist (and I am one), I should name what I have called the aboriginal intuition of God, *the instinct of Causality under the impulsion of Wonder, Ideality, and Veneration*.

P. S. No. 2.—18th June.—The glimpse into the system I embrace, contained in Observation 3, will show that it is a sort of synthesis of Spinosaism and phrenology. of Christianity and paganism, of idealism and realism; at least it unites and reconciles these opposing elements of human theory. Be so kind to me as not condemn it for incoherent on account of any incongruities at first sight. I do not know if it be truth; God only knows that; but I do know it is not mystical in the sinister sense of the word, and that it is at least coherent in all its parts. In addition to it, at present, let me add that I consider the sum and procession of perceptions, conceptions, ideas, emotions, desires, remembrances, and anticipations which do result phenomenally from the action and reaction upon one another of my bodily conformation on one hand, and the Divine common soul of you and me and all beings on the other; I say I consider that procession of human phenomena to be, and to constitute, my proper self. There is not any need, philosophically speaking, of hypostatising that living series, although, practically speaking, the imagination and the heart demand such an impersonation of it; and we always hypostatise or impersonate phenomena until we are better taught; witness the phenomena of heat hypostatised by Black, in the form of *caloric ;* those of animal and vegetable life, in that of a *vital principle*, by a set of physiologists ; those of morbid or occult sensibility, in that of *Od*, by Reichenbach ; and so on, *ad infinitum* almost. For any sake, excuse my long-windedness ; and be so good as let me know your judgment on these views of mine, if you have time before your departure.

No. VIII.—Note on Dr M'Cosh's "Method of the Divine Government."

The Rev. James M'Cosh, LL.D., in an elaborate work on "The Method of the Divine Government, Physical and Moral," has honoured my book "On the Constitution of Man" with a long note of criticisms, chiefly in condemnation of it. The following is his concluding paragraph :—" We have so far noticed this treatise, because there is an air of extraordinary wisdom about it, which has made many regard it as superlatively profound. The author has seen and endeavoured to count the nice wheels of the machine, but has overlooked their relation to one another, and the moving power by which they have been set in motion. His views are about as profound as those of a factory-girl, explaining, with looks of mysterious wisdom, to her companion who has just entered the work, the movements of some of the straps or wheels, telling her how to use them, and pointing out the danger of not attending to them. The information is all very good and useful, provided always that it be not hinted, that in knowing the motion of these few wheels, we know all about the machine, its end, and its mode of operation."

If I am the "factory-girl," it is to be inferred, I presume, that Dr M'Cosh is the head engineer under God, and that in his "Method of the Divine Government," he has elucidated far better and more extensively than I have done "all about the machine, its end, its mode of operation, the moving power by which the wheels have been set in motion," and "their relations to one another." The reader will judge of the success of his exposition, when I add that he ignores the brain and the nervous system of man as instruments in the moral government of the world!

Again, Dr M'Cosh says, "A very little observation suffices to discover the wonderful pains which have been taken with man in creating him at first, in endowing him with bodily organs and mental faculties, in opening to him sources of knowledge, and placing a multitude of resources at his command. What high intelligence! What far-sighted sagacity! What fields, rich and fertile, placed around him, inviting him to enter that he may dig for treasures and gather fruits! It does seem strange, that in endowing man with such lofty powers, God should not have furnished him with faculties to communicate directly with his Maker and his Governor." · (P. 41.) In my opinion, God communicates with man through nature; and in Chapter V. I have pointed out that while our faculties are adapted to the constitution of this world, and it to them, and are capable of discovering the existence of God, some of His attributes, and His Will, in so far as it relates to ourselves, nevertheless, He may so far transcend our faculties as to render us incapable of receiving more direct communications. Man can communicate with the dog, because they have some faculties in common; but he cannot communicate with the oyster, because its powers of comprehension are too far below his faculties to render this possible.

Dr M'Cosh's view is different. "Now," says he, "combine these two classes of facts, the apparent distance of God, and yet his nearness intimated in various ways, his seeming unconcern and yet constant watchfulness; and we see only one consistent conclusion which can be evolved, *that God regards man as a criminal, from whom he must withdraw himself, but whom he must not allow to escape.*" (P. 45.) If I rightly understand these words, they imply that the conclusion at which Dr M'Cosh has arrived from his study of "The Method of the Divine Government," is, that this world is a great prison, the human race a collection of criminals, and God the Head-Jailor and Executioner! Whatever his meaning may be, his words grate harshly on my sentiment of Veneration when applied to the Supreme Being. Dr M'Cosh was a minister of the Free Church of Scotland, and apparently he holds fast by its dogmas, and sees man and nature only in the light in which they are represented in the Catechism quoted on p. 186.

No. IX.—FAITH IN GOD AND MODERN ATHEISM COMPARED : BY JAMES BUCHANAN, D.D., DIVINITY PROFESSOR IN THE NEW COLLEGE, &c.

Dr Buchanan, in this liberal and philosophical work, has criticised "The Constitution of Man." It is necessary here to advert only to two of his objections—"That the physical and organic laws" says he, "cannot be broken or violated in the same sense in which the 'moral law' may be transgressed, is evident from the simple consideration that the violation of a natural law, were it possible, *would be not a sin but a miracle.*"

Answer—In "The Constitution of Man" (8vo edition, published in 1847), p. 20, it is said—"A law of nature is not an entity distinct from nature. The atoms or elements of matter act invariably in certain definite manners in certain circumstances; the human mind perceives this regularity, and calls the action characterized by it, action according to law. But the term 'law,' thus used, expresses nothing more than the mind's perception of the regularity."

It is erroneous therefore, to say that I have taught that man can alter the modes of action imposed on the atoms or elements of matter, which is what Dr Buchanan charges me with. Such a mode of breaking the "natural laws" would certainly imply miraculous power in the transgressors.

Again, Dr Buchanan says—Mr Combe "speaks as if the physical and organic 'laws of nature' possessed the same authority and imposed the same obligation as the 'moral' laws of conscience and Revelation; and as if the breach or neglect of the former were *punishable* in the same sense, and for the same reason, as the transgression of the latter."

In the same edition of "The Constitution of Man," p. 24, I published the remarks contained in page 97 of the present work, which form an answer to this objection; and in page 208 of this work I have endeavoured to shew that the rules of conduct which we are capable of deducing from the action of every natural force, and its relationship to ourselves, ought to be regarded by us as containing a *moral and religious sanction;* and that it is Dr Buchanan and his friends who, in regarding these rules as matters of merely prudential consideration, are in error, and require to take the beam out of their own eyes. They do not practically regard nature as a Divine Institution, and do not reverence the lessons which it teaches. He also, like Dr M'Cosh, ignores the brain and nervous system as instruments employed by God in the moral government of the world!

No. X.—SPEECH OF LORD JOHN RUSSELL ON TEACHING NATURAL THEOLOGY IN COMMON SCHOOLS. (Referred to on p. 246.)

Lord John Russell, in a speech delivered by him in the House of Commons on 4th April 1853, in introducing a scheme of National Education, is reported by *The Times* to have said, "The scheme" (of giving secular instruction in schools and omitting sectarian religion) "is developed by many of the writers on the subject, especially by Mr Combe, whose name, no doubt, will be well remembered by the House. What he holds out is this, —that very imperfect views are taken with respect to religious subjects; that very often those rules which the Almighty has laid down for our conduct in this life, so far from being followed, are wilfully or blindly set at nought; and that it is the business of the schoolmaster to teach those laws of social economy and of physiology by which the people of this kingdom may be better instructed in conducting themselves, so as to enable them to avoid that course of vice and misery into which too many of them fall. It will, however, be obvious to the House that this is a proposal different from what was the apparent proposal, as at first put forth, of the advocates of the secular system. The proposal, as it stands nakedly in the first declaration of their views, amounts to this,—give exclusively secular instruction in the schools, and leave religion to be taught elsewhere by the ministers of religion. The second view of the subject, however, is this,—there is a natural theology which should be taught in the schools, but Christianity should not be taught there. Now, that appears to me a view certainly more extensive, and undoubtedly far more dangerous, than that which the advocates of secular education first set out with. My belief is that the people of this country acted with a right instinct, when, upon associating together and devoting their money for the purpose of education, they declared openly that there should be a religious training in the schools, and that that religious training should comprise all the great doctrines of Christianity."

Lord John Russell commits an error if he means, that while the advocates of a purely secular education proposed that Christianity should be taught by the clergy, or by teachers authorized by them, in a separate school, I proposed to exclude such teaching altogether. In none of my published works does any such proposition appear, but the reverse. I have advocated teaching Christianity in separate schools, and I do so still; because the people are Christian, and I should outrage every principle of religious liberty and common sense, should I propose that persons, whose highest hopes and fears are bound up in the Christian religion, should in any way be precluded from having it taught to their children.

The real state of the question is this. When purely secular instruction in one school, and sectarian religious instruction in another, were proposed, the religious public objected, "In your secular schools you propose 'a godless education.'" When we answered, "Nature is a Divine institution, and in these schools we shall teach God's natural laws established to regulate human wellbeing, leaving you to teach sectarian dogmas in a separate school," Lord John replied, "This is far more dangerous!" More dangerous than what? Apparently, from the context, than the purely secular instruction, which, however, many had denounced as "godless." Lord John appears to me, by implication, to deny that Nature is a Divine Institution, that it reveals rules for the guidance of human conduct, and that these rules are entitled to our reverence as Divine!

No. XI.—TEACHING PHYSIOLOGY IN COMMON SCHOOLS.
(Referred to on p. 257.)

Extract from the General Laws relating to Public Instruction, passed by the Legislature of Massachusetts, in the year 1850.

Chapter 229, entitled "An Act requiring Physiology and Hygiene to be taught in the Public Schools."

SECT. 1. Physiology and Hygiene shall hereafter be taught in all the Public Schools of this Commonwealth, in all cases in which the School Committee shall deem it expedient.

SECT. 2. All School Teachers shall hereafter be examined in their knowledge of the Elementary Principles of Physiology and Hygiene, and their ability to give instruction in the same.

SECT. 3. This Act shall take effect on and after the first day of October One thousand eight hundred and fifty-one. (*April* 24, 1850.)

Medical Opinion on the Importance of Teaching Physiology and the Laws of Health in Common Schools.

Our opinion having been requested as to the advantage of making the Elements of Human Physiology, or a general knowledge of the laws of health, a part of the education of youth, we the undersigned have no hesitation in giving it strongly in the affirmative. We are satisfied that much of the sickness from which the working classes at present suffer might be avoided; and we know that the best-directed efforts to benefit them by medical treatment are often greatly impeded, and sometimes entirely frustrated, by their ignorance and their neglect of the conditions upon which health necessarily depends. We are therefore of opinion, that it would greatly tend to prevent sickness and to promote soundness of body and mind were the Elements of Physiology, in its application to the preservation of health, made a part of general education; and we are convinced that such instruction may be rendered most interesting to the young, and may be communicated to them with the utmost facility and propriety in the ordinary schools, by properly instructed schoolmasters.

Thomas Addison, M.D., Senior Physician, and Lecturer on the Practice of Physic, Guy's Hospital, &c.
James Alderson, M.D., F.R.S., Fellow, Curator, and Lumleian Lecturer to the Royal College of Physicians.
J. Moncrieff Arnott, F.R.S., Member of the Council and of the Court of Examiners of the Royal College of Surgeons, &c.
Neil Arnott, M.D., F.R.S., Physician Extraordinary to the Queen, Member of the Senate of the University of London.
Benjamin Guy Babington, M.D., F.R.S., Physician to Guy's Hospital, &c.
T. Graham Balfour, M.D., Surgeon, Royal Military Asylum.
William Baly, M.D., Lecturer on Forensic Medicine at St Bartholomew's Hospital, &c.
Archibald Billing, M.D., F.R.S., Member of the Senate and Examiner in Medicine, University of London, &c.
Golding Bird, M.D., F.R.S., Professor of Materia Medica and Assistant Physician to Guy's Hospital, &c.
Francis Boott, M.D., Member of the Council of University College.
W. Bowman, F.R.S., Professor of Anatomy and Physiology at King's College, &c.
Richard Bright, M.D., F.R.S., Physician Extraordinary to the Queen, Consulting Physician to Guy's Hospital, &c.
Sir Benjamin C. Brodie, Bart., D.C.L., F.R.S., Sergeant Surgeon to the Queen, Surgeon to H.R.H. Prince Albert, &c.
George Budd, M.D., F.R.S., Professor of Medicine at King's College, and Physician to King's College Hospital.
Sir William Burnett, M.D., K.C.B. and K.C.H., F.R.S., Director-General of Naval Hospitals and Fleets.
George Burrows, M.D., F.R.S., Physician to St Bartholomew's Hospital, &c.
Wm. B. Carpenter, M.D., F.R.S., Examiner in Physiology, &c., University of London, Professor of Forensic Medicine at University College.
Sir James Clark, Bart., M.A., M.D., F.R.S., Physician in Ordinary to the Queen and to H.R.H. Prince Albert, &c.
James Copland, M.D., F.R.S., President of the Royal Medical and Chirurgical Society.
John Davy, M.D., F.R.S., Inspector-General of Army Hospitals.
John E. Erichsen, F.R.C.S., Professor of Surgery, University College, and Surgeon to University College Hospital.
William Farr, M.D., of Registrar-General's Office.
Robert Ferguson, M.D., Physician Accoucheur to the Queen, &c.
William Fergusson, F.R.S., Professor of Surgery at King's College, Surgeon in Ordinary to H.R.H. Prince Albert, &c.
John Forbes, M.D., D.C.L., F.R.S., Physician in Ordinary to H.M. Household, Physician Extraordinary to H.R.H. Prince Albert, &c.

R. D. Grainger, F.R.S., Lecturer on Physiology at St Thomas's Hospital.
William Augustus Guy, M.B., Physician to King's College Hospital, Professor of Forensic Medicine at King's College.
Cæsar H. Hawkins, President of Royal College of Surgeons, Surgeon to St George's Hospital, &c.
Francis Hawkins, M.D., Registrar of Royal College of Physicians, and Physician to Middlesex Hospital.
Thomas Hodgkin, M.D., Member of the Senate of the University of London.
Joseph Hodgson, F.R.S., Member of Council of Royal College of Surgeons, Examiner in Surgery in University of London.
Sir Henry Holland, Bart., M.D., F.R.S., Physician in Ordinary to the Queen and H.R.H. Prince Albert.
William Jenner, M.D., Professor of Pathological Anatomy at University College.
H. Bence Jones, M.A., M.D., F.R.S., Physician to St George's Hospital.
Francis Kiernan, F.R.S., Member of Senate and Examiner in Anatomy and Physiology, University of London.
P. M. Latham, M.D., Physician Extraordinary to the Queen.
William Lawrence, F.R.S., Surgeon Extraordinary to the Queen, and Examiner Royal College of Surgeons.
Charles Locock, M.D., First Physician Accoucheur to the Queen, &c.
Thomas Mayo, F.R.S., Physician to the St Marylebone Infirmary.
Richard Owen, F.R.S., Hunterian Professor of Physiology to the Royal College of Surgeons, &c.
James Paget, F.R.S., Assistant Surgeon and Lecturer on Physiology at St Bartholomew's Hospital, &c.
John Ayrton Paris, M.D., F.R.S., President of the Royal College of Physicians.
E. A. Parkes, M.D., Professor of Clinical Medicine, University College, Physician to University College Hospital, &c.
Richard Partridge, Professor of Anatomy and Physiology, King's College, Surgeon to King's College Hospital, &c.
Richard Quain, F.R.S., Surgeon to University College Hospital.
G. Owen Rees, M.D., F.R.S. Assistant Physician and Lecturer on Materia Medica at Guy's Hospital.
Edward Rigby, M.D., Examiner in Midwifery to the University of London.
P. M. Roget, M.D., F.R.S , Member of Senate of University of London, Author of "Bridgewater Treatise on Physiology," &c.
H. S. Roots, M.D., Consulting Physician to St Thomas's Hospital.
John Scott, M.D., Examining Physician to East India Company.
Edward James Seymour, M.A., M.D., F.R.S., formerly Physician to St George's Hospital.
William Sharpey, M.D., F.R.S., Professor of Physiology, University College, Examiner in Physiology, University of London.
Alexander Shaw, Surgeon, and Lecturer on Surgery to Middlesex Hospital.
Andrew Smith, M.D., Director-General, Army Medical Department.
T. Southwood Smith, M.D., Physician to London Fever Hospital, and Member of General Board of Health.
H. H. Southey, M.D., D.C.L., F.R.S., Gresham Professor of Medicine.
Edward Stanley, F.R.S., Surgeon to St Bartholomew's Hospital.
R. Bentley Todd, M.D., F.R.S., Professor of Physiology at King's College, Physician to King's College Hospital.
Benjamin Travers, F.R.S., Surgeon Extraordinary to the Queen, and Surgeon in Ordinary to H.R.H. Prince Albert.
Alex. Tweedie, M.D., F.R.S., Physician to London Fever Hospital, Examiner in Medicine to University of London, &c.
W. H. Walshe, M.D., Professor of Medicine at University College, and Physician to University College Hospital.
Thomas Watson, M.D., Consulting Physician to King's College Hospital.
Charles West, M.D., Physician Accoucheur, and Lecturer on Midwifery at St Bartholomew's Hospital.
C. J. B. Williams, M.D., F.R.S., late Professor of Medicine at University College, and Physician at University College Hospital.
James Arthur Wilson, M.D., Senior Physician to St George's Hospital.

LONDON, *March* 1853.

For EU product safety concerns, contact us at Calle de José Abascal, 56–1°,
28003 Madrid, Spain or eugpsr@cambridge.org.

www.ingramcontent.com/pod-product-compliance
Ingram Content Group UK Ltd.
Pitfield, Milton Keynes, MK11 3LW, UK
UKHW041951230426
12048UKWH00008B/276